The Riddle of America

Essays Exploring North America's "Native Expression-Spirit"

edited
by
John Wulsin

Contributors:

David Adams
Christy MacKaye Barnes
Henry Barnes
J. Leonard Benson
Norman Davidson
Tom Dews
Virgilio Elizondo
Juan Flores
Joe Glosemeyer
Hikaru Hirata
Gertrude Reif Hughes
Michael Miller
David Mitchell
Hilmar Moore

Julia E. Curry Rodriguez
John Root, Sr.
Barbara Schneider-Serio
Virginia Sease
Jeanne Simon-Macdonald
Rick Spaulding
Edward Warren
Thornton Wilder
Linda Williams
Michael Winship
Dorit Winter
John Wulsin
Lara Wulsin

Published by:
 The Association of Waldorf Schools of North America
 3911 Bannister Road
 Fair Oaks, CA 95628

Title:
THE RIDDLE OF AMERICA
Essays Exploring North America's "Native Expression-Spirit"

Editor: John Wulsin

Executive Editor: David Mitchell

Cover: Hallie Wooten

Proofreaders: Judy Grumstrup-Scott, Ann Erwin

© 2001 by AWSNA

ISBN # 1-888365-32-3

Table of Contents

Acknowledgments vi

Introduction vii

Mythology

Oraibi
Edward Warren.. 1

Awakening Spiritual Consciousness through Legend:
The Legend of Huitzilopochtli
David Mitchell 3

The Ramapo Salamander
David Adams 9

Geography

The Etheric Geography of North America
David Mitchell 21

North of the Border
Philip Thatcher 55

Oklahoma
Joe Glosemeyer 68

Texas
Hilmar Moore 79

Music, Art, and Literature

Reflections on Early Sacred Music of New England
Michael Winship 82

Music and Manners: The American Experience
Tom Dews 89

What Is American Light?
J. Leonard Benson 92

What Is "American" in American Art? A Summary Survey of Two Centuries
David Adams 99

The Birth of American Literature:
The Altering of the Early American Mind
John Wulsin 148

Vishnu's Pursuit of Maya in the Life of Ralph Waldo Emerson
John Wulsin 158

Emerson's Epistemology with Glances at Rudolf Steiner
Gertrude Reif Hughes 178

Toward an American Language
Thornton Wilder 183

The American Loneliness
Thornton Wilder 207

Emily Dickinson
Thornton Wilder 217

The Creative Use of Language by Some of America's Great Writers
Christy MacKaye Barnes 228

The Thief Who Kindly Spoke
Michael Miller 237

Mary Oliver, Inspired Teacher
Jeanne Simon-Macdonald 245

To Each Her Honey
Lara Wulsin 247

Immigration

Choosing America as a Place for Incarnation or Immigration
in the 21st Century
Virginia Sease 251

Immigrant Contributions: las contribuciones de los emigrantes
Julia E. Curry Rodriguez 258

The Sacred in Latino Experience: lo sagrado en la experiencia latina
Virgilio Elizondo 260

Latinos, Too, Sing America: los latinos, también, cantan américa
Juan Flores 262

Who Is Truly a Westerner Today?
Henry Barnes 264

Education

Waldorf Education in North America: The Curriculum and the Folk Spirit
Norman Davidson 272

Movement in America: And So—What's Moving Us?
Barbara Schneider-Serio 279

Multiculturalism and Waldorf Education in America
Linda Williams 282

Columbine . . . Afterthoughts
Hikaru Hirata 288

More Riddles

Feminism or Humanism? Women's Studies Meets Spirit Studies
Gertrude Reif Hughes 300

America – The Price of Greatness
Edward Warren 306

Freedom, Thinking, and Individuality: Ways to a New Style in Culture
John Root, Sr. 317

Anthroposophy and the Spirit of America
Rick Spaulding 335

America's Gold Rush: Can It Be Redeemed?
Dorit Winter 342

Biographies of Contributors 349

Acknowledgments

I am grateful to many people who considered possible articles for this book and to others who pointed me in the right direction. David Sciarreta led me directly to *Americanos;* Edward James Olmos and Dr. Lea Ybarra encouraged me to solicit official permission from Little, Brown, and Co., to reprint three articles from *Americanos.* Tappan Wilder was extremely encouraging, urging me to solicit permission from Nicole Verity, of the Barbara Hogenson Agency, to reprint three Charles Eliot Norton Lectures that Thornton Wilder gave at Harvard University in 1952. Sherry Wildfeuer, editor of *Journal for Anthroposophy,* generously allowed us to reprint "American Light," J. Leonard Benson, 1981; "Emerson's Epistemology with Glances at Rudolf Steiner," Gertrude Reif Hughes, Spring/Summer 1986; "Reflections on Early Sacred Music of New England," Michael Winship, Spring/Summer 1987; "The Thief Who Kindly Spoke," Michael Miller, Summer, 1988; "Anthroposophy and the Spirit of America," Rick Spaulding, Fall 1998; and "Choosing America as a Place for Incarnation or Immigration in the 21st Century," Virginia Sease, Fall 1999. *The Waldorf Education Research Institute Bulletin* gave permission to print Dorit Winter's address, "America's Gold Rush. . . ,"given at the 1999 national AWSNA conference. Susan Stephenson led us to Joe Glosemeyer's "Oklahoma." Gosha Karpowicz, James Vaughn, and Dale Hushbeck teamed up on the cover, completed masterfully by Hallie Wooten. David Sloan and Jane Wulsin (who has, more importantly, given me sustenance throughout) helped edit the editor in the introduction. And most important, David Mitchell has been a dedicated partner, helping to co-conceive the notion of the book, consulting well along the way, asking tough questions, making good suggestions, and engaging in Paul Bunyonesque labors, helping the language and manner of these many streams become, as well as possible, one mighty river.

Introduction

by

John Wulsin

     In 1997 the Association of Waldorf Schools in North America focused on America as the theme of its annual conference in Wilton, New Hampshire, at the Pine Hill and High Mowing Waldorf Schools. When there are over eight hundred Waldorf Schools in many parts of the world, what does it mean to be a Waldorf School in America? In 1999 AWSNA focused again on America at the annual conference at the Toronto Waldorf School. That year a resource for study was the newly published edition of Carl Stegmann's *The Other America*. John Gardner's *American Heralds of the Spirit* has also given many people helpful insights into America. In a conversation with David Mitchell, the idea arose to collect various articles that had been written on America and to publish them in one volume. Hence, *The Riddle of America*.

     Initially, I combed sources familiar to people who had some relationship to Waldorf education. In time, however, in true American fashion, the trails started leading in many directions, such as Thornton Wilder's *Charles Eliot Norton Lectures* at Harvard, 1952, and Edward James Olmos' new book, *Americanos*, 1999, the first book fully about and by Latin Americans. Some people were willing to write new articles about particular aspects of America. And, of course, dimensions are missing.

     The Riddle of America endeavors to explore and reveal what Walt Whitman, in his essay "Democratic Vistas," calls America's "native expression-spirit." This term, original, slightly rough-hewn, nevertheless is the most distilled seed-name I can think of for the subject of this book. I hope all the articles, some implicitly, some explicitly, will shed light on America's especially mysterious "native expression-spirit."

     The Riddle of America begins with three articles exploring the mythic background of America. "Oraibi" is the Hopi story of the evolution of the world until the arrival of the first white settlers, as distilled by Edward Warren. David Mitchell then considers one of the Americas' primary myths, "Huitzilopochtli," the feathered serpent, as a key to understanding American consciousness. An old American folk-tale "The Ramapo Salamander," with a strange blend of Native American and European settlers, geology, and Rosicrucianism yields an esoteric glimpse at America, with the help of David Adams.

What does the "body" of America suggest? Four articles look at America geographically. David Mitchell presents an expanded version of his talk at Wilton in 1997, "The Etheric Geography of North America," a broad view culminating with exercises one can do to better understand one's particular geographic region. Philip Thatcher pays attention to the geographical influence of western Canada in "North of the Border." Joe Glosemeyer explores the geological, geographical, and cultural dimensions of Oklahoma. Then Hilmar Moore sets a geographical background for waves of interaction between Native and European, Mexican and Anglo, Catholic and Protestant in neighboring Texas.

How do the music and the art of America reveal some of its character? Michael Winship notices specific qualities of "Early Sacred Music of New England," as they reflect traits of soul of the early American settlers. Tom Dews characterizes America's improvisational music, particularly bluegrass and jazz. J. Leonard Benson, through attention to the Hudson River School's Luminist Movement, 1850–1875, considers the possibility of a particularly "American Light" in painting. Then David Adams explores "What Is American in American Art?" in an arcing spread from that Hudson River School through architecture, sculpture, and abstract expressionism to pop art and minimalism, with illuminating perspective.

A series of seven articles explores the emerging American mind as revealed and evolved through its literature. John Wulsin first articulates Coleridge's influence on two preacher-predecessors who stir the pot; then he focuses on essential polarities and developments in Ralph Waldo Emerson's thinking as reflected in both his public essays and private journals. Gertrude Reif Hughes looks at Emerson's epistemology, especially in relation to Rudolf Steiner's. Thornton Wilder illumines the process of forming an American language in three articles, focusing first on Herman Melville, then on Henry David Thoreau, and finally on Emily Dickinson. Christy MacKaye Barnes touches on particular linguistic traits of a number of our writers, from Walt Whitman through Carl Sandburg. Michael Miller contemplates the art and mystery in the lyrics of the song, "All along the Watchtower" by Bob Dylan, perhaps the most popular poet of the English language since Shakespeare. Jeanne Simon-Macdonald introduces Mary Oliver's poetry, in which nature so often reveals humanity. Lara Wulsin shows how sound reveals sense in three of Mary Oliver's poems.

We inhabitants of the Americas, even Native Americans, know ourselves as immigrants. Virginia Sease ponders what it might mean to be born in America or to immigrate to America. Three articles consider the Latin-American experience particularly. Julia E. Curry Rodriguez offers a panorama of immigrant contributions. Virgilio Elizondo reveals essentials of "The Sacred in Latino Experience." Juan Flores sketches Latino musical contributions to American culture. Henry Barnes, reflecting on our land and some of its most characteristic thinkers, wonders what is the real spirit of the West; "Who Is Truly a Westerner Today?"

To ponder the future of America, one must consider, in the light of all these dimensions explored so far, how can education best meet what lives in America? Four articles consider riddles of education in America. Scotsman Norman Davidson casts a fresh eye on how the spirit of America might inform an American Waldorf curriculum. Barbara Schneider-Serio, a German-born American dancer/eurythmist, portrays particular traits of contemporary American movement. Linda Williams, from Detroit, articulates possible multicultural dimensions of an American Waldorf curriculum. Hikaru Hirata uses the tragic shootings at Columbine High School as a catalyst for reflections on contemporary challenges and how Waldorf education might best meet them.

The final five articles explore a number of other riddles of America. Gertrude Reif Hughes illuminates American feminist thought in the light of Rudolf Steiner's epistemology. Edward Warren begins with the Native Americans, notes waves of immigration and development, and, using Whitman's perspectives, follows the United States of America right up through Martin Luther King, Jr., and the Vietnam War, questioning the price of America's greatness. John Root considers contemporary questions of cultural freedom in light of the Constitution of the United States. Rick Spaulding looks at America though the lens of the more contemporary folk tale, *The Wizard of Oz*. And Dorit Winter's talk in Toronto in 1999 presents the Golden Gate Bridge in San Francisco Bay as an image for the question, "Where is the West Heading?"

Part of the American nature of this collection of articles is that while some are clustered appropriately together, chronologically, geographically, or thematically, elements of one article may appear in one or more other articles, differently emphasized. Readers will eventually experience a quite wide, overlapping, almost topographical tapestry, with articles echoing and further revealing the various themes.

Readers unfamiliar with Waldorf education may be surprised by references to the Austrian philosopher and educator, Rudolf Steiner (1861–1925). Rudolf Steiner referred to his extensive understanding of the human being as Anthroposophy, or the wisdom of humanity. Steiner had a profound interest in and understanding of America's past, present, and future and what it might bring the world, sooner and later. In 1919, Steiner was asked to form the first Waldorf school, for the children of the workers at the Waldorf-Astoria factory in Stuttgart, Germany. At present there are over two hundred Waldorf schools in the Americas and over eight hundred in the world. Anyone interested in learning more about Waldorf education might contact:

> The Association of Waldorf Schools of North America
> 3911 Bannister Road
> Fair Oaks, CA 95628

The spirit of this collection, like the spirit of America, is eclectic. The editor certainly hopes that this collection may be of help as a resource to all kinds of teachers, not only in the Waldorf movement. Above all, may *The Riddle of America* serve the interests of anyone who ponders the mysterious nature of this hemisphere. Of course, how we understand our past and present will affect our future. May these articles help us not only to better recognize but as well to better clarify the "native expression-spirit" of America. Ideally, these articles will both reveal and catalyze others.

Oraibi

by

Edward Warren

Oraibi—the center of the world—is a small Hopi Indian village placed on the great rocky spur of Third Mesa. Here the people settled after their great migration to the North, South, East and West of the North and South American continents. Here they waited for centuries for their Lost White Brother. Here they received prophecies about the use of valuable minerals under their land. Why would they settle on the North American continent's most barren land? Why do they live in one of the most difficult climates? Why should they settle on ground that contains vast quantities of uranium? Who is their Lost White Brother? Why is he missing? How could universal brotherhood be a central motive in the lives of a few Hopi on the Arizona desert?

Answers to some of these questions were made public by Hopi traditionalists shortly after the bombings of Hiroshima and Nagasaki, as a contribution to world peace. Their oral traditions—creation myths, legends and prophecies—which vary greatly, were published by Frank Waters in *The Book of the Hopi*, by Harold Courlander in *The Fourth World of the Hopi*, and by Albert Yava in *Big Falling Snow.*

The Hopi creation myths tell of a people who are now living in the Fourth World, one of good and evil, beauty and bareness, heat and cold, height and depth. In this world humans must choose between good and evil if the next three worlds are to pursue.

At the beginning, Taiowa, the creator, gave a being called Sotuknang the task of creating the First World, Tokpela. Sotuknang gathered from the endless spaces the solid substances, the waters, and the air. He then created Spider Grandmother, who created the animals, plants, and minerals before forming male and female human beings. These people understood and followed their guardian, Mother Earth.

She taught them the Song of Life. They learned that if they used their forces selfishly or stopped singing the Song of Life, they would lose their harmony with Mother Earth. This happened to some of the people in the First World. After saving those who still sang the Song of Life, Taiowa destroyed the First World with fire. Harmony was also lost in the Second World because of some of the people's egotism, and it was destroyed by ice. War and revenge abounded in the Third World so that Taiowa destroyed it with great floods, which broke the continents asunder.

When the survivors of the great floods emerged into our world, the Fourth World, they were met by Masauwu, the God of Death and the Underworld. He had given the people the knowledge of fire in the Third World but had chosen to go his own way in the evolution of the worlds, so he was doomed by Taiowa to be protector of the land in the Fourth World. Appearing as a handsome young man, Masauwu told the people to migrate to all four corners of the world in order to claim the land for the Creator and Mother Earth. He warned them that if they lost their harmony with Mother Earth by not singing the Song of Life, he, as protector and guardian of the land, would take over the world. Some of the people completed the migrations to all four corners of the continents without preferring to settle down on rich land in a favorable climate. They were sent by their prophecies to the Three Mesas on the desert, where they live today. In their villages a simple life was won through the collection of water at distant wells in the desert and by growing special kinds of corn in the valleys. Walpi and Oraibi are still inhabited today. Here they received the prophecy of their Lost White Brother, called Pahana, who would appear to them from the East bringing with him a true brotherhood of humans, which would enrich their lives and the whole world. They were told to submit to the new culture, which Pahana would bring with him, and to carry out ceremonies through the years to prepare themselves for his arrival. They also received a striking prophecy, which told them not to release the minerals (uranium) from their home under the ground before humanity has achieved the consciousness to use them peacefully.

History has shown the Hopis that the true Pahana did not come to their lands in the person of Pedro de Tovar, a Spanish conquistador, dispatched by Francisco de Coronado in 1540. Neither did the first Franciscan missionaries bring with them true brotherhood when they began christianizing the Hopis in 1629. The Hopis knew that this "slave church" was from the false Pahana and that they would have to wait a long time before the true Pahana would come to them.

Awakening Spiritual Consciousness through Legend:

The Legend of Huitzilopochtli

by

David Mitchell

Myths and legends connect us to the evolution of humanity, provide us with courage to endure hardship in life, and present us with a perspective to understand the geographical message emanating from the area where we live. Joseph Campbell refers to myths and legends as the "literature of the spirit." In myths we find symbols imbued with messages available to educate us toward the higher impulses of humankind. They have the purpose of bringing the reader to a spiritual and eternal level of consciousness.

Mesoamerica and the Holy Land have congruent legends. These myths can be found inscribed on both the walls of buildings of ancient cities and temple pyramids of Mexico and on their corresponding forms in Gaza and other Egyptian mystery centers. The Egyptian epoch laid a foundation for Western civilization. In North America the lowlands of Chiapas was the center of the most advanced early American civilization, that of the Mayas. The oldest known American skeleton, the Tepexpan man, was unearthed in the Yucatan Valley of Mexico. Some 6,500 to 8,000 feet above sea level stands the oldest pyramid in Middle America, Cuicuilco, as well as the largest human-made structure in the world, the pyramid of Cholula, where unusual and powerful religious rites were practiced.

North America has many myths and legends, but there is one in particular to which I would like to draw attention. It comes from the Mexican mysteries. I first encountered it while studying Rudolf Steiner, and I found it so incredible that I packed my suitcase and set off for Mexico City to do research at the National Museum of Anthropology and then travelled to the sacred site of Monte Alban (White Mountain) by Oaxaca. All that I discovered confirmed what I had read in Steiner's writings.

Mesoamerica

In North America we are assaulted by materialism. The mythological spiritual picture of this is embodied in the being of a personality known as Ahriman, the personification of darkness, mentioned in the ancient Persian mythology as the archrival to Ahura Mazdao, the god of light. The influence of Ahriman spread throughout the Near East and Europe. North America, according to Steiner, escaped the Ahrimanic destruction in an outwardly earthly reality; however, the Ahrimanic influence was established there as a ghost-like, or phantom-like, presence able to impress itself into the will impulses of human beings.

A discrete population of people lived in North America before history was recorded. It was isolated from the influences of both East and West because it had special characteristics which it needed to develop spiritually. They were able to cultivate a particular capacity in their thinking based upon specific initiation rituals that were directly experienced. They worshipped a specter-like Spirit who was related to the Great Spirit of Atlantis who had assumed an Ahrimanic disposition. This spirit had a name that sounded akin to Taotl. He was a powerful but not totally incarnated being. All of this took place before the "discovery" of America by emissaries to the West.

There were many gods that were worshipped in Mesoamerica. One of the most important was Quetzalcoatl. Depicted as a feathered serpent, he was a half-mythical ruler and cultural hero of the Toltecs. As a ruler he was especially benevolent and had great compassion. Possessing a combination of animal and human attributes, he went by the name of Kukulkán in the Yucatan, where

Stella of the good god Quetzalcoatl

he created the center called Chichen Itza. Following his death there was a succession of Quetzalcoatls throughout the centuries. At a certain juncture, a personality who went by that name became heavily influenced by dark powers.

Many people were initiated into the mysteries of Taotl, which were Ahrimanic in character. These Ahrimanic forces caused a hardening of the human being. The ultimate effect was as if the soul was squeezed and pressed out of its being. The victims would give up the control of their own souls and excarnate. All of this happened through rites of black magic.

No one was initiated into these mysteries unless they had taken part in a murder. Progression on this ritualistic path required additional murders, after which additional Ahrimanic "truths" were imparted. These murders had to be performed in a particular ceremonial manner. The victim was bent over a rounded stone such that the thorax and the abdomen were extended upward.

In this position, a knife would cut out the still-beating heart. (Rudolf Steiner suggested that it was the stomach.) The initiate would psychically breathe in the soul-life forces of the victim and would incorporate these astral forces into himself. The organs were then further sacrificed to the god Taotl in a special ceremony. The victims to be murdered had been religiously prepared to die and often willingly accepted their fate as part of a higher law of sacrifice. They were told that they were being released from the drudgery of life, and their souls would fly upward toward everlasting peace. They were also told they would live on, in a strengthened form, through their murderer, with whom they would conduct a steady conversation between the threshold of life and death. Repeated sacrifices increased the astral capacities of the initiate and allowed for heightened powers of black magic.

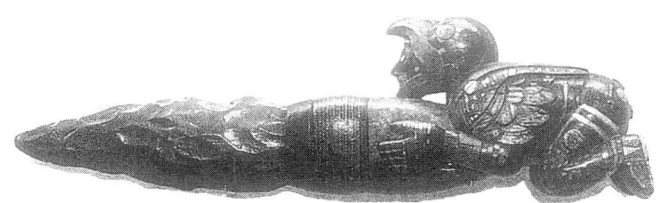

Obsidian ritual knife

The Legend

An Aztec maiden, Coatlícue, wearing a skirt fashioned from living snakes, was sweeping and tidying on the holy hill of the serpents when a puff of bird-down softly descended from heaven. She gathered the down in her hands, balled the feathers up, and stuffed them into her waist band. Later that evening she discovered that the feathers had disappeared and she had become pregnant.

After his birth the child was given a name which sounded like "Huitzilopochtli." (Rudolf Steiner translated this name as Vitzliputzli.) Born in the year 1 A.D., he lived to be thirty-three years old. He was born with a task—to work against the horrible Ahrimanic mysteries—and his early years were spent in preparation for, and devotion to, this task.

At the time of Huitzilopochtli's conception, the Ahrimanic powers, recognizing his mission, incarnated a being to be his earthly adversary. This being was all-powerful as a black magician. As he walked through the countryside, he could perpetuate malignant diseases amongst the people through magical forces. With a wave of his hands he could cause standing water to become foul. He was a feared master of all of the black arts and had a Mephistophelean character, according to Steiner. He was called Quetzalcoatl, after the original Quetzalcoatl, who was a being of profound goodness and had been revered by the people as a god. Thus confusion was promoted through the name given. His symbol was the caduceus—twin snakes winding up a staff. He was the greatest black magician ever to have walked the face of the earth. He had penetrated these secrets of black magic through ritualized murders and the exorcizing of human hearts.

A struggle between this black magician and Huitzilopochtli ensued for three long years. The battle ended with Huitzilopochtli wrestling his opponent into submission and nailing him to a cross. The cross was inverted and set into the earth where it was set on fire—thus banishing the black magician's soul forever so that he was rendered powerless in his deeds. His acquired black knowledge was made impotent. Huitzilopochtli thus acquired the capability for winning back for the earth all those souls who had forsaken the earth previously through the mysteries of Toatl.

Thus, in the Western Hemisphere we have a legend of an event that took place that has remarkable reversed similarities with the mystery of Golgotha in Palestine. It is of further interest that these two distant events took place at the same exact time in world history!

The Legend as Teacher

In spite of the great gulf that separates pre-Columbian thought from our own, there is a great deal in this legend of Huitzilopochtli that can illuminate us in the spiritual tasks presented in our modern times. The message is meaningful to those who care to take the trouble to penetrate the essence of the myth.

The holy battle engaged in by Huitzilopochtli was a psychological war waged within the consciousness of a specially trained man who was capable of conquering his own base, lower nature. He was one of a group called the White Brotherhood. When successful in the accomplishments of their inner work, this group of men was rewarded by being allowed to look behind the gossamer veil of reality to a place of dazzling whiteness. There they saw a white eagle (a representation of Huitzilopochtli), a white cypress, white willows, white reeds, white frogs, white fish, and white water snakes. This mental image gave them a feeling of blissfullness.

Do the Ahrimanic influences manifest in us in North America today? The qualities of the black magician can be experienced wherever we find mechanistic thinking. It is present when we meet sclerotic diseases and souls who deny the existence of the higher soul qualities of humankind. Its counterpart is experienced through the pervasive world of

Image of the "Black Magician"

fantasy which titillates us from Hollywood. Life itself is not felt to be worthwhile, and souls are lured away from reality.

The earth heaviness and materialism offered by North America was necessary for human evolution because it provided a balance for the intellectual spiritualization which threatened to excarnate people in Europe and the East. The earth requires a balancing of forces that become too predominant.

All human beings must create their own balanced "house of the spirit." We can never become truly upright and good until we cultivate a warm interest in our fellow human beings. All spiritually cultivated inner life will be merely egotistic and seductively false unless we take a kindly loving interest in other people. It is this social task that calls for our attention today, and this is a message that is hidden within the legend of Huitzilopochtli, the feathered serpent!

Bibliography:

Anton, Ferdinand and Frederick Dockstader. *Pre-Columbian Art.* New York: Abrams Inc., 1998.
Campbell, Joseph. *The Power of Myth.* New York: Doubleday, 1988.
Krupp, Dr. E. C. *Beyond the Blue Horizon.* New York: Oxford University Press, 1991.
Le Plongeon, Augustus. *Sacred Mysteries Among the Mayas and the Quiches.* Minneapolis: Wizard, 1973.
Mitchell, David. Unpublished notes, Mexico National Museum of Anthropology, Mexico City, Mexico, July 1992.
Nicholson, Irene and Paul Hamlyn. *Mexican and Central American Mythology.* London, 1968.
Sabloff, Jeremy A. *The Cities of Ancient Mexico —Reconstructing a Lost World.* New York: Thames and Hudson, 1989.
Steiner, Rudolf. *The Inner Evolutionary Impulse of Evolution.* Lecture 3, Spring Valley, New York: Anthroposophic Press, 1984.
Tagle, Silvia Gómez. *Mexico National Museum of Anthropology Catalog.* Mexico City: GV editores, s.a. de c.v., 1986.
(Willboruoghy, ed.). *Mexico.* Alexandria, Virginia: Time-Life Books, 1986.

The Ramapo Salamander

by

David Adams

  The creators of the world wanted to protect human beings from evil spirits of greed and lust, so they imprisoned them beneath a steep mountain called High Tor. Much later the youngest of the three wise men, Amasis, heard the story of their imprisonment and decided to test his faith in the infant Christ by finding the mountain and changing these spirits from evil to good.

  In a dream he saw the location of High Tor in New York and undertook the long journey there overland across Asia, Alaska, and North America. When he arrived at High Tor, he built an altar on the mountain top. Because he refused to take the sun-worshipping faith of the Native American tribe there, they attacked him. He would have been killed in the attack except a sudden earthquake tore the ground at his feet, and everyone fell into the crevice except Amasis.

  To him was revealed in a magic vision the earth spirits in caves below the mountain, heaping up jewels and offering to give them to him if he would speak a word that would bind his soul to the earth forces for a thousand years. He refused, but he also was not able to change the spirits from evil to good.

  Later, in 1740, a band of ironworkers led by Hugo came from the Harz Mountains in Germany to settle at High Tor in order to mine the rich iron ore near there. When the Native American tribes saw their houses of stone and their skill at forging knives and other wonderful metal tools from the ore they took out of the rocks by fire, they went away from the area, thinking the ironworkers to be divine beings.

  When Hugo, who was a Rosicrucian, heard of the Magus Amasis's earlier efforts with the spirits under the mountain, he had his men build a forge where Amasis's altar had stood. He, too, began to pray over the spirits below, trying to turn them to good. It had been the custom in Germany to put out and restart the forge fire every seven years, but Hugo felt this was unnecessary. However, his men spoke of the fire salamander that once every seven years grows to full size in an unquenched flame and then goes forth doing mischief.

On the last day of the seven years, Hugo entered the forge and saw his men gazing into the furnace at a pale form that seemed made of flame. As he stared transfixed into the forge, the earth spirits told him he could set them free by reading aloud the letters burned in a triangle on the back of the giant salamander forming in the flames. But Hugo refused, although they offered him great riches, as they had also offered to Amasis.

Hugo and his wife had two children, a boy Hugo and a girl Mary, who stood beside him as he gazed into the furnace and prayed for the spirits. The children begged him to leave. His daughter was pure and unspotted by the world, and it was her prayer that brought Hugo to his senses and made the scene below grow dim when he stared at the evil light of the salamander clinging to the rocks below.

One night Hugo left his wife, who was too ill to move, and went with his son to the forge on High Tor. The salamander rose out of the flames below and burned Hugo's son to death. Hugo felt fire burning at him as well, until he felt water being sprinkled on his face and saw his wife standing beside him casting holy water into the furnace and speaking a magic prayer. At that moment a storm arose, and rain fell and put out the forge fire—but as the last glow faded, the lady fell dead. After this, Hugo went mad with sorrow and often wandered through the woods, leaving Mary alone in their hut.

A few days later, a young man of unusual beauty came to the hut asking for shelter. Mary made him welcome and told him of her family's distress. He promised to help her, and over the next days a tender feeling grew between them. One day he saved her from the attack of a panther, and, as he carried her in his arms, she wanted to declare her love for him. However, he placed her away from him and told her he was really an Angel of Fire sent by God to help human beings. He trod the darkness of the earth testing his obedience to God.

He had yielded to his love of the earth, and the evil spirits had changed him into a fire salamander with the secret letters inscribed on his back. If spoken aloud by a human being, they would set the evil spirits free from their imprisonment under the mountain. When Hugo refused to speak the letters, the evil spirits had ordered him to destroy her brother and mother and to drive her father mad. Then he only had power over the element of fire, which either consumes or hardens to stone. "Now water and life are mine," he proclaimed. "Behold! Wear these, for you are worthy." Upon saying this, he changed her tears to lilies and placed them on her brow. "When your mother came to me with the power of purity to cast me out of the furnace, I turned into a human form and came to you. If you were not so pure, I would again have been corrupted and turned into an earth spirit. The wish for power led me away from my mission to the suffering. Now I must pass the last test—the gate of fire."

Suddenly Hugo and the other men came up to the house and saw the young man holding his daughter. Filled with anger, Hugo cried, "He has ruined my house and my daughter!" He grasped the young man and threw him into the fire. But Mary saw how, because of his love for her, he rose upward in robes of silvery light in the form of an angel again and vanished in the sky above. Her fear and horror died away, and a peace came to her that lasted until the end.

Composite version compiled by David Adams from the composite version in Jane McDill Anderson, Rocklandia: A Collection of Facts and Fancies, Legends and Ghost Stories of Rockland County Life *(Nyack, NY: privately published, n.d.); and the version in Charles M. Skinner,* Myths and Legends of Our Own Land, Volume 1 *(Philadelphia: J. B. Lippincott, 1896). The sources used by Jane McDill Anderson included Elizabeth Oakes Smith,* The Salamander *(New York: Putnam, 1848).*

Esoteric America

At the beginning of the 1980s when I first came across the above legend while living near High Tor in Rockland County, New York (near the Ramapo Mountains), I exclaimed to myself, "Why, this story is really about America!" But only now, nearly twenty years later, have I found an opportunity to try to articulate more specifically just how this fairy tale of the "Ramapo Salamander" concerns the esoteric nature of America. Many aspects of this fascinating tale remain mysterious, but I hope here at least to begin to explore its meanings with the help of anthroposophy. As with most fairy tales, a variety of valid interpretations is possible.

Rudolf Steiner has explained how the true European fairy tales spread by the minstrels from about the eighth to the thirteenth centuries originated, in fact, with the Rosicrucians (or, better said, their immediate ancestors). "It is a superficial view to believe that such tales can be invented by human fancy," he says. "The old tales which give expression to the spiritual secrets of the world came into being because those who composed them gave ear to others who were able to impart the spiritual secrets."

The "Salamander" tale is likewise specifically associated with a German Rosicrucian source (Hugo and perhaps the other German ironworkers), even if rather a latter-day version. The fact that several versions of the "Salamander" exist (some of which I have not yet been able to locate) indicates that the story was modified or added onto as it was passed along through the years (like most legends). Sorting out these revisions to arrive at the original and essential elements of the legend probably more than two hundred years later is no easy task, and work remains to be done in this regard. Unlike most fairy tales, this story is a curious mixture of historical and geographical specificities, imaginative narrative, and occult lore and imagery. It is my suspicion that, in particular, the segments about the Native Americans were later additions, so they will play little role in my interpretation. As with most fairy tales, the various characters and events are likely to represent members or faculties of the human being, revealing an unfolding drama of human psychological and spiritual development.

The story begins with the journey of Amasis, said to be the youngest of the three wise men. His overland route is especially emphasized to indicate his origin from the East (even though he had to travel across the American West to arrive at High Tor). I have not been able to trace the name Amasis in connection with legends of the three magi, but it seems that this opening reference is intended to indicate a relationship to an impulse connected with Christianity (which was opposed to the atavistic "sun worship" of the local Indian tribes). That an event from beneath the earth saved Amasis is a curious development, considering the subsequent emphasis on the sub-earthly realm as the locus of evil spirits. In any case, it is Amasis the magus who brings to America the original inspiration to redeem the evil spirits under the earth, to change their evil to good. To attempt it he must resist the temptation of the evil spirits to bind his soul to the earth.

To help understand this, I will summarize some spiritual scientific background information from Rudolf Steiner that is related in Carl Stegmann's helpful book, *The Other America*. Stegmann depicts a tragic inner battle being fought within the unconscious soul depths of America: between the possibility of humanity being chained to the earth and its true longing for the spirit, ultimately between the Michael-Christ forces of spiritualized heart thinking and the Ahrimanic forces that would direct human beings one-sidedly toward the earth through materialistic thinking and willing.

Stegmann describes a number of factors that, more than in other regions of the world, work to connect American humanity more strongly with the forces of the earth below. In general, the metabolic-will nature of the human being, the psychosomatic aspect within which Americans tend by nature to live most strongly, is more closely connected with the physical organism and, thereby, with its earthly surroundings. The impulse of the pre-Christian Ahrimanic mystery center among the ancient Aztecs, as described by Steiner, has united with the elemental forces of the western world and even today rises up out of the subsensible inner depths of the earth in America. Another factor concerns the especially strong American presence of the human Double, an Ahrimanic astral being with no ego that lives below conscious awareness within every incarnated human being, from just before birth until just before death. Although the Double had the originally beneficial task to help us as spiritual beings to harden and adapt to the earthly world, today the Double is completely penetrated by Ahriman and works to make dense the human body and to bind human beings to the lower powers of the earth.

The Double subconsciously opens human beings to those elemental earth forces to which it is intimately related, attempting to make human beings into materialistically-oriented beings not led by their own egos but guided from outside by Ahrimanic powers. In the depths of human souls, the Double acquires ever greater power over the unconscious life of human will, binding souls with powers that derive entirely from the earth itself—rigidifying forces of mechanization and subnature (especially gravity, electricity, and magnetism). Indeed, Steiner stated that in America those sub-earthly magnetic forces that connect the human being more closely with the Double rise up most strongly. These forces are connected with the fact that on the American continents, most of the mountain ranges run in a north-south direction.

Of the three powers of the human soul (thinking, feeling, and willing), Steiner describes the will as the youngest and strongest. Thus, we can associate Amasis, the youngest of the three magi, with the human will. Aside from the will's generally instinctive and unconscious nature, today the human will is typically directed toward the earth and is more or less cut off from the creative powers of the macrocosmic world will. It is one of the great tasks of the West to recognize the will in its true being. To rediscover the lost cosmic connections of the human will, it is necessary to undertake inner cognitive-meditative work so that the will can be recognized as permeated by the higher, spiritual ego. The will must be harnessed to thinking, and thinking to the will, in order to revivify and heal both faculties.

Only the higher ego can achieve and maintain a balance between the various human soul powers as well as between other polarities, such as Lucifer and Ahriman, and East and West. As opposed to the Ahrimanic powers of death ruling modern materialistic, intellectual civilization, humanity, especially in America, must discover the secret of life, of resurrection, that lies within the mysteries of Christ and the higher ego and which also beckons from the depths of the will. If the will is not consciously grasped by Americans in its spiritual richness, it will be used by the opposing Ahrimanic forces that work particularly strongly in America. That there are both good and evil spiritual powers within the unconscious depths of the will was once strikingly related by Rudolf Steiner to the images in this legend specifically in connection with America.

We can picture the Ahrimanic forces as being active below the threshold of consciousness like lava, like volcanic forces under a soil that emits smoke if one sets fire to paper above it. This shows that beneath the soil there are terrifying forces that pour from every aperture under such circumstances. So it is with the forces of the soul.

So Amasis, the representative of the East, where human beings particularly live within the soul forces of thinking, struggles to resist the attempts of the subearthly spirits to bind him to the earth forces and attempts over his altar to redeem these same spirits. Although he fails, his quest becomes an ideal that centuries later is resumed by Hugo. As Steiner's Foundation Stone Meditation says, "Let there be fired from the East / What in the West is formed."

The band of ironworkers led by the Rosicrucian Hugo who came to High Tor in 1740 represents the other large region of the world, the "Middle" of Europe. As a Rosicrucian eighteenth-century impulse, they also represent a more mature Christianity than Amasis could bring, one already within the period of development of the Consciousness-Soul. Their skill in mining and working iron can perhaps be related to the spiritual-cognizing forces of the Archangel Michael, although this legend occurs more than a century before the beginning of the Michael Age in 1879. Perhaps we should just take it as a sign of the ironworkers representing a more intellectual, historically advanced, scientific civilization, using the cue in the story of the contrast drawn between the atavistic Native American civilization and the newer European immigrants.

The metal iron is connected with the qualities of the planet Mars, such as strength, courage, aggression, masculinity, independence, and egotism. Iron has the beneficial functions of helping better adapt human souls to the earth (partly through its connection with magnetism), supporting the activity of the formative forces, assisting several processes of "breathing," and helping the self-conscious ego to incarnate and freely to will within the blood circulation. These are typical qualities of the modern, western, self-consciously incarnated human being within the Consciousness-Soul Age. The ironworker also recalls the type of the smith from mythology and fairy tales, about whom Wilhelm Pelikan writes:

> Externally, the smith works with fire, bellows, and hammer, a son of Prometheus shaping iron into tools that enable him to master the physical plane. Internally, we kindle the blood's fire with our breath; with every pulse-beat we develop the thrust of the will in our organism and let this will stream into our active limbs. What is happening here except that the "inner smith," latent in all of us, is bringing forth the iron-forming smith as his external counterpart?

Hugo takes up Amasis's quest to turn the subearthly spirits to good, likewise resisting their temptations to set them free into the world of human beings by using his cognitive powers to read the mysterious writing on the salamander's back. However, the longer he continues living on the American continent, the more entranced he becomes by the evil forces rising up from the earth, by the scene in the furnace below. What could be the meaning of the giant salamander that forms when the forge fire is not extinguished and restarted after seven years? Steiner tells us that rhythms of seven years are particularly connected with the astral body but in a more general sense constitute any larger or smaller period of temporal evolution or metamorphosis, being also connected with a cycle of influence of the seven traditional planets. In addition, we know that our bodily organism is completely renewed every seven years, which is primarily a function of our metabolic-will system, of the forces of life within us.

Hugo's refusal to renew the forge fire could be an image for letting these living metabolic-will forces grow too strong and one-sided without being renewed and rebalanced. Another possible understanding is that Hugo, by not respecting the tradition based on the cosmic rhythms, has severed his will from its heavenly influences and connected it all the more closely to the earth—a continual tendency in America, Steiner tells us. In either case, this deed results in the dangerous force of the fire salamander, externally a kind of unusually large and powerful fire elemental being in the subearthly realm.

But we also learn later in our fairy tale that the salamander is in reality an angel of God enchanted by the subearthly evil spirits. Perhaps we can take this figure of the angel as an image for the human soul or the higher self. Having the task to help suffering human beings, a mission of love, the angel is seduced by love of the earth and the desire for power—both temptations of the will particularly associated with the American continent. What is needed to redeem the fallen or enchanted force represented by the angel, that is, the soul of the human being in America?

In the story it is first the sacrifice of her life made by Hugo's loving wife that rescues him from the burning fire of the subearthly salamander and brings the rain that puts out the unrenewed forge fire (but not before his son—or perhaps younger alter ego—Hugo is consumed in flames by the salamander). It was the purity of his daughter Mary who through her prayers rescued him from the salamander's mesmerizing spell and who later is essential for the redemption of the fallen angel. Although one can take Mary to represent something like Goethe's Eternal Feminine or the divine Sophia (in which case her name Mary is not coincidental), we should also consider that Steiner said in 1918 that especially in Americans, an ever greater contrast will become apparent between male and female qualities. Whereas the more earth-bound American male will tend to create a materialistic and mechanistic civilization through one-sided emphasis of the intellect, will, and physical body (including sports), "Anglo-American spiritual life will pass over into the world of the future through 'womankind.'..." Through their stronger heart-forces of feeling, American women will more easily open themselves to spiritual influences and provide a necessary balance to the male tendencies. I will take Mary in particular as the figure of the femininely spiritualized American soul, or at least of that element within the soul—a kind of counterpoint or complement to Hugo's masculine qualities.

Steiner also emphasized the need for moral purity of heart in the meditative verse he provided for the St. Mark's Group, the original American Anthroposophical Society group in New York City. This verse has often been taken as a general meditation for unfolding spiritual work in America:

> May our feeling penetrate to the center of our hearts
> And seek in love to unite itself
> With human beings seeking the same goal,
> With spirit beings bearing grace,
> Who are strengthening us from realms of light,
> Illuminating our love and gazing down
> Upon our heartfelt, earnest striving.

When the handsome angel saves Mary from the panther (read mountain lion or cougar), this is yet another indication of a purification or strengthening of the forces of the heart. Steiner more than once described the close relationship between the feline family (typified by the lion) and the human heart and rhythmic system. He also pointed out that the Double is entirely lacking in warmth of heart.

As the angel explains to Mary, when he was in the form of the salamander under the power of the evil subearthly spirits, he had power only over the element of fire. This "fire" could be interpreted anthroposophically in various ways—as warmth-ether, as the "subnature" fires of electricity and magnetism used by the Double, as the "fiery" qualities of the astral world, perhaps even as the warmth/heat processes generated by the human metabolic-limb system (the bodily counterpart of the will). Because of the sacrifice of Hugo's wife and the purity and selfless love of Mary, the angel has now acquired a power beyond fire, the power over "water and life," which he demonstrates by turning Mary's tears to lilies (a traditional symbol of purity associated with the Virgin Mary). In anthroposophical terms, this might signify an ascension from warmth-ether to life-ether (the etheric generally being associated with water), or from a transformation of the astral (Spirit-Self/Manas) to a transformation of the etheric (Life-Spirit/Buddhi), or from knowledge of subnature forces to that of life-forces.

Steiner has pointed out that everything concerned with the forces of growth and life is will-related, and such forces are particularly strong in America. The American mastery of modern technology, driven by the electromagnetic forces of subnature as well as manufacture of iron and steel, can ascend to mastery of the life-forces only through a moral purity of heart. In addition to being related to the future development of a morally conditioned technology of etheric forces that Steiner discussed on several occasions, this development in the legend can be read either as an initiation of the will or as a general spiritual advancement through rebalancing one-sidedness.

When the last test of the "gate of fire" is passed, the angel, because of his love for Mary, ascends to the spirit in robes of silvery light, bringing a lasting peace. Through the influence of spiritual purity of heart as well as those highest powers of the will, love and sacrifice, the American soul can be redeemed or resurrected both from its overly strong attachment to the earthly and from a one-sided inner life within the will. In the unconscious will, human beings are connected with the cosmic spiritual world, united in love with all beings (as experienced every night during sleep). This, too, belongs to the potentials of the purified will. This story of the "Ramapo Salamander" may be taken as a general warning tale for American humanity to cultivate purity of soul and the spiritual willpowers of love and sacrifice in order to avoid becoming too bound up with the Ahrimanic earth forces and subearthly fire processes that rise up so strongly from beneath this continent. As Steiner once admonished us, "Whatever is acquired from the subnatural must be sacrificed to the supersensible."[1]

---

1. *Art History as an Image of Inner Spiritual Impulses*, manuscript translation by Gertrude Teutsch, twelfth lecture of October 23, 1924, p. 29. It is also relevant to note Steiner's statement that human beings can only understand subnature for what it really is "if he rises, in spiritual knowledge, at least as far into extra-earthly Super-Nature as he has descended, in technical sciences, into Sub-Nature." *Anthroposophical Leading Thoughts*, trans. George and Mary Adams (London: Rudolf Steiner Press, 1973), p. 218.

A particularly promising alternative interpretation is suggested by Rudolf Steiner's fifth lecture in *The Temple Legend* (London: Rudolf Steiner Press, 1985), pp. 49–59, given November 4, 1904. There Steiner relates the temple legend of Hiram and Solomon originally told by Christian Rosenkreutz at the beginning of the fifteenth century and passed down particularly in Masonic circles. Steiner draws attention to the "Cain" stream of humanity who knows how to handle and understand fire and its related technologies (as Hugo and his men understood the working of iron in the forge). In addition to the "mysteries of fire," this stream also represents "the masterful wisdom which is achieved through the overcoming of earthly passions and desires," in contrast to the "Abel" stream, "the detached piety which does not concern itself with worldly conquest" (p. 58). Similar to the "Ramapo Salamander," this legend includes images of a golden triangle and a combination of mastery over fire and water, which are explained by Steiner. Hiram is enabled to perfect the casting of the "Molten Sea" (or "Brazen Sea") by learning spiritually "the mysteries of fire" so that he is able properly to unite water and fire, which refers to uniting "the water of calm wisdom" with "the fire of the astral world, with the fire of passion and desire" (p. 58). The Golden Triangle, which represents the development of the three higher human members of Spirit Self, Life Spirit, and Spirit Man (or Manas, Buddhi, and Atma), stands for the future sixth epoch achievement of humanity. It is not clear why this image of the triangle would be associated with freeing the evil fire spirits in the "Salamander" tale, unless perhaps the original intention of the tale was to indicate how the achievement of such higher powers of knowing (which neither Amasis nor Hugo carries out) allows one to freely converse with the fiery astral world and its spirits. An alternative translation of this lecture as well as a wealth of other material on Rosicrucianism with interpretations by Steiner may be found in Paul M. Allen, ed., *A Christian Rosenkreutz Anthology* (Blauvelt, N.Y.: Rudolf Steiner Publications, 1968).

Rudolf Steiner indicated this esoteric lineage in "The European Mysteries and Their Initiates," *Anthroposophical Quarterly* 9:1 (Spring 1964). In this lecture given May 6, 1909, he speaks of the legend of Flor and Blancheflor as well as the school of the Holy Grail as signs from a stream of esoteric Christianity that was continued and carried further with the founding of Rosicrucianism in the fourteenth and fifteenth centuries. His explanation of the figure of Flor is also relevant to an understanding of the story of the "Ramapo Salamander."

Bibliography:

Hauschka, Rudolf. *The Nature of Substance*. trans. Marjorie Spock and Mary T. Richards. London: Rudolf Steiner Press, 1983.
Mees, L. F. C. *Living Metals*. London: Regency Press, 1974.
Pelikan, Wilhelm. *Secrets of Metals*. trans. Charlotte Lebensart, Spring Valley, NY: Anthroposophic Press, 1973.
Stegmann, Carl. *The Other America: The Western World in the Light of Spiritual Science*. Oakland, California: privately published in two volumes, n.d.
Steiner, Rudolf. *Background to the Gospel of St. Mark*. trans. E. H. Goddard and D. S. Osmond, London: Rudolf Steiner Press, 1968.
—————. *Geographic Medicine*. Spring Valley, NT: Mercury Press, 1979.
—————. *Inner Impulses of Evolution: The Mexican Mysteries and the KnightsTemplar*. Spring Valley, NY: Anthroposophic Press, 1984.
—————. *In the Changed Conditions of the Times*. trans. Olin D. Wannamaker, New York: Anthroposophic Press, 1941.
—————. *The Karma of Untruthfulness*. vol. 1, trans. Johanna Collis, London: Rudolf Steiner Press, 1988.
—————. *The Karma of Vocation*. trans. Olin D. Wannamaker, rev. Gilbert Church and Peter Mollenhauer, Spring Valley, NY: Anthroposophic Press, 1984.
—————. *Man as Symphony of the Creative Word*. trans. Judith Compton-Burnett, London: Rudolf Steiner Press, 1970.

———. *Rhythm in Man*. Lecture of December 21, 1908, manuscript trans., Ghent, NY: Rudolf Steiner Library.

———. *Rhythms in the Cosmos and in the Human Being*. Lectures of December 20, 25, and 28, 1923, manuscript trans. M. Thornton, Ghent, NY: Rudolf Steiner Library.

———. *A Sound Outlook for Today and a Genuine Hope for the Future*. Lectures of June 25 to August 6, 1918, manuscript trans., Ghent, NY: Rudolf Steiner Library.

———. *The Temple Legend*. trans. John M. Wood, London: Rudolf Steiner Press, 1985.

———. *The Wrong and Right Use of Esoteric Knowledge*. rev. trans. C. D., London: Rudolf Steiner Press, 1966.

The Etheric Geography of North America

by

David Mitchell

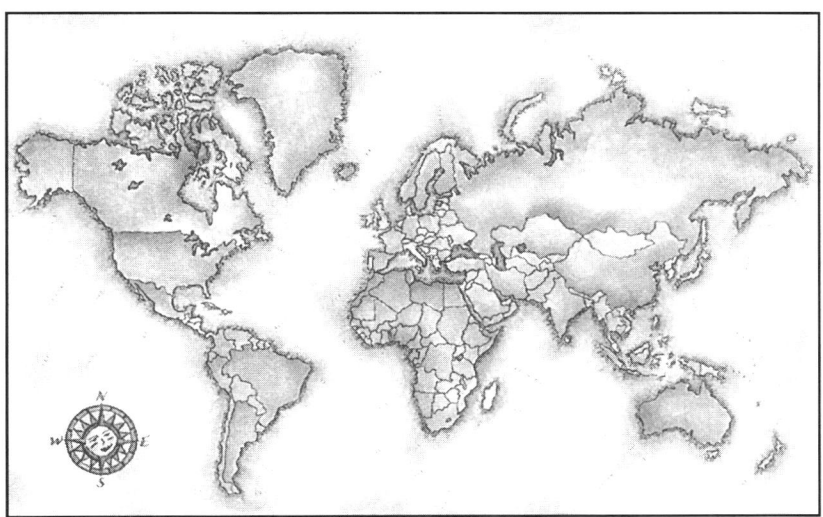

What is the geographic and spiritual uniqueness of North America? Are human beings physically and spiritually affected by their geography? How is geography an expression of living forces, and how can we become aware of these forces in our daily tasks as striving human beings?

These are questions to be considered as we play imaginatively and artistically with the geography of North America. First, look carefully at the map of the world above and observe it phenomenologically. How do the landforms and oceans speak to you? Can you discern an underlying threefoldness in the land formation?

There is a mystery connected with threefold patterns found on the earth, as well as a relationship to the threefold aspects of the human being as described by Rudolf Steiner.[1] By contemplating this connection along with the etheric geography, we become more attuned to our own unique place on earth. This acquired consciousness allows us added effectiveness in our social interactions. It is only when we come to terms with the forces emanating from our locality that we find our individual self.

The Physical Geography of North America

The earth consists of six continents distributed amongst three major oceans—the Pacific, Atlantic, and Indian. Observing a world globe, we quickly recognize that the Northern Hemisphere is predominantly land while the Southern Hemisphere consists of vast amounts of water. We see that the earth has a mountain cross; the mountain ranges in North America, like the fault lines, run mostly South to North while in Eurasia the mountain ranges and the faulting run East to West.

North America stands out as the third largest continent in land mass on the earth, covering about one sixth of the land area. It has the world's largest island, Greenland, and the world's largest freshwater lake, Lake Superior. Forests cover about a third of the land area.

North America has a longer total coastline than any other continent. Except for the large East Coast harbors and the fjord-like coastline of British Columbia and Alaska, the coastline is relatively undifferentiated. Including the continent's many islands, it is approximately 190,000 miles long.

On the west side of the continent, the warm currents of the Pacific create a mild climate year around. The world's largest ocean, the Pacific, rolls immense waves, surging with pounding elastic energy, against North America's west coast. They provide

Crane's Beach in Ipswich, Massachusetts, part of the East's coastal plain

a dynamic life far more untamed than the Atlantic's, which roll with civility on a far fuller longitude. The western mountains tickle their toes in the surf. The Pacific waves seem subtly aware that they are at the edge of earth's shifting sutures, a meeting of margins. Stand at Point Reyes on a foggy morning, and you cannot escape feeling the presence of the etheric realm.

Paradoxically, the Pacific sends the California Current of cold water to the South while the Alaska Current of warm water flows north. Thus, Alaska has a warmer climate than corresponding parts of Canada. Nature is behaving contrary to what one might expect!

Big Sur, California where the coastal range tickles its toes in the surf

Warm, moisture-filled winds from the Pacific Ocean bring a heavy annual precipitation. The clouds accumulate and are held back by the coastal mountains so that rains develop and come down on the wind side of the mountains, creating a climate reminiscent of Niffelheim in the Norse Mythology. Giant sequoias and massive redwoods stretch to heroic proportions in this ideal growing environment. Behind the coastal mountains, we have salty steppe and bone-dry desert, over which the winds race until they reach the Rockies, where the remaining moisture is squeezed out.

The Morphology of North America

We quickly observe that the continent is roughly triangular in shape. (See diagram above.) In the North, the continent's shoulders measure 5,400 miles wide from the Aleutians to the Canadian province of Newfoundland. At its southern point it is 30 miles wide at Panama. Interestingly, it is equally 5,400 miles tall from northern Greenland to Panama. There is a recognizable correspondence in the morphology of both North and South American continents. The overall form is repeated in miniature. Both continents are broad in the North, while in the South their peninsulas are drawn out at their southern tips like pulled taffy. Both continents have young, high mountains in the West and less high, older mountains in the East. Between these are mighty river systems that have deposited vast alluvial plains. Both continents thereby repeat the anatomy of the entire earth, which consists of a northern hemisphere dominated by land and a southern dominated by ocean.

    The North American plate rests atop a magma sea. What is under the magma? In the October 1997 issue of *Scientific American*, geophysicists acknowledged that in the center of our earth there exists a spinning crystalline structure the size of the moon. Immense pressure on the inner core has solidified the iron and caused it to take on a hexagonal crystal form that has inherent directional/physical properties. Some unknown force apparently keeps the hexagonal iron crystals all in close alignment.

> This gargantuan single crystal is more than 2,400 kilometers across. The internal stress caused by the earth's rotation is strongest along the north-south axis. Thus, the hexagonal iron that constitutes the inner core could crystallize in parallel with the spin axis as do mica flakes that form in rocks squeezed by tectonic forces. The tumultuous churning of the outer core's liquid iron creates the magnetic field, but the inner solid core is needed for proper stability. [2]

Glaciated land and lakes of the Canadian shield

Effects of Geography on the Physical Body

In *The Mission of the Folk Souls,* Rudolf Steiner states that every geographical region has not only a physical, but also a psychic and spiritual, topography or aura. This aura is the sphere of activity for the folk spirit. In America one does not find oneself only in the midst of nature; one finds oneself constantly confronting nature. Nature appears to face human beings as a power, a creative force, that forms and transforms their entire being—even to the point that it influences their physical structure.

In dealing with the threefold nature of the world, one has to come to grips with many levels of geographical phenomena. On one level are the forces connected with the earth itself. These can be observed by their influence on the geography and the life forms of a particular spot on the earth. The land influences people, culture, physical proportions, and moods.

Sociologists have observed that certain evolutionary changes of bodily structure are to be found in successive generations of immigrants to North America, regardless of national or racial origin.[3]

The changes are:

- The arms and hands achieve a greater length like the Native American Indians'.

- The facial structure becomes particularized, characterized by a broadening of the lower jaw.

- The head becomes more oval.

The continent of North America is thus forging a unique physiology. In general, the individuality can be characterized as youthful and emotionally vital. It has strong will-forces, is altruistic, playful, able to laugh at itself, and able to ask questions without inhibition. The shadow side is that it is aggressive, materialistic, competitive, and overly concerned with power and control.

A Continental Imagination of a Living Earth from East to West

The East has a fertile coastal plain. Streaming up the East Coast from the Gulf of Mexico is the Gulf Stream. It joins itself with the North Equatorial Current between Florida and the Bahamas, where it sends more water flow per second than all the rivers of the world together empty into the ocean. This current warms the entire East Coast and creates fertile fishing centers like the Grand and Stellwagen Banks. It then flows across to Iceland and Norway, curves toward Scotland into the Inner Hebrides, and concludes around the island of Iona, making a pathway reminiscent of the shape of a giant ear. Iona is the island of Saint Columba, who brought Christianity to Europe.

Imagine the first settlers of North America confronted by the massive virgin forests. The landscape was not particularly inviting. It was pagan, and even frightening at times. Even today, if you walk in the fields unaware, you may contract a violent rash brought on by poison ivy, poison oak, or poison sumac, insidiously passing their oils on to you.

The secondary growth in forests is overpowering. Today the state of New Hampshire is ninety percent forest. In 1900 it was ninety percent cleared fields. The forces of growth are so powerful that you feel always the need to take a stand against it, or else it may swallow you up. There is variety, too. In the combined states of North Carolina and Tennessee, there are more species of trees than in all of Europe.

A prominent land feature on the East Coast is the Canadian Shield, a huge basin of ancient rock consisting of gneiss and granite that covers most of Canada east of the Great Plains and north of the Great Lakes. Here we find many pothole lakes and glacial, carved rivers. The Hudson Bay, like a giant bib above the shield, is not deep; it is a scoured depression made by the ice. Imagine the force and power produced by the four ice ages as they shaped and reshaped the land! For example, Mount Washington, New England's highest peak at 6,288 feet, had one mile of ice above its summit. The weight of this ice and its movement shaped the earth, as a potter's hand kneads clay.

The Ipswich River, an auburn, slow-moving river moving through the coastal plain by Middleton, Massachusetts

Few people live in this region because of the poor soil and cold climate. However, many valuable minerals lie beneath its surface. The days are intense with sunlight, and the nights are inky in their darkness. Here the continent breathes light and darkness. As a rule, the people in this region possess a strong consciousness and wakefulness, necessitated by both the severity of the environment and unpredictable weather. At the southern portion of the shield stretch the arms of an immense boreal forest.

The word boreal means "northern" and refers to the land area just below the tundra, a region that has extremely cold winters and a short growing season. Boreal forests have the simplest structure of all forest formations. They have only one uneven layer of trees, which reaches up to about seventy-five feet (twenty-three meters) high. In most of the boreal forests, the dominant trees are needle-leaf evergreens, either spruce and fir or spruce and pine. The shrub layer is spotty. However, mosses and lichens form a thick layer on the forest floor and also grow on the tree trunks and branches. The vast boreal forest on the lower edge of the Canadian Shield is constantly engaged in photosynthesis, releasing oxygen into the atmosphere and then consuming carbon dioxide. It is the primary respiratory region of North America.

Boreal Forest in Canada

The folded Appalachian Mountains, which stretch lazily up the East Coast, are worn stumps of ancient rock that once stood higher than the Himalayas! They project an old wisdom, and their valleys provide a haven for the East's many hamlets and villages. The many rivers have tree-crowded and grassy banks, and they amble slowly but steadfastly toward their destination.

The predominant generalized etheric gestures expressed in the Easterner are a heightened mental alertness, a strongly developed feeling realm or appreciation of culture, and a more inwardly contracted personality. Appropriate adjectives would include taciturn, earnest, and nonsuperfluous.

The Midwest is strung like an inclined hammock between the Appalachians and the Rockies. At the ninety-eighth meridian, the grass prairies and savannas begin, and a region of big weather, big sky, and an annual twenty-inch rainfall begins. Here is the continent's balance point. The landscape balances between the forces of earth, sun, water, and air. It is much like the balance our circulatory system achieves. This region is the heartland. The people, like the landscape, are generally open, warm, and welcoming.

A road in Kansas stretches forever across the flat plain.

The Midwest contains a plethora of lakes, ponds, rivers, and streams. Some of these lakes are the largest freshwater reserves in the world—the Great Lakes. It also has long, deep, glacially-gouged finger lakes filled with fresh water. The presence of an abundance of water creates an etheric balance. This area provides the continent with a circulatory experience, because of movement of water through the uncounted rivers, streams, brooks, ponds, and lakes. It is the circulatory center of North America.

This Midwest, all great plains and thick topsoil, is the breadbasket of the world. Here corn, wheat, and oats grow in abundance.

Whereas wheat is the crop of Europe, and rice is the crop of Asia, corn is the principal crop of North America. As a plant, it is well suited to the geography of North America and contains some interesting parallels within its morphology. Multipurposed, it is used for feed for animals, as a source for sweetener; it can be distilled into alcohol and consumed as a vegetable or flour for humans. The form of the corn stalk is tall and spindly; it is a plant of light and air. It has a minimal relationship with the earth—the roots even seem inadequate to sustain it. The plant requires adventitious roots to come out of the stalk inches above the ground and support it, as flying buttresses support cathedral walls. As the plant feeds, it draws an enormous quantity of nutrients from the soil, and the farmer must take care to rotate crops so the soil is not totally exhausted.

In the Midwest, we find the earth's magnetic north located in the Parry Islands, northwest of Resolute, District of Franklin, Northwest Territories, Canada. The earth's largest magnetite deposits are located in Saint Joseph, Missouri, the Mesabi Range in Minnesota, and Sudbury, Ontario, Canada. The area surrounding the Great Lakes has large copper deposits, as does the area by Morenci, Arizona. The metals iron and copper predominate in the middle. All of these resources have allowed the area around Detroit to become an industrial center of the United States and Canada, the resources placed there as a kind of geographic gift.

The predominant etheric gestures expressed in the Midwest are wide open spaces, vast proportions, intense light, rhythmically circulating water, and accessible, welcoming, deep topsoil.

Five-hundred-acre cornfield in Nebraska

As we go over the Rocky Mountains, the gateway to the West, we encounter high altitude plateaus, scrubby, parched deserts, and finally the two coastal ranges. In the West, the mountains are more rhythmically patterned, but are rough, pointed, crumbly, and younger than the Eastern mountains. The orientation is upward. Everything seems to point to the heavens—the pointed pines, the upthrusted sandstone, and the sparse, sharp, snowy peaks of the 14,000-foot mountains. Rabindranath Tagore captured this heliotropic surge when he said, "Trees are the earth's endless effort to speak to the listening heavens." The horizon seems to stretch forever and the dome of massive azure sky and the billowing white clouds that gallop by give one a feeling of humility and awe.

Because of the moving air masses traveling from west to east, we have collision points east of the Rockies, where the lighter, quicker, warmer air masses meet the heavier, slower, colder air, creating swirling vortices that evolve into cyclones and tornadoes that wreak havoc in Kansas and neighboring states. The West Coast has mud slides caused by torrential rains, and the East Coast has its late summer/early autumn hurricanes.

The Rockies herald the beginning of the West. They begin in Alaska like a hand raised to a teacher with three fingers up, then contract into a wrist at the Yukon, British Columbia, and Alberta. They expand again through Montana, Idaho, Wyoming, Utah, Colorado, New Mexico, and

Arizona and then contract again as they enter Mexico. The widest section is five hundred miles between Denver and Salt Lake City. Seen in its entirety, it is like the lumbar region of the spinal column of the earth's skeleton. It is aligned with curving force lines between the Earth's vagrant and reversing magnetic poles; the polarity is further experienced from the chill of Alaska's frozen polar region to its ending in the solitary coccyx of Tierra del Fuego—the land of earthly fire.

Rocky Mountain National Park

On the eastern flanks of the Rockies once roamed the ancient dinosaurs. A high inland salty sea existed before the earth's volcanic forces erupted, transformed, and drained it. On the western slope of the Rockies, we find yet a second basin that stayed much longer beneath the ocean and became covered with layers of dead fish, plants, and sediment on top of the gneiss/granite. This became compacted and provided later generations with coal, oil, and natural gas. Within the Colorado Rockies we also find a valuable pegmatite zone that stretches from Durango in the south to Boulder in the north. Here massive amounts of gold, silver, and tungsten have been removed. In the land under the connected cities of Blackhawk and Central City, so many valuable minerals were extracted that it was called the richest square mile on earth.

The gray, moonlike landscape of Nevada and the uranium-rich fields around Moab, Utah, breathe a dry, hot breath, suggesting an atmosphere of approaching death. Here the U.S. military has silos with missles poised and ready. Further west, we find active volcanoes and sliding faults. In 1857 the San Andreas Fault slipped thirty feet toward Alaska in one hiccup, and the Santa Cruz Mountains around San Francisco have warped several inches higher in the last three decades. In Los Angeles we have a desert artificially made to appear abundant. It is a fragile, dependent life that is home to the center of universal fantasy—Hollywood!

Gray desert of Nevada

A chain of volcanoes forms a mountainous spine along the Pacific Coast, from the Aleutians past Central America to the tip of Chile. Most of the Caribbean islands were created by volcanic eruptions. Others are coral and other limestone formations.

Like natural cathedrals, huge conifers dominate the Pacific coastal forests. In the Sierra Nevada, the sequoias are the bulkiest, though not the tallest, of all the world's trees. The largest sequoias measure about one hundred feet (thirty meters) around at the base. They live between 3,000 and 4,000 years. Forests of redwood, one of the world's tallest trees, grow along a narrow coastal strip from central California to southern Oregon. Many of these giants tower more than three hundred and fifty feet (ninety-one meters).

The predominant etheric gestures expressed in the West are a moveable land influenced by earthquakes, volcanoes, and fire; a parched, wasted land holding rich resources underneath, a feeling of something new or

Sandstone weathering in Utah

The hard core of ancient volcanoes remains.

unexpected always capable of happening.

In summary, the predominant etheric gestures are these:
- The East, where the continent breathes and tradition dominates
- The Center or Midwest, where the continental circulation happens; steadiness, balance, and evenness predominate
- The West, where the continent dies and becomes reborn, where every mountain and pointed evergreen lifts your gaze to the heavens, where new ideas and insights are quick to appear and fade away

The threefold activities of respiration, circulation, and death/rebirth allow North America to have a cosmic consciousness and allow it to communicate with the stars. The Native American Indians centered their cosmologies on this reality.[4]

Natural History Appears Most Emphatically in the Vertical: North-South

What are the polarities that have built our continent? In the North the land is broad and extended and has the most differentiation, but people are the most contracted. In the South where the land is pinched and contracted, the people are, generally, open and warm. Tourist advertisements tout southern hospitality. The North has water in abundance. The South has one major river, the Mississippi.

There are also polarities built into the continent's geography. In the South where warmth prevails, we have the strongest contraction of the land mass. In the North where the cold contracts nature, we have the greatest extension and differentiation. In the North, water abounds and is held in bogs, lakes, and ponds. In the South, we find the deltas of two major rivers, the Mississippi and the Colorado, draining the continent. They split their bounty, one emptying into the Atlantic and the other into the Pacific. The geology of the North American plate also has its polarities. Gneiss and granite provide the foundation in the East, which spreads out in the continental shelf all the way to the mid-Atlantic ridge. Northwest of Manchester, New Hampshire, you can pick up pieces of rock that originated in Africa and were left behind after a great collision of the plates during ages past. On the West Coast, you find the Pacific plate pushing under the North American plate in a process called subduction. Here we find the geologically unstable environment of faults, volcanoes, and earth rumblings known as part of the "ring of fire" that forms around the shores of the Pacific Ocean. Here we stand at the edge of earth's shifting sutures, a meeting of margins. The rocks are crumbling sandstone and unstable mountains which cast down boulders after every downpour.

The greatest differentiation in nature shows up in a north–south direction. In this polarity, in connection with the cycle of the year, a strong dynamic prevails—the bird migrations in the North, the schooling of herring in the spring at Cape Cod, the whale migrations from Baja, the hurricane seasons, and the southern monsoons. These are all rhythmic processes in a differentiated spatial structure—breathing processes of an immense organism, Earth.

Below are some generalized polarities connected with the vertical:

North	South
Contains and holds water	Drains water
Solid rock layers dominate	Swamps, deltas
Jet stream in the upper atmosphere	El Niño in the Pacific
Temperate climate	Warm/hot climate
Wakeful	Siesta, sleepy, dreamy
Industrial, scientific, technical	Agricultural, rural
Consonants stressed	Vowels stressed
Clipped speech	Southern drawl
Somewhat estranged from nature	Nature pervades and invites
Subrock technically rigid	Land susceptible to tectonic movement

The mountain ranges run predominantly north to south. This allows warm air to be pulled north during the winter and cold air to drop unexpectedly to the south. Our seasons are not constant, and North Americans are constantly watching the approaching weather from the west. This unpredictability of the weather, due to the absence of east/west mountain ranges, affects our soul breathing and our meditative life, making it more difficult to become quiet and inwardly focused. Rhythm is hard to maintain; peacefulness is constantly disturbed. Americans live with an enormous will to act within the material world of the external. Recent examinations of North America's prehistory with connection to the etheric geography illuminate this reality.

An interesting way to gain a mental picture of the magnitude of currently known earth time was suggested by the geologist Don Eichler in his booklet *Geologic Time*. He compressed the entire 4.6 billion-year history of Earth into one year. Considered this way, our current generation would fit in the last fraction of the last second. Go back three seconds and you would come to Columbus setting sail across the Atlantic, which itself would be an instant after the Aztecs built their capital, Tenochtitlán. Extend back ten seconds, and you would see the end of the Roman Empire. Look back for a minute or so, and you would come across the close of the Pleistocene Ice Age, when the most recent continental ice sheets began to recede from northern Europe and the Great Lakes area of North America, coinciding with the beginnings of agricultural pursuits by humankind and civilization. During the rest of the 364 days, 23 hours, and 59 minutes, the Earth was forming. The history of civilization, as we know it, takes place in roughly the last single minute.

Early History of North America

Professor Barry Fell was a Harvard professor of marine biology, ethnographer, and etymologist. Originating from New Zealand, he made some very controversial claims relating to the prehistory of North America.[5] He claims that visitors were coming to North America as early as 5000 B.C. They came for two purposes: first to gather silica-enriched herbs that grew nowhere else in the world and were needed in Europe to prepare medicines, and second, to make astronomical observations through the clear skies over the northern midwestern states that could not be made anywhere else. (It has even been suggested that these people might have been able to converse with the stars here, as Laurens van der Post claims the Bushmen did in Africa.)

Who were these people who made the journey to North America? They were Libyans, Carthaginians, Celts, Greeks, Romans, Phoenicians, Iberians, and Norsemen.

What is the evidence they left behind to convince Fell of their presence? He has located hundreds of rocks in the Northeast with gouges cut in

35

them. These cuts represent letters of an Iberian language called "Ogam," a system of writing used by the ancient Celts and thought to exist only in the British Isles. He has located early Arabic petroglyphs, phallic symbols, dolmans, cromlechs, prehistoric temples (Mystery Hill in New Hampshire), Egyptian hieroglyphics in caves by the Mississippi River at Memphis, evidence of Roman shipwrecks along the East Coast, existing correspondence between Pueblo Indian and North African cultures, the presence of a Norse tower in Newport, Rhode Island, and other evidence as far west as Colorado. He has suggested that the Algonquin Indian language is akin to Basque from northern Spain and has found root words from the Phoenician language in the language of Maine's Mic-Mac Indian culture. He postulates that during the Dark Ages, the strife in Europe stopped the supply boats, and certain colonies were stranded, having to intermingle with Indian tribes to survive. He points out that the word "America" is an ancient Libyan word which means "land across the ocean" and that it was used in the third century B.C. by medieval navigators.

These first visitors were confronted by an overpowering wilderness that transformed men and women from iron into steel, as North America later began to be colonized and new nations were born. This process was reflected in the contemporary literature of the colonies.

The Influence of Geography on European Literature

The English poet William Wordsworth portrays nature as landscape for the eye's appreciation; his wilderness is never too far from civilization. The English landscape is meticulously ordered and tamed. In his poem "Lines Composed a Few Miles Above Tintern Abbey," Wordsworth potrays nature as a landscape. Nature is tamed. Everything is ordered and in its own place.

While tromping through England, I visited Wordsworth's home at Dove Cottage, in Grasmere. It was late afternoon when I arrived. I was the only guest and got into a lively discussion with the caretaker. He invited me to tea to continue our conversation. At the end, I asked him to show me the room and the desk where Wordsworth did his writing. He led me out to the back garden. When I protested, he told me that Wordsworth did not always write down his work. Most often he would go to the garden or on walks and when he returned would call for his sister Dorothy or one of the other women of the house. They would say to each other, "William is kindled!" and go to him with pen and paper.

Once, Samuel Taylor Coleridge was amazed, at the end of a four-days' ramble, to find Dorothy sitting on a bench, waiting. Wordsworth promptly dictated "Tintern Abbey" to her. He had received his inspiration as he walked through the gentle, accommodating landscape of the Lake District.

Lord George Gordon Byron described the Alps as merely a part of his journey. The Alps assisted him in achieving his transcendental experience, yet they appear geographically to only be mountains wedged in between civilizations. Nature was seen merely as an aid to human enlightenment. A contrary experience was addressed by the first novelists in North America.

Hoodoos at Bryce Canyon

The Influence of Geography on American Literature

In North America, civilization is squeezed between vast tracts of wilderness. According to Emerson, nature wipes out individuality. Nature is described in terms of self. Amidst the fierce wilderness, Emerson explores the capacities of the human being. According to Thoreau, wilderness is at the heart; it is where things happen! According to Hawthorne, wilderness is a problem. His home of Salem, Massachusetts, is situated between the wilderness and the sea. Its very existence was a fragile one. Uncontrollable forces (the passion of Reverend Dimmesdale and the bloodthirstiness of the pagan Indians) are out there waiting to devour an impious soul. The first thought one had upon awaking each day was survival. The early pioneers had a need for identity and an urge to test their existence. They asked themselves, how do we come to grips with nature? The answer was, with physical force! This became the task of the early Americans, and it is still a theme today.

Geographical Inspiration—the First Novels in North America

The French émigré, Jean de Crèvecoeur, popularized the idea that America was a "melting pot" and that Americans constituted a new race. The settlers of North America entered a land free from a preexisting dominating folk soul, where new social ideals could be established.[6] The three western nations that played the most significant role in the colonization of North America also represented the three soul types spoken about by Rudolf Steiner:

> The Spanish — representing the Sentient Soul, settled in Mexico, as well as the American South and West. They brought horses, established ranches, and nourished a rich family life. Their initial interest was the earth, in collecting gold.
> The French — representing the Intellectual Soul, settled in the North and explored the Midwest, opening up the continent's interior as trappers and hunters. Their initial interest was in the animals. They collected fur for fashion apparel.
> The English — representing the Consciousness Soul, settled along the East Coast and gave to the new nation form, government, and commerce. Their initial concern was with the plant realm. They planted seeds and established farms.

Crèvecoeur's *Letters from an American Farmer* is the first American novel. Like Henri Rousseau, Crèvecoeur was a romantic on a search for paradise. In his novel he describes America as a paradise. He said he felt a personal resurrection upon coming to America. He observed that hard work brought joy and that America was a place where everyone helped each other. He saw the farmer as a person of virtue, attached to the soil; this helped Americans to become better human beings. The environment was there to purify, but it was necessary to impart an ideology on the wilderness. When

Crèvecoeur looked at the frontier, the West or the wilderness, he superimposed civilization over it.

In Europe in the eighteenth century, there was an argument against John Hoopes, who stated that man has an innately wicked disposition, that he was merely a social animal. America offered Europeans the opportunity to test this view. In Europe, man had become fully civilized; he did not represent original man and nature. America offered raw wilderness—it offered a total experience.

Crèvecoeur saw cruelty and wildness in nature. He favored the farmer. His farmer was a man of feelings with a liberal education. This farmer projected human attitudes onto nature. This resulted in a person able to control the universe, to humanize and anticipate nature by superimposing himself or herself on the environment. D. H. Lawrence called Crèvecoeur "the great meddler" because he tried to humanize the American environment.

On the other hand, James Fenimore Cooper favored the frontier. In his novels *The Pioneers* and *The Leatherstocking Tales*, the hunter comes out on top. Natty Bumpo, called Hawkeye, becomes one with the environment. He becomes an "earth-god." There exists in the frontier a mystery that must be solved, an all-wrong which must be righted. In Crèvecoeur, the hunter never has a chance; in Cooper, he is allowed to speak. The frontier is finally given a spokesperson who later becomes a cultural hero.

So in the first American writings, we have the conflict of the following:

- frontier openness vs. new needs of the community
- individuality vs. sovereignty of law
- unlimited freedom vs. restrictions

To Cooper the basic issue was settlement vs. wilderness.

Ralph Waldo Emerson, considered America's first major writer, might say that Hawkeye was the ideal American Scholar! Emerson asks questions that had never been asked before. He does away with any obstacle between one and his environment. He asks, "What is the focal point which makes one go?" Emerson works in terms of dichotomy:

self	—	spirit
soul, mind, spirit	—	nature
me	—	not me
inner	—	outer

He is trying to prove that the individual is God. He tries to make an accordion of the dichotomies. They go in and out and touch each other. In *Nature,* Emerson makes a case for active contemplation. Contemplation for Emerson is growing. Emerson says that the universe is wide open, whereas Cooper and Crèvecoeur both say that it is closed.

Henry David Thoreau completely interacts with his environment; he was on a quest for reality. Nathaniel Hawthorne was intent on probing the complexity of the human condition.

One day, Thoreau stopped by Hawthorne's house and persuaded him to take a boat out on the Concord River. It was early spring, snow was on the ground, the ice had just started to break up on the river, and from the azure sky shone a golden sun. It was a perfect day for an adventure.

After they had launched, Thoreau had an idea. Why travel by boat when they could travel more in harmony with nature on a large ice floe? Carefully they rowed the boat to the side of a thick, large, ice slab floating freely and very carefully they boarded it. Balancing in the center, with legs akimbo, they noticed a puddle where the ice was beginning to melt under the intense spring sun. Within the puddle was a crystal clear reflection of all above. Gazing into the puddle and seeing within the billowing clouds and the passing willow trees, Hawthorne remarked, "Henry David, if this puddle is able to reflect the majesty of the heavens, what is the soul of man capable of reflecting?"

The early novelists and the transcendentalists established a tone for the American conscience. This tone helped set the characterological disposition expressed by foreigners when they describe Americans.

The American People

Every visitor is immediately struck by the warm, friendly humor which, at least on the surface, prevails everywhere. The American calls a mere acquaintance a "friend," while at the same time he wants to be seen as an individualist. Americans appreciate being able to express their independence through gesture, clothing, music, architecture, politics, and just about anything else. It is the unique destiny of the United States to be a nation founded entirely upon ideas.

North America is the home to young nations. Only seven generations old, Canada, the United States, and Mexico are still in the process of discovering themselves, and there exist a lot of contradictions. There still is idealism and altruism, yet one also finds hedonism and violence. It is the land of Home Depots and McDonalds. Every bookstore boasts shelf after shelf of fix-it and self-help books. Self-sufficiency is available for everyone.

You can quick order "fast food" for every meal to save time in the rush to do more, and you may never have to leave your car to bank, eat, see a movie, or even, in California, attend drive-in church services. There is an atmosphere of restlessness, a need to be entertained, and a nervous mobility. A modern culture jogs on, lacking spiritual health and moral constraints.

The June 8, 1997, edition of the *New York Times Magazine* was a special issue on America, "How the world sees us." Over a dozen authors from around the globe were asked to contribute. Josef Joffe noted that America's wealth comes from production and from relentless adaptation and innovation. "If steel falters, then they shift to microchips, if the Japanese grab the camera market, then Hollywood will flood the world with movies. The United States is a gambler that makes a stake at every table that matters—and does so with more chips than anyone else."

America's destiny is connected with the ultimate mastery of force. In our modern world, America experiences the destiny of force (in terms of economic, military, and technological force) as her own.

This force was born from conquering the aggressive hardness of this continent's geography. The land has imbued the people who live on it with certain qualities; North America's nature and its landscape have nothing soft, inviting, comfortable, but rather offer constant resistance. The land fosters a pioneer spirit, inspiring such characteristics in human beings as courage, tenacity, perseverance, and self-reliance, but also calls forth recklessness, thoughtlessness, and ruthlessness.

Force requires the strengthening of the "will." The will of North Americans can be experienced through the many scientific discoveries made on this continent. This is seen most strikingly through the history of electricity and its technical application. The pioneering work of Benjamin Franklin, Nikola Tesla, and Thomas Edison are outstanding examples.

Nikola Tesla, for example, as a child in Croatia in 1868, was shown a postcard with a picture of Niagara Falls on it. He is reported to have said that he would harness those falls some day, a prediction that he later fulfilled by selling the patent rights to his system of alternating current dynamos, transformers, and motors to George Westinghouse in 1885, after emigrating to America in 1884. Before coming to America, he developed his first working model of the induction motor, the motor which made his AC power system superior to Edison's DC system. Tesla brought forth his original ideas in Middle Europe. He then produced his first working model in Western Europe, and finally had to come to America to bring his ideas into fruition.

Another example of this phenomenon is the development of the atom bomb. The theories and ideas necessary for its production came out of Europe in a threefold way. Polish-born Marie Curie discovered uranium, the necessary ingredient for its production. Albert Einstein and others in middle Europe developed the theoretical foundation for it. Ernest Rutherford and Niels Böhr in western Europe did the principal experimental work. What was begun in middle Europe was carried to the United States by several European nuclear physicists, including Einstein, Enrico Fermi, John von Neumann and Edward Teller, in order to be brought into physical production. These are examples of the practical application of the will as applied in North America. Is it mere coincidence? Are there other mirrorings of the will or threefoldness in America?

The characteristics of a nation are represented and symbolized in the memorials they construct in their capitals. Visitors to Washington, D.C., are met by the trinity of three national monuments—a manifestation of the threefold human being. Piercing the sky is an obelisk, reminiscent of ancient Egypt, built by the Masonic order as a symbol of George Washington. This monument is both an external and internal symbol of "will."

To the west, mirrored in the reflecting pool, is the Lincoln Memorial. Within classical Greek pillars and an open architecture, sits William French's white marble sculpture of Abraham Lincoln, so alive in its expression that the eyes seem to follow you as you walk through the horizontal space before it. There is a sense of goodness which prevails. Here we have an image of the purity of our life of "feeling."

Across the tidal basin, alone on a peninsula that juts into the Potomac River, sits a domed edifice—the Jefferson Memorial. Thomas Jefferson, perhaps the most inspired thinker of the new nation, is memorialized in a building whose very architectural form is representative of the contemplative.

These three individuals and their monuments stand as testament to a wisdom we can only imagine today, but what are the hidden forces within the earth that affected them and everyone who lives here?

Electricity/Magnetism

It would be impossible to discuss the geography of North America without consideration of the subterranean forces of electricity and magnetism that are especially strong in North America. The magnetic pole of the earth is situated in the Western Hemisphere in northwestern America.[7] This means that the western hemisphere is the electromagnetic hemisphere. This disposes the human mind to discover there the secrets of magnetism and electricity and of other forces of the physical, material world.

Electricity is the Earth's light, the opposite to sunlight. It is generated from the combustion of coal, gas, and oil, which are made to reveal their hidden light. Electricity is the force derived from matter.

Electricity in the human organism is connected with the physiological processes at the foundation of the action of will. No movement of a muscle is made without electrical current, nor is any breath or heartbeat. In normal health, we regulate the electricity within us, and movement results.

Magnetism, however, seems to have something to do with the activity of the brain. Paul de Rochas found in his experiments with mediums that through the application of a magnet, the thoughts of one person can be conveyed to another. Scientists experimenting with brain function in Russia have found that through the application of a magnet the thoughts of one person can be conveyed to another. Today, in catalogs throughout North America, there are magnet-inserted pads, belts, shoe inserts, and so on, advertised to redirect the body's energy to relieve pain.

Static electricity, which occurs in low humidity, is a phenomenon where stationary electric shocks are produced as a result of friction. Static electricity is especially prevalent in different parts of North America. It is so plentiful in Washington, D.C., that many federal office buildings have rubber door handles to prevent people from becoming shocked.

Our nervous system is permeated by electrical forces created by the salt ions in our body. These salts, imbued with elemental forces, originally come from the earth.

The very deepest basement rock of the North American continent's crust, revealed through the erosion caused by the Colorado River at Granite Gorge, Grand Canyon, Arizona, bears the inspiring name: Zoroaster granite. From mythology we know that Zoroaster was the first to name Ahriman as the destructive prince of darkness whom Ahura Mazdao, the Sun Being finally defeats. From January 1, 1909, Steiner uses the name Ahriman to refer to this Being.[8] He describes Ahrimanic beings as Mephistophelian in intelligence.

Mythologically, it is said that the Ahrimanic beings did not want to live in the sphere they were destined to live in by the higher hierarchies. The Ahrimanic beings wanted to conquer the earth, but they had no bodies, so they entered the earth by permeating salts and minerals.

As humans metabolize the salts and minerals, the Ahrimanic beings enter our bodies before we are born. When in our body, they represent what we call our Double, which lives beneath the threshold of our conscious life, and is nothing less than the author of our organic illnesses. In this manner the Double acts as a karmic conditioner.

The role of the Double is to help us into incarnation by placing our lower nature in an affinity with the Earth. The Double is in our unconscious and cannot be driven away. It only leaves us before we pass through the threshold of death. Magnetism enhances the Double and makes it more prominent. The Double wants humans to forsake their spiritual nature and wants them to develop only the cold parts of their intellect, to reject all spiritual knowledge for earthly knowledge, to reject our souls.

Different parts of the earth are more influential in this regard. The Double chooses to be related to those forces that ray forth from the Earth. These forces are most clear in the North American continent, so here they exist in mass. As the inherited body is about to die, the Double streams back to the mountains and again re-enters the mineral world through the salts!

The intellect in Europe needed to be protected from these forces. Steiner points out, along with Professor Fell, that many journeys across the Atlantic took place to study the diseases that occurred in American Indian cultures as a result of their special relationship with the Double.[9]

Among those authors who have written about this concept of the Double are: Feodor Dostoyevsky in *The Double*, Oscar Wilde in *The Picture of Dorian Grey*, Nathaniel Hawthorne in *The Birthmark* and *The Scarlet Letter;* Edgar Allan Poe in *William Wilson,* and Robert Louis Stevenson in *The Strange Case of Doctor Jeckyll and Mr. Hyde*.

Consider the Double and the ruthless will activity of the settlers moving west, not, as is often described in history books, as a river of humanity, but rather as a confluence of human bulldozers. They allowed nothing to stop them. They could do any action without being called to task. This same quality exists today in our last frontier, Alaska. Only now it is the government of the United States that is responsible.

High-Frequency Active Auroral Research Project—HAARP

In Gakona, Alaska, 140 miles north of Prince William Sound, 200 miles east of Anchorage, is a $100 million facility operated by Phillips Laboratory of the U.S. Air Force and the Naval Research Laboratory and overseen by the U.S. Department of Defense. Built by ARCO Power Technologies, owners of twelve patents of the aforementioned Nichola Tesla, this project, HAARP, is being funded through military "black budgets," DOD appropriations that are allowed to be hidden by the blackness of night and are, thus, not accountable to Congress.[10]

The area looks like a large football field with a grid of tall radio antennas. The ionosphere, created by the sun's radiation, stretches from about thirty-five miles above the Earth's surface and extends out to beyond five hundred miles. This thin band of atmosphere contains both neutral gas and charged particles known as ions and electrons. This ionized medium can distort, reflect, and absorb radio signals.

HAARP's activity is to zap the upper atmosphere with a focused and steerable electromagnetic beam. When 10,000 watts are sent out, energy returns at levels from 12,000 to 18,000 watts. The apparatus is a reversal of a radio telescope: antennas send out signals instead of receiving. The expectation is that a superpowerful radio-wave beaming technology will be able to lift areas of the ionosphere by focusing a beam and heating those areas. Electromagnetic waves then bounce back onto the earth and penetrate everything—living and dead. This is the most dramatic geophysical manipulation of the atmosphere since the atmospheric explosions of nuclear bombs. No one knows exactly what is going to happen.

Private individuals investigating HAARP have discovered that this system has been used to manipulate and disrupt the human mental process, through pulsed radio-frequency radiation over large geographic areas. They have observed local caribou running in circles, confused, and walking backwards desperately trying to get away from something unseen. The activity appears to have a profound effect on the migration patterns of fish and other animals which rely on an undisturbed energy field to find their routes. They have noted that the internal body temperature of humans in the vicinity of the restricted area rises, road flares are ignited inside the trunks of cars, car batteries explode, and aircraft instrumentation is scrambled when in the air space near the experiment.

The device also functions as an earth-penetration tomography (a sort of CAT scan). It is possible to create an x-ray picture of a section of the earth.

It has been discovered that there are atmospheric rivers 420 to 480 miles wide, 4,800 miles long from equator to pole about 1.9 miles above the earth. There are five of these in each hemisphere. Weather could be exploited and changed through manipulation of these streams by HAARP.

Electromagnetic exposure is known to cause changes in the chemistry of the brain, fatigue, memory loss, cataracts, birth defects, and cancer. Is this the genesis of America's new military arsenal? North America has a unique position on the earth with regard to electromagnetic forces, their manipulation, and their service to humanity.

The Peruvian shaman Carlos Castaneda wrote about power spots emanating from the Southwest and Mexico.[11] These power spots are geographic locations where an individual receives a feeling of power and strength bestowed upon him or her from the earth. It is as if the earth passes over an inner gift. When you return to this spot, you feel regenerated and invigorated. There are stories of the Northeast Indians standing in the middle of a river and staring upstream as the water surges toward them. This gave them a feeling of abundant strength. Conversely, they looked downstream and allowed the river to pull out of them extra energy when they needed to rest. When I think of Plum Island, a barrier island off Newburyport, Massachusetts, I always experience a feeling of joy and energy. This is one of my power spots. When I go there, I am able to re-create myself. It is important that we find such places in our lifetime.

Nature and Culture

Our task in the new millennium is to bring culture to nature. No longer is nature to be feared. We have fully explored our planet. No longer is nature to be conquered. It is busy re-creating itself constantly as a result of our abuse. No longer should nature be pitied, a modern sentimental paradigm prevalent in our postmodern culture of comfort wherein we decry exploitation of the earth's resources. What is called for is a sensible stewardship wherein we bring knowledge and culture to the protection of a living, sustainable planet. Culture brings with it form and discipline. Wendell Berry supports this when he writes about the need to create an art of nurture, a culture of a nurtured habitat, not as a romantic dream, but rather as an alternative to a possible nightmare.[12]

What is Missing?

Consider a citadel of American cities, Las Vegas. Its entire commercial purpose is to attract tourists with a threefold intent—to amuse them, to feed them, and to shock them. Then it keeps their money and sends them home. A cultural heritage is missing in America; instead we must create one for ourselves. The lack of culture hinders the individual from developing a capacity for spiritual discrimination. What we have is a continuously evolving pop culture of shifting images at the cinema or on the television, which attacks our imagination and floods us with untrustworthy inspirations coming at us through ubiquitous advertising and rap and popular music. Our intuition is distorted by the prevalent and hedonistic view of sexual gratification and the presence of a pill to self-medicate to avoid any pain.

We are pulled between two powerful forces. One seeks to lead us off the earth, to live in fantasy, happily ever after, where life lacks importance, and personal happiness is the only objective. The other force locks us to the earth, denies the existence of the spirit, espouses behaviorism instead of true education, and offers instant packaged solutions for every situation.

It becomes obvious how etheric geography affects human culture and vise versa. We begin to understand why Rudolf Steiner placed such importance on connecting geography and history.

Conclusion

Rudolf Steiner indicated that, in the future, the study of geography would prove as fruitful to the understanding of human destiny as the study of the stars has been in the past. It is my hope that this essay will contribute toward thinking of the earth etherically as a living being and will help people understand their individual social situations through examining their local surroundings and gain a true sense of place.

Humanity must come to terms with what comes from the Earth. The Earth produces forces that can overwhelm you and can create a one-sidedness if you do not meet what comes toward you with wakeful consciouness.

Practical Exercise

The exercise that follows is intended to bring about geographical consciousness and an understanding of the effects of environment on our social striving. Increased consciousness allows us to meet our "geographic place" in a new way. Increased awareness allows us to rise above environmental forces. While I created this for Waldorf school communities, it can be used by any individual or group who would like to recreate a relationship to locality.

The exercise is fairly simple. In general, you:

1. Spend time to study your particular place where you are striving.
2. Find out where you are.
3. Identify the human experience of your area. Create a characterization of the problems.
4. Determine what the one-sidedness in your local picture is.
5. Decide what you need to work on to balance things out.

Once you bring consciousness to the challenges, you will be on the pathway toward overcoming them. Specifically, a study group would write the four main areas (the physical land, the bioregion, the cultural heritage, and human destiny) with the subheadings on a blackboard. Individuals would then volunteer to research an area of interest and then present it to the full group for discussion. It is best to intensify the final sharing over a few successive days so that conversations can evolve and new ideas can be illuminated.

Each presentation would have specific, overall qualities that could be drawn from it by the full group. (Do not look only at the obvious facts but probe for a quality that rests behind the gossamer veil of reality!) The intention is to paint a portrait of the physical, etheric, and astral bodies, and the ego of the area. This exercise can offer a group a more objective view of its situation, problems, and particular destiny.

– Practical Exercise –
A Development of Consciousness of Place

1. Physical land (geography, geology, mineralogy)   **Physical character**

    What does the land look like?

    Geology of the land

    Weather/Climate

2. Bioregion/Etheric life   **Etheric character**

    Plants?

    Water?

    Influence of light and warmth ethers

3. Cultural heritage   **Astral character**

    History

    Native Americans

    Early settlers

    War years

    What is the astral character of the region?

4. Human destiny   **Ego**

    Biography of the school

    Children of the new millenium

    Influence of the Double

    Beginning of the new millenium

By working through the research on the four major topics, we come to an imagination of the being of our unique location. By developing consciousness of this being, we are no longer surprised by outer events. Rather, we become able to understand them in light of the greater whole. In this way, we can use our consciousness to rise above the environmental forces.

Example: Boulder, Colorado

Profile: New-age community. University town with 25,000 students, average age: 29. A lot of people are therapists of one sort or another. Sharp criticism within and without the schools. Opinions and judgments formed quickly. A lot of fear. A lot of astrality. A lot of neediness in the parent body—what is in Waldorf for me? A pervasive arrogance that says, "Boulder is special."

1. Physical land (geography, geology, mineralogy) Physical character

What does the land look like? The vistas are breathtakingly beautiful. At the boundary of the sedimentary structure of the plains and the upthrust of the crystalline granite, there is a lot of visible quartz and silica. The Rockies are young, craggy, decaying peaks, wind whipping and howling at 90mph. Canyons have rushing, white-capped water. There are violent and sudden electrical storms and flash floods.

Overall quality: On the edge, youthful, powerful earth forces feel close at hand.

Geology of the land One end of a rich pegmatite zone that stretches to Durango. Gold, silver, coal, oil, and natural gas are or were abundant. Land is cratered with tunnels from mining.

Overall quality: Silver is reflective and is used to back glass to make mirrors. Boulder has cognitive qualities, piercing intellect.

Weather/Climate Thin air, high altitude (over a mile above sea level), hard to breathe. Takes two weeks for the hemoglobin to adjust and take in the proper amount of oxygen. Sun shines over three hundred days per year. Chinook winds up to 120mph come from out of nowhere. They produce headaches. Dry air, electrical storms. Lightning goes horizontal as well as vertical.

Overall quality: Intense weather. Astral

2. Bioregion/ Etheric Life Etheric Character

Plants Conifer forests (saturnine, dry, fragrant [warmth ether]), semi-arid, Century cactus, succulents. Major growth of plants to be used to combat arthritis: devil's claw, yucca, datura. There is a lot of silica in the plants; this is good for the skin and for the lungs. A number of plants aid respiration. Arnica—good for bruises and healing.

Overall quality: Small amounts of water. Weak etheric.

Influence of light and warmth ethers / Air and fire and earth are strong forces, but there is no water. Oscillating clear light, sun very strong, glare powerful, need sunglasses. Sweeping horizontal vistas out over the plains.

Overall quality: Intense, overwhelming light, sweltering heat in summer.

3. Cultural heritage   Astral character

History Indians came to Boulder to make peace treaties. Hundreds of thousands of buffalo used to migrate up and down the plains here; was a buffalo kill site. First university west of the Mississippi established here. City planners from the beginning. Cerebral—many federal research and science offices.

Overall quality: Organized, entrepreneurial, perhaps too much, throws us out of balance.

Native Americans Utes, Arapahoes, Comanches. Cultural rituals consisted of performing coup on an enemy.

Early settlers Pioneers, miners—Boulder became a supply center for the miners.

What is the astral character of the region? There is an unconscious mingling of East and West Coasters. It is a crossing point. Stephen King wrote *The Stand* about the last city on the earth, patterned on Boulder.

4. Human destiny   Ego

Biography of the Waldorf school The school was started by parents. The first year five teachers were hired. At the end of the year, four teachers were fired. Strong teachers were attracted to the school. Precocious—grew rapidly right into a high school. Funds readily available.

Children of the 2000s The children come from wealthy homes. A task is to help them develop altruism because life has placed them in a situation to help other people.

Friendships The soil is shallow for the most part. Plants don't send roots very far into the earth. This is reflected in the difficulty to establish deep friendships.

Influence of the Double Powerful—the electrical force field of the Rockies can be experienced strongly.

The new millenium The area has a strong influence of soft tech business and is a center for government and private sector research.

If we were to apply the overall qualities to a description of a human being, what would he/she look like?

Physical		Youthful, not stable, with a lot of power
Etheric		Weak etheric
Astral		Very intense
Ego		Cerebral, over-organized—strong head and will forces but needing development of the heart and heart-felt, mature thinking

1. The principle of threeness can be found throughout the human body: the human form is composed of a head, a torso, limbs; there are three types of teeth (molars, incisors, canines), three types of muscle (cardiac, striated, smooth), three types of bone (flat, long, curved), three parts of a long bone (ball, shank, hinge), three major parts of the brain (left hemisphere, right hemisphere, corpus callosum), three vessels for blood (veins, arteries, capillaries), etc. See Rudolf Steiner's *Study of Man* and *Occult Physiology* for more information.

2. See *Scientific American*, "A Spinning Crystal Ball," pp. 28–33, October, 1996.

3. See *Rediscovering Geography: New Relevance for Science and Society*. Commission on Geosciences, Environment, and Resources, National Academy Press, 1997. See also Juan Carlos Garavaglia. *Human Beings and the Environment in America: on Determinism and Possibilism*. International Social Science Journal, November 1992.

4. I am deliberately avoiding going into depth on the relationship of the American Indian to the etheric geography of North America. They had a very different relationship than the settlers from Europe and Asia, and a separate consideration would be necessary to do justice to this relationship.

4. See *America BC*. Barry Fell. Simon & Schuster, Pocket Books, 1989.

5. *Ibid.*

6. See Jean de Crèvecouer's novel *Letters from an American Farmer*.

7. Information about the magnetic center of the earth and ore deposits comes from The Rare-Earth Information Center, 112 Wilhelm Hall, Iowa State University, Ames, IA 50011-3020.

8. See Rudolf Steiner. *The Influence of Lucifer and Ahriman—Man's Responsibility for the Earth*. London: Rudolf Steiner Press, 1954.

9. See Richard Schmitt. *The Double*. Sacramento, February 1981, and *The Other America*. Carl Stegmann. Rudolf Steiner College Press, 1997.

10. To learn more about HAARP, look at the following web sites:

http://www.xyz.net/~nohaarp/pandora.htm
http://www.conspire.com/haarp.html
http://www.earthpulse.com/haarp/background.html
http://www.ufomind.com/place/us/ak/haarp/

Official "HAARP" site of the U.S. Government:
http://server5550.itd.nrl.navy.mil/haarp.html

or read the book *Angels Don't Play This HAARP* by Dr. Nick Begich and Jeane Manning, Earthpulse Press, 1997.

11. See Carlos Casteneda, *Journey to Ixtlan*. Simon and Schuster, 1972. In the summer of 1960, Carlos Casteneda, a UCLA anthropology student,

traveled to the Southwest to do research on medicinal plants. While at a bus station, he met an extraordinary man. His name was Don Juan Mateus, called "Don Juan." Don Juan, a Yaqui "brujo" or shaman, decided to teach Carlos the "Yaqui way of knowledge." It is not known if these stories are fiction or non-fiction, and many critics still debate the writings. They can be viewed as "modern myth."

      12. See *The Unsettling of America*, Wendell Berry, Sierra Club Books, San Francisco, 1986.

Bibliography:

Benesch, Friederich. *Observations of North America*. Stuttgart: Sept 17–18, 1976.

Berry, Wendell. *The Unsettling of America*. San Francisco: Sierra Club Books, 1986.

Cheney, Margaret. *Tesla, Man Out of Time*. New York: Dell, 1981.

Cook, Grace. *The Sun Men of the Americas*. New Lands, England: White Eagle Publishing, 1978.

Fell, Barry. *America BC*. New York: Simon & Schuster, Pocket Books, 1989.

Mavor, James and Byron Dix. *Manitou, Sacred Landscape*. Rochester, Vermont: Inner Traditions International, 1989.

Richardson, Thomas, *Nikola Tesla*, New York: Heath, 1985.

Schmitt, Richard. *The Double*. Fair Oaks: Steiner College Press, February 1981.

Steiner, Rudolf. *Mission of the Folk Souls*, Oslo: June 7–17, 1910.

_____. *The Destinies of Individuals and of Nations*. Berlin: Sept. 1, 1914 and July 6, 1915.

_____. *The Inner Evolutionary Impulses of Mankind*. Dornach: Sep. 18, 1916.

_____. *The Karma of Vocation*. Dornach: Nov 19, 1916.

_____. *The Reappearance of Christ in the Etheric*. Stuttgart: March 6, 1910.

_____. *The Tension Between East and West*. Vienna: 1922.

_____. *West and East—Contrasting Worlds*. Vienna: June 1–12, 1922.

_____. *Wrong and Right Use of Esoteric Knowledge*. Dornach: Nov 1917.

_____. *Geographic Medicine*. St Gallen: Nov. 15–16, 1917.

Stegmann, Carl. *The Other America*. Fair Oaks: Rudolf Steiner College Press, 1997.

_____. *America and the Threefold World*. Carmichael, CA.: Emerson Study Newsletter.

van Emmichoven, Zeylmans. *America and Americanism*. Fair Oaks: St. George Books, 1986.

Periodicals:

Scientific American, "A Spinning Crystal Ball," October, 1996, p. 28–33.

The New York Times Magazine, "How the World Sees America," June 4, 1997.

North of the Border

by

Philip Thatcher

At the age of 21, on my way from Massachusetts to summer work in British Columbia, I traveled via the Canadian Pacific Railroad from Montreal through the Canadian Shield and along the north shore of Lake Superior, across the prairies, and into the mountain ranges of Canada's most westward province. The images from that first journey across what has since become my country by adoption continue to work into my picture of Canada itself, and into the question, what are the differences, as well as the similarities, between my country by adoption and my country of birth, which lies south of the 49th parallel?

Before that first trip, my image of Canada was like that of many Americans—a non-image. As a Washington, D.C., bus driver expressed it, "Canada? I don't know nothing about it. This bus just goes to Farragut Square." Or the store clerk in Albuquerque: "Canada, that's up north, near New York State, isn't it? Only it's not a state, it's a whole country. Is that right? Do I win a prize?"[1]

Indeed, Canada is up north, a whole country, and not simply an extension of its southern neighbor. But, one might ask, why not? Why is there an English-speaking, French-speaking country in the northern part of our continent that throughout its history has refused to join its destiny with that of the United States? What has been, and what might become, Canada's task within the world community of nations—within the cosmic community of folk souls, or to put the question in the light of Anthroposophy, in this Michaelic time? In the course of this article, I want to make some observations that may give these questions clarity and resonance.

Geography

If one looks at a map of North America, certain geographic features clearly bridge the Forty-ninth Parallel: the rain forests of the Pacific Northwest, the Rocky Mountains, the prairies, the Great Lakes. There are other across-the-border similarities that are more than geographic, such as the West Coast way of life that prevails from Los Angeles to Vancouver.

Yet, look again. The seaboards of the southern part of the continent are compact, allowing few incursions from the sea. There are many rivers, but these are held firmly in their courses by the surrounding land mass. There are few large lakes other than the Great Lakes, and they too are clearly contained by land. Here the element of earth seems dominant.

Moving northward, the picture changes. From the Atlantic one travels past Newfoundland, Cape Breton, and other islands to enter Canada through the long waterway of the Saint Lawrence. The approach to the Pacific coastline is even more confounded by islands, and large inlets thrust themselves far into the coastal mountains. The sea begets a fog that reaches right across British Columbia to the western flanks of the Rockies. The Canadian prairies, in turn, are covered with lakes, great and small, while the waters of the Hudson and James Bays bring Arctic waters to within a few hundred miles of the American border. The Canadian Shield comprises some 2 million of Canada's 3.845 million square miles. Extending southward through most of Quebec, curving around James Bay and then spreading northward to the Arctic, it is a maze of pre-Cambrian granite, muskeg, and lakes that has profoundly affected the physical development of Canada, as well as the Canadian imagination.

If the element of earth prevails in the southern part of the continent, the element of water prevails in the north.[2] To the south, the land contains the water; northward, the land is contained by water, held together by a vast network of rivers and lakes and encroaching seas. The transition from the one configuration to the other corresponds to the border between the United States and Canada.

A second observation: the crossing of geographical frontiers such as the Appalachian Mountains, the Mississippi River, or even the Rocky Mountains, which is central to the westward movement of American history, has no counterpart in the history of Canada. The Canadian Shield was never a frontier to be crossed but rather a space to be entered, explored, and named. It was not a matter of crossing it but of learning to survive within it. That picture holds true, as well, for the prairies, and even for the mountains of British Columbia, where the Rockies are but the threshold to further ranges, "poured like seas" all the way to the Pacific coast.[3] Likewise, no river was given status of a frontier to be crossed. The Mackenzie, the second-longest river on the continent, empties unobtrusively into the Arctic Ocean. Having borne something of Canada's history upon its waters, it nonetheless gives evidence that Canada's geography to a great extent stands apart from its history and even overshadows it:

> The Arctic shore
> receives the vast flow
> a maze of ponds and dikes
> In land so bleak and bare
> a single plume of smoke
> is a scroll of history.[4]

From their earliest days, Canadians have experienced themselves as a people few in number in an immense land. From this experience, the question has arisen, in varied forms: how do we enter into and live humanly with this space? How do we form links with one another across it? How do we prevent ourselves from being overwhelmed by it? Canadians had little sense of having a "manifest destiny" to cross the continent, frontier by frontier, and subdue it. It was a matter of finding passages, often watery ones, into the continent and through it, and having the will to do that.[5]

It is significant that many of Canada's artists have taken up the question of how one meets and comes to terms with an immense and often daunting landscape. Poet Al Purdy imagines the thoughts of two Gaels set ashore along the north Atlantic Coast by the Viking explorer Karlsefni (ca. 1000):

> Brother, the wind of this place is cold,
> and hills under our feet tremble,
> the forests are making magic against us–
> I think the land knows we are here,
> I think the land knows we are strangers.[6]

In his long poem, "Towards the Last Spike," E. J. Purdy pictures the Canadian Shield as a great serpent whose tail "swished / Atlantic tides, whose body coiled itself / Around the Hudson Bay, then curled up north." Asleep in her pre-Cambrian folds, the serpent is awakened, and annoyed, by the railroad builders busily driving spikes into her backside:

> Now was her time. She took three engines, sank them
> With seven tracks down through the hidden lake
> To the rock bed, then over them she spread
> A counterpane of leather-leaf and slime,
> A warning, that was all for now.[7]

In "Bushed," Earle Birney shows a man trying to settle down beside "the lake-lap of a mountain / so big his mind slowed when he looked at it." But the settler found "the mountain was clearly alive / sent messages whizzing down every hot morning / boomed proclamations at noon." Ospreys fell on the lake "like Valkyries" and "moosehorned cedars circled his swamps and tossed / their antlers up to the stars."

> then he knew though the mountain slept the winds
> were shaping its peak to an arrowhead
> poised.

In the end, the settler bars himself into his cabin and waits "for the great flint to come singing into his heart."[8]

I could bring other examples to show that the themes and mood of these three poems are representative of an awareness that can be found in much of Canadian literature—that the land is alive with elemental forces that rise up before human beings, surround, and challenge them, that often wear a hostile mask upon first meeting, yet which must somehow be met if human beings are to survive within that land.

Another, yet similar, perspective is found in Douglas Le Pan's "A Country without a Mythology." Here the explorer is a stranger going among savage people with no monuments, landmarks, or traditions to guide him. He soon sheds the graces and ceremonies of his European heritage, shaking berries from the bushes as he goes and plucking pickerel from the rivers. Saints' days, festivals, and abbey clocks, once familiar markers of the passage of time, no longer have meaning, where "months, years, are here unbroken virgin forests." Sometimes the explorer cherishes a vain hope that around the next bend in the river he may meet something, some mark or sign, that will allow him to link this land with those lands rich in myth and history that he has left behind:

> And now the channel opens. But nothing alters.
> Mile after mile of tangled struggling roots,
> Wild-rice, stumps, weeds, that clutch at the canoe,

> Wild birds hysterical in tangled trees.
> And not a sign, no emblem in the sky . . . .[9]

In Le Pan's poem, the elemental world does not confront the traveler in its midst but rather retreats before him, sometimes in the form of passive anger, yet closes in behind him and cuts him off from the myths and meanings of the old world. There are some similarities here to the American experience, in that many of those who came to the United States left things European on the far side of the Atlantic but seemed to have done so at least semiconsciously in their desire to take up a new life in a new land. In contrast, the experience pictured by many Canadian writers is the newcomer's finding that the forms and meanings he tries to bring with him are simply swallowed up in the vastness of Canada and are proved incapable of helping him chart a course into it.

A number of Canada's painters have also tried to engage and reveal what lives hidden in the elements of earth, water, and light. In the work of A. Y. Jackson, J. E. H. MacDonald, Lawren Harris, and others of the Group of Seven, one experiences the artist standing reverently and expectantly before the Canadian wilderness with the thought that, in the words of Lawren Harris, "this North of ours is a source of spiritual flow which can create through us . . . a flow of beneficent informing cosmic powers behind the bleakness and barrenness and austerity of much of the land."[10]

The imagination that a Spirit worth meeting lies hidden behind the wild, barren, and even hostile mask of the land is also evident in the work of Emily Carr. Born in Victoria, British Columbia, in 1871, this eccentric, indomitable woman tramped the forests of the Pacific coast, spent lonely and sometimes terrified nights in abandoned Indian villages, traveled the inlets in fragile canoes, and once found herself at 3 A.M. climbing in pitch blackness up the slimy ladder of a northern cannery wharf, in order to release onto her canvases the unseen realities that revealed themselves to her through the elements

Emily Carr, *Forest Landscape (1)*, c. 1938

of earth, water, and light. Especially the light: Emily Carr captured it not only through the sweep of her skies, but also from the depths of her forests, a hint of Something to be met and known, simply for Itself.

In her journal she wrote:

> I am painting a flat landscape, low-lying hills with an expanding sky. What am I after—crush and exaltation? It is not a landscape and not a sky but something outside and beyond the enclosed forms. I grasp for a thing and place one cannot see with these eyes, only very, very faintly with one's higher eyes.[11]

I have considered the geography of Canada, its effect upon Canadians, and responses to it at some length because there are few places in the country where the impact of the wilderness is not immediate and immense. If I face southward from my home in North Vancouver, I stand within a metropolis of well over a million people; if I face northward, I stand at the edge of forest, mountains, and waters that stretch to the Arctic Ocean, an expanse through which I could conceivably travel without ever meeting another human being. The rural zones separating the two realities are few. Thus this ever-present experience of raw, and to a great extent unnamed, wilderness is part of being a Canadian, even if that is not always acknowledged or welcomed.

What, however, is being asked of Canadians who are willing to wake up with this elemental world? Who recognize that they live in a country not ready to be easily settled or domesticated or reduced to a setting within which human beings make history? The act of naming may provide one clue toward an answer. In the Book of Genesis, Adam gives names to the animals. In Canada many places—mountains, lakes—are still unnamed. Yet Canada's artists, at least, have recognized the act of naming to be essential to their art, and many are committed to understanding more fully what the act of naming both gives and reveals. Could that commitment be taken up and understood in a wider sense?

Here I think of Gurnemanz's words in Wagner's *Parsifal*, that the beings of nature cannot of themselves see the Redeemer but look toward "Man redeemed" to make that seeing possible for them.

History

> In mid-river we join the ancient force
> of mud and leaves moving in their journey
> down the face of the continent and after
> the first dance of leaving
> one element for another we fall quiet,
> waiting for silence to give us a
> glimpse of history.[12]

Canada has a history, even though it might from one point of view seem to be but a plume of smoke in a vast land or a handful of leaves floating upon the surfaces of its rivers. Here I want to offer a few glimpses of that history and how it differs from that of the United States.

From the first colony at Jamestown in 1607, the Atlantic seaboard to the south was populated by men and women who came to settle, however varied their backgrounds or reasons for coming to the New World. In fact, settling into the space between the seaboard and the Appalachians was the primary work of Americans throughout the 17th century. There were exploratory probes through the Appalachians into the territory west of them, but it was not until well into the 18th century that there was any significant movement across that frontier. The Ohio Company began its work in the 1740s, and Daniel Boone crossed into Kentucky in 1767.

One consequence of this early and clear pattern of settlement was an almost inevitable conflict with the Indian tribes along the Atlantic seaboard, once an initial period of mutual goodwill had passed—inevitable, because many of these tribes had abandoned their earlier hunting patterns to become farmers themselves.

In contrast, the French who arrived north of the Great Lakes were the main explorers and fur traders with little interest in settlement. Thus, settlement as such proceeded slowly. Acadia (Nova Scotia) was founded in 1605 and Quebec City in 1608. Yet by 1663 there were only three thousand inhabitants in New France, most of them still engaged in the fur trade.[13] Because of the fur trade, however, exploration westward proceeded throughout the 17th century and into the 18th, both on the part of the Coureurs de Bois and the Hudson Bay traders, as distinct from the slower movement westward from the Atlantic seaboard to the south. By 1673, Jolliet and Marquette were exploring south of the Great Lakes, down the Mississippi to the Gulf of Mexico, and by 1795 the northern waterways had brought Alexander Mackenzie first to the Arctic Ocean and then to the Pacific coast.

Because the northern pattern was primarily one of trading, there was little conflict between the French and most of the Indian tribes north of the Great Lakes. In fact, these Indians became partners with the French in the trading enterprise and were also receptive to the Christianity of the Jesuit missionaries who traveled with the Coureurs de Bois. This was especially true of the Hurons and Algonquins. Relations with the Iroquois south of the Great Lakes became another matter, and the decision of the French to side with the Hurons and Algonquins was to prove costly later in the 17th century. But the conflict with the Iroquois lay elsewhere than in a dispute over the possession of land.[14]

It is also worth noting that the English colonists who came to the Atlantic seaboard left a motherland in the throes of change. Seventeenth-century England was the time when Parliament wrested power from the king, and when there was no king for twenty-one years. Not surprisingly, those who came to the American colonies brought something of the struggle with them, expressed in a strong wish to found new and independent institutions of government. Seventeenth-century France, on the other hand, was the time of Louis XIV, who established New France as a royal province directly under his control, although the practical running of the colony was delegated to a Superior Council of three members in Quebec City. Nonetheless, the habitants who settled in the Saint Lawrence Valley were not inclined to break their ties with France, or with French institutions, even though they were capable of resisting the demands of a government uncongenial to their own welfare. Thus the kinds of issues further south that eventually led to the American Revolution were simply not issues in Quebec, and the stresses upon the value of authority and order there at the beginning continued until French rule ended, only to be reconfirmed under British rule through the Quebec Act of 1774.[15]

This northern emphasis upon order and authority extended westward in the 19th century and affected the settlement of the Canadian West. The first attempts to establish a colony west of the Canadian Shield from 1812 onward were ordered and regulated by the Hudson Bay Company, which up to 1869 owned one-third of Canada. At that time, two years after confederation, the Bay Company sold its holding of Rupertsland (including areas of present-day Quebec, Ontario, Manitoba, Saskatchewan, Alberta, and the Northwest Territories) to the newly formed Dominion of Canada. Its authority, however, was soon replaced by that of the Northwest Mounted Police. Formed in 1873, the Mounties were given the task of securing the West for Canada until it could be properly settled. That meant helping new arrivals dig in, ordering relations between settlers and Indians, and convincing in particular those settlers from the south that the pattern of lawlessness with law and order dogging its heels was not going to be repeated north of the border.

In the colonies of Vancouver Island and British Columbia, also once owned by the Hudson Bay Company, the task of ordering settlement was undertaken by the governor, James Douglas, and Judge Matthew Baillie Begbie. When eight thousand (or so) American miners streamed north in 1858 to the gold fields along the Fraser and Caribou Rivers, Begbie, who came to be know as "the hanging judge,"[16] made sure that the gold fields of the north would not fall victim to the lawlessness that had plagued those to the south. In brief, the pattern in the Canadian West was one of law and order that arrived during the first stages of settlement, or even preceded it, in contrast to the pattern that seems to have been typical in many parts of the American West.

A third historical glimpse: throughout its history, Canada has clearly and consciously rejected not only union with the United States but also some of its key institutions and emphases. Not all Canadians along the way have agreed with that decision, but Canada as a whole has consistently stood by it.

Prior to and during the American Revolution, the Continental Congress sent envoys to Quebec to persuade that colony to join forces with it. Quebec refused. In both 1775–76 and 1812–14, attempts by Americans to invade Canada and bring it into the Union failed (although neither attempt had the wholehearted support of the American people, especially in 1812). The peoples of Canada—French, English, and even some immigrated Americans—stayed loyal to British North America, whatever differences they had with one another.

The Americans fought their Civil War while Canada was laying the groundwork for confederation, which became a reality two years after the war ended. During that time, the men who were shaping confederation looked southward and noted that the American constitution left to the individual states those powers not specifically given to the federal government, and that this provision was being used by Jefferson Davis, among others, to justify the right of individual states to secede from the Union. So the founders of Canada decided that it should work the other way around, that those powers not specifically delegated to the provinces would be reserved by the federal government, in an effort to make impossible north of the border the kind of civil war that was rending the United States asunder.

Other examples could be given to show how consistent this Canadian refusal of American identity has been, at least politically. The question is, to what end has Canada made that refusal? To what have Canada, and Canadians, been trying to say "yes" throughout their history and into the present time?

Canadian Identity

The United States has often been described as a melting pot; Canada is more of a mosaic. Pressure upon ethnic groups to become "Canadian" is low-keyed, at the most. So it is difficult to say who is really a "Canadian," or of what that would consist, other than being born in Canada or having taken out citizenship. There have been a variety of responses by Canadians to this interesting situation, two of which are especially typical.

On the one hand, Canadians have gone through recurring identity crises, with groups around the country crying out for the protection of Canadian industry, the preservation of Canadian culture, and the ensuring of sufficient Canadian content in magazines or on radio and television. The current talks on free trade between Canada and the United States have provoked cries of this nature. At such times, voices begin to ask, "But who are we, really?"

This groping for a clear sense of national selfhood, seriously meant and sometimes worth taking seriously, can also become laughable. As a one-time mayor of Calgary quipped, "Canadians are the only people I know who keep pulling themselves up by the roots to see if they're still growing."

When identity crisis subsides, however, Canadians show a remarkable lack of concern about who they are and treat matters of national identity very casually. Canada did not have a distinctive flag until the mid-1960s. During the flag debate in the House of Commons, many of those outside the House wondered in passing what the fuss was all about. Even more remarkable is the fact that Canada waited for more than a hundred years after confederation to extract its constitution from the British House of Commons and bring it across the Atlantic.

National identity? It hardly seems to be an issue, unless someone decides it should be an issue. Canadian content? Canadian newspapers would shrink to a few pages if they concerned themselves with things purely Canadian. In fact, it would appear that whatever identity Canada has comes, to some or perhaps a great extent, from being willing to look beyond its borders and concerns to the world at large. A lack of self-concern opens the way to being concerned about the concerns of others, something that Canadians have, on the whole, done well.

The life of Norman Bethune provides one example. A maverick doctor who poked and prodded the medical establishment in Canada, Bethune's concern for others led him into the Spanish Civil War and eventually to China in the late 1930s, where he spent the last years of his life with the armies of Mao Tse-tung, designing field hospitals able to provide essential medical treatment, yet mobile enough to be packed up and set down elsewhere whenever the Japanese came too close. The Chinese consider Bethune to be one of their national heroes. Perhaps his destiny reveals something of his country's destiny—to become a nation capable of living beyond the confines of nationalism, and even nationality.

CODA
Hidden in wonder and snow, or sudden with summer,
This land stares at the sun in a huge silence
Endlessly repeating something we cannot hear.[17]

Yet emptiness is also openness, and possibility. Living in a country whose history has been more concerned with guarding its spaces and keeping them open rather than filling them with national content, Canadians have an opportunity to listen closely to their silences, to search out what their land endlessly repeats, to let its mountains, lakes, and rivers come singing into their hearts, and to discern those signs and emblems capable of speaking to a people whose identity is characterized more by possibility than by content.

In the poem cited earlier, Douglas Le Pan warns Canadians not to search their rivers or skies for the signs, emblems, or "golden-haired Archangels" that have informed peoples on the other side of the Atlantic.[18] Yet the channels and skies are nonetheless open for a meeting with those cosmic powers interested in informing the present and future work of Canada within the world and cosmic community. In the lecture cycle, *The Mission of Folk Souls*, given in northern Europe, Rudolf Steiner said:

> In order that, distributed amongst the various peoples of the Earth, the progressive development of successive epochs may be realized, in order that the widely differing ethnic types may be molded by a particular geographical area or community of language, in order that a particular form-language, architecture, art or science may flourish and their various metamorphoses receive all that the Spirit of the Age can pour into mankind—for this we need the Folk Spirits, who, in the hierarchy of higher Beings, belong to the Archangels.[19]

How then to wake up to and work with that Archangel concerned with a people who entered nationhood only twelve years before the start of the Michaelic Age, and whose national symbol, recently adopted, is but a maple leaf upon a clear, white space?

Emily Carr, *House Posts, Tsatsinuchomi, B.C.*, c. 1912, watercolor over graphite on wove paper, 55.4 x 76.6 cm.

---

1. Walter Stewart. *As They See Us.* Toronto: McClelland and Stewart Limited, 1976.
2. Denis Schneider, a Quebecois Anthroposophist, observes that the language of French-speaking Canadians has lost its original crisp clarity and has become more watery.
3. E. J. Pratt. "Towards the Last Spike," in *Poets between the Wars.* ed. Milton Wilson. Toronto: McClelland and Stewart Limited, 1977, p. 63.
4. F. R. Scott. "Mackenzie River."Toronto: McClelland and Stewart Limited, pp. 101–102.
5. The hope of finding a Northwest Passage through the continent remained alive until well into the 17th century, and the building of the railroad was seen as essential to the survival of confederation. Noteworthy, also, is the theme of the world's fair now taking place in Vancouver: Transportation and Communication.

6. "The Runners," *Purdy Selected.* Toronto: McClelland and Stewart Limited, 1972, pp. 21–23.

7. *Op. cit.*, pp. 61–63, 71–72.

8. Margaret Atwood, ed. *The New Oxford Book of Canadian Verse.* Toronto: Oxford University Press, 1982, p. 115.

9. *Ibid.*, pp. 168–169.

10. Bess Harris, and R.G.P. Colgrove, eds. *Lawren Harris.* Toronto: Macmillan, 1969, p. 11.

11. *Hundreds and Thousands: The Journals of Emily Carr.* Toronto: Clarke, Irwin and Company Limited, 1966, p. 61. See also Klee Wyck Toronto: Clarke, Irwin and Company Limited, 1971.

12. Dale Zieroth. "Baptism," *Mid-River.* Toronto: Anansi, 1981, pp. 7–8.

13. A hundred years later, the population of New France was a mere eighty thousand while that of the English, soon to be American, colonies was already two million.

14. Eventually land did become an issue and has remained so—but not until settlement had truly begun. The pattern on the Pacific coast was a similar one. See Robin Fisher, *Contact and Conflict: Indian-European Relations in British Columbia, 1774–1890,* Vancouver: University of British Columbia Press, 1980.

15. The Quebec Act therefore became one of the immediate causes of the American Revolution, lest that unwelcome form of government be extended southward.

16. Evidence shows that he sentenced only two men to be hanged.

17. F. R. Scott. "Laurentian Shield," *Poets between the Wars.* p. 91; also found in *The New Oxford Book of Canadian Verse.*, p. 95.

18. *Op. cit.* "A Country Without a Mythology."

19. Given at Oslo, Norway, June 7–17, 1910: Lecture One. London: Rudolf Steiner Press, 1970, pp. 21–36. Also: Kenneth McNaught, *The Pelican History of Canada*, Penguin Books, 1983.

Oklahoma

by

Joe Glosemeyer

In his "Epistle to Burlington," Alexander Pope advises us to "consult the genius of the place in all." Rudolf Steiner tells us that the forces of the living earth "influence the human being in various ways according to the geographical formation." He has also pointed out that it was the etheric geography of Tintagel that inspired King Arthur and his knights in their missions. With this background, the following considerations are offered in the hope of stimulating a conversation that will shed light on this "genius"— in this particular case, the one for Oklahoma.

Rudolf Steiner has said that the human body and the world around it are related as microcosm to macrocosm. Close examination reveals the same care that has formed the body as a temple of the spirit has also formed the geography as a temple for a chosen people. Work on the temple for Oklahomans first emerged from the primeval waters during the Paleozoic age.

At a time when most of the North American continent was covered by a shallow sea, an island known as the Ozark Dome emerged in the middle of this sea. Land in northeastern Oklahoma is a part of that formation. Later, new formations began to appear in southern Oklahoma. Limestone deposits were buckled upward to a height of two miles. Today, what remains of that effort is known as the Arbuckle Mountains. During the same period, west of the Arbuckles, granite peaks emerged, now known as the Wichita Mountains. Another region arose from the sea during the Permian period: the sandstone ridges of the Ouachita Mountains made their appearance to the east of the Arbuckles. These three ranges, the Arbuckles, the Wichitas and the Ouachitas, stretch across southern Oklahoma almost from border to border, the only mountains in this country that run east and west in alignment with the solar forces.

It was also during the Permian period that a vein of unique red sandstone crystals, called "rose rocks," were formed near the existing seashore in central Oklahoma. These barium sulfate crystals, deposited in the Garber sandstone, can be found in a few other places, such as California, Kansas, and Egypt, but nowhere so abundantly as in Oklahoma, and only here are they red, so far as is known.

By the end of the Paleozoic age, significant mineral deposits had been formed throughout Oklahoma: zinc in the northeast, enough to supply half of the world's need for a time; coal in the southeast; salt in north central Oklahoma; gypsum in the west. Northwestern Oklahoma's Alabaster Caverns is the largest gypsum cave in the world, with its rare and beautiful rose-colored alabaster. Oklahoma also has an abundance of many other materials but is most famous for the vast deposits of oil and gas that are found throughout the state.

A sudden loss of the old life forms marks the end of the Paleozoic era. The Mesozoic era that followed is widely recognized as the age of reptiles, in particular the dinosaurs. In Oklahoma, this period began with an event whose significance persists to this day, for it was then that the iron oxide sediments that give Oklahoma soils their red color were laid down. Rudolf Steiner indicates that iron is present on earth because of the influence of Mars. It is significant for us because it is due to iron's presence that we would eventually be attracted to earth.

During the Jurassic period that followed, evidence of the strength of the polar forces surfaced with the uplift of a line of granite mountains, known as the Nemaha Range. These extended through central Oklahoma and up to the northern border of Kansas. They were later submerged, only to be discovered because of the rich deposits of oil found there.

Towards the end of the Mesozoic era, the shallow seas that had continuously flooded Oklahoma, finally receded altogether, along with the dinosaurs. This completed the fundamental geology. It remained for a time to perfect the flora and fauna of this region.

Equatorial conditions had prevailed here during the preceding eras, but now the poles shifted those conditions farther to the south. The scene of major geological changes moved to the west with the upsurge of the Rocky Mountains. This change brought drier conditions to the central plains. Where once were seas and swamps, a wide savanna emerged with a variety of grasses. These grasses now supported great herds of large grazing mammals instead of giant reptiles.

The dawn of the Ice Age brought further restrictions to the life forms in this region. The vast herds of buffalo and other animals that remained required large amounts of available water as well as food. Although not a single lake remained after the land dried out, Oklahoma was blessed with a system of rivers to support this abundant life.

Like the sacred Ganges springing from an ice cave ten thousand feet up in the Himalayas, the Arkansas River, half-a-world away, arises from the glacial ice ten thousand feet up in the Sangre de Christo Range of the Rocky Mountains. The Arkansas and its tributaries (the Cimarron, the North Canadian and the South Canadian Rivers) all flow eastward across Oklahoma, along with the Red River that forms Oklahoma's southern border.

Life-giving water also springs up in many places throughout the state, but nowhere more abundantly or dramatically than near Sulfur. There, some thirty springs burst forth with both fresh and mineral water, according to the first written accounts. Although not all of those can be found today, millions of gallons of water still pour daily from those that remain.

If the genius of a place abides in a certain architecture that is characterized by its land formations, mineral deposits and water resources, then the temple decor, that is, its qualities of color and warmth, can be felt in its weather and climatic conditions. Endowed with a rich geologic diversity, Oklahoma is also adorned with weather conditions that can be described as not only diverse but also volatile and turbulent. Three different air masses frequently meet over Oklahoma: 1) cold, dry air from the north, 2) warm, moist air from the south, and 3) low pressure storm systems moving eastward from the Pacific. Occasionally, the remnants of a hurricane from the Gulf of Mexico or even farther east will move over Oklahoma.

Particularly in the spring, these systems can collide with enough energy to produce massive storms. These storms can generate tremendous lightning displays, wherein space is rent in two, revealing its etheric life-blood, according to Steiner. Because of the frequency of these storms, central Oklahoma has been designated "tornado alley." These atavistic forces keep Oklahomans from getting too comfortable.

Rainfall amounts diminish rapidly from eastern Oklahoma (average of fifty inches per year) to western Oklahoma (average of fifteen inches per year). The 98th meridian, near Oklahoma City (97.3 W), represents the dividing line between the big bluestem of the tall-grass prairie and the buffalo grass of the short-grass prairie, or the beginning of what has been classified as a "brittle" ecology. This line marks the end of the acid soils of the eastern woodlands and the beginning of the alkaline soils of the West. On a current map, interstate highway 35 is in approximately the same location.

This is also the approximate location of the ancient Nemaha mountain range. A significant feature of a different kind marked this line by the time the white man arrived here. A band of scrub oak (largely blackjack and post oak), from five to thirty miles wide, stretched completely across Oklahoma from north to south, hindering passage to the west. This region came to be known as the "crosstimbers" because of the dense nature of this growth. A government map 9 of 1834 called it the "western boundary of habitable land."

Oklahoma is, also, a transition zone between the short growing season of the North, and the long-season South. Bluegrass can be grown in Oklahoma City but not much farther south. On the other hand, live oaks can be found just south of Oklahoma City, in Norman, but no farther north. This approximate dividing line can be identified on a map along highway #140.

Above all, Oklahoma's climate is characterized by abundant sunshine—it is a part of the Sunbelt. Oklahomans expect to have sunshine every day. More than three days in a row of overcast weather is rare. The wind, however, is not—the days without wind are few.

In summary, the world creative powers laid down an abundance of materials in Oklahoma that could be of great benefit to mankind, or of great harm. From the gypsum emerged beautiful alabaster and an endless supply of selenite crystals—even a region called the "Glass Mountains." From sandstone grew a multitude of rose rocks. A line of diverse mountain formations arose along and near the Red River. Four Rocky Mountain headwaters birth rivers that flow through Oklahoma, from Black Mesa on the western high plains to the swampy lowlands of the eastern coastal plains. Adding to this water supply are other important rivers and copious springs. This structure is blessed by a climate that is generally warm and sunny, but can quickly turn unpredictable, violent and extreme.

As these conditions evolved over time, the teeming life of the tropical seas and swamps was replaced by the dinosaurs. They, in turn, had to yield to the large mammals of the Ice Age until, finally, the grasslands emerged to support the buffalo herds by the millions in historical times.

What then is the human significance of this geographical setting characterized by vitality, bounty, diversity, and transition? With these conditions, all was in readiness for the arrival of post-Atlantean man. We know that in the milder climates to the south, the people established cultures of great power, but their mystery knowledge became decadent. In the northern climate of the United States, although the cultural achievements were not as marvelous, the people maintained a high degree of spirituality, in connection with Mother Earth.

The first culture in Oklahoma of widespread significance centered on trade between the many different peoples in this country and in Mexico. This was a culture of mound builders. The largest site, near Spiro, flourished from 500 to 1500 A.D. As that culture ended, to the east broke the dawn of the consciousness soul age, from whence came the first European explorers.

In America at that time, a culture had arisen on the Great Plains among the peoples whose life and spirituality were closely connected to the buffalo, who thrived on those wide seas of grass stretching to the west from the crosstimbers. The nomadic, symbiotic cultures that lived by these wandering herds lived also by a spiritual ideal that was an organic part of the individuality of this land.

Children in these cultures learned that life is a healing journey that moves in a great circle (Medicine Wheel). Life begins for each one at a point on that circle corresponding to one of the four directions. For example, one may begin in the South, that is, with virtues of innocence and warmth. This is symbolized by the astral nature of a mouse and the color green. This initial quality of life is the first gift that one brings to the whole people, but it is one-sided. So one must travel around the circle to learn the gifts of the West (introspection, black, bear), North (wisdom, white, buffalo), and East (illumination, yellow, eagle). This journey is the vision quest.

The trail is not marked. Each person finds his own way through the life of nature around him. One discovers his individual medicine mirrored in the circle of life. This is the new gift that he can give away to his people, as the buffalo has taught through his sacrifice. One has, thus, found his place in the great circle of life and can dance with his people in the Sun Dance. In the words of T. S. Eliot,

> We shall not cease from exploration
> And the end of all our exploring
> Will be to arrive where we started
> And know the place for the first time.

In their connection to the life around them, these people learned the virtues of courage, self-sacrifice, and harmony as their highest ideals. By their attunement, we see that the spirit of this land strengthens the heart forces. Out of such forces, they met the approaching white man.

A second characteristic of life in Oklahoma is revealed by what happened next. Forty-eight years after Columbus' first voyage, Coronado passed through central Oklahoma. The Spanish influence, however, remained largely to the south and west, except for one important fact: the horse returned to the Americas with the Spaniards. This was a boon to the Plains Indians.

French trappers and traders arrived 150 years later. The goods that they brought, especially guns, also made life easier, in some ways, for Native Americans. However, their lives in this region took a turn for the worse at the beginning of the 19th century. Land in what was to become Oklahoma passed from the Spanish to the French to the United States. The first settlers had arrived in Oklahoma just prior to Thomas Jefferson's purchase of the Louisiana Territory in 1803. Jefferson soon won approval from Congress to send out men to explore this vast new territory. Shortly thereafter, he conceived the idea of making a place there for the "Five Civilized Tribes," who were in the way in the South: the concept of "Indian Territory" was born, which would eventually lead to Oklahoma as we know it today.

"Removal" became the official government policy in 1816. The Choctaws were soon on their way to Oklahoma. Sixty-seven other tribes would be settled in Indian Territory before the government was done. Their re-settlement pattern in Indian Territory mirrored their original distribution across the country. Indian Territory, thus, became a microcosm of the country as a whole. This is the second characteristic of life here: it is a contraction and concentration of life spread out over the entire continent.

This phenomenon was to repeat itself toward the end of the century when Indian Territory was opened up for white settlement. The original impulse that brought white settlers to this country resurfaced in the opening of Oklahoma: the hope of freedom and fresh opportunity for the unfortunate and the outcast. The process of settlement that took place over a period of centuries for the country as a whole took place in a matter of days and weeks in Oklahoma.

This contraction appears to be a metamorphosis on the human plane of the architectural forces that created such diversity in the physical landscape and arranged a climate where wet meets dry, warm meets cold: Native Americans from the four corners were assembled here, and then people from the four races and nearly every culture. Within this circle of life, a force is working to "compress" the human relationships in our society. Just as the forces in leaf and stem are concentrated in the calyx to hold the budding flower, so here astral forces are at work to create a chalice, or "heart region," to hold the etheric waters of life. Given their sensitivity to Mother Nature, the Kiowa and others who lived in this "heart-land" would naturally idealize the practice of the virtues of the "heart," enshrined in their culture.

One other etheric quality, that of "sound," or chemistry, remains to be examined. We have seen that at a very early stage, this region was uniquely susceptible to the creative powers, as in the formations of rose rocks. This same force appears later in formations of alabaster and selenite crystals. Just as we hear in the booming thunder of an Oklahoma storm the power of God's thought, so we see in her rocks an openness to the creative Word. One wonders if this characteristic of Oklahoma's geology hasn't found expression in the significant contribution that Oklahomans have made to culture and the arts. This contribution has been made, first of all, by many of the Native Americans: Sequoias, Jim Thorpe, Walter Richard West, "Doc" Tate Nevaquaya, the Kiowa Five, the five Indian ballerinas and many others, some of whom have gained international recognition. The annual Red Earth Festival in Oklahoma City is the premier celebration of Native American culture. Reduced almost to extinction, the Indian spirit has found new life, creative power, and honor once again through art, music, and dance. What the skill of their statesmen and the courage of their warriors could not accomplish, the inspiration resident in Oklahoma achieved by releasing the spirit of their peoples through their artists.

This same resonant quality then found expression among the settlers, most notably in the songs of Woody Guthrie. He countered the cowboy myth, which some Oklahomans had helped to popularize, by singing from the heart of a common man. With a courage gained in the "Oklahoma hills" that he sang about, the truth rang out in his music. Since his time, Oklahoma has produced an unending string of musicians—black, red, and white—who have followed him from the hills of Oklahoma to the concert stage of America and the world and placed an indelible stamp on the emerging American culture.

If Oklahoma's heartstrings are tuned to the creative Word, there is another aspect of Oklahoma's geography that stirs up discord. As we have seen, Oklahoma is bisected from north to south by a line running generally through Oklahoma City. First marked by an ancient mountain range, which later submerged, it is now marked by the change from the ecology of the East to that of the West, along with scattered remnants of the infamous crosstimbers, over which broke the advancing wave of European immigration. The crosstimbers was indeed the end of "habitable land" as European culture understood it. Here stands a threshold at which the rules change, not only on the level of ecology, but at higher levels as well. This the Plains tribes understood well. Beyond this crossing, buffalo roamed by the millions before the white man came, so the astral forces here were intense. Mastery of these forces was essential for harmony to prevail, according to the Sun Dance teaching. They knew that courage and self-sacrifice were the rules here.

Oklahoma has extracted a heavy sacrifice, wittingly or not, from its inhabitants. The forced removal of the Five Civilized Tribes to Oklahoma has become known as "The Trail of Tears" because of all those who suffered and died. A generation later, those same tribes were drawn into the Civil War at a terrible price.

That, however, was only the beginning. All of the other tribes in Oklahoma endured great hardships as well. The Kiowa elders even decided to give up the Sun Dance because it raised the threat of violence from the whites. In perhaps one of the most infamous battles in the west, Black Kettle and his band of Cheyenne were massacred by General Custer in their winter camp in western Oklahoma. Blacks have been certainly no strangers to suffering either, but in 1921 the worst happened when dozens were killed in a race riot that destroyed their section of Tulsa. It was the farmers' turn in the 1930s. Many of the settlers had plowed up the prairie after the buffalo had been destroyed and the Indians nearly so. In little over a generation, the work of centuries was undone, and they could only reap the whirlwind as dust storms swept over the plains.

This was, indeed, meant to be Indian Territory in that the crosstimbers stood in the way to remind the newcomers to lay aside their old mentality and put on the wisdom of those who had been carefully taught by the spirit of Mother Earth. There is a great "wildness" in the astral forces of the West, just as there is great vitality in the etheric forces, which could drive the grasses up over a man's head and feed sixty million buffalo. Then there is the strength of the magnetic polar forces with which to contend. Without a strong sense of the "people," in the face of these conditions, the heroic rugged individual of American folklore can become the wild renegade instead. Stories of renegades abound in Oklahoma.

Just as Oklahoma gathers the forces of North and South within its borders, so it also draws together the forces of East and West. The broad Arkansas River forms a natural gateway as it passes between the Ozark plateau and the Ouachita Mountains, beginning its long westward climb until its tributary, the North Canadian, passes by the heights of Black Mesa as it leaves the panhandle for its birthplace in the Sangre de Christo mountains. These solar-oriented rivers, as well as the mountains of southern Oklahoma, cross the crosstimbers. This picture, perhaps, speaks to the geographical support available here for the development of the needed heart forces, along with support from the iron-red soil and abundant sunshine. A modern indicator of such heart, as big as the buffalo heart, can be seen in the existence of two charitable institutions in Oklahoma City with global impact, World Neighbors and Feed the Children.

This cross of forces is erected in the hearts of Oklahomans. Those solar forces of dedication and self-sacrifice contend with the polar forces of lawlessness and greed for the upper hand within each individual. Rudolf Steiner reminds us of the poetic imagination of Anastasius Grun, who could see a time when the cross as a symbol of suffering would fade from memory after strife had been laid to rest. The ancient stone cross would be overgrown by the roses of a long peace. In Oklahoma, however, the image is reversed, for hidden underneath the crosstimbers that stood as a barrier to the expansion of 19th century, European civilization lies a vein of red rose rocks, extending for thirty miles both north and south of Oklahoma City. This "cross" stands here, as a guardian, to open our eyes to the genius living in these temple grounds—in the mountains, rivers, and prairie grasses sweeping up to the west—to a life that is not lived in a "place," as in the 19th century European model, but to life lived as a journey. The temple of Oklahoma is a slowly spinning wheel, like the wandering hooves of the former buffalo herds: not a wheel of suffering, as in the oriental tradition, but a Medicine Wheel of wisdom. The wheel of wisdom takes us in every direction so that we may receive the gifts of each one in order to heal our infirmities. Over Oklahoma the air from every direction spins in a vortex, alternating first one way and then the other with the passing highs and lows, sometimes with great ferocity. So, also, the various peoples and cultures have been vigorously mixed here to create a chalice of opportunity and creativity.

We are also stirred by atavistic southern warmth forces, manifesting as fundamentalism, racial arrogance, and self-righteousness that would "lord it over" others. At the opposite pole, we have taken every materialistic turn of the cold, calculating mind, which would plow the soil, drill for oil, or fly to the moon, despite the harm it does to one's neighbor, and justify it as for the greatest good. These two extremes mark the polar current.

However, this stream is crossed by forces that can reveal the eastern light of the spirit and shape that sensitivity through the dark western forces of the will. Consequently, Oklahoma has produced people of purpose who have been able to reach around the world with their social vision, as well as artists who have reached around the world with their artistic vision in color, music, and dance. The crosstimbers of suffering rise up "at the still point of the turning world." When that suffering enters a heart warmed to willing sacrifice by the Christ-Sun and stirred by creation's dance, that is, a heart courageously ready to dedicate one's life to one's brothers and sisters, and in tune with the musical spirit that shapes this land, then the calyx stands ready for the flower. Buried beneath the cross lie the roses, the Word in the works of humankind.

A particularly significant expression of the spirit of Oklahoma and its effect on the destiny of its people was revealed during Easter week of 1995. The polar forces of opposition, using events to the south of Oklahoma City in Waco, Texas, and to the north of Oklahoma City in Herrington, Kansas, unleashed a deadly attack aimed at kindling a firestorm of hatred. What they did not reckon with was the strength of Christ within the faithful, who opened their hearts in love, not anger and hate. As the blood of a rainbow of 168 victims poured onto the streets, the rescuers rushed in by the hundreds with their own blood and sweat, and mourners by the thousands wiped their tears and poured out aid in a spirit of sacrifice: they learned what it means to give away. As the Cherokee saw the blood and tears of their people turned to rose rocks by the gift of God at the end of their trail, so the Oklahoma spirit can enable us today to transform suffering into works of beauty.

When you have struggled through the crosstimbers of this land and dug down below all of those gnarly roots, then you are fit to "be-hold" the red roses of spirit recollection that drew you here. Above the winds of Oklahoma, you can hear the notes of a rainbow people gathered here to give away their all at the altar of the heartland. In the transforming love that flamed around that gift, we feel the warmth of Christ playing on our heartstrings to create a rose of peace to adorn the hearts of those who passed this test. With the passing of the storm, the rainbow of peace vaults this temple to encourage the hearts of people seeking their way through our time.

Hopefully, these remarks will encourage others who share an interest in this field to respond so that together we can learn more about our etheric geography.

Bibliography:

Boeger, Palmer H. *Oklahoma Oasis: From Platt National Park to Chickasaw National Recreational Area*. Muskogee: Western Heritage Books, 1987.

Eliot, T. S. *The Complete Poems and Plays 1909–1950*. New York: Harcourt, Brace, and World, Inc., 1952.

Morris, John W. and Edwin C. McReynolds. *Historical Atlas of Oklahoma*. Norman: University of Oklahoma Press, 1965.

Oklahoma Museum of Natural History. "The Cross Timber," 1988.

Steiner, Rudolf. *Geographic Medicine*. Spring Valley: Mercury Press, 1986.

———. *The Festivals and Their Meaning*. London: Rudolf Steiner Press, 1975.

———. *Karmic Relationships*. London: Rudolf Steiner Press, 1975.

———. *Inner Impulses of Human Evolution*. Hudson: Anthroposophic Press, 1984.

Storm, Hyemeyohts. *Seven Arrows*. New York: Harper and Row, 1972.

The WPA Guide to Oklahoma. Kansas City: University of Kansas Press, 1986.

Texas

by

Hilmar Moore

Texas joined the United States in 1845, the first and only independent nation to become a state. Texas had been a territory in Mexico until the revolution of 1836, when it won its independence. A historian told me that the real significance of Texas' independence from Mexico was that this assured that Texas would be under Protestant rule rather than part of a Catholic nation. Perhaps the recent resurgence of fundamentalism around the world and the rise of the "Religious Right" in the United States can give us a picture of the difference that religion makes in the life of people. If you travel or read widely, you can form an impression of the differences in Catholic, Protestant, Muslim, or Marxist nations.

Texas reserved the right to divide itself into five states. Obviously it has not done so yet, but its great size does pose problems. People in the far reaches of the Panhandle or El Paso or the Rio Grande Valley often feel far removed from their state government in Austin. I live in Austin, and the geography here stretches into the distance like a five-pointed star. Austin is approximately in the center of the state. If you travel an hour or so in any direction, you come into a considerably different region. To the north, you soon meet the Great Plains, the land of prairies that undulates from Hudson Bay to the Gulf of Mexico. To the east, you meet the edge of the mighty southern forest that stretched from the Atlantic coast to east Texas. It is said that before European settlement, a squirrel could jump into a tree in South Carolina and not touch the ground until it was near Austin!

Just to the west of our city, you find the Balcones escarpment, where the uplift that formed the Rocky Mountains drained the huge ocean that existed in ancient time into what is now the Gulf of Mexico. This uplift caused massive rifts in the limestone that resulted from eons of ocean life, and these rifts created powerful springs that are so indicative of the Texas Hill Country. As you go west, you are on a continuous rise until you meet the Rocky Mountains in New Mexico. I feel that Santa Fe is the top and Austin is the bottom of a bio-region characterized by increasing aridity and altitude. An outgrowth of the Rockies exists in Big Bend National Park and the Guadalupe range near El Paso.

Interestingly, as one moves from the Louisiana border to the New Mexico border, you lose one inch of annual rainfall every thirty miles, so you go from well over forty inches of annual rain to less than ten inches! Texas' twelve great rivers and many creeks and springs are truly a life-giving element where water is never a sure thing.

If one heads southwest from Austin, you are soon in the Sonoran Desert that comprises much of northern Mexico. It is a desolate region of great power and beauty. If you drive southeast, you meet the coastal plain that takes you to the beaches of the Gulf.

Culturally, Texas mirrors its geographical diversity. The first settlers were quite a variety of Native American tribes, from the adept Comanche and Kiowa Apache raiders to the more sedentary farming tribes, the fierce and feared Karankawas of the coast (said to be cannibals), the Tonkawas of central Texas, and many others. The first European settlers were Spaniards, led by soldiers and Franciscan priests, whose presidios and missions are still standing and are marvelous to visit. The Spanish rulers and later the government of Mexico began to make land grants to American "empresarios," who hyped the glories of free land and a new start in Texas. Trouble soon arose because the American settlers never felt comfortable under the Mexican government, under which slavery was illegal and whose provincial capital was far away. That a war began is not surprising; what is surprising is how easily Texas won it, due in large part to the incompetence of the Mexican dictator, Santa Anna, who led his troops unwisely, to the disgust of the excellent professional soldiers who would have easily beat the "Texian" revolutionaries.

One of the largest and most interesting of the immigrant groups came from Germany. They are responsible for Texas' first newspaper, the first opera company, and other cultural gifts, and they settled from west of Houston out to Fredericksburg to the west. They seemed to live easily with the Indian tribes, were excellent farmers and businessmen, and took great care to conserve natural resources. Their old stone houses are in great demand today. In their communities, a large dance hall was central to life, and many exist today, still in use. The fundamentalist Protestant Texans had grave doubts about the Germans' love of dancing, beer drinking, and frolics on Sunday! In the 1880s, large numbers of Czechs and Poles arrived, lured by land sold by railroads. In the 1890s, numbers of Russian Jews fled pogroms and became active merchants in many towns and cities. Another group, without which Texas culture is unthinkable, are the African Americans who came first as slaves of the American settlers. Their contributions to Texas would take many pages to describe.

The final group to mention is Mexican. The last decades of the 19th century saw the American Texans take lands and rights away from the Mexicans, and South Texas had a civil rights movement that paralleled that of America, only it was the Mexican Texans regaining rights. Today, of course, the picture is far different from when I was a child. Then the actual border, the cultural border with Mexico, was just south of San Antonio. Today it is near Austin!

Texas had its Protestant, northern European century; now it is rapidly becoming more Mexican by the day. In another century it will be a far different place. Even the geography has changed under the environmental damage of the coastal petrochemical industry and the ravages of improper farming elsewhere. The dominant feature is urban growth, no longer limited to Mexican, European, and African peoples, but now including Caribbean, Central and South American, Vietnamese, and many others. The dominance of oil, which superseded cotton farming, now gives way to high tech in Austin and Dallas. Today the diversity of Texas' culture is becoming more extended than ever before, even surpassing its geography.

Reflections on Early Sacred Music of New England

by

Michael Winship

Music serves as an indicator both delicate and profound of a person's or a people's relationship to world and cosmos. As such, it has great capacities for historical revelation. The re-creating and experiencing of music, for performer and listener alike, can be a readily accessible gateway to the spiritual and historical impulses of the past.

With such revelatory capacities latent in musical composition, it is unfortunate that American art music has had such difficulties in finding its way as an authentically American mode of musical expression. Until recently, such music looked away from America towards Europe for its models and techniques, and consequently, it has not been able to integrate itself comfortably into American culture. The role it has played has been as much one of a cultural icon as of a living experience.

However, there existed in the early days of this country a group of composers, little known today, whose art did not suffer from this confused orientation. These composers produced a varied body of music uniquely American in orientation. Their style of music flourished from the last third of the 18th century through the early years of the 19th century. It was centered in New England, from whence it radiated out along the Eastern seaboard.

What was it about New England that allowed an indigenous style of music to arise? At the end of the 18th century, New England was, by American standards, unusual in its ethnic, cultural, and spiritual homogeneity. The original European settlers had come to the region for the most part out of religious impulses, and a stern and serious Christianity still held sway. A geography textbook[1] written around 1800 in New England described the New Englanders with an equal mixture of accuracy, hyperbole, and insularity, as:

An industrious and orderly people; economical in their livings, and frugal in their expenses, but very liberal when called for valuable purposes, or by brethren in distress. They are well informed in general; fond of reading, punctual in their observance of the laws . . . jealous and watchful over their liberties; almost every individual pursuing some gainful and useful calling. They are humane and friendly, wishing well to the human race. They are plain and simple in their manners, and on the whole, they form perhaps the most pleasing and happy society in the world.

Such a unity of people, place and culture evokes the working of a folk soul. Deeply rooted in the New England experience, and spread out across the continent by the massive emigration that took place in the 19th century, were many impulses that were to have great significance in the shaping of America's destiny. These included the strong emphasis on self-reliance, self-government, and individual liberty; the concern for education; the famous—and infamous—Puritan work ethic; and perhaps a moral approach to life that can too easily become moralistic.

The earnest and pragmatic nature of the New England soul did not encourage an early or easy blossoming of nonutilitarian culture. The Transcendentalists and other related 19th-century movements, the high point of New England culture, were two hundred years in gestation. However, the unifying religious and recreational roles that music played in a community gave earlier rise to the music that we are to consider.

The church-singing tradition that the Puritans brought with them from England had become all but moribund at the time of a resurgence of choral singing in New England in the second half of the 18th century. Fostering this resurgence were the "singing schools" across the region. Singing schools were set up in villages and towns usually during the winter months when the pace of farm life had slackened. In these schools, the students learned the rudiments of sight-singing and a number of sacred choral pieces, mostly by now-forgotten 18th century English composers. The schools were often led by peripatetic singing masters, mostly self-taught, who pursued this avocation as a sideline to another profession.

In their enthusiasm for their craft, some of these singing masters wrote their own compositions, undeterred by their formidable lack of music training. No need to be restrained by an almost complete absence of training! They were in the New World, where all things were possible to the enterprising. The greatest of these singing masters, William Billings, wrote in the preface to his collection, *The New England Psalm Singer*, words that foreshadow that later New Englander Emerson's famous essay "Self-Reliance":

> Perhaps it should be expected by some, that I should say something concerning rules for composition; to these I answer that Nature is the best dictator, for all the hard, dried, studied rules that were ever prescribed, will not enable any person to form an air . . . It must be Nature, Nature must lay the foundation, Nature must inspire the thought . . . For my own part, as I don't think myself confined to any rules for composition, laid down by any that went before me, neither should I think (were I to pretend to lay down rules) that any one who came after me were in any ways obligated to adhere to them, any further than they should feel proper; so in fact, I think it best for every composer to be his own carver.

And so, as the 18th century drew to a close, in villages and towns across New England, compilations of music came off the presses in great numbers, in oblong-shaped, leather-bound editions that, in battered and bruised condition, can occasionally still be found in used bookstores today. Much of what was produced is of little artistic merit, as one might expect under such circumstances. The compositions consisted of the reworkings of European clichés or attempts that reached beyond the technical prowess of the composer. Yet in the finest of this music, a new sound was created, one with Old World roots but grown and formed in the New World atmosphere.

These Yankees wrote mostly sacred vocal music, usually in three or four parts. The pieces were short and structurally simple. The three major forms used were the plain tune, in which a melody was harmonized, the anthem, and the fuging tune, a two-section piece, with voice entrances of the second part more or less imitating the voice of the first.

The composers' melodic sense was colored by the Anglo-American folk music around them. Harmonically they had little interest in the intricacies of their European models. Their pared-down style included unprepared dissonances, parallel-perfect intervals, unconventional voice leadings, and idiosyncratic and modal-tinged chord progressions. These and other such sounds had long been banished from the conservatories of Europe but probably existed in the folk harmonizing of New England. When counterpoint was attempted, it was of a rough and ready nature.

What is the effect of this music? Drawing on the memories of her childhood in Litchfield, Connecticut, Harriet Beecher Stowe wrote in a story called "Poganuc People":

There was a grand, wild freedom, an energy of motion in the old "fuging times" of that day well expressed the heart of the people courageous in combat and unshaken in endurance.... Whatever the trained musician might say of such a tune as "Old Majesty" [by Billings], no person of imagination or sensibility could hear it rendered by a large choir without deep emotion. And when back and forth from every side of the church came the different parts shouting,

> On cherubim and seraphim
> Full royally He rode,
> And on the wings of mighty winds
> Came flying all abroad,

there went a stir through many a stern and hard nature, until the tempest cleared off in the words:

> He sat serene upon the floods
> Their fury to restrain,
> And He as Sovereign Lord and King
> For evermore shall reign.

    To Stowe's account, I can add my impressions of a few characteristic pieces, impressions that might give a further insight into the nature of the New England folk soul. Billings' anthem "The Rose of Sharon" has a freshness and exuberance, a spring-like joy, coming from the folk-colored melodic lines and the dance-like rhythms as well as from the enthusiasm with which he attempts his compositional devices. In Swan's fuging tune "Montague," or the anonymous "New Jordan," the rugged modal harmonies and the rough, vigorous cascading and colliding of the voices in the contrapuntal sections build an impressive effect of homespun grandeur. A mood of stillness, of inward listening and openness to the spirit, is created by the haunting, reflective quality of Goff's fuging tune "Sutton-New," or Morgan's plain tune "Amanda." These pieces, and others like them, can have a powerful effect on singers today.
    The music was usually conceived independently of any specific set of words. Although the words of some old hymns can offer much on which to contemplate, many seem remote and irrelevant today. The music itself, however, can make accessible the living sources of the spiritual impulses that inspired the people of New England and so helped to shape American destiny.

The reasons for the decline of the New England style are as instructive in their own way as the music itself. As the Eastern seaboard grew more "civilized," people became more self-conscious about their cultural standards. Their native music was just not proper, compared with the European "scientific" music that a man or woman of any cultivation would acknowledge as taste-setting. Consequently, the collections of sacred music published in 19th-century New England showed a steady decline in the native style. By the 1850s, a typical collection might have had only two or three of the most popular old tunes, and these were often reharmonized to make them "correct."

This transformation had an imposed, self-conscious quality and was certainly not universally accepted. I found a torn and tattered old hymnal, *The American Vocalist*, published around 1850 in Boston, which contained an unusual amount of old American music. Its editor had written about the earlier Yankee composers with feeling: "Many of them were holy men, and their music, composed among the hills and forests . . . will make the eyes of a congregation weep, while modern compositions have little or no effect." However heartfelt, such sentiments constituted rearguard opinion in a region rapidly altering its character under the impact of massive emigration, immigration, and industrialization.

No longer welcome in their native New England, the singing masters followed the pioneers south and west, flourishing as long as they stayed a few steps ahead of civilization. Today a tiny, much-altered remnant of this music survives in the sacred harp singing that still exists in isolated patches of the Deep South.

Although this music disappeared relatively early from the American musical mainstream, it can have a place in our schools and communities today. Besides its inherent and easily accessible musical qualities, it has a unique appropriateness as part of our American spiritual heritage. Just as we are accustomed to seeing the Transcendentalists as a precious flowering of the New England spirit, so may we see this somewhat earlier musical outpouring as a similar flowering—one manifesting in the world of thought and the other in the world of tone. These gifts of the American spirit can continue to inspire us into our future.

---

1. Dwight, Nathaniel. *A Short but Comprehensive History of the World*. 6th edition, 1805.

2. Lo, what a glorious sight appears
   To our believing eyes!
   The earth and seas are passed away,
   And the rolling skies.

3. From the third heaven, where God resides,
   That holy, happy place,
   The New Jerusalem comes down
   Adorn'd with shining grace.

◆◆◆

These pieces show two contrasting moods. One, "Northfield," is outward and exuberant. The other, "Sutton-New," is inward and reflective. In both cases, the melody is in the tenor line. They are satisfying to sing, and were sung, in two [T,B] three [S,T,B], or four [S,A,T,B] parts. Both pieces appeared in a number of tune books of the period, in slightly varying forms. The present versions are taken from The Village Harmony, *5th ed., Exeter, New Hampshire, 1800.*

2. I cry 'til all my voice be gone;
In tears I waste the day:
My God, behold my longing eyes,
And shorten Thy delay.

3. Shine into my distressed soul
Let Thy compassion save:
And though my flesh sink down to death
Redeem it from the grave.

The pieces should be sung in a natural and unaffected way, with care taken that the melody does not get buried. It was sometimes suggested that a few sopranos and tenors double each others' parts. The pieces can be pitched in whatever key is comfortable for the singers.

Music and Manners:
The American Experience

by

Tom Dews

    I would like to explore what this music and its performance may have to say about the American way of feeling, thinking and doing—or what could be called the American manner.

    What distinguishes jazz and bluegrass from other folk/popular music of the world? In both jazz and bluegrass there is a strange and fragile democracy at work among the members of the ensemble playing together. Each member supports the others, careful to complement but also dedicated to leading innovatively when soloing. A subtle communication must be operative between players; the "conductor" is the spirit among them. The social and musical achievement manifests in sound, so if the sounds are good, we say the music is "moving." As with all good music, the right balance of melody, harmony and rhythm is present—we "feel" the harmony, the melody captures our thinking, and the rhythm may move us to tap our feet.

    One may say that jazz was born through the meeting of a number of cultural streams, but most would acknowledge that it is largely an African-American creation, and this may have assured that it would have a strongly improvisational nature. (It may be a gross oversimplification to say that African rhythms and musical form met European notions of harmony and structure—but somehow something new was born with elements of both.) Some scholars have stressed that Black people in early American experience could not depend on law or institutions, and so for sheer survival had to "live by their wits." Life itself had to be improvised, and there was little margin for error. Therefore, the music was necessarily improvisational. The improvisational nature of jazz can not be overemphasized. When Wynton Marsalis was asked if there could be jazz without improvisation, he said, "Yes, but it won't sound as good." In the same interview Marsalis likens jazz without improvisation to playing basketball without the basket.[1] Indeed, while other folk music around the world may provide an opportunity for masterful improvisation, in American jazz, the improvisation is both "heart" and reason to be.

The jazz soloist leads innovatively; he strikes out into an unknown musical landscape. He has a progression and/or established melody but must chart a particular and original path, taking risky steps that other ensemble players may never have imagined. Hours of practice, knowledge of scales, chord progressions, and an understanding of repertory are necessary here, but imagination and courage to innovate through improvisation are also essential. Yet this is not a one-person performance. The soloist charts a course, but he must be in constant communication with ensemble members. He can go into uncharted waters, but it must be done with the other musicians or the boat sinks.

Bluegrass music is also difficult to define. It developed with less of an African influence and was dependent on European folk music in the beginning. These, however, were reworked and Americanized in subtle ways. The practice of various ensemble players taking a "break" or solo is certainly akin to jazz practice, and many of the same social and musical necessities pertain here as in jazz. Bill Monroe, father of bluegrass, is reported to have said that bluegrass is like baseball—it is a team sport, but everybody has to come up to bat. Jazz and bluegrass composers are often struck by what happens when their compositions are played in these conductorless ensembles. They experience their own musical ideas augmented, embellished, and often completely transformed by their fellows. Often this is such an intense experience for the composer that in the process he will get new ideas and may spontaneously do something he has never done with the piece.

Last summer I went with a friend to a fiddlers' picnic near Lancaster, Pennsylvania. After making several wrong turns, we found the gathering in a small town park—a single policeman was directing traffic to parking in a field across the road. As we walked closer to the picnic grounds, the cacophonous buzz of stringed instruments mixed with harmonizing voices became louder. At one end of the park, several hundred people were seated in front of an outdoor stage listening to performers who had signed up to play, but quickly we could see that the real heart of the festival was elsewhere. Arranged in constantly changing groups of three, four, or five players

—all over the acre of park grounds, under every large tree and against the wall of every picnic shelter or pavilion—were small folk ensembles making music which ran the gamut from old time to folk, with bluegrass and early country holding the mid-ground. There was no admission, and one could play with whomever one could find.

A festival like this is an interesting experience. You walk around with your instrument, milling with dozens of other musicians, looking for a likely pairing. Rarely are introductions made. People may play together two hours before speaking enough to share names or hometowns. I stop beside a fiddler who is tuning up. He has attracted a banjo, with my guitar we make a threesome, and with barely a nod we are off into "Soldiers' Joy" at breakneck speed, followed by an extremely free version of the Beverly Hillbillies theme ("Ballad of Jed Clampett"). We are working on "Blackberry Blossom" when a young autoharp player joins us, and when we start "Wildwood Flower," a guitarist in his seventies steps into the group.

My friend and I played with different groups through most of the day, connecting in the late afternoon in a group that featured an eleven-year-old fiddler. While many of the players were over age fifty, a surprising number were under twenty—a tribute to the appeal of the music making.

A feature of these music fests, which are held all over North America, is that ninety percent of the material is the same, with the exception of some regional differences. A large corpus of diverse folk music is shared by millions of people in America, and they also share the free and improvisational manner of performing it. Most of it is never seen in printed form, yet the complexities of performance, vocal and instrumental, and the virtuosity needed are considerable.

These musics, then, are in some ways emblematic of the American endeavor—the music is democratic, egalitarian; it is constantly "new," and within carefully prescribed guidelines it allows for infinite imaginative creation by a group. The nature of the collaboration, improvisation and decentralization in practice—the democratic approach—and the eternal search for the new both in material and in how ensembles are constituted—these characteristics in the American musics are indicative of the American manner.

---

1. Interview with Tony Scherman, *American Heritage*, October 1995.

What Is American Light?

by

J. Leonard Benson

First of all, "American Light" is the title of one of the most important exhibitions (Spring, 1980) of mid-19th century American painting ever to be assembled. Appropriately enough, the setting for this was a suite of rooms in the National Gallery in Washington D.C., a city which has, in its own right, rich resources for the study of American art. The subtitle of the exhibition helps to clarify the main title: "The Luminist Movement, 1850–1875."

The sumptuous scale of the show and its book-length, well-illustrated catalog[1] with contributions by leading historians of American art offered delectation for those who knew what to expect and must have brought admiring surprise to many visitors who did not.

The term "luminism" is a relatively recent invention (1948) and has only in the last few years become somewhat popular. It designates a major development—probably *the* major development—within the stream of landscape painting generally known as the Hudson River School. The working out of the concept of "light consciousness" behind the term has been a large concern of the present generation of mature scholars.

In attempting to assess the experience these paintings gave me, I distinguished two levels: a formal art historical and a "metaphysical" or, more specifically, an Anthroposophical one. The following thoughts concern particularly the latter, but some mixing of the two is necessary. Indeed, the thoughtful installation of the exhibit itself proposed that the visual arts of the mid-19th century, represented particularly by F. H. Land, J. F. Kensett, M. J. Heade and F. E. Church, have a direct relationship to great American thinkers of the same time, such as Emerson and Thoreau, quotations from whom were lettered above the carefully arranged canvasses (usually a large one flanked by two smaller ones).

Nevertheless, the title allows a rather simple-minded doubt to arise: what is *American* light? Is not light all over the world scientifically the same, given that an identical mixture of atmospheric elements (moisture, winds, clouds, dust, and so on) should produce identical effects wherever they occur? This should happen especially in coastal or marine settings. Theodore Stebbins in his contribution to the catalog ("Luminism in Context, A New View") demonstrated that 19th century painters in northern Europe and Russia on occasion achieved light effects very similar to those of the American luminists. His examples are overwhelmingly marine scenes, and he is careful not to claim that paintings from all these countries have identical stylistic features. The more one postulates inland settings involving varying altitudes, flora, and other local features that modify climate, the less likely are such coincidences; this means that American light itself includes many nuances, from the White Mountains of New Hampshire to Yosemite Valley of California. Yet these are usually quite distinguishable from European counterparts. (Stebbins noted this in connection with a painting of the Bavarian Alps.)

It is possible, therefore, in a qualified physical sense, to speak of "American" light. In another sense, however, Anthroposophy can offer a finer criterion for appreciating the quality of landscape painting in this era of realism in art:

> To clairvoyant consciousness there extends over every region of the Earth a peculiar spiritual cloudlike formation that we call the etheric aura of that particular region. This etheric aura varies according to the landscape: in Switzerland it is different from Italy and again different in Norway, Denmark or Germany. Just as every man has his own etheric aura, so a kind of etheric aura hovers above every region of the earth's surface.[2]

In common parlance, the expression *genius loci* refers to something larger than, but surely including, what Rudolf Steiner is describing here. In the greatest luminist paintings, particularly in the landscapes of Church and Heade, there seems to be an added dimension that eludes words. I take this to stem from an ability of these artists to include in a mysterious way some hint of the etheric aura of the places they were depicting.

Contributors to the catalog trace the development and interaction of the various artists who originated, brought to culmination, and then ushered out the luminist movement. An American style underlying this is assumed, and intermittent efforts are made to define this group phenomenon. There is a sort of consensus that certain features or combinations of features run through the stream of art in this country like a *leitmotif*. In particular reference to this exhibition, its organizer[3] cites the analysis of a colleague:

> Seeing luminism as especially (though not exclusively) American, Novak grounds the style in a native tradition that gave preference to measurement, factuality, and scientific values. She persuasively links to Emersonian transcendentalism the luminist's distillation of light to a concretion of divine presence—more in pictures of calm, glassy clarity than ones of vibrating, exotic color.

The abiding interest of American artists in measurement, factuality, and scientific values is developed further in technical art historical terms by Novak herself in a contribution to the catalog ("On Defining Luminism") and most particularly by her student, Lisa Andrus, in a separate contribution ("Design and Measurement in Luminist Art").

If taxed as to why American art has the characteristics just mentioned, most art historians would probably follow Lloyd Goodrich in his introduction to a 1971 exhibition entitled "What is American in American Art?"[4] Goodrich proposes the specific and unique geographical and cultural situation of the United States as the source of the qualities that inhere in the country's art. Without doubting the importance of these factors, one may nevertheless ask why the cultural situation developed in the particular way it did. Why did religious concerns, discussed eloquently by several contributors to the catalog, remain a decisive factor in 19th century American art and life at a time when materialistic values were undermining the traditional culture of the European peoples? Anthroposophy suggests a way of thinking about this problem on a level beyond the disjunctive (Cartesian) academicism of our time. It points out the parallel between the identity of an individual human being, which remains the same throughout life, and the more elusive but undeniable identity of a people during its creative historical existence. The real and ideal motives that bring the founders of a people together in a geographical unit are of interest to a certain community of supersensible beings, the archangels, from whose ranks folk souls (the term in common parlance) are drawn:

> [T]he rise and fall of a nation is something which (the Archangel) feels to be independent of him and for which he is not directly responsible, but which gives him the occasion to incarnate in a particular people at a definite time. When the opportunity for incarnation

occurs, when a people can be found in the full vigour of youth, in the creative period of life, then the Archangel incarnates in that people just as man incarnates after passing through the period between death and rebirth. Equally, the Archangel senses its impending death, feels the need to withdraw from the people in question when he perceives the individual centers beginning to be less productive, less active and to lose their inner vitality. Then comes the time when he withdraws from the particular national community, enters into his Devachan, the life between death and rebirth, in order on a later occasion to seek out another community. Thus, the springtime of a people, the youthful vigour and vitality testifies to the youth of the Folk Spirit, which he experiences as a living vitalizing force within him. He experiences the decline of the life of a people as the withering of the centers in his inner field of perception.[5]

Further details about the activities of such beings are given by Steiner:

We must think of (the Archangel) as a higher Being, two stages higher than man in evolution, hovering over the whole people, issuing directives concerning what this people as a whole has to fulfill. The Archangel knows what steps must be undertaken during the creative period of a people when the youthful vigour and vitality are the strongest. He knows what aims must be pursued by a people during the period of transition from youth to age in order that his directives may function in the right way.[6]

The principle of a divine guidance in human affairs is stated here with unmistakable clarity. Yet the application of it to specific historical cases is not simple. One gains the impression from reading Steiner that the forming of a people under a folk soul in the normal way has much—but perhaps not everything—to do with the formation of a separate language. Since no new language has evolved in the settlement of the New World by Europeans, it is not clear that a "normal" folk soul has associated itself with this country. As if to support this, Steiner says, rather cryptically:

A study of the character of the North American people shows a people who, for the time being, are under an abnormal Spirit of Personality (Archai).[7]

What does emerge clearly from a consideration of American painting and its context is that a distinct and original culture had emerged in the northeast part of the United States by the end of the third quarter of the 19th century. One gets the impression that a strong concern for—one might almost say an infatuation with—religious values dominated this culture. On the one hand, its bearers had escaped from what they undoubtedly felt was an undesirable constraint on religious life in Europe. On the other hand, their sheer awe before an as yet unspoilt sublimity of Nature on a new continent produced an apocalyptic mind-set, as Albert Gelpi has implied in his contribution to the catalog ("White Light in the Wilderness"). The temptation to rape this virgin beauty could neither be resisted nor morally justified —a dilemma that only accelerated in the 20th century and left a fundamentally tragic flaw in the American character. Undoubtedly it is this flaw that gave an opportunity for Luciferic and Ahrimanic beings to infiltrate American consciousness with spectacular results, particularly since about 1830.

Inasmuch as an increasingly analytical concern with the interaction of atmospheric conditions, light and color characterized Western art as a whole in the 19th century, it does not seem feasible to attribute this specific impulse to the sphere of any one folk soul. Instead, in such spheres must have existed a general formula, common to all nations, for the mental and emotional set within which individual artists of one or another folk extraction approached this problem.

Whence, therefore, is the inclination of artists of all nationalities at this time to pursue the problem of light? For an insight into this phenomenon anthroposophy refers us to an even deeper level of the human consciousness and, accordingly, to an even higher realm of the spiritual world. Out of this deep level the thought may sometimes form itself in the minds of the cultural vanguard: now is the time for. . . . And again common parlance has a word that haunts Western historians: *Zeitgeist*, of which Steiner says:

> In every age there is something that transcends the Folk Soul, which can bring various Folk Souls together, something that is more or less universally understood. This is the Zeitgeist . . . to use an unfortunate term which is in common usage. Each epoch has its particular Zeitgeist. . . . [That] of the Greek epoch is different from that of our age. . . . To the materialist of today the Spirit of the Age is an abstraction, devoid of reality; still less would he be prepared to accept the Spirit of the Age as an authentic entity. Nevertheless, the term "Spirit of the Age" conceals the existence of a real Being who is three stages above men. It conceals the identity of . . . the Archai.[8]

It is not necessary to speculate about the ultimate mission or purpose of the Spirit of the Age who was in charge from the beginning of the Renaissance until 1879 when, according to Steiner, a change of regency took place. It is sufficient for our purpose to notice that, in general, artists in the Egyptian and Graeco-Roman epochs (including the Middle Ages) tended to draw or paint objects in the flat two-dimensional sense, either shadowless or even bathed in a supernal light as indicated by a gold background. There are some exceptions to this, but they do not alter the general point being made here. It was not until the beginning of the Renaissance that the depiction of physical objects in simulated three-dimensional space, made possible by the discovery of the laws of perspective, began to dominate the consciousness of artists. This corresponded to the awakening of the scientific spirit, which enabled man to explore the purely physical aspects of objects with increasing acuity. This one-sided concentration partook of the illusion that artists conjured out of pigments, colors, and shadows in a simulated, increasingly more realistic light. At first both scientists and artists remained aware of a divine framework within which these endeavors took place, but this factor gradually became elusive in the course of the 18th and early 19th centuries in Europe. It is of great interest that artists in the United States retained an awareness, which they applied to their work, of the divine ground of existence right through to the 1870s —and, indeed, to a high degree.

From the standpoint of Anthroposophy, it seems appropriate to point to the temporal juxtaposition of the Luminist movement (dated roughly 1850–1875 in this exhibition) with the succession to regency of the Archangel Michael in 1879. Doubtless, the America of the third quarter of the 19th century, tortured as it was by the moral agony of the Civil War, was the only place in the civilized world where light could still have been distilled "as a concretion of divine essence" by a group of major artists. This looks like the last triumph of what I should like to call traditional spirituality. The coming of Michael signified the call to create a new morality out of the situation growing from the irresistible momentum of a triumphant materialistic science and technology in the Western world.

---

1. February 10–June 15, 1980. Edited by John Wilmerding. Published for the National Gallery of Art, 1980.
2. Rudolf Steiner. *The Mission of the Folk Souls*. Eleven lectures given in Christiania (Oslo) from June 7–10, 1911. Translated by A. H. Parker, London: 1970, p. 38.

3. Wilmerding, p. 17. An earlier American painter is described by T. Stebbins (p. 215) as "objective, realistic, linear, non-painterly." Another definition of luminism by A. Gelpi (p. 301).
4. Kennedy Galleries, New York, 1971. Goodrich found the diversity of artistic trends (he is including the 20th century) to be the key factor (p. 21):

> "There are many diverse qualities that can be called characteristically American; for ours is a pluralistic art, the expression of a diversified, democratic society, giving free rein to wide individualism in artistic creation." This latter statement underlines the increasing complexity and, one may hope, maturity in the American scene.

5. Steiner, Rudolf. *The Mission of the Folk Souls.* p. 59. The incarnation of the Archangel is presumably into the higher members, not the physical bodies, of the people.
6. *Ibid.*, p. 61.
7. *Ibid.*, pp. 50–51.
8. *Ibid.*, p. 32.

What Is "American" in American Art?
A Summary Survey of Two Centuries

by

David Adams

  The first century and a half of American visual artwork was conducted in dialogue with artistic styles developing in Europe during the same time period. With the exception of architecture, it was only after the Second World War with the development of the New York School that within North America a fully original style arose that also influenced artists of Europe and elsewhere. This was followed by pop art and a series of other expressive inventions that marked the beginning of a continuing American hegemony in the visual arts—or, from another point of view, which marked the point at which American art became continuous with the art of the rest of the world (at least the parts of it influenced by Western culture).

  What follows is far from a complete survey of the history of American art. I have omitted many worthy artists and stylistic developments, have concentrated primarily on painting, and have continued the story only through the 1960s, after which American art became more completely pluralist in style. I have ignored photography, film, video, computer art, the influence of these "technological media" upon painting, and the increasing role of critical theory in art production; and I do not discuss such more recent developments as op art, superrealism (or photorealism), conceptual art, process art, performance art, kinetic sculpture, installation art, body art, earth works (or site art), neo-geo, graffiti art, neo-expressionism, and postmodern architecture. In what I have written, I have tried to focus on those artists whose work could convey the qualities that are most essentially or originally "American" within the course of American visual arts. If this narrative inspires readers to acquaint themselves more thoroughly and directly with the richness of the American visual arts, it will have accomplished its primary aim. I should not neglect to acknowledge the extensive help I have derived from a few fundamental and pioneering studies of American art, which are listed in the references at the end and to which the reader can also be profitably referred (particularly the books by Novak, Sandler, and Tomkins).

John Singleton Copley and an American Art

John Singleton Copley (1738–1815) was probably the first American artist to rise above the limitations of the New World environment and begin to construct a foundation for an enduring American vision concerning the relationship of object to idea. Preceding him lay a long tradition of "limners," anonymous artisans with no formal artistic training, sometimes referred to as "folk artists." Their art was rooted in the practical arts of sign-making and the crafts, but stylistically it owed something to the Dutch and English painting traditions dating back to the seventeenth century. The painting of the limners was characterized by linear, flat, hard-edged forms and an equal emphasis on all of the parts of a picture. They seemed to present reality as an idea pinned down onto specific objects rather than as an observation of passing optical effects of light and atmosphere.

In contrast to European art, there was a clear American tendency to avoid obvious, broad brush strokes that could express both the sensuousness of paint and the personal activity of the artist. It has been suggested that one reason for this was rooted in the Puritan heritage of distrust of subjectivity, emotion, and the entire sphere of the sensuous. This intense religiosity, in a nation founded by those seeking religious tolerance, combined with democratic principles that presumably favored a more realistic and even practical artistic expression related to everyday life. The course of American art inevitably reflected this juxtaposition of a tendency toward an objective, literal understanding of the world with a deeply religious orientation toward life that also was expressed in the somewhat pantheistic philosophy of transcendentalism.

Copley's art grew from the soil of this tradition and preserved many of its characteristics well into his maturity—especially a linear distinctiveness to figures and objects, an equalization of parts, and a tendency to emphasize the flat picture plane. Like the limners, he often used visual "formulas" to render certain poses or landscape backgrounds, but he also added the impression of a certain specific solidity. In his portrait paintings (such as his famous image of Paul Revere), he developed an almost fanatical concern for exact likeness and clarity. Out of repeated encounters with his sitters, he would conceptually synthesize an expression of their personality frozen in time and firmly locked into space, almost like a still life painting.

Yet Copley longed most of all to master and paint in the European courtly and academic style, especially after he finally left for London in 1774 (just as the Boston Tea Party was dumping his Tory father-in-law's tea into Boston Harbor). He took a "grand tour" of the Continent to learn the essence of the European practice of painting—that is, as he put it, sacrificing "the small parts to the General Effect" and constructing a tapestry of quick, visible brush strokes that approximated the sensory effects of light, color, and atmosphere. The emphasis on a distillation of individual tactile sensations and depictions of specific material objects and figures from his American experience were relaxed, as Copley struggled to paint less from memory and idea and more from actual, specific perception.

He also expanded his work into "history painting," the grandest and most esteemed of the European genres of art. Although this turn led to some of his worst, most overblown images, it also produced a few of the masterpieces of early American art, especially *Watson and the Shark* of 1778 and *The Death of Major Peirson* of 1782–84. Although based on a historical incident and framed in the visual language of heroic history-painting going back to the Renaissance (think *Michael Fighting the Dragon*), the quite palpably rendered *Watson and the Shark* can also be read as an early Moby Dick-like image of the American struggle with the "powers below" (Figure 1). Such a picture provided its primarily European audience with the appeal of new adventures and unfamiliar places in the New World.

The Turn toward Landscape: The Hudson River School

Another important early figure in American painting was Washington Allston (1779–1843), who

Figure 1. John Singleton Copley, Watson and the Shark, 1778, oil on canvas, Museum of Fine Arts, Boston

after his return in 1818 from seven years in England, adapted to American landscape painting his strong impression of the coloristic painting of Venice. His controlled luminosities, atmospheric richness, and resonant tones created new standards of subtlety in American painting. Using multiple glazes and underpaint to achieve a diffuse glow, Allston used his magic to soften the edges of facts and create a suggestively poetic, nostalgically brooding reverie on nature that was imitated by many later American artists.

The American artist's turn toward the landscape was much expanded by the Romantic painting of Thomas Cole (1801–1848) and the Hudson River School of painters that he is usually considered to have founded. In contrast to the Puritan view of art as immoral, the Romantics helped Americans view art as a civilizing, moralizing, and, indeed, elevating experience —although the Hudson River School was also in part a reaction against the growing city life and industrialization of the first half of the nineteenth century. These painters saw nature as beautiful, not threatening. Respect for the natural world as evidence of God's handiwork was a major aesthetic belief of the nineteenth century—at least until the end of the Civil War.

Rather than for its purely artistic qualities, this landscape painting was primarily appreciated for its literal realism and the stories its could tell. The American Romantics of the Hudson River School never developed the truly imaginary Romanticism seen in Europe. Perhaps this was due to the continual critical caution in their ears against tampering too much with God's world. Their need to grasp factual reality, to pinpoint the physical thereness of things appears as an essential aspect of the American experience. As a consequence of this factual, realistic orientation, the characteristically American approach to painting was overwhelmingly linear, emphasizing the boundaries of clear, luminous form.

Nationalist sentiments noted that, rather than the specialized knowledge needed for history painting, landscape painting required only the natural experience that was democratically available to everyone. Ralph Waldo Emerson's writings on nature had paved the way for a further moralistic understanding of the benefits of contemplating natural landscape (as well as art), an experience where, Emerson wrote, "the currents of the Universal Being circulate through me. . . . In the woods is perpetual youth. Within these plantations of God, a decorum and sanctity reign. . . . In the woods we return to reason and truth." (*Nature*)

Cole was clear that the emphasis on subject matter, the story—even the idea or ideal—took precedence over any sensuous or atmospheric evocations of the artist. In a world that insisted on strong realism, the paradox was that Cole was nonetheless an imaginative dreamer and an idealizing artist who sought to express the inner essence rather than the outer appearance of nature. He wrote poetry of "nature's purer love divine" and was often as sensitive and artistic a painter of nature in words as he was in pigments. His painting thus offered an initial statement of one of the recurring dramas in American art—a polarity of the real and the ideal (Figure 2).

Cole preferred imaginative "compositions" rather than the specific "views" of nature favored by most of his patrons. He preferred to rearrange what he saw in the natural world in order to convey a more definite, dramatic, or concentrated mood of nature that would make a stronger impression. He filled many books with sketches from the field but always selected and recombined them in the studio to produce his usually somewhat grander landscape paintings. It was not so much the evidence of his sight as his mind's eye picture of a scene that he tried to convey through his artwork. He wanted to imitate "true nature" and not "accidents nor merely common imitation that takes nature indiscriminately." After returning from a European tour in 1832, Cole turned much more strongly to allegorical painting on the passage of time, from which arose his famous series from the 1840s on the four ages of life, *The Voyage of Life*. It was felt that Cole had managed to transfer the heroic aims of traditional history painting to the art of landscape.

Cole seems to have been largely successful in disguising from his patrons his true idealistic, nonrealistic interests and methods. His often sweeping landscapes present an ordered, serene, balanced world governed

Figure 2. Thomas Cole, The Notch of the White Mountains (Crawford Notch), *1839, oil on canvas, National Gallery of Art, Washington, D.C.*

by a benign Creator (who is nonetheless immanent in His creation). Cole's compromise solution was taken up by a number of other succeeding landscape painters who are referred to collectively as the Hudson River School—Asher B. Durand, Thomas Worthington Whittredge, and Jasper Francis Cropsey, among others of the first generation. Their collective style was famously characterized by critic James Jackson Jarves as "idealizing in composition and materializing in execution," whereby they recomposed details of their sketches so that "though the details of the scenery are substantially correct, the scene as a whole often is false." Gradually a few of the Hudson River School painters—especially Durand—broke away from Cole's formula to let the compositional structure of their pictures take shape from the components of a landscape themselves (Figure 3). By the mid-1850s, Durand advised younger artists to study nature, not the work of other artists, to learn to paint landscape.

Luminism

The national predilection for the specific and recognizable reached its greatest but most paradoxical expression in the peculiarly American style of painting known since the 1950s as luminism. This approach is usually associated with landscape painting (as a kind of further development of the Hudson River School), but its supporters argue that it is more fundamentally an indigenous American way of seeing that can also be identified in still life, portraiture, and genre (scenes of everyday life) paintings. In mid-nineteenth century luminist landscapes nature was presented on a smooth, mirror-like surface that showed barely a trace of the artist's hand. The aim was artistic anonymity, to remove all visible traces of the artist's activity so that the spectator could confront the image as directly as possible. This was not an approach of "mere realism" but arose from a subjectivity

Figure 3. Asher B. Durand, The Hackberry Giant, 1864, oil on canvas, Yale University Art Gallery, New Haven, CT

that strove powerfully to transfer the artist's feeling directly to the object with no intermediary. Luminism pursued an increased intensity of realism, which perhaps could be termed a "super-realism" or "impersonal expressionism."

As John I. H. Baur's pioneering essay on luminism in 1954 already made clear, this stylistic category referred not just to an attitude toward light but also toward things. In contrast to the Hudson River School, luminism created its own internal world. Here time seemed to stop, and the moment was locked in place, especially by a strong horizontal picture organization and by an ordering of planes stepping back in space from and parallel to the picture surface. There was little sense of the continuous sweep of the Hudson River School's landscape vision; rather, a containment of each part within its own spatial unit arrested the moment in what Emerson called a "concentrated eternity." Expressed again through linear, two-dimensional tendencies in rendering forms, the traditional American artistic concern with the integrity and fact of the physical object (its "thingness" or "thereness") reached its most intense development in luminism. This again reflected a reliance on more of a conceptual or "mind's eye" image than on the actual sensation of the eye. As another indication of a conceptual bias, the detail shown on distant objects was often unnaturally precise.

The somewhat mysterious quality of luminist light (from which its name derives) was largely due to how it was contained within clearly defined spatial geometries, its very subtle modulations of tone, and the way that most luminist landscapes contrasted a foreground area of ultra-clear detail with a luminous, hazy—and sometimes dazzling—background. Here again the transcendentalist musings of Emerson on light have been cited as a significant influence. Consider, for example, Emerson's comment that light was "the first of painters," and how "a jet of pure light" is "the reappearance of the original soul." Or: "And the stimulus it [intense light] affords to the sense, and a sort of infinitude which it hath, like space and time, make all matter gay." In a luminist landscape or seascape, the hazy, glowing distance is simultaneously a realistic rendering of an atmospheric effect, a finite spatial termination to the picture, and a suggestion of the infinite and divine. Luminism became the most effective artistic solution to the dual American need for the real and the ideal, for science and faith.

Fitz Hugh Lane's *Off Mount Desert Island* of 1856 is a good example of the luminist approach (Figure 4). This Maine coastal scene includes the typical contrast between a sharply rendered but basically empty foreground and a firm horizon line surmounted by a radiant, misty wall of clouds. Between these two features, the space seems trapped, as if within a hermetically sealed shadowbox. Unlike the impressionist style that was soon to be imported from France, Lane's precisely formed painting does not allow its light to mingle with the atmosphere and circulate about. It creates a glass-like plane that is somehow both tangible and intangible. His unusual light reminds us both of atmospheric realism and of spiritual qualities. Indeed, it is quite possible that Lane, like his contemporary luminist genre painter William Sidney Mount and other artists of the time, may have been involved with the popular movements of spiritualism or Swedenborgianism.

Although there are other interesting luminist painters I will not discuss, including Mount, Martin Johnson Heade, John Frederick Kensett, Sanford Gifford, and George Caleb Bingham, I cannot leave this topic without

Figure 4. Fitz Hugh Lane, Off Mount Desert Island, 1856, oil on canvas, Brooklyn Museum of Art

mentioning Frederick E. Church (1826–1900), the best known Western landscape painter of the 1850s and 1860s. Cole's only pupil, Church gradually turned from the lyric landscapes of the Hudson River School to more epic expressions. Some of these wildly popular paintings not only expanded the range of common American taste, but widely exhibited works, such as *Niagara* of 1857, and the chromolithograph, *Our Banner in the Sky*, also expressed a nationalistic connection that seemed to suit a nation rapidly expanding under "Manifest Destiny." In the 1850s Church made two trips to South America, producing many dramatically panoramic paintings of the Andes mountains and the Ecuadorian volcano Cotopaxi that expressed simultaneously his scientific and spiritual interests in such phenomena (see Figure 5). Often combining various perspectives in one picture, he visually drew the spectators into the foreground of his pictures only to dazzle them with a grand, frequently elevated (and thus, disembodied) landscape perspective. While Church used a number of luminist elements for his theatrical effects, they are not always used consistently and are often mixed with other approaches. In later years, he traveled worldwide (accompanied by a photographer, who shot the subjects Church also sketched), becoming perhaps most known for his colorful and imposing paintings of Arctic icebergs.

Before leaving luminism, I should also briefly mention the remarkably palpable and intensely observed, non-painterly, *trompe l'oeil* still lifes of the late nineteenth century by William Michael Harnett (1848–1892), John Frederick Peto (1854–1907), and John Haberle (1856–1933). Their composed assemblages of everyday objects seem in luminist fashion to be sealed in stillness within the shallow boxes of their frames and presented in an impersonal way controlled by the artist's knowledge of their tactile and conceptual properties rather than their precise optical appearance.

Figure 5. Frederick E. Church, Coto-paxi, 1862, *The Detroit Institute of Arts*

Painterly Realism

From after the Civil War through the early twentieth century, the general trend in American art was, in imitation of such European styles as the Barbizon School and impressionism, toward the painterly—that is, the broad, obvious brush stroke used to build up forms in a fluid, coloristic way rather than through line drawing. Three notable later nineteenth-century American realist painters who were able to integrate this painterliness —and the outdoor painting usually associated with it—with Native American tendencies were Winslow Homer (1836–1910), Thomas Eakins (1844–1916), and John La Farge (1835–1910).

Homer used everyday, local subjects as vehicles for compositional experimentation. Already in his early twenties, he was acknowledged as the country's leading illustrator, although he began to work more and more with oil paints during the later 1860s and then marvelously with watercolors in the early 1870s. He showed a keen sense for capturing the lifelike appearance of things in a particular light at a specific time, but he also introduced flat areas of color as well as diagonal and asymmetrical compositional features, probably under the influence of Japanese prints. Unlike the French impressionists, Homer's light never challenged the fundamental integrity and weight of the material objects within his realistic pictures.

After an 1881 visit to England, Homer began to see nature, especially the sea, as a challenging antagonist necessary to engage on a daily basis. In 1883 he built a seaside studio in Maine with a large balcony breasting the sea like a ship's bridge. There he lived and worked in increasing solitude, pursuing his personal battle with the vast forces of the sea, gradually developing the spare but powerfully epic style of his later years. The rich colors he had used previously were replaced with a more somber oceanic palette. In *Undertow* of 1886, two half-drowned young women are dragged from the sea by lifeguards (Figure 6). In this picture, one feels a kind of unresolved tension between the three-dimensional elements of the figures and the flatter elements of the ocean and the overall narrative representation—or, more simply, between the right and the left sides of the scene. Flesh and foam seem to share a similar texture of paint, indicating the rougher paint application that characterized his last two decades of work. In these late oils, human figures recede, and the drama focuses on the battle of the marine elements—rocks, waves, wind, and weather. He painstakingly studied these outdoor scenes, simplifying his images to express the stark power of his somewhat deterministic view of humanity's dominance by forces of wild, impersonal nature.

Figure 6. Winslow Homer, Undertow, *1886, oil on canvas, Clark Art Institute, Williamstown, MA*

If Homer could be called an "objective realist," Thomas Eakins would have to be labeled a "subjective realist." Passionately involved with the world around him, Eakins expressed both an American respect for material fact and a vision tempered by his interest in science, mathematics, and artistic technique. His genius expressed itself in two modes—a somber-colored Rembrandt-like style charged with emotional empathy that he used mostly for his sensitive, intimate portraits (including his famous *The Gross Clinic*) and a more original, rather luminist style used for his outdoor sporting pictures. *Max Schmitt in a Single Scull* of 1871 demonstrates a condition of stopped motion and measured containment of space due to Eakins' carefully studied composition and the use of photography for preliminary studies (Figure 7). The brutal realism of Eakins' paintings of medical dissections, his graphic but mechanical instruction on anatomy as a drawing teacher at the Pennsylvania Academy of Fine Arts, and his insistence on drawing from naked models before mixed-sex classes shocked many of his contemporaries and eventually led to his dismissal as director of the Academy in 1886. His influence as a teacher extended this painterly realism into the so-called Ashcan School painters of the early twentieth century, who introduced banal and everyday aspects of life as valid themes for art.

The brilliant but uneven work of John La Farge set him apart from all of the other artists of his time, making him the most curious, contradictory, and transitional figure of nineteenth-century American art. As a separate but parallel (and sometimes preceding) development, La Farge's work independently exhibited most of the progressive features of contemporary French art during the same periods: all the main features of impressionism (but realized in a different way), the post-impressionist love of the primitive and exotic, a decorative flattening tendency, a desire for new forms and ideas, and a wish to reevaluate phenomenologically the basic nature of sensation and expression. He collected Japanese prints before Whistler, painted outdoor landscapes before the first impressionist exhibition, and painted in Tahiti a year before Gauguin. He created a new, atmospheric approach to wood engraving, a new mood of imaginative fantasy in illustration, and an original, psychologically aware type of art criticism. He introduced new effects in American painting derived from Japanese art: asymmetrical composition, use of large areas of empty space, and flattened forms and colors. At the same time with surprising eagerness, he revived Renaissance style painting and decoration with its old-fashioned idealistic and allegorical themes, was a weak draftsman, and frequently worked in a conservative figural style. Puzzlingly, his work can be both strikingly original and dully formulaic.

Figure 7. Thomas Eakins, Max Schmitt in a Single Scull, *1871, oil on canvas, Metropolitan Museum of Art, New York*

La Farge used the visible brush stroke of the European tradition but made his landscapes and flower paintings vibrant with the impression of real and specific light, air, and space. Reacting against American materialism and Civil War violence, he pioneered an introspective concern with the ambiguity of sensation, evoking the underlying, ever-shifting unity of inner and outer experience, of subject and object. For this aspect of his painting, we could call him a "phenomenological realist" (in the sense of the phenomenology of Henry and William James, whom La Farge inspired). His contemporaries acclaimed him as one of the greatest living artists.

Opalescent Stained Glass and Sculpture

La Farge was also the inventor of opalescent stained glass windows, a revolutionary development within the staid craft of stained glass. This was a peculiarly American contribution to turn-of-the-century Western art and craft. In contrast to the traditional, transparent "pot metal" or "antique" colored glass used in leaded windows since the Middle Ages, opalescent glass is cloudy and translucent. Opaque particles within the glass modulate the opacity of the glass and scatter light, sometimes giving an iridescent effect. The layered structure allows two or more different colors to be blended irregularly within one sheet of glass, giving rise to a variety of paint-like effects. La Farge developed the art of flat opalescent window glass in the quest for more sophisticated pictorial means in stained glass. Avoiding light-obscuring painting on the glass, American artists used the new opalescent medium to attain a luminosity and intensity of color greatly surpassing what was possible with the reflected light of pigment painting. Here the pigment was suspended in glass rather than in oil or water.

In opalescent glass window murals, the milky texture, streaky soft blends of color, subtle color modulations (useful for depicting rounded forms and receding space), and varied transitions in value caused by differing glass opacity and surface thickness can remind us of tonal effects of oil painting, while the combination of colors from overplating two or more differently colored sheets of glass is reminiscent of multiple watercolor washes. Moreover, an array of new techniques and applications further expanded the paint-like repertoire of the American glass artist: cast or molded glass forms, chipped and faceted glass nuggets and jewels, "confetti" glass, mottled glass, folded "drapery glass," three-dimensionally patterned or "corrugated" glass, graphic use of different widths of lead strips between glass sections for linear and chiaroscuro effects, and many more. Art critics of the period spoke of "painting with glass" on "crystal canvases" (Figure 8).

Figure 8. John La Farge, Hollyhocks and Cherry Blossoms Windows, *c. 1882, leaded opalescent glass, originally on the stair landing, Ames-Webster House, Boston; now St. Louis Art Museum*

The initial glass types, innovative techniques, and original expressions worked out by La Farge were further expanded by Louis Comfort Tiffany, his wealthy contemporary and rival. Both artists also used the new medium to explore the flatness and asymmetrical composition they were observing in Japanese prints. The hundreds of opalescent glass artists, known collectively as the American School, could be said to have combined a heavier, more material medium than paint with a lighter, more transcendently luminous effect—perhaps once again expressing that paradoxical American combination of realism and idealism, matter and spirit.

There was little nineteenth-century American sculpture that did not merely imitate European work in a less effective way—with perhaps two exceptions. The first was the small quantity of brilliantly eccentric work by William Rimmer (1816–1879), a teacher of La Farge. His figures typically expressed some kind of romantic agony or defeat and showed both a skillful knowledge of anatomy and a powerful feeling for naturalistically modeled form that looked ahead to the sculpture of Auguste Rodin. The other, later sculptor of note was Augustus Saint-Gaudens (1848–1907). Although strongly identified with the retrospective American Renaissance movement stylistically, Saint-Gaudens was able to rise above this context in a few of his greatest works, notably in the Admiral David Glasgow Farragut monument of 1878–1881, the monument for Colonel Robert Shaw and his regiment of black soldiers (1884–1898), and the Adams Memorial funerary monument (1886–1891). The latter depicts in bronze a shrouded, brooding figure seated on a rugged boulder, an image inspired by Buddhist statues and executed for author Henry Adams with guidance from La Farge.

Early Modern Architecture

In architecture, some of the first original American developments can be perceived during the 1880s in the designs of Henry Hobson Richardson (1838–1886). His early work beginning in the 1870s was designed either in the picturesque American "Shingle Style" (where a house's walls are covered with wooden shingles) or in a particularly solid revival of the round-arched Romanesque style. He drew freely on a variety of historical styles, reorganizing them between 1877 and 1887 in over sixty buildings that had a tremendous influence on American architecture. By the mid-1880s probably no sizable city in the United States did not have at least a few prominent buildings imitating Richardson's style.

Richardson focused on the Romanesque style because it was direct, solid, and simple—characteristics that he thought reflected the American approach to building construction. He emphasized the sense of weight and massiveness in his buildings by the depth of the windows, the broad planes of the roofs, use of heavy, usually rough-surfaced masonry, and a general largeness and simplicity of form. This rusticity was, in turn, ennobled and formalized by elements added from various design traditions. Eventually his concentration on a clear relationship of solid to void, of wall to window, became a harmonious, abstract composing that hardly referred to any past style. Probably his most important building for later architecture was the Marshall Field Wholesale Store in Chicago, built between 1885 and 1887 (and demolished in 1930; see Figure 9). This austere, massive granite block was articulated only by the shape, scale, and rhythm of its openings. Like a Roman aqueduct without any classical ornament, three rows of ever smaller arcades doubled, then quadrupled up the building, creating a tree-like unfolding of the motif. U-shaped around a central court, this refined distillation of other commercial architecture in Chicago created a somber, modernized renaissance palace for the business world.

Figure 9. Henry Hobson Richardson. Marshall Field Wholesale Store, Chicago, IL

Louis Sullivan (1856–1924) praised Richardson's design and showed its influence in the famous auditorium that he built in Chicago with partner Dankmar Adler in 1886–1889. Like many other late nineteenth-century architects in Chicago, Sullivan pondered the best solution to the new design problem of the tall office building. While the development of the modern "skyscraper" that resulted from their efforts was really a group project including as much engineering as architectural expertise, Sullivan contributed not only a large share of the key building designs but also devised an appropriate functional design theory.

The famous aphorism of Louis Sullivan, "Form follows function," has often been taken as a motto for the entire modernist movement in architecture and design. Although Sullivan is usually credited with the first definite statement of an architectural theory based on an analogy between the form-function relationship in living nature and in architecture, his ideas were strongly influenced by the conceptions of nineteenth-century German architectural writers going back to Goethe, as transmitted by the many German immigrant architects in Chicago. In Sullivan's architectural theory, the functionalism necessary for life in nature was considered necessary for beauty in architectural design. Sullivan had also derived this analogy from his own nature studies and from contemplation of Herbert Spencer's biological writings, which discuss earlier debates among biologists about the relative roles of form and function in living organisms. Also, Sullivan's grandfather, a follower of transcendentalist George Ripley, nurtured in the young Sullivan a love of nature and free thinking. Sullivan's conceptions, in turn, were passed on to his influential assistant Frank Lloyd Wright, the most visible twentieth-century advocate of "organic architecture."

Sullivan made penetrating efforts to discover and then create according to the underlying principles or laws by which the visible forms of nature come about. That Sullivan felt he had grasped an essential and universal verity is indicated in his 1901 article, "Function and Form": "The interrelation of function and form. It has no beginning, no ending. It is immeasurably small, immeasurably vast; inscrutably mobile, infinitely serene; intimately complex yet simple." As applied to the tall commercial building, Sullivan attempted to express its practical functions: a ground floor of stores requiring ready access, light, and large areas; a second story of large, accessible, well-lit rooms; an indefinite stack of identical offices; and, at the top, a large attic for pipes, tanks, valves, and other equipment related to the building's utilities. In addition to these, he wanted to represent the overall character of "loftiness" of such a building as "a proud and soaring thing" with no dissenting lines. A look at Sullivan's Wainwright Building in St. Louis of 1890–1891 or his destroyed Guaranty Building in Buffalo of 1894–1895 indicates that these structures arose directly from this functional and expressive program (Figure 10). The first two stories use a different stone sheathing and feature an obvious entrance and larger windows; above this rise several uniform tiers of offices pierced by unbroken vertical lines; and on the top story, a large projecting slab terminates the ascension above a profusion of curving terra cotta ornament. Veering from Sullivan's functionalist foundation, the later development of the American skyscraper pursued the imitation of abstract European aesthetic and geometric factors introduced by architects such as Mies van der Rohe and Le Corbusier.

Sullivan perhaps recognized that the essential functions of plants exist more in time than in space. The visible form of the function "oak" is one that changes through the seasons. Sullivan reflected this botanical metamorphosis of form in the method for generating his unique style of organic architectural ornament. This was pictorially described only late in his career in the publication he finished in 1923, *A System of Architectural Ornament According with the Philosophy of Man's Powers.* Therein several sequences illustrate the production of an intricate, stylized design through a progressive transformation of a simple geometric or organic form abstracted from nature (Figure 11).

Figure 10. Louis Sullivan. Guaranty Building, *Buffalo, New York, 1894–95. Chicago Architectural Photographing Company*

In his 1914 *In the Cause of Architecture,* Frank Lloyd Wright (1867–1959) stated the basic concept of his organic approach to design: "By organic architecture I mean an architecture that develops from within outward in harmony with the conditions of its being as distinguished from one that is applied from without." Wright worked out this general principle in many directions, developing a quite varied application of an organic approach to architecture that included, in addition to his mentor Sullivan's functionalist concepts, the shaping of a building's exterior by its interior space (i.e., by its living uses), the uniqueness of every structure, a complete integration of parts and whole, plan and/or ornament forms based on local minerals and plants, use of local materials with designs appropriate to their nature, a more flexible division of internal spaces by screens and panels (rather than the house as a box), horizontality to express both kinship with the ground and the sheltering function of the low, spreading roof (especially in his "prairie houses"), use of human scale for all proportions, and a close—even intimate—relationship of design to site and client (Figure 12). It should be mentioned that Wright conceived form and function as interdependent concepts, rather than viewing function as a deterministic cause of form. He also argued that the use of standardization and mass production in architecture must always be "humanized and made flexible in design" so that architecture will continue to express "a deeper sense of human life values" (*The Natural House*, 1954).

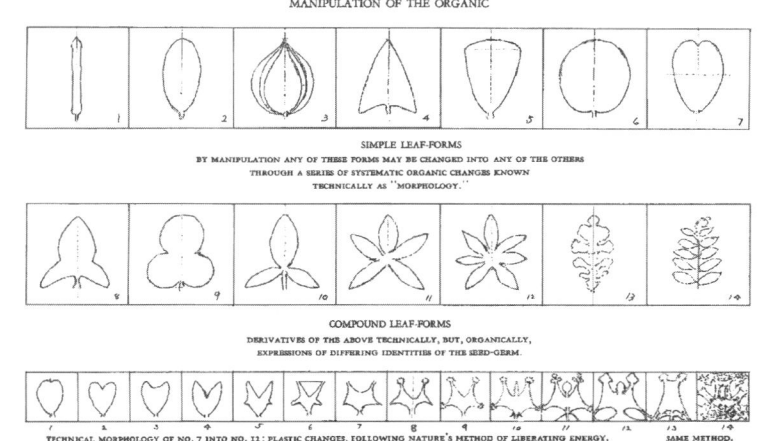

Figure 11. Plate 2 from Louis Sullivan, A System of Architectural Ornament According with the Philosophy of Man's Powers. *New York: AIA Press, 1924*

In a democratic spirit, Wright hoped to bring better design to everyone, as in his Usonian houses and his mass-produced furniture designs. The Usonian houses were smaller, simpler versions of his prairie style homes, which he cast into a few standard plans. Just after the Second World War these seemed to capture the mood of the emerging middle class and were quickly adapted by building contractors, speculators, and women's magazines. For the next several decades—and even today—they set the tone for most modern domestic architecture in the United States. But where Wright always adapted his standard plans to different sites and aesthetically proportioned his designs, most imitators were less sensitive, resulting in endless, clumsy, monotonously similar housing tract developments of "shoebox" or split-level "ranch" houses.

Always looking to nature for guiding principles of architecture, Wright's later work moved from his earlier horizontally and rectangularly based style to a more varied, flexible, and eclectic world of forms, often emphasizing a specific formal theme ("grammar") used throughout a building, especially rounded elements. This later work, which included the spiraling Guggenheim Museum in New York City, employed the representational function of architecture, conceived as an art of infinite possibilities "expressive far beyond mere function in the realm of the human spirit" (*The Natural House*).

Early Twentieth-Century Modern

The first half of the twentieth century saw American painters and sculptors more or less imitating avant-garde stylistic developments in Europe. Beginning already in the last decade of the nineteenth century, French impressionism was well received and much imitated in America. Its brightly colored palette, cheerful sensuousness, and secular light gradually replaced the more divine light and a temporal effect that had been expressed in luminism. Along with this arose a greater attention to the individual expression of the artist's self (which had been carefully removed in luminist pictures). However, the American impressionists were more reluctant than their French counterparts to fracture solid objects into a web of individually "broken" brush strokes. Solidly based in the absolute of "God's blueprint" in nature, American culture was not yet

Figure 12. Frank Lloyd Wright. Robie House, *Chicago. 1909. Chicago Architectural Photographing Company*

ready to decompose the appearance of reality under the broken impressionist brush stroke. American painters adopted mainly the painterly technique of impressionism (broken brushwork, brighter color, a lively surface), while forms generally maintained their volume, structure, and contoured shapes under the "quieter" American version of impressionism. A few of the leading American impressionist painters were Mary Cassatt, John Singer Sargeant, William Merritt Chase, Theodore Robinson, Childe Hassam, John Henry Twachtman, and Thomas Dewing.

Although a large segment of the American art community continued for many decades to resist the early twentieth-century modernist styles of abstraction (such as cubism, futurism, and constructivism), these were introduced to American shores by the famous New York Armory Show of 1913 and by a series of exhibitions beginning in 1908 at 291, the New York City gallery of pioneer modern photographer Alfred Stieglitz. In addition to synchronism (to be discussed later) and some flashes of commercial label imagery that appeared in the colorful works of Gerald Murphy, Stuart Davis, and Charles Demuth (prefiguring the pop art of the 1960s), I would like to point to three early modernist American artists who introduced an independent expression of line and color as well as elements of abstracted form in order to express something more originally American in relation to the experience of nature: Arthur Dove, Georgia O'Keeffe, and Charles Burchfield. Their abstractions ranged from the cellular, musical, and even spiritual, on the one hand, to the inventively formal and aesthetic on the other—but always primarily conveying their experience of the qualities of a particular natural reality or a spirit of place. Although having a few formal qualities in common with these early modernists, the precisionist movement of the 1920s and 1930s in painting and photography was perhaps the opposite manifestation. Precisionism admired and tried to express the formal qualities of modern technology and industrialized society in a somewhat revamped luminist language (e.g., clean lines, sharp edges, anonymous surfaces, geometric planar shapes, flat colors).

Both Dove and O'Keeffe were part of the Stieglitz circle of artists, and other artists from this group, such as Max Weber, John Marin, and Abraham Walkowitz, used stylized and abstracted elements more to express the exciting, bustling qualities of New York City than the being of nature. Arthur Dove (1880–1946) invented a highly personal style of painting, informed on the one hand by contemporary discoveries in science and on the other hand by the occult. The Stieglitz circle regularly discussed such scientific developments as Einstein's theory of relativity showing the interdependence of matter and energy, the concept of nature as permeated by electromagnetic "force fields," and related phenomena such as Χ-rays and radio waves. Dove and some other artists linked these ideas to interests in the conceptions and practices of Theosophy, Vedanta, the Kabbalah, and other occult philosophies, with Dove claiming to himself possess a degree of clairvoyance. The Theosophical Society, for example, taught that the universe was a continuous medium of energy, mind and matter both being different levels of vibrations, and even provided colored paintings of the clairvoyant appearance of illustrative "thought forms."

However, Dove was unique in transposing these ideas into the context of landscape, although he was perhaps somewhat influenced in this direction by the writings and paintings of Vasily Kandinsky in Germany. Dove explained in interviews along with his first exhibition in 1912 that his work also was based on the mathematical and geometric laws he "sensed" within nature (later expanded to include projective geometry). Use of more or less geometrical shapes provided him a certain structural order in the realm of nonrepresentational art, but he also colored and composed them to suggest nature's order. In a pastel such as *Nature Symbolized No. 2*, of 1911 (also titled *Wind on a Hillside*, after its immediate inspiration; see Figure 13), it could be said that Dove both geometricized nature and naturalized geometry. He typically used a geometry of curves that related to organic forms more to evoke the inner order or formative forces of nature than to depict any specific thing. Using repeated or radiating shapes that were lightly shaded and progressively scaled to suggest expansive motion, he sought to

Figure 13. Arthur Dove. Nature Symbolized No. 2 (or Wind on a Hillside). *1911. Pastel on paper mounted on plywood. Art Institute of Chicago*

achieve a quality of charged picture space and an interaction between form and surface that paralleled the scientific-occult ideas of nature as an integrated field of forces.

In a 1916 exhibition catalog, Dove made clear that he tried to capture more the inward human reaction to nature within an "inner space," "the reflection from my inner consciousness." Rather than using abstraction to try to liberate art from nature, as was often seen in European modernism, Dove used it as a way to discover how art and nature can be one, to suggest the presence of the supernatural within the natural. In this sense, Dove's work can be linked to the ideals of divine immanence characteristic of the earlier Hudson River School. In turn, Dove's work has strongly influenced several late-twentieth-century painters, such as Bill Jensen and Gregory Amenoff.

Georgia O'Keeffe (1887–1986) turned to abstraction in painting shortly after seeing an exhibition of Dove's paintings at 291 in New York in 1914. Her own somewhat similar paintings were exhibited there two years later by Alfred Stieglitz, whom she married in 1924 to form one of the great artistic partnerships of American culture. Many of her early non-representational paintings were inspired by music, but others developed a simplified way of conveying the more grandiose and sublime aspects of the American landscape, especially the West (Figure 14). Rather than expressing the landscape itself, she was trying to paint her own inner experience of it. Beginning in 1924, she expanded this theme to intense, closeup but large-scale views of specific, emblematic objects of the landscape—especially flowers and later, after she began living in the southwestern desert in 1929, bleached animal bones. These paintings seemed to relate to the American tradition of solid forms, precise linear feeling, and local colors. However, O'Keeffe imbued

Figure 14. Georgia O'Keeffe. Blue and Green Music. 1919. Oil on canvas. Art Institute of Chicago

them with her previous interests in abstract composition and limited but other-worldly colors so that the flower forms evoked invisibly active growth processes, and the iconic bone forms, products of death, ironically seemed filled with life. She thus created a visual world that was simultaneously remote and familiar, chastely severe and delicately sensuous, a uniquely American combination of Puritan simplicity with aesthetic sophistication.

    The watercolors of Charles Burchfield (1893–1967) were primarily stimulated by an intensely emotional and visionary experience of nature. Influenced, like Dove, by Theosophy, he invented imaginative visual forms to represent his experience of the invisible aspects of the natural world—its sounds and forces as well as the emotional or elemental qualities of a particular place. These were then appropriately inserted into more or less realistic landscape pictures. By the early 1920s he had shifted focus to mastering the realistic depiction of the visible world in terms of light, color tone, and firm solidity. In 1939 he began to return to his earlier visionary watercolors, revising some and creating new ones, enriching them with the monumentality of style and confidence he had gained in his realistic middle period. These later paintings often reflected the cosmic aspect of the natural world and conveyed a sense of the awe-inspiring power and mystery of nature (Figure 15). In 1961 he commented, "An artist must paint, not what he sees in nature, but what is there. To do so he must invent symbols, which, if properly used, make his work seem even more real than

Figure 15. Charles Burchfield. Moonlight in June. 1961. Watercolor. Amherst College, Amherst, MA

what is in front of him. He does not try to bypass nature; his work is superior to nature's surface appearance, but not to its basic laws." Burchfield here seems to summarize the alternative modern approach to American idealist realism that the development of nonobjective painting made possible for artists like Dove, O'Keeffe, and himself—the possibility to evoke a higher level of realism than the merely material.

Before turning to American art after World War II, I must mention briefly the first American avant-garde style to attract attention in Europe, synchronism, which was created in 1913. Inspired by the correspondences between colors and musical tones taught by Canadian Ernest Percyval Tudor-Hart as well as other color theories, synchronist painters explored a language of non-representational spectral color: "its rhythms, its contrasts, and certain directions motivated by color masses," in the words of its founder, Morgan Russell. Although the synchronists advocated painting principles of color perspective and generation of form out of color qualities that were similar to those of Rudolf Steiner, they also pursued the creation of a spatial solidity out of color and analogies to anatomical and Baroque sculptural form (especially Michelangelo's) in color composition.

Abstract Expressionism (The New York School)

The broad, painterly handling of paint that John La Farge first essayed was only accepted by a wide spectrum of American artists with the arrival of the first American impressionist painters in the late nineteenth century. It could be said that it took American painters more than forty years to fully absorb, digest, and transform this traditional European technique, when it surprisingly reemerged just after World War II in a radically Americanized form as abstract expressionism. This was the first and perhaps still the most significant major artistic style to originate wholly within the United States. Although strongly stimulated by the automatist and biomorphic abstraction of European surrealists exiled in New York, this new American style came to overwhelm the previous European modern traditions not only in America but in Europe itself. Abstract expressionism, also known as the New York School, became the first and most renowned of many international triumphs of American art during the later part of the twentieth century.

Reacting against any suggestion of impersonal or machine-made pictorial elements as well as allegiance to any fixed larger "style," the New York School artists experimented with the spontaneous, the indeterminate, the dynamic, the open and the unfinished in their artwork. The pioneering abstract expressionists more or less selectively combined what were seen at the time as the two major developments in modern art, cubism and surrealism. In particular, they extended the "automatic" drawing techniques of nonrepresentational surrealism as a way to try to bypass the artist's conscious mind and reveal more archetypal or "mythic" content. "True art is an adventure into an unknown world," wrote painters Mark Rothko, Adolph Gottlieb, and Barnett Newman in a 1943 letter to *The New York Times*.

The new approach launched by these artists in the mid-1940s was characterized by critic Harold Rosenberg in 1952:

> At a certain moment the canvas began to appear to one American painter after another as an arena in which to act—rather than as a space in which to reproduce, redesign, analyze, or "express" an object, actual or imagined. What was to go on the canvas was not a picture but an event.

As explained by Rosenberg, Clement Greenberg, Meyer Schapiro, Robert Motherwell, and other prominent critics of the period, the most important aspect of the new American painting was the activity of self-exploration—the opportunity given by painting to realize a more genuine self-knowledge as a result of the difficult, open-ended challenges of finding each correct painterly gesture to add to previous gestures on the canvas. Although the emotion and meaning expressed were more important for the gesture painters than formal qualities of line, color, and design, they refused to preconceive particular meanings or styles, believing that a significant resolution would grow out of their total involvement in the act of painting.

Viewing the painting as a spontaneous improvisation (similar to the jazz music most of these artists listened to), the gesture painters favored the broad brush stroke that seemed direct and honest, rather than artificial and thought out. They employed a variety of devices as signs of the artist's active presence: the stroke, the brush, the calligraphic mark, the splatter, the drip, and even the pour—as well as a general emphasis on the qualities of the paint itself as substance and the surface of the canvas as texture.

Focused solely on the "performance arena" of the canvas and immersed in the unpremeditated process of painting, the artist remained alert to possibilities of a new coherence as "events" accumulated on the painting surface—sometimes over months or even years. Painter Robert Motherwell described this way of working in 1947: "I begin a painting with a series of mistakes. The painting comes out of the correction of mistakes by feeling." This occurred through a series of existential choices or "moral" decisions involving much contemplation, anxiety, doubt, and passion, out of which a hard-won order and wholeness would be constructed. The painted product was primarily a record of this existential process, which could be more or less successful for both artist and spectators.

The development of New York School painting has been classified (somewhat arbitrarily) into two main tendencies: gesture painting and color field painting. Gesture or "action" painters organized their canvases as open, expressive accumulations of excited painterly "gestures," each painted with equal emotional intensity to form a unified "all over" image that seemed to dynamically expand beyond the framing edge. Color field painters, who developed slightly later, concentrated on the overall effect of the painting as a single shape, presenting more refined, unified, consistent, and expansive optical textures or "fields." A number of younger artists took up the color-field wing of abstract expressionism, eventually leading it toward simpler, flatter, and hard-edged forms, and a number of different names were given to these later tendencies in painting (which continued into the 1970s and beyond), including post-painterly abstraction, hard-edge abstraction, cool art, stained color-field abstraction, and minimalism.

The Gesture Painters

Of the original gesture painters, I would like to briefly consider two pioneering and leading figures, Jackson Pollock and Willem de Kooning. More than any other artist, it was Pollock (1912–1956) who opened the way to a new kind of direct, improvisational, large-scale American abstraction. Raised in several locations in the Southwest, Pollock absorbed early influences both from the expansive desert landscape and its Native American inhabitants and from his introduction to the teachings of Theosophy and Krishnamurti by a high school art teacher in Los Angeles. Although he absorbed many artistic influences after moving to New York City at age seventeen in 1930 (especially cubism), he particularly gravitated to Jungian ideas of mythic or totemic content and imagery drawn from the unconscious. Between 1942 and 1946 he increasingly suppressed overt references to mythic images in his paintings and concentrated more on making the process of painting itself into a kind of mythic or ritualistic act.

In the years just after 1946, Pollock achieved his major breakthroughs, eliminating all recognizable imagery and relying exclusively on free-wheeling painterly gestures interlaced to generate an allover frontal surface (Figure 16). He found the actual procedure of paint application to be increasingly expressive. He felt the need to expand the size relations between canvas, brush, and the painter's arm and shoulder to acquire more "room to paint in." He then stretched his large canvases out on the floor and increased the distance of travel of the paint by using new drip and splatter techniques that brought paint onto the canvas from all sides from dried-out brushes, sticks, and trowels. Paint was "aimed" at the canvas rather than "carried" there on the tip of a brush. Balancing with remarkable control from the hips (rather than from the shoulders, as was typical), Pollock himself became the source of energy imparted to the painting, and he painted with motions of his whole body in order to act "within" the painting itself.

In traditional painting, the artist's inner processes are experienced as moving faster than outer processes. Pollock's approach made the painter's movements nearly as fast as the speed of inner processes, allowing an unprecedented amount of direct emotional expression to be transferred directly to the canvas. "I want to express my feelings rather than illustrate them," Pollock explained. The archetypal or mythic element he had previously sought to express representationally he now tried to embody within his own spirit, externalizing it on the canvas in terms of energy, force, and intensity. "The source of my painting is the unconscious," he asserted. As Pollock described, "The painting has a life of its own. I try to let it come through. It is only when I lose contact with the painting that the result is a mess. Otherwise, there is pure harmony, an easy give-and-take, and the painting comes out well."

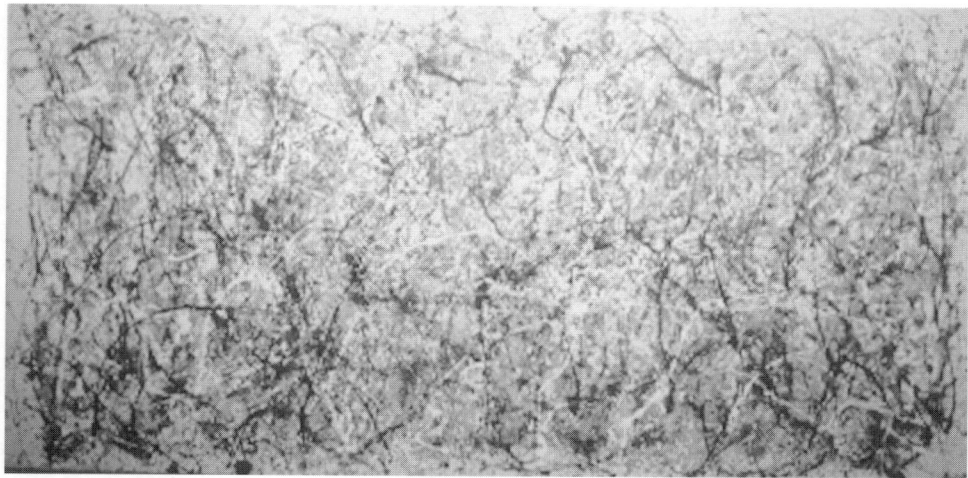

Figure 16. Jackson Pollock. One (No. 31, 1950). *1950. Oil on canvas. Museum of Modern Art, New York*

For the observer, too, Pollock's large-scale paintings tend to be experienced more as environment than isolated object. The viewer is less detached from such a painting than from a more traditional artwork. Viewers relate their impressions of his paintings to a wide range of phenomena: the American landscape, New York City, the night sky, atomic energy, jazz music, American transcendentalist ideas, existentialist ideas of risk and chance. Freed from the traditional functions of drawing, Pollock's line trajects freely as an autonomous element, building an expansive web of forces suspended in front of the canvas, seeming to project a sense of space out from the picture surface. Throughout each picture, there is a continual tension between picture surface and the dissolving marks, between the frontal plane and receding space, between wall and veil. Greenburg comments that the picture surface of Pollock's paintings seems to open up from the rear. Actually, it is the quality of flatness of the picture surface, not that material surface itself, that becomes dissolved by an element of pictorial illusion—a very subtle experience where the difference was indistinguishable between the literalness of surface and the illusionistic "spatial" presence of the painting conveyed through how the paint was applied.

The most emulated and influential painter during the 1950s, Willem de Kooning (1904–1997), had studied art for eight years in his native Holland before moving to New York City in 1926. His later reputation was largely based on his masterful syntheses of intense personal expression with a certain pictorial finesse and virtuoso handling of paint, or, in terms of formal innovation, on his combination of traditional figural subjects with an energetically structural but flat surface. De Kooning later admitted that he was often jealous of Pollock, who told him, "You know more, but I feel more." His painting was strongly influenced by Pollock's allover, dripped-paint style, but de Kooning also felt himself linked to the Western artistic tradition.

In the early 1940s de Kooning began to "draw" directly with his paint-loaded brush, applying an often vehemently expressive brush stroke to increasingly complex compositions that seemed to reflect the dynamic, anxious, and restless qualities of modern urban living. He allowed his raw, gestural brush strokes themselves ("color drawing") to carry the burden of his meaning. For many critics and fellow artists, his dynamic, open-ended canvases seemed to convey an honesty of expression and risk-taking that gave new meaning to the creative process.

De Kooning's work was also an illustration of how abstract expressionism represented more of an attitude and approach to painting in general than only a commitment to pure abstraction. Constantly measuring himself against the work of past masters of art (especially Picasso and Ingres), de Kooning sought to absorb the achievements of European modernism into the qualities of his fast-paced, action-oriented urban life style. Out of these influences emerged his most famous and long-lived subject, "the Women."

De Kooning has confessed both the compelling attraction and the traditional sources of this image, which called up in him "anxiousness . . . fright maybe, or ecstasy": "The *Women* had to do with the female painted through all the ages, all those idols, and maybe I was stuck to a certain extent; I couldn't go on." In an interview, he further described how the attempts to seize the reality of woman as subject presented endless possibilities for him to test his "performance" against that of past artists. As part of his fascination with banal qualities of American popular culture, he has also related his *Women* to the giant women on billboards and trucks and on pin-up posters—the ubiquitous and iconic public goddesses of sex and sales-pitches.

In his earlier paintings of women, de Kooning used obvious gestural brush strokes and a faceting of the figure into small overlapping planes to assert the reality of the flat picture surface and the physicality of the canvas supporting the paint, while at the same time he refused to completely deny the illusion of bulky volume of the figure's body and the illusionary deep space of the room she was seated within. Beginning with his *Woman I* painting of 1950–1952, de Kooning rejected both traditional illusory picture space and modernist composition in flat planes. He developed his concept of "no environment" to express the shifting lack of specificity of the urban scene, how both interior and exterior city scenes can seem so similar to related scenes in other parts of the city. He added to this a kind of "no environment" of the woman's body, which he termed "intimate proportions." In other words, he came to equate the changeability and multiple meanings of his woman image with the perpetually changing impressions on the streets of Manhattan. Thus, she also was apprehended simultaneously as a complex of passing sensations, passions, moods, and symbolic meanings.

To express this in his post-1952 *Women* paintings, de Kooning destroyed the boundary between the figure and the setting, so that the two elements more or less merged into a single overall image—all fragments of similar importance in the continuous stream of visual encounters (Figure 17). The central mystery of his art lies in the expressive tension he sets up between the ordering powers of the artist and the mysteries of ambiguity and multiple meaning in our lived experience. He seems to suggest that there is a continuity of both reality and meaning between the outer and inner worlds of our experience. Such ambiguities can also be observed in his purely nonrepresentational works, which sometimes recall anatomical parts freed from their familiar figural context, densely compacted within his pictures so that they are continually, dynamically interacting with each other within a kind of eternal becoming that weaves across the picture surface.

The Color-Field Painters
The formal problems of the color-field painters within the New York School were, in a way, more difficult than those of the gesture painters. They wanted to maximize the visual impact of specific colors and found that, to do so, they had to simplify or eliminate any other figures or symbols and apply the colors in large expanses that would saturate the eye. Most of them also found it necessary to suppress any evidence of their own autobiographical process or painting activity. But then how were they to avoid formlessness?   This was a more radical abandonment of the familiar structural basis of existing Western art, that is, of the use of modulated dark and light values to produce the illusion of mass in space. Their solution was to find ways to adjust the colored areas to create a unified and contained field, each zone of which is of equal chromatic intensity and value. The surface of the painting was treated as an active "field" with a unified texture for an allover, "single image" effect.

Figure 17. Willem de Kooning. Woman on Bicycle. *1952–1953. Oil on canvas. Whitney Museum of American Art, New York*

Some observers seemed to grasp landscape sensations within color-field paintings, but the artists themselves had something different and more visionary in mind, which they might have termed the "abstract sublime." Like the gesture painters, their work arose out of an interest in a universal mythic expression. They wanted to create a nonrepresentational art that suggested transcendence and revelation, which took art back to its origins in mystery and magic. To overcome the perceived loss of power and predictable responses from traditional religious symbols and rituals, they tried to eliminate all references to familiar images, whether in nature or art. They wanted, in Newman's words, to make "cathedrals ... out of ourselves, out of our own feelings." They wanted their fundamentally simplified paintings to create an effect of infinity and boundlessness, but also an elemental impact akin to that evoked by the primitive, tribal, or ancient sacred art that they admired.

In the early 1940s Mark Rothko (1903–1970) began using oil paint as if it were watercolor, thinning the paint and applying it in freely brushed, overlapping background glazes. This created a subtly luminous atmospheric impression enhanced by minute surface changes in the stained and blotted color. However it was not until the later 1940s that he came to spread simple washes of this color across his canvases, eliminating any vestiges of figural or symbolic imagery. To solidify these rather diffuse pictures, Rothko made his large color areas into roughly rectangular shapes, but with loose, undefined edges to give them a sense of movement and depth. In 1949–1950 he first limited the number of such elements in a picture to two or three, arranging them as large rectangles of similar width, one above the other (Figure 18). He placed the contours of the rectangles close to the picture edges in order to make his design unobtrusive and to stress the outer borders of the entire picture as one entity. There were no strong movements or abrupt divisions, and the bleeding of the shapes into the ground fused both into a single plane, further reinforcing

Figure 18. Mark Rothko. November 22, 1949. 1949. Oil on canvas. Museum of Modern Art, New York

the overall unity of the painting. Often the lower layers of atmospheric color seemed to radiate through the upper layer and/or create a glowing "halo" effect around the rectangular forms.

Despite these formal simplifications, Rothko emphasized: "I'm not interested in the relationship of color or form to anything else. I'm interested in expressing basic human emotions—tragedy, ecstasy, doom, and so on. And the fact that a lot of people break down and cry when confronted with my pictures shows that I can communicate those basic emotions. . . . The people who walk before my pictures are having the same religious experience I had when I painted them." It is impossible to pin down any specific meanings to Rothko's paintings. When seen from a close distance as intended, their huge size and sense of engulfing color suggest that the viewer transcend his or her ordinary feeling of self. This self-transcendence can lead to a mystical sense of cosmic identification or to a more tragic, death-like loss of self. The subtle color modulations seem to dematerialize both surfaces and edges so that the rectangular planes become floating blocks of ethereal color that gradually envelop the viewer in a total color experience. By an alternate impression, the rectangles seem to recede, turning into layers of veils that hide some mysterious presence the viewer is challenged to penetrate. Spending time with a Rothko painting makes observers more aware of themselves as involved in the act of perceiving and invites them into a kind of silent inner dialogue or drama. It is appropriate that one of Rothko's last works was the hexagonal meditation chapel in Houston whose walls are filled with fourteen huge panels in deep red-brown colors.

Barnett Newman (1905–1970) drew a fundamental contrast between his approach to a painting based only on a lofty "pure idea" and the external, formative beauty of European art, which wanted "to exist inside the reality of sensation." Instead, Newman aimed for a "formless form" to suggest the mysterious sublime and "the impact of elemental truth." Perhaps as early as 1945 he realized that a straight line need not evoke a geometric abstract world but could merely divide the surface of a picture while still suggesting the subjectivity of the artist. For Newman, the simple line was a primordial, universal, archetypal gesture of human creation, and he felt his independent vertical line could serve as a simple personal gesture within the picture-space of his extremely simplified and color-focused paintings.

In Newman's wall-sized "zip paintings" beginning in 1948, his blurred vertical lines blend into their surrounding color-field and echo the vertical framing edges of the picture, giving the actual, material edge of the painting a compositional function and identity (Figure 19). The vertical

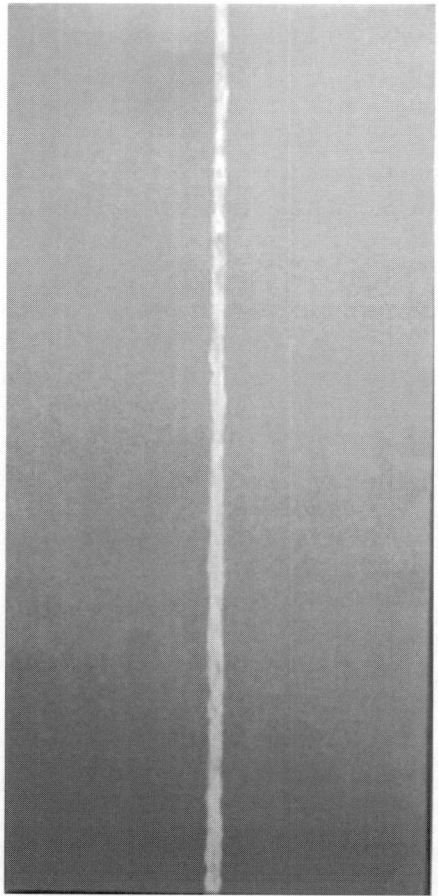

Figure 19. Barnett Newman. Onement III. *1949. Oil on canvas. Museum of Modern Art, New York*

"zips" or "stripes" are not seen as separate from the ground but as accents, energizing the field and helping open out the picture plane to vast dimensions while still giving it form. He used lines not to outline shapes but to "declare space." At the same time the zips can recall other associations: earlier significant vertical artistic traditions (for example, crucifixions), modernist elongated or eroded human figures, or human aspirations toward something higher. In contrast to Rothko, Newman suppressed atmospheric and tactile details in order to de-emphasize the physicality of the paint and point more easily to the metaphysical meanings that were his main intention. His pictures were likewise intended to be contemplated at a near distance, absorbing the viewer in a kind of communion, "to hold the emotion, the unanswerable cry." Newman also acknowledged a possible association between his paintings and the sublime qualities expressed in many nineteenth-century American landscape paintings.

Abstract Expressionism and Welded Sculpture

There was also in sculpture a sort of equivalent to abstract expressionism in painting, based upon the post-war development of the hotter-burning oxyacetylene torch. A group of American sculptors latched onto welding and brazing (high-temperature metal soldering) as a kind of sculptural version of the expressionist brush stroke. The new technology enabled sculptors to induce metal to run, drip, and splatter. They used metal rods and built-up textures to construct their hulking, abstractly organic or mechanical sculptures with odd extrusions and jerky, often awkward-looking assemblages. Among the original pioneers of this "braze and weld" approach were Reuben Nakian, Theodore Roszak, Seymour Lipton, Ibram Lassaw, and Herbert Ferber. With the addition of either found objects or a larger scale, other sculptural approaches developed from this beginning— especially the welded assemblages or constructions (sometimes called "junk" or "funk" sculpture) of Richard Stankiewicz, John Chamberlain (crushed automobiles), Mark di Suvero, Anthony Caro, and George Sugarman; and the huge-scale "primary structures" of Tony Smith, Ronald Bladen, David Black, and Mathias Goeritz.

The pioneering sculptural work of David Smith (1906–1965) encompassed more than one of these approaches. Learning to weld in an automobile plant and a Second World War locomotive factory, Smith first applied his technical expertise to larger welded sculptures during the later 1940s on his upstate New York farm. From the beginning, he took up the theme of landscape or wilderness (both natural and psychological) with an emphasis on a central American theme: the relationship of the heroically isolated individual to the vastness of nature (especially the encounter of earth and sky). In this connection, he executed a number of works on the theme of flight or levitation, involving bird-like forms and complexes of rising metal arcs. In the early 1950s he began incorporating pieces of agricultural equipment, integrating their original function into the total structure of his designs. A few years later he discovered that highly reflective metal surfaces (sterling silver, polished stainless steel) created gestural light-reflection designs that "pictorialized" the surfaces of his sculptures, creating a moving, allover calligraphy of light effects that caused them to appear nearly as immaterial as light itself (especially outdoors).

But it was only in his last four years of life that Smith began producing his group of almost thirty monumental *Cubi* sculptures that integrated these various concerns (Figure 20). Assembled from modular units of hollow steel boxes and cylinders and polished to create vibrant sunlight reflections, these standing forms were composed of floating cubical "clouds" suspended between heaven and earth. These gravity-defying figures continued the image of the lonely hero actively confronting the universe (or at least an infinite landscape) with the defiant gesture of an Ahab. Yet these *Cubi* images seem to be equally internalized, subjective visions, achieving a dynamic ambiguity between sculptural volume and pictorial reflectivity. As with most of Smith's work, much of the vitality of the *Cubi* figures derived from his imitation of the functioning of natural forces, such as movement, tension, resistance, gravity, balance, and growth. Smith's figures showed in a modern way what sculpture can do that painting cannot: create a concentrated incarnation of forces and values within a symbolic freestanding object.

Predecessors of Pop Art

It was in 1948 that Robert Rauschenberg (born 1925) enrolled at the unusual, innovative Black Mountain College in North Carolina, where he would learn important lessons from art teacher Josef Albers and radical musician John Cage. From Albers, the color theorist, Rauschenberg learned that one color was as good as another, so that it became almost impossible for him to decide to use one color instead of another, because to do so would express a personal preference—something that he did not want to do. In opposition to Albers' highly ordered approach to art, Rauschenberg came to find his own freedom to "do something that resembles the lack of order I sense." Influenced by Zen Buddhism and the *I Ching*, the much older Cage sought to create sounds as well as silence in such a way as to extinguish the artist's personality, memory, and desires. The purpose of art was not creating personal masterpieces but a perpetual process of discovery, of "purposeless play," in which anyone could participate. Rather than being something separate from life, for Cage art was a way of waking up to the very life one was living. With a series of all-white and all-black paintings in the early 1950s, Rauschenberg, like Cage,

Figure 20. David Smith. Cubi XX. *1964. Stainless steel. Murphy Sculpture Garden, University of California at Los Angeles*

explored ways to limit the artist's control over the final result, mainly by trying to make the viewer work harder and become more involved in the process.

A couple of years later, Rauschenberg had progressed to incorporating collage elements and found objects into his paintings. Imitating his idol de Kooning, Rauschenberg integrated the added objects by quick, agitated brush strokes, drips, and splatters. He was using collage elements to bypass his own personal taste and to reproduce the nonorder he perceived in life around him. He wanted to let materials be (or become) themselves without his own personality interfering. His artwork was a form of collaboration with materials. He used such items as mirrors, umbrellas, pages from magazines, electric light bulbs, windows, and dirt. Juxtapositions of such unrelated objects seemed to reflect the breakdown of linear, cause-and-effect thinking in modern science and philosophy as well as the all-at-once lifestyle of New York City (where he now lived). He began to think of himself as a reporter, bearing witness to the tense, constantly changing life around him.

Rauschenberg became close friends with artist Jasper Johns in 1954–1955, leading to an intense aesthetic interchange. They were also influenced by the early experimental "popular imagery" paintings of Larry Rivers, who in 1953 combined a parodied image of *Washington Crossing the Delaware* with the spontaneous, sketchy, gestural painting of abstract expressionism. By 1955 Rauschenberg had begun incorporating still larger objects into his paintings, which spilled out into the space around them. Turning Renaissance perspective illusion inside out, he built his pictures out into the viewer's space, using objects such as automobile wheels, electric light fixtures, stuffed animals and birds, pieces of furniture, and pillows. These new works, somewhere between painting and sculpture, were called "combines" or "combine-paintings" (Figure 21). Although often taken as jokes, many of these were actually arch, subtle commentaries on the ideals of the New York School. For example, *Factum I* and *Factum II*, two virtually identical collage paintings of 1957, were intended as a satire on abstract expressionism's elevation of spontaneity and unique personal expression.

While Rauschenberg's use of everyday and commercial objects in his combines (as well as in several theatrical "happenings") helped prepare the way for the pop art of the 1960s, he used them more indiscriminately than the pop artists would. He also continued to use paint in the spontaneous style of de Kooning, whereas most pop artists tried to imitate the slick, impersonal surfaces of commercial art. Rauschenberg intentionally avoided exerting total control over his creative work, trying to accept the world and

Figure 21. Robert Rauschenberg. Inlet. 1959. Combine painting. Los Angeles Museum of Contemporary Art

its disorder as it was and collaborate with it, thereby loosening the boundary between art and life. The pop artists wanted to create art, not work in Rauschenberg's gap between art and life.

By the early 1960s Rauschenberg's palette became bolder and brighter, and he began experiments with commercial silk screen and lithography that would continue for the rest of his career. But he still used these new mediums to reflect the visual chaos of contemporary urban life. He reproduced photographs, art prints, and magazine images on photosensitive silkscreen, which was then printed on canvas, promiscuously mixing, merging, superimposing, and painting over images jumbled together in a more complex continuity than was possible with the three-dimensional combines. He created similar collage-like images adapted to the revived medium of lithography. A few years later, he helped spearhead Experiments in Art and Technology (E.A.T.), an organization of about six thousand engineers, scientists, and artists that undertook experimental collaborations between art and technology. He even created artworks that combined lithographic and silkscreen imagery with electrified mechanical constructions of Plexiglas and aluminum. In all of these mediums and others up to the present day, Rauschenberg managed to produce memorable artworks based on his ability to capture lively compositions within the tension between beauty and ugliness or between form and chaos.

The original personal images developed by Jasper Johns (born 1930) had an equally revolutionary effect on the art world beginning in the mid-1950s. However, Johns' works are difficult to explain briefly, partly because they deal with the vocabulary of modernist artmaking, criticizing, subverting, and commenting upon the discipline itself. He complicates matters by working with a repeated set of subjects over up to four decades, shifting his meaning and interactions within a medium on each occasion. Like words in a private language, each object or motif carries for him complex, private meanings, secret codes, and unconscious attitudes about the world. The viewer is challenged to interpret these densely layered creations full of nuance and mystery. Ultimately, his works show how an emphasis on the kind of lively, "modernist" surface emphasized by abstract expressionism can also carry vivid subject matter—while pretending not to do so.

Primarily a self-taught artist, Johns was also strongly influenced by John Cage. His first original, repeated theme came to him in a dream: the American flag. In *Flag*, of 1954–55, he used the ancient wax-based medium of encaustic to create a beautiful, translucent surface whose calm, controlled structure contrasted dramatically with the emotional expressionism of the New York School. However, a flag shared most of the typical qualities of abstract expressionist art; it was flat, a unified allover image with no hierarchy of forms. But it also was a mundane, mass-produced, popular image that would never have appeared in an abstract expressionist painting. The flag image fills the entire canvas with no "background" around it. According to the critical thought of the time, the development of modern art had succeeded through a victory of emphasis on flat surface over illusionistic subject matter. But a flag was both a subject matter image and a flat surface. Johns' seemingly simple flag was paradoxical: it was neither a real flag nor an artist's representation of a flag. It simultaneously represented its subject and was the subject represented. Like all of his work since, it posed a question about the relationship between art and reality and how we differentiate between the two. Once it was realized that the question, "Is it a flag or is it a painting?" had no answer and didn't matter, the way was open to pop art, that is, for any popular image to enter painting.

The use of the ready-made flag image also allowed Johns to make an artistic statement while avoiding personal self-expression. "I didn't want my work to be an exposure of my feelings, " he said in a famous statement. As with Rauschenberg, this sentiment was not just shyness but a sophisticated reappearance of the characteristically American allegiance to a simultaneously conceptual and material reality of the object. "I'm interested in things which suggest the world rather than suggest the personality," Johns elaborated. "I'm interested in things which suggest things, which are, rather than in judgments." He found something artificial about deliberately trying to suggest a particular psychological state, and he wanted his paintings to be literal objects, "as a real thing in itself." Johns' systematic studies of the philosopher Ludwig Wittgenstein around 1961 furthered his interest in the ambiguous interactions of art objects and real objects and led to his conceptions of painting as a kind of language or a model of reality. From these reflections a new level of complexity of meanings emerged within his ever more elusive paintings, and he occasionally made more telling statements about his aspirations to render "the condition of presence," of "being here." "I personally would like to keep the painting in a state of 'shunning statement,'" he commented in 1965, ". . . that is, not to focus attention in one way but to leave the situation as a kind of actual thing, so that experience of it is variable."

As an example of the later work in which Johns carefully veils his complex meanings, we can consider briefly *In the Studio* from 1982, an encaustic painting on canvas with attached objects (Figure 22). The painting began when Johns saw an empty canvas propped against the wall in his studio, represented here by the tilted rectangle painted in the lower picture, which also implies perspective recession in space. However, this impression is disrupted by the actual attached board, which projects outward from the canvas at a reverse angle to the illusory recession. A three-dimensional wax cast of a child's arm is painted in a multi-colored flagstone pattern, which refers to a similar pattern used in two paintings by French surrealist René Magritte, who also philosophically explored the differing meanings and reality of visual, verbal, and mental images as well as how a painter can create illusions of all three. The mysterious arm is repeated in a painted "drawing" illusorily "pinned" to the canvas by painted nails casting shadows (which, in turn, refer to similar nails used in Georges Braque's cubist still lifes). Also "pinned" to the studio wall is one of Johns' cross-hatch "paintings," a multi-referential motif he introduced in the early 1970s as part of a re-evaluation of Picasso and Pollock. He derived the pattern by combining a regularization of Pollock's allover brush strokes and the colored decorative hatching used by Picasso to organize and control his surfaces. The motif usually relates to Johns' interest in concealment of meaning (especially concerning sexuality and death), his efforts to camouflage subject by surface. Below, another "pinned" cross-hatch "painting" is seemingly melting away into the surface of the wall (and the picture). These three pairs of opposites depicted in *In the Studio* relate to Johns' struggles within the context of modern art to reconcile real and illusory space and objects, surface and subject, idea and thing. As with most of his enigmatic artwork, they refer more to processes of his own inner creative activity than to a still life scene of his studio.

Pop Art

The high seriousness of abstract expressionism seemed very out of place within the positive, optimistic, open, and irreverent mood of the 1960s. With its giant scale, bright colors, and familiar images, pop art arose with a broad appeal during this decade to reflect the shift in national sensibility. But pop art equally expressed an element of mocking hostility toward the serious, refined emotionalism of its immediate artistic predecessors. Its point of departure in North America was the pictorial irony, depersonalized action-painting techniques, and use of images from everyday culture seen in the works of Johns and Rauschenberg. The pop artists chose to depict everything previously considered unworthy of art: every level of advertising, magazine and newspaper illustrations, tactless bric-a-brac, ordinary consumer goods, film stars, pinups, and comic strips. Nothing was sacred. The pop artists were the first to expand the realm of visuality in art to include the wide-open field that was later (today) called "visual culture"

Figure 22. Jasper Johns. In the Studio. *1982. Encaustic on canvas with attached objects. Philadelphia Museum of Art*

and has led to the incorporation of all manner of popular imagery in works of art.

Nor did the pop artists honor traditional methods of creating art. Their aim was generally to alter the images they found in popular culture as little as possible rather than emphasizing the activity of the artist as an original genius. Not primarily social commentary or critique, pop art merely tried to accept and reflect what was found visually in the modern world rather than retreating from it to an ivory tower of fine art. Humor or even satire may have been included, but the main purpose was a kind of exploration of the boundaries between the images of art and those of everyday life, especially commerce. Among others, the styles of pop art included Roy Lichtenstein's blown-up paintings of comic book scenes and comic-style rendering of gestural brush strokes, Tom Wesselman's *Great American Nudes*, Robert Indiana's colorful traffic signs conveying messages of the *American Dream*, James Rosenquist's gigantically scaled billboard-figure collages, Mel Ramos's brand-name pinup ads, the ironic road signs of Edward Ruscha and Allan D'Arcangelo, and the comically constructed urban environments of Red Grooms.

What pop art celebrated was not so much the commercial objects themselves as the look of media representations of such everyday objects. By the 1960s, the advertising and marketing of mass-produced consumer goods had reached an unprecedented level in the United States. Pop artists used such images for their art, but they repeated and magnified them on a huge scale usually with flat garish colors or different materials so that the viewer's perception of them was inevitably altered and intensified. The subjects were basically interchangeable: Elvis Presley could substitute for Chiquita bananas, a car crash, Marilyn Monroe, or a bottle of Coca-Cola. The subject lost its weight, another intentional deflation of the ideals of abstract expressionism. At its most radical, pop art helped fuel growing calls toward the end of the 1960s for the end of art as an isolated practice, for the merging of art and life in general as a kind of cultural revolution.

The most prominent pioneer of pop art was Andy Warhol (1927–1987). As an awkward, uneasy child of relatively poor immigrant parents, the young Warhol saw the grocery store's endless rows of canned food as something beautiful, signifying wealth, abundance, and psychological security. His art came to feature these kinds of commercial images as well as movie stars and other mass media imagery. "Don't look beneath the surface," he said in one of his many provocative statements about his artwork, "There's nothing there."

As one of the top illustrators on Madison Avenue in the early 1950s, Warhol developed a fine sense of how to give an image graphic clout. He began employing this skill in 1960 in a series of large paintings of comic strip figures and cheap advertisements. But when he saw how much better Lichtenstein's similar comic strip paintings were done, he switched to pictures of multiple representations of Campbell's soup cans, Coca-Cola bottles, and dollar bills (Figure 23). By the end of 1962 he was using silkscreen to speed up the process and achieve something of the impersonal, "cool," and mechanically reproduced look of commercial products. He then expanded his imagery to include a variety of other mass-media images, including movie stars, celebrities, and newspaper photographs and stories. People found something hypnotic about his endless repetitions of these images, and they were even imitated in fashion design.

Warhol does not seem to have intended any negative connotations regarding mass-produced goods or acquisitive consumerism. He appeared to simply accept everything. His explanation was deceptively simple: "Pop art is liking things." He called his famous New York studio The Factory to demystify the idea of the special environment of the artist's studio and to shift the emphasis in art from the producer to the consumer. His repetitive, film-like treatment of a single image gave his sometimes emotional images (for example, electric chairs and car crashes) a certain detachment, relativity, and anonymity that they would not otherwise have had, also reflecting the modern apathy for media imagery. It has been suggested that contemporary

Figure 23. Andy Warhol. Green Coca-Cola Bottles. 1962. Oil on canvas. Whitney Museum of American Art, New York

141

senses are so overloaded with artificial emotion from bad movies, politician's speeches, canned music, soap operas, and sitcoms, that a stark, mechanical repetition like Warhol's can mean more than a hyper-expressionistic portrayal of accident victims ever could.

Warhol modified this effect somewhat in his later paintings, primarily colorful portraits of the wealthy and fashionable, who became his friends. For these works, before he silk-screened photographic images of his subjects onto his canvas, he first underpainted each panel with bright polychrome paints in a loosely abstract expressionist style. Thus he juxtaposed in one somewhat contradictory picture the mechanically reproduced image and the hand-painted, expressive brushwork—anticipating a combination that the younger neo-expressionist artists of the 1980s (who admired Warhol) would find increasingly popular.

In addition to his painting, Warhol produced a variety of other kinds of art that predicted many of the directions art explored during the rest of the twentieth century: multimedia events, performance art, films, videos, sound pieces, and relationships between visual art and the latest rock music. He redefined the role of the artist in late twentieth-century terms as a medium who lets the events of the day act on and through him or her, stamping a specific persona on everything he or she does. Somehow the ever-detached Warhol himself was always the real work of art; paint, canvas, films, and video tape were just the material means to make it manifest. Warhol ultimately made it clear that art today must itself be seen as part of the mass-culture industry, which actually shapes the artist's relationship to an audience.

In 1961 pop artist Claes Oldenburg (born 1929) opened *The Store* in a shop on the Lower East Side of Manhattan, laying out over a hundred art objects for sale. These were bumpy plaster shapes imitating common consumer goods covered splashily with bright household enamel paints. In a second version the following year he also made large-scale versions of some items, including some in "soft" forms of painted canvas: blue pants, a piece of cake, a hamburger. The rest of his career was largely devoted to the direction indicated in this second *Store*: recreating everyday technological or consumer objects in isolated, usually greatly enlarged forms composed of different materials. For example, a "soft toilet" would be made of stuffed vinyl (Figure 24) or a steel baseball bat would be made a hundred feet high. By creating these variant versions of objects, he decontextualized and, in effect, dematerialized their original everyday versions by spotlighting the aspect of their form. He ignored the uses and materials of the baseball mitts, three-way plugs, clothespins, and pay phones he pulled out of their everyday contexts and instructed viewers to observe them purely as forms. "I'd like to turn people on to the fact that the world is form, not just function and money," Oldenburg said. "Think of the fun it would be to sit on your porch and look at the world as form." Through this almost mystical approach to form, Oldenburg attempted to wake up viewers to the subtle but powerful influence of the everyday functional forms around them and continued in a new way an older American artistic dialogue on the visual relationship between form and matter, idea and substance.

Minimalism

I will conclude with a short discussion of minimalism, a style that did occur in the flat, monochrome paintings of Frank Stella, Ad Reinhardt, Robert Ryman, and Agnes Martin, but was primarily centered on sculpture.

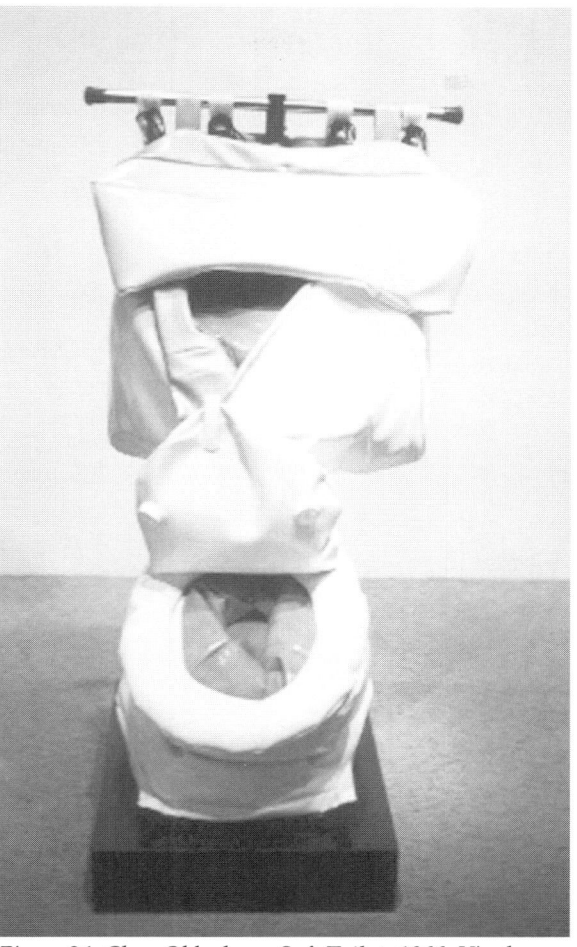

Figure 24. Claes Oldenburg. Soft Toilet. *1966. Vinyl filled with kapok painted with liquitex. Whitney Museum of American Art, New York*

Almost the opposite of the flamboyance of pop art, minimalism first emerged in the one-person shows of Donald Judd and Robert Morris in 1963, although none of the somewhat different artists involved liked the label minimalism. Minimalist sculpture consisted of elementary geometric volumes or symmetrical and serial sequences of modular geometric volumes placed directly on the floor or wall (Figure 25). Their nonrelational designs featured uninflected, usually unpainted surfaces with no signs of the process of their making. They were often fabricated in factories out of industrial materials such as fiberglass, formica, Plexiglas, chrome, aluminum, or plastic. The emphasis was on the literal objecthood of the work, and this extreme physicality was based on preconceived ideas.

Using the term "specific objects," Judd argued that only when the eye perceives objects that actually exist in all three dimensions (as opposed to the illusionism in painting) does the eye's vision match what the mind knows to be true from experience. Thus, the two-dimensional art of painting had reached a dead end. Objects now should be presented rather than represented. Minimalists seemed to be literally realizing critic Clement Greenberg's call for a radical reduction of each art form to its most pure essentials—in the case of sculpture, a literal, monolithic physicality with properties of scale, proportion, shape, and mass. Simple forms, which Greenberg called unitary objects, could be more readily apprehended as constant, known shapes. Since the essential creative act was the artist's idea, and not the activity of construction, minimalist objects were typically preplanned and prefabricated rather than developed by the improvisational welding process of the constructionists. Out of a peculiarly American drive for absolute clarity and simplicity, they sought the most direct relationship possible between idea and object.

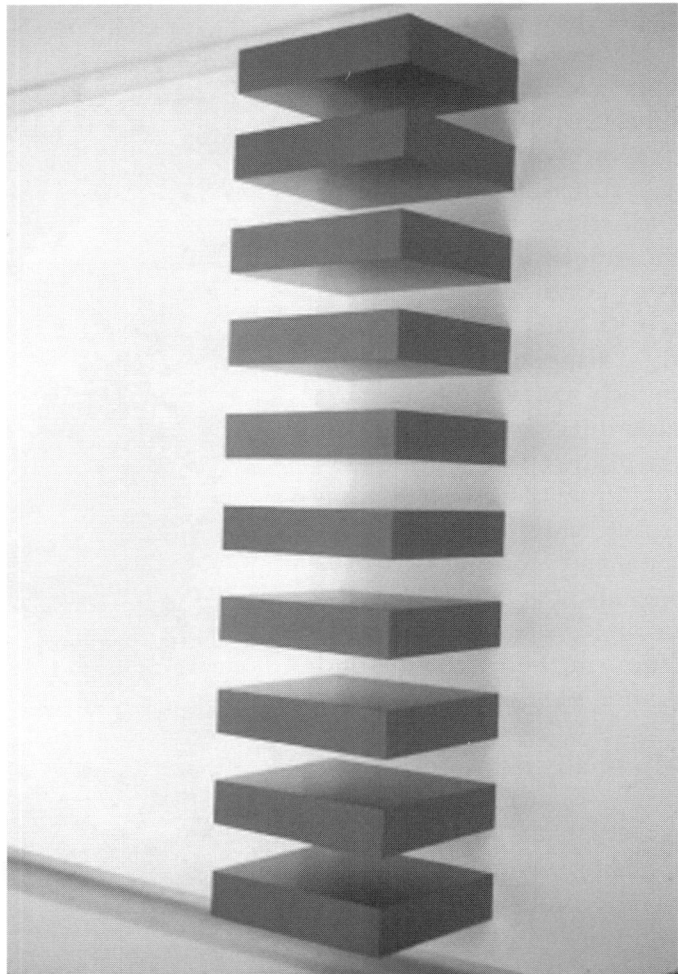

Figure 25. Donald Judd. Untitled – Ten Stacks. 1969. Anodized aluminum. Walker Art Center, Minneapolis.

Despite criticisms of being boring and monotonous on the one hand, and despite the sculptors' attempts to empty their forms of all emotional and historical "debris" on the other hand, critics began to notice minimalist sculptures' elegant proportions and beautiful, reflective surfaces, especially as they were subject to varying conditions of light, atmosphere, and material. Ultimately, the very physicality of these objects called up inescapable aesthetic reactions from observers, ever defeating the sculptors' utopian quest to completely purify their medium of such subjective involvements (although conceptual art soon tried to carry this quest for purification a step further back to the idea itself, while other sculptors relocated their activity to physical transformations of the earth itself [the natural landscape] in the form of large-scale "earthworks" or "siteworks").

An Anthroposophical Afterthought

I would like to add a final observation based on a statement from the spiritual-scientific research of Rudolf Steiner. In a lecture of December 14, 1920, published as *The Soul's Progress through Repeated Earth Lives*, Steiner describes how human souls who lived in Asia during the period just before, during, and after the time of Christ and absorbed the "fine spiritual culture" of the Orient have generally reincarnated as the majority of the North American population. These "old souls" have spent a comparatively long time between their death and a new birth and now, with their spiritual inclinations, feel less comfortable in heavier American bodies. Because of this, they tend to apprehend and relate to their new bodies more from the outside than from the inside, leading to the characteristic American external view of life. As a result, the former living spirituality of these souls tends to become either abstract or weak, tending toward a more materialistic conception of the world. The spiritual ego is not properly and firmly embodied within these typical Americans, leading, for one thing, to a characteristic kind of thinking more by passive association than by active meaningful relationships.

In addition to whatever else can be said from the points of view of spiritual geography, history, and culture, is this perhaps not one deeper explanation for that curiously paradoxical American combination of an intensely, objective physical orientation to objects and art and a sense for a more timeless, transcendent spirituality or conceptuality? We have seen this odd kind of fusion appearing in a variety of forms throughout the history of American art from Luminism to Minimalism. This inner-outer disjunction might also help to explain the recurring American literary and visual imagery of the lone ego defiantly confronting the vast cosmic and earthly physical expanses of the continent. A key question for the future of America is whether or not it will now succeed in learning to see the spiritual within the physical, as essentially united with the physical. For this reason also it is particularly important in America that people are able to regularly encounter the spiritual in external sensory form, as it can exist above all through works of art and architecture.

Bibliography

Adams, Henry, et al. *John La Farge.* New York: Abbeville, 1987.
Baigell, Matthew. *Thomas Cole.* New York: Watson-Guptill, 1982.
Baur, John I. H. *The Inlander: Life and Work of Charles Burchfield 1893–1967.* Cranbury, N.J.: Associated University Presses, 1984.
Boyle, Richard. *American Impressionism.* Boston: Little, Brown and Company, 1974.
Bush-Brown, Albert. *Louis Sullivan.* New York: George Braziller, 1960.
Cohn, Sherrye. *Arthur Dove: Nature as Symbol.* Ann Arbor: UMI Research Press, 1985.
Davidson, Abraham A. *Early American Modernist Painting 1910–1935.* New York: Harper and Row, 1981.
Francis, Richard. *Jasper Johns.* New York: Abbeville, 1984.
Fry, Edward F. and Miranda McClintic. *David Smith: Painter, Sculptor, Draftsman.* New York: George Braxiller, 1982.
Gerdts, William H. *American Impressionism.* New York: Abbeville, 1984.
Greenthal, Kathryn. *Augustus Saint-Gaudens: Master Sculptor.* New York: Metropolitan Museum of Art, 1985.
Homer, William Innes. *Alfred Stieglitz and the American Avant-Garde.* Boston: Little, Brown and Company, 1977.
Howat, John K. *The Hudson River and Its Painters.* New York: Viking Press, 1972.
Lippard, Lucy R. *Pop Art.* New York: Oxford University Press, 1966.
Lisle, Laurie. *Portrait of an Artist: A Biography of Georgia O'Keeffe.* New York: Washington Square Press, 1980.
Morgan, Ann Lee. *Arthur Dove: Life and Work.* Cranbury, N.J.: Associated University Presses, 1984.
Novak, Barbara. *American Painting of the Nineteenth Century,* second edition. New York: Harper & Row, 1979.

O'Connor, Francis V. *Jackson Pollock.* New York: Museum of Modern Art, 1967.
Prown, Jules David. *American Painting: From Its Beginnings to the Armory Show.* New York: Skira/Rizzoli, 1977.
Rose, Barbara. *American Painting: The Twentieth Century.* New York: Skira/Rizzoli, 1986.
Sandler, Irving. *American Art of the 1960s.* New York: Harper & Row, 1988.
_____. *The Triumph of American Painting.* New York: Harper & Row, 1970.
Steiner, Rudolf. T*he Soul's Progress through Repeated Earth Lives.* New York: Anthroposophic Press, 1944, especially pp. 13–16.
Sullivan, Louis. *Kindergarten Chats and Other Writing*s. New York: George Wittenborn, 1947.
Tomkins, Calvin. *Off the Wall.* New York: Doubleday, 1980.
Wright, Frank Lloyd. *The Natural House.* New York: Horizons Press, 1954.

The Birth of American Literature:
The Altering of the Early American Mind

by

John Wulsin

Acknowledging that the stories of Native American culture have been rich for ages, the fact that Sequoyah, in the mid-1820s, first created a Native American alphabet (Cherokee) means that written stories emerge as "Native American Literature" primarily in the twentieth century. While Native American culture has influenced "European/American" culture more subtly than most people realize, this exploration will focus on the emergence of a stream of literature in America.

When one thinks of Spanish settling in Saint Augustine, Florida, in the 1580s, and of the English pilgrims settling in Plymouth, Massachusetts, in the 1620s, it is perhaps astonishing to find little literature in America in the 1600s. While an image such as Governor Winthrop's "City upon a Hill" (from his lay sermon) certainly dominated the imaginations of the early Puritans, the poet Anne Bradstreet, writing in Boston in the 1640s and 1650s, was an exception.

THE FLESH AND THE SPIRIT

In secret place where once I stood
Close by the banks of lacrim flood,
I heard two sisters reason on
Things that are past and things to come.
One Flesh was called, who had her eye
On worldly wealth and vanity;
The other Spirit, who did rear
Her thoughts unto a higher sphere.[1]

In one poem, to her book, she writes,

> I cast thee by as one unfit for light,
> Thy visage was so irksome in my sight. . . .[2]

Anne Bradstreet writes uncomfortably, almost guiltily, in a discouraging environment. Generally New England in the seventeenth century fostered no drama, little poetry, no fiction; the most creative word-work was sermons and letters. Why so little literature in the New World? The settlers established geographic independence from the Old World, with an ocean between. They secured their own religious independence, while not often being tolerant of others' religious independence. In addition, of course, they were preoccupied with survival, clearing wilderness, and forming various and changing relationships with Native American tribes. And the religion of most of the northern settlers puritanically discouraged, even forbade, the arts, as tending to be temptations of the devil.

And American literature of the 1700s? In the first decades, one minister in the little western town of Northampton, Massachusetts, was secretly writing poetry, which Thomas Johnson discovered in a Yale library and published in 1939. Edward Taylor's preface of *God's Determinations Touching His Elect* shows some potent word-work.

> Oh! What a might is this! Whose single frown
> Doth shake the world as it would shake it down!
> Which all from nothing fet, from nothing all:
> Hath all on nothing set, lets nothing fall.
> Gave all to nothing-man indeed, whereby
> Though nothing, man is embossed the brightest gem,
> More precious than all preciousness in them.
> But nothing-man did throw down all by sin,
> And darkened that lightsome gem in him
> That now his brightest diamond is grown,
> Darker by far than any coalpit stone.[3]

However, in the first half of the century, most literary energy was devoted to sermons. Two polarities generated much of the tension and energy of the Great Awakening of the 1730s and 1740s. While one stream of the Congregational and Presbyterian churches, led by Rev. Chauncy of Boston, felt all religious consideration should remain within reason, Jonathon Edwards, also from Northhampton in the wild West, led those eager to fan the passions beyond reason. Edwards, in his sermon, "Sinners in the Hands of an Angry God," did not hesitate to proclaim that the "God that holds you over the pit of Hell, much as one holds a spider, or some loathsome insect over the fire, abhors you, and is dreadfully provoked."[4] In the other polarity of the mid-eighteenth century, Edwards defended the Calvinist doctrine of predestination against the "insidious" but irresistibly spreading Arminian doctrine of free will. (Jacobus Arminias was a Dutch minister and divinity professor in Leyden around 1600.)

As the Great Awakening subsided by the 1750s, the settlers were consumed with their struggles for economic, legal, and political independence. One could say that the essential literary energy of the nation fighting to be born was distilled into two documents, The Declaration of Independence, July 4, 1776, and the Constitution, 1789. One articulated the spirit of the new nation; one articulated the form of the new nation. It is as though the political thinkers of the time worked with their rational minds and their imaginations, in accord with each other, with the spirit of the English language, and with the being of the new nation, in a mighty labor to fashion a conceptual body that would allow the new nation to form and to grow in a balanced way, honoring both individual and democratic mass, working toward executive, legislative, and judicial interaction, restraint, and support.

At this time in world history, the great ideals of the French Revolution, "Libertè, Egalitè, Fraternitè," exploded into terrorizing bloodshed, begetting the ideals' opposite, Emperor Napoleon, within ten years. One has to imagine the quality of concentration, imagination, and clear thinking that allowed a number of individuals in this raw, uncultured frontier nation to find the words to embody the ideas that would allow them to live healthily in what has become the longest enduring democracy in world history. Not many poems, stories, plays, novels have been written during labor. What a great, future-engendering labor that was. Nevertheless, long after geographical and religious independence, it was to be a whole lifetime after the declaration of economic, legal, and political independence, a whole lifetime later, that the new United States of America finally called for, and began to articulate, artistic independence.

Before paying attention to that call for literary independence, let us first become aware of the American frame of mind in relation to language in the late 1700s and early 1800s. The Declaration of Independence and the Constitution, perhaps two of the best offerings of the age, were fashioned during the height of the Age of Reason, the Age of Enlightenment. In order to understand the mind being born, we must understand the mind of the mother, England. Literally, after the unparalleled, extraordinary expansions of Elizabethan drama, of the lyric metaphysical poets, and of Milton's epic *Paradise Lost* in the 1600s, England in the 1700s settled back into an "Augustan Age," characterized as a reflection of Rome, epitomized by the skillful wit of Dryden and Pope. The rhyming couplets that fourteenth-century Chaucer had initiated and thrived in, which Shakespeare and Milton had both outgrown, reappeared in the Age of Reason, as an ebbing back to an Intellectual soul mentality, which both Dryden and Pope mastered. The only epic possible then was a mock-epic, Pope's "The Rape of the Lock." Dr. Johnson created the first dictionary of the English language, published in 1755. Johnson, in his *Rasselas*, warn against "the hunger of the imagination, which preys on life," interfering with seeing things as they actually were.

Dr. Johnson's celebration of prose coincided with the emergence of the new form of literature, the novel, in the late 1600s and the 1700s. Novels such as Daniel Defoe's *Robinson Crusoe* and *Moll Flanders*, Henry Fielding's *Tom Jones*, and Richardson's *Pamela and Clarissa*, generally portray and explore middle-class characters making their rational and emotional ways through contemporary society, in which human nature functions in the context of the normal laws of both linear time and three-dimensional space. However dynamic the characters and stories may be, the stage is limited. Lunatics, tragic lovers, poets, and certainly supernatural gods are outside the scope of the essentially rational English novel of the 1600s and 1700s.

The Royal Academy of Science had been maturing, tempered strongly by Galileo's discovery of the sun as the center of our universe, by Descartes's distinctions between matter and mind, by Newton's demonstrations of man's ability to calculate mathematically the course of the planets through the heavens, according to the laws of gravity. One could say that for many, Newton's clockwork universe marked the shift, as Heaven, or even the heavens, started to become, simply, space.

In America, in the late 1700s and early 1800s, the theological thinking was also very rational. For those who feel a little confused about the religious origins of the "American Mind," perhaps a summary would be helpful. The primary source of the early American mind (of New England settlers) was John Calvin (1509–1564), a major Protestant leader, in Geneva, Switzerland. Especially his beliefs in the universal priesthood of all believers, the importance of faith over good works, and predestination became a source for the Huguenots in France, the Presbyterians in Scotland, and the Puritans in England. The original Puritans in America considered themselves Congregationalists, compatible with Presbyterians, as more Scots poured into the colonies. In the Boston area one of the dominant influences, streams, became the Unitarians in the 1700s. Believing in one God, denying the divinity of Christ, oriented toward social deeds, inspired by John Locke, the Unitarians felt the Calvinist emphasis on the sinfulness of man to be inconsistent with reason. Eventually the Unitarians split from the Presbyterians in 1805, and, led by Rev. William Ellery Channing, formed their own American Unitarian Association in 1825. The scope of this article does not include attention to the Catholic culture of Maryland, because it does not seem to have contributed in any primary way to the altering American mind which gave birth finally to an American literature in these early centuries.

It is fair to characterize the general American theological mind of the turn of the century as earnest, thoughtful, rational, relatively literal in relation to the Bible, cautiously extending beyond reason at the most to allegory, in which one image in the Bible or in nature, serves as a type for one spiritual truth. A good example of this frame of mind appears in the recent novel, *Cold Mountain*, by Charles Frazier, portraying the attitude of a Civil War wife toward nature and God. Ada is venturing through the Blue Ridge Mountains; her husband Monroe has been away in the war for several years.

> After a time they crossed a black creek, stepping with care on the dry backs of humped stones. Ada looked at the way the creek was seizing up with a thin rim of bright ice along its banks and around rocks and fallen trees and nubbles of moss, anything that hindered the flow. In the center of the creek, though, the fast water ripped along as always.
>
> Where it ran shallower and slower, then, were the places prone to freezing. Monroe would have made a lesson of such a thing, Ada thought. He would have said that the match of that creek's parts would be in a person's life, what God intended it to be the type of. All God's works but elaborate analogy. Every bright image in the visible world only a shadow of a divine thing, so that earth and heaven, low and high, strangely agreed in form and meaning because they were in fact congruent.
>
> Monroe had a book wherein you could look up the types. The rose—its thorns and its blossom—a type of the difficult and dangerous path to spiritual awakening. The baby come wailing to the world in pain and blood—a type of our miserable earthly lives, so consumed with violence. The crow—its blackness, its outlaw nature, its tendency to feast on carrion—a type of the dark forces that wait to overtake man's soul.

> So Ada quite naturally thought the stream and the ice might offer a weapon of the spirit. Or, perhaps, a warning. But she refused to believe that a book should say just how it should be construed or to what use it might be put. Whatever a book said would lack something essential and be as useless by itself as the dudgeon to a door hinge with no pintle.[5]

Ada recognizes that her husband's book of equivalencies lacks something essential. Frazier's representation of Monroe's mind in the Blue Ridge Mountains in the 1850s probably works as a pretty fair characterization of the bent of the American mind in New England in the early 1800s.

Whereas in Boston the Unitarians were emerging, in Connecticut the Congregationalists remained dominant, feeling, as their name implies, neither the need for a priest as mediary between God and man, nor the need for a hierarchical bishop to direct the church, rather trusting the people of the congregation to carry together the word, the spirit of God.

Two young American Congregationalists in the 1820s and 1830s struggled to reconcile their inner experience of the divine with the language available to articulate that experience. In their frustration, each independently found himself reading Samuel Taylor Coleridge's *Aids to Reflection*, philosophical notes. Coleridge's little book almost single-handedly catalyzed a linguistic, if not revolution, then evolution in the American mind. The two young Congregationalists, James Marsh and Horace Bushnell, are similar in several ways. Both, through Coleridge's influence, pioneered beyond the thinking of the time. Both nevertheless managed to remain within the boundaries of the Congregational Church. Each did, however, go in a different direction from the other.

How did Coleridge's thinking affect their thinking? Back in England in the 1790s, the young poet-preacher, Samuel Taylor Coleridge, fourteenth and favorite child of a minister, was assuming he would become a Unitarian minister, until the poet in him felt too stifled by the Unitarian single-mindedness. The artist in Coleridge felt so dynamically the relationship between poet, poem, and inspiration that the theologian in Coleridge became a Trinitarian, absolutely experiencing the parallels between the triads of poet, poem, and inspiration on the one hand, and Father, Son, and Holy Spirit on the other hand.

A keen philosophical thinker, Coleridge was also an astute observer of nature and a close friend of scientists, such as J. B. Priestly, who discovered oxygen. What poet/philosopher/theologian Coleridge realized was that if the divine Creator is immortal, limitless, then His living creation has also its limitless, unpredictable dimensions, beyond the grasp of man's measuring mind. However, Humanity, the primary creature, made in the image of the Creator, could conceivably use words (use the Word) in ways that reflect the infinitely mobile, multidimensional capacity of the original Word to create the living world. If the Spirit is multidimensional, endlessly vital, does not our language need to be multidimensional, endlessly vital?

Hence, the human language that will be able to do justice to the living spirit will not be simply rational exposition, nor will it be simply the almost arithmetic allegory, "rock equals steadfastness." No, the human language that will reflect the divine spirit, in kind, will be quickening, suggestive, with layers of meaning coexisting, facets simultaneously reflecting, symbols suggestive in numerous directions, a language luminous, numinous, not fixed but flowing, as the imagination of the ultimate I AM flows.

Now, let us return to the Unitarian influence, because, as Philip Gura has said, "Ralph Waldo Emerson, Bronson Alcott, Theodore Parker, Elizabeth Peabody, and other Transcendentalists who became concerned with the problem of language (albeit to various degrees) were nurtured within the cocoon of the Unitarian Church."[6] The Unitarian religion was based on John Locke's empiricist philosophy. Just as Locke viewed the soul as *tabula rasa*, a blank slate to be filled with impressions, so, echoing the medieval nominalists, Locke viewed language as an arbitrary group of signs arranged for external convenience.

Elaborating upon Locke, the Scotsman Thomas Reid and other fellow "Common Sense" philosophers valued observation of the world through the senses, experiencing language therefore as reflecting the human particulars of time and space, not as reflecting any eternal reality. Such attitudes, rooted in Locke, elaborated by the Scottish Common Sense philosophers, promulgated through the Unitarian Church, powerfully permeated Harvard, Yale, and Princeton in the early 1800s.

By the 1820s though, some Harvard students were becoming excited by Kant and Coleridge, who articulated a knowing that preceded experience. One young Vermonter studied Divinity in both Andover and Cambridge, Massachusetts, publishing in fact an edition of Coleridge's *Aids to Reflection* in 1829. James Marsh wrote an essay exploring how an emerging modern sensibility resulted from a new relationship between faith, reason, and imagination.[7] Marsh saw the Enlightenment's emphasis on logical rationality leaving faith weakened. He felt Coleridge's understanding of imagination was the key to healing the spiritual anemia of early 19th century America. Coleridge, reflecting on recent church history, recognized that,

"Too soon did the Doctors of the Church forget that the heart, the moral nature, was the beginning and the end: and that truth, knowledge, and insight were comprehended in its expansion. This was the true and first apostasy—when in council and synod the divine humanities of the Gospel gave way to speculative systems, and religion became a science of shadows under the name of theology, or at least a bare skeleton of truth, without life, or interest, alike inaccessible and unintelligible to the majority of Christians."[8]

Through Coleridge's acknowledgment of the crucial validity of the feeling life, Marsh experienced that the will's wellspring of faith could be rejuvenated, that reason could be illuminated with the greater vitality of higher reason, a faculty limited not to the mere mind of man, but capable of shining with the light of the creator. Hence one's language, rather than being a collection of stickers stuck on the things of the world, could in fact bear the things of the world with such an artful care that they revealed the spirit of their creator. The language of theology could in fact livingly reflect the living spirit.

James Marsh became a Congregationalist minister, and the wise trustees of the University of Vermont invited him in 1826 to become president of their university. As president and professor, he devoted the rest of his life to establishing a college curriculum based on a Coleridgean foundation. Partially through Marsh's interests and efforts to heal the rifts between America's Calvinists and Unitarians, Coleridge's *Aids to Reflection* became, as Perry Miller said, the "book which was of the greatest single importance in the forming of the Transcendentalists' minds."[9]

A generation younger than James Marsh, Horace Bushnell was a country boy who had carded wool with his father. When he arrived at Yale, he realized that he had no language with which to express his religious experiences. Reading Coleridge's *Aids to Reflection*, Bushnell found that "writing became, to a considerable extent, the making of a language, and not going to dictionaries." He became aware of how, "the second, third, the thirteenth sense of words, all but the first physical first sense belong to the empyrean, and are given, as we see in the prophets, to be inspired by."[10] As early as 1839, he published his *Preliminary Dissertation on Language*. During the ensuing decade he continuously strove to develop language shimmering with inspiration, like that of the prophets, language enspirited, enthused, vibrant with multidimensionality beyond the limitations of logic, in short, language that was like life.

Bushnell's collection of sermons, *God in Christ*, published in 1849, articulates "a Logoism in the forms of things, [so that things] serve as types of images of what is inmost in our souls [because] God, the universal

Author, stands EXPRESSED everywhere."[11] Bushnell experienced that rather than being embroiled in the logical battles between the Unitarians and the Trinitarians, rather than being locked into Swedenborg's arithmetical one-to-one correspondences, people needed to accept that the things of the world only imperfectly reflect the Spirit of the creator of that world. In the same manner, the words of our language only reach toward accurately reflecting (doing justice to) both the world and the creator. But, said Bushnell, through the activity of the Logos in human language, our language was in fact constantly improving upon itself "by multiplying its forms of representation. . . . As form battles form, and one [word] neutralizes another, all [their] insufficiencies are filled out, . . . the contrarieties liquidated, [and the mind can then] settle into a full and just apprehension of the pure spiritual truth."[12] Bushnell articulated that truth was "not two-dimensional but spherical, to be apprehended thorough a multiplicity of forms."[13]

In short, Horace Bushnell, the Congregational theologian, experienced that, just as man was but the image of the Creator, so man's language was but the image of the original Word. But, as such, man's language could, and indeed should, glow with symbolic multiplicity of meaning, of connotation, immeasurably limitless possibilities, as anything living in fact is.

James Marsh and Horace Bushnell, while liberating language from the flat, rational equation of logical limit, maintained such a flowing, multiplicity of language permeated with the image of the Judaeo-Christian Creator. They strove to activate language through the activity of imagination, imitating in kind, though not degree, the imagination of the infinite I AM, as it is presently active in the creation. One could say that through imagination's rescue of language from the limits of rationality, Marsh and Bushnell were attempting, with Coleridge as a guide, nothing less than the rejuvenation of American protestantism, which was the dominant frame of mind in the still new nation. From another perspective, these two good ministers began the process of galvanizing the American mind out of the Age of Reason, which, in its distilling clarification, had served so well the conceiving of the United States of America. Nevertheless, long after the separate geography had assured religious "freedom," a lifetime after political and legal independence had been accomplished, these two men experienced that in fact the American individual was not yet spiritually free within the confines of the religious mind of the time. Since American theology had become trapped in what one might call a rational soul eddy, these two Congregationalists recognized, experienced, the imagination as the medium that might allow the Christian to experience the spirit at the time, in time, the spirit of the time, as fully, as vitally, as human language can allow.

If the influence of Calvin can be seen as a taproot of early American consciousness, perhaps it is time to acknowledge Coleridge's crucial role as a light that led leaf to flower, in what Van Wyck Brooks called, "The Flowering of New England, "in what F. O. Matthiessen called "The American Renaissance," the extraordinary gift to world literature. Coleridge's inspiration persevered a couple of decades into the works of Emerson, Thoreau, Hawthorne, Melville, Poe, Whitman, and Dickinson, and appeared long after geographical, religious, political, legal, and economic independence. It is also time to acknowledge the role, in bringing that light to America, of two little-known Congregational ministers, James Marsh and Horace Bushnell, who helped to make possible how our American artists could think, imagine, and write, beyond the confines of the church. Marsh and Bushnell helped the early American mind to alter, so that Hawthorne's scarlet letter could evolve, could mean variously, so that Melville's doubloon in *Moby Dick* could be read so many different ways by so many different people.

1. Miller, Perry, ed. *The American Puritans*. Anchor Books, 1956, p. 267.
2. *Ibid*., p. 266.
3. *Ibid*., p. 304.
4. Faust, Clarence and Thomas Johnson, ed. *Jonathon Edwards*. Hill and Wang, Inc., 1935, p. 164.
5. Frazier, Charles. *Cold Mountain*. Atlantic Monthly Press, 1997, pp. 298–99.
6. Gura, Philip. *The Wisdom of Words*. Wesleyan University Press, 1981, p. 18.
7. *Ibid*., p. 41, note 18.
8. Coleridge, S. T. *From Aids to Reflection*. Aphorism IV, *Selected Poetry and Prose of Coleridge*, ed. Donald Stauffer, Modern Library College Editions, 1951, p. 530.
9. Gura, p. 45, note 32.
10. *Ibid*., p. 53, note 54.
11. *Ibid*., p. 60, note 72; *God in Christ*, p. 22, 24.
12. *Ibid*., p. 63, *God in Christ*, p. 55.
13. *Ibid*..

Vishnu's Pursuit of Maya in the Life of Ralph Waldo Emerson

by

John Wulsin

He in whom the love of truth predominates will keep himself aloof from all the moorings, and afloat. He will abstain from dogmatism, and recognize all the opposite negations between which, as walls, his being is swung. (December 1835)

This quotation is keynote to our exploration of Ralph Waldo Emerson's experience and understanding of Man and Nature as expressed in his private journals and his public essays. Even when unexpressed, the content of this quotation remains the active principle that induces the transformation of words used in expressing the relation between man and nature, much as Vishnu and Maya in the Hindu myth metamorphose through ascending incarnations from insect to elephant to become Man-God and Man-Goddess.

The element running through entire nature, which we popularly call Fate, is known to us as limitation. Whatever limits us we call Fate. If we are brute and barbarous, the fate takes a brute and dreadful shape. As we refine, our checks become finer. If we rise to spiritual culture, the antagonism takes a spiritual form. In the Hindu fables, Vishnu follows Maya through all her ascending changes, from insect and crawfish up to elephant; whatever form she took, he took the male form of that kind, until she became at last woman and goddess, and he a man and a god. The limitations refine as the soul purifies, but the ring of necessity is always perched as the top. (R. W. E., "Fate," 1852)

Vishnu, both the Primeval Cosmic Man and the Lord of Being, pursues Maya, the Mother of Existence, throughout the cycles of lives much as man pursues nature in the cycles of Emerson's protean mind. We will follow the transformation of this relationship between the human being and nature through selected private and public writings in three periods of Emerson's life: his young adulthood up to the age of thirty-five (1838), the next state until he was forty (1839–1843), and the nine years until he was forty-nine (1844–1852).

What is Emerson the man by the age of thirty-five? Born on May 25, 1803, in Boston, Massachusetts, Ralph Waldo Emerson grew up in a "poor but educated family." He lost his pastor father at the age of eight and, subject to tuberculosis which separated him from normal games and sports, young Emerson found fulfillment in the companionship of his three brothers and in books. Poor health after his graduation from Harvard College delayed his becoming a minister of the "rational Christianity" of the Unitarian Church until 1828. In the interim, his reading of various contemporary philosophers, especially Coleridge, was weakening the intensity of his commitment to the dogma of the church as he discovered the revelation of a God within his heart, not just on historical and scriptural record. At the age of twenty-eight, Emerson lost his wife of eighteen months, Ellen Tucker, to consumption. One year later, in 1832, Emerson resigned as minister over his parish's and the church's attitude toward the celebration of the Lord's Supper, feeling by now that in the ministry as a profession, "instead of making Christianity a vehicle for truth, you make truth only a horse for Christianity."

A year of travel, including meetings with Coleridge, Wordsworth, and Carlyle replenished his health and confidence. Soon after, Emerson settled in Concord, soberly married Lydia Jackson in 1835, and at the age of thirty-three, suffered the death of his dearest brother Charles. During these years, Emerson's explorations of his age and its ideas led him to Plato and the Platonists, Swedenborg and the Swedenborgians, George Fox and the Quakers, Goethe, Shakespeare, Coleridge, and Carlyle, always seeking the illuminating moment. He partially supported himself by giving lectures to adults on the Lyceum lecture circuit as far away as Maine. In 1836, the year of Charles' death, he published his first book, *Nature*. The following year, in "The American Scholar," his address to the Phi Beta Kappa Society at Harvard College, he sounded the trumpet blast of cultural, literary, and artistic independence from Mother England and the Old World, sixty years after political independence. Students and professors alike charged forth like warriors with a renewed mission. In 1838, at the age of thirty-five, Emerson told the graduating class of the Harvard Divinity School to declare its spiritual independence from the old religion, to realize "that God is, not was; that He speaketh, not spake." Some students walked forth charged, but Harvard closed its doors to Emerson as a speaker for twenty years. He never regretted speaking those truths.

What was Emerson's concept of man at the age of thirty-five? In *Nature*, 1836, he speaks of beauty as threefold. The Greeks called their whole world order "beauty." What Emerson himself means by beauty is not clear, but he asserts that "the world . . . exists to the soul to satisfy the desire of beauty. . . . Beauty, in its largest and profoundest sense, is one expression for the universe." Beauty is threefold because man's, the soul's, experience of the beauty of the world is threefold. Aesthetically, man perceives the delight of natural forms. Through man's will or virtue "an act of truth or heroism seems at once to draw to itself the sky as its temple, the sun as its candle." Man through "the intellect searches out the absolute order of things as they stand in the mind of God, and without the colors of affection."

> The intellectual and active powers seem to succeed each other. . . . There is something unfriendly in each to the other, but they are like the alternate periods of feeling and working in animals; each prepares and will be followed by the other. Therefore does beauty, which in relation to actions . . . comes unsought, remain for the apprehension and pursuit of the intellect; and then again, in its turn, of the active power.

Emerson suggests man's soul is composed of three faculties: the intellect, the feeling perception of beauty, and the will—the first and last in potent polarity.

If man is threefold, what is nature? "Strictly speaking . . . all which Philosophy distinguishes as the Not Me, that is, both nature and art, all other men and my own body, must be ranked under this name, Nature." But Emerson is no philosopher strictly distinguishing; he never fixedly defines either Man or Nature. As "nothing is quite beautiful alone," neither is anything quite true alone, but only in relation to other partial truths. The closest he comes to early definitions is that "the world is emblematic . . . the whole of nature is a metaphor of the human mind." By mind he means the whole human soul. Nature is macrocosm, man microcosm. The objects of nature cannot be understood without man, nor can man be understood without the objects of nature. "The beauty in nature . . . is the herald of inward and eternal beauty, and is not alone a solid and satisfactory good," for it is but the embodiment of what once existed in the intellect as pure law. As the last issue of spirit, nature's "every object rightly seen, unlocks a new faculty of soul."

How did Emerson experience the human being's relation to nature through his own will? His journal reveals himself at the early age of twenty-one to feel overwhelmed by some force, not me. "I am the servant more than the master of my fate. I shape my fortunes, as it seems to me, not at all. For in all my life I obey a strong necessity." Eight years later, in 1832, he has begun a glowing though cautious commitment to the terrible freedom of his own inner life. Yet in 1835 he still struggles for words to describe the force prohibiting him from shaping his life at his own will.

> We only row, we're steered by fate. The involuntary action is all. See how we are mastered. . . . With desire of poetic reputation, we still prose. We would be Teachers, but in spite of us we are kept out of the pulpit, and thrust into the pew. Who doth it? No man: only Lethe, only Time; only negatives; indisposition; delay; nothing.

To the public, however, in *Nature* in 1836, at the age of thirty-three, he wrestles to portray a world of possibility, without limitation. Nature can be the unfallen bride of man, uniting with him. There is no "not me" which is not potentially me. Nature is the virginal ally of religion. "Prophet and priest, David, Isaiah, Jesus have drawn deeply from this source. This ethical character so penetrates the bone and marrow, as to seem the end for which it was made." As Nature's beauty heralds an inward beauty, so Nature's ethical character seems its *raison d'etre*.

Every natural process is a version of a moral sentence. The moral law lies at the center of nature and radiates to the circumference. . . . The laws of moral nature answer to those of matter as face to face in a glass. The axioms of physics translate the laws of ethics.

So with nature as beneficent catalyst for the opening of the soul, "the exercise of the will is taught in every event." Emerson only hints of any weakness in man's capacity to "'build his own world" when stating that "with the prevalence of . . . secondary desires—the desire of riches, of pleasure, of power, of praise . . . the power over nature as an interpreter of the will is in a degree lost." But the wise man pierces these secondary desires. For the wise man, Nature is not at all a mastering Fate. "Nature . . . is made to serve . . . as the ass on which the Saviour rode . . . one after another his victorious thought comes up with and reduces all things, until the world becomes at last only a realized will—the double of man."

But privately Emerson continues to recognize a tension. In May of 1837 he pleads, recognizing society's deterioration, "Let me begin anew. Let me teach the finite to know its master. Let me ascend above my fate and work down upon my world." In early October he acknowledges the pull of some force greater than his own will. "We are carried by destiny along our life's course, looking as grave and knowing as little as the infant who is carried in his wicker coach through the street." Yet within the same month he asserts his own push against the pull: "There ought to be, there can be nothing to which the soul is called, to which the soul is not equal." From this sincere impulse rises the exhortation in the 1838 Harvard Divinity School address that "the remedy to the deformity of the forms already existing is first, soul, second, soul, and evermore, soul . . . a whole popedom of forms one pulsation of virtue can uplift and vivify." Virtue is an attribute of will or action. Deeds for Emerson are not the glories of war or the fighting of forest fires. "The preamble of thought, the transition through which it passes from unconscious to the conscious, is action." Emerson means not outwardly directed action, but inward action, action intimately related to thought. Through thought the world becomes a realized will—the double of man. At this stage Emerson focuses on the two polar faculties of man's soul, less concerned with the mediating feeling realm.

How did Emerson through his thinking experience man's relation to nature in this period? In 1831, at the age of twenty-eight, he writes in his journal, "Suicidal is the distrust of reason; this fear to think. . . . To reflect is to receive truth immediately from God without medium. That is living faith. To take on trust certain facts is a dead faith, inoperative." Encouraged by Coleridge, Emerson knows early on the need for the sword of thought, to distinguish without dividing. One must think actively or succumb to dead usages that scatter one's forces. In *Nature,* Emerson declares, "Nature stretches out her arms to embrace man, only let his thoughts be of equal greatness . . . only let his thoughts be of equal scope, and the frame will suit the picture. . . . In proportion to the energy of his thought and will, he takes up the world into himself."

In proportion to the energy of man's thought, nature will unlock the thinking faculty of his soul. Action, mutual activity, thinking action. As nature exercises man's will in every event, it also is "a discipline of the understanding in intellectual truths. Our dealing with sensible objects is a constant exercise in the necessary lessons of difference, of likeness of order." Nature hones the edge of the discerning sword. Yet Emerson senses and is helped again by Coleridge to articulate that the sharp, cold steel of understanding does not suffice. For,

> to the senses and the understanding belongs a sort of instinctive belief in the absolute existence of nature. In their view man and Nature are indissolubly joined. Things are ultimates, and they never look beyond their spheres. The presence of Reason mars this faith. The first effort of thought tends to relax this despotism of the senses which binds us to nature as if we were a part of it, and shows us nature aloof, and, as it were, afloat. When the eye of Reason opens to outline and surface are at once added grace and expression. These proceed from imagination and affection.

Through understanding, man perceives nature as it appears. In the light of reason nature is revealed as phenomenon, not substance, not more than the accident or effect of spirit. Understanding, the knowledge of man, is an evening knowledge, *vespertina cognitio*; reason is akin to the knowledge of God, or morning knowledge, *matutina cognitio*. As Emerson had asserted to himself that the lover of truth must keep himself aloof from all moorings and afloat, so for the lover of truth must nature remain aloof, afloat, protean, unfixed. Otherwise it falls. Vishnu's Maya must elude Vishnu. Kindled by the fire of holiest affections, man's "reason" becomes flaming sword, instrument of the artist, of the uplifting, uniting creator.

Preceding the necessity of the active soul to "realize the world," to take up the world into himself, is the need of the faculties of the soul to act in relation to each other. It is not enough to be a thinker, understanding. One's thinking must be imbued with the warmth of affections, of imagination, must be engaged in the action of raising pre-existing ideas from the unconscious into consciousness. In his address, "The American Scholar," in 1837, Emerson asserts more clearly that man cannot afford to fall into particular faculties or functions. Then "the priest becomes a form, the attorney a statue-book; the mechanic a machine . . ." Man must sustain his faculties, his latent functions that his whole soul be engaged, that he be man thinking, not "a mere thinker, or still worse, the parrot of other men's thinking." The faculties of the soul, thinking, affections, action, only compose the whole, which he suggests in the word "character." "Character is higher than intellect. Thinking is the function. Living is the functionary. . . . This is a total act. Thinking is a partial act."

Yet throughout this early period of Emerson's adult life, the strongly asserted images of the whole man and the marriage of man and nature face-to-face momentarily tremble like a prematurely open rose at the piercing, winter-like sound of the keynote. The keynote declares that man cannot rest on the vision of the rose, of wholeness, of marriage, but must remain afloat, suspended between the opposite poles, "between which, as walls, his being is swung." In May 1838 he writes in his journal,

> I complain in my own experience of the feeble influence of thought on life, a ray as pale and ineffectual as that of the sun in our cold and bleak spring. They seem to lie—the actual life and the intellectual intervals—in parallel lines and never meet. Yet we doubt not that they act and react ever. . . . How slowly the highest raptures of the intellect break through the trivial forms of habit. Yet imperceptibly they do. Gradually, in long years, we bend our living toward our idea, but we serve seven years and twice seven for Rachel.

The path toward wholeness is one of undulation. In 1834 he writes, "Love compels love; hatred, hatred; action and reaction are always equal." In *Nature* two years later, he writes on the one hand that "nature is the organ through which the universal spirit speaks to the individual, and strives to lead back the individual to it." Then he says on the other hand that "the Supreme Being does not build up nature around us, but puts it forth through us, as the life of the tree puts forth new branches and leaves through the pores of the old."

Man and Nature are mutual means. Through each the Spirit engenders the other. In "The American Scholar" he balances the ancient Pythagorean call, "Man, know thyself" with "Study nature," that modern man's inward and outward senses become aligned in an ebbing and flowing. Yet he acknowledges in *Nature* that "we are as much strangers in nature as we are aliens from God. We do not understand the notes of the birds. The fox and the deer run away from us . . . What discord is between man and nature." Emerson's "Orphic Poet" sings that

> Man is dwarf of himself. . . . Once . . . out from him sprang the sun and moon . . . But, having made for himself this huge shell, his waters retired. . . . He sees that the structure still fits him, but fits him colossally. Say, rather, once it fitted him, now it corresponds to him from far and on high. Man . . . perceives that his law . . . is not inferior but superior to his will . . .

Thus spake the "Orphic Poet." Emerson himself speaks resolutely, positively, to the public to take up the sceptre of reason to make the world a double of himself. Yet in May 1837 he writes to himself, "A believer in Unity, a seer of Unity, I yet behold two. . . . Cannot I conceive the Universe without a contradiction?"

Between the ages of thirty-six and forty, supposedly solitary Emerson actually enjoyed the frequent company of a group of outstanding individuals, a concentration almost rivaling in quality and surpassing in friendship that of Shakespeare and his contemporaries, Marlowe, Jonson, etc. Closest to Emerson were Bronson Alcott, "who . . . makes . . . the Platonic world as solid as Massachusetts to me; and Thoreau [who] gives me in flesh and blood and pertinacious Saxon belief, my own ethics."

Ellery Channing, Margaret Fuller, and Nathaniel and Sophia Hawthorne were among other liberal thinkers looking to find a way through the pervading empiricism, rationalism, and realism of the time. Somehow dubbed the Transcendentalists, this extended circle both generated and came to embody a movement of cultural awakening, which spread through the Northeast in all levels of society. Nevertheless, Emerson, at the age of thirty-seven, refused to join in 1840 the opening of Brook Farm, the communal experiment to find the ideal combination of manual and intellectual labor. Although Brook Farm might well have provided the ideal environment for Emerson's Man Thinking, Emerson felt he still needed to get his own house in order first. In 1840 he helped found, contribute to, and finally edit *The Dial*, the publication of the Transcendentalists. In 1841 he published *Essays*,

First Series. The following year, his six-year-old first son, Waldo, died, leaving Emerson's faith deeply shaken. The prophet's voice regained some of its power only gradually, through writing poetry and through a lecture tour to Washington,D.C., Baltimore, Philadelphia and New York in 1843, at the age of forty.

In these years of 1839 through 1843, the pendulum swings between the human being and nature, between Vishnu and Maya, but not back and forth, for the focal point is not fixed; it moves; the pendulum spirals. Emerson writes in his journal in the summer of 1841, "The metamorphosis of Nature shows itself in nothing more than this, that there is no word in our language that cannot become typical to us of Nature by giving it emphasis." Several months earlier, in April, he writes, " I am of the Maker not of the Made. . . . Through all the running sea of forms, I am truth, I am love, and immutable I transcend form as I do time and space."

As Emerson recognizes that the intellect and active powers seem to succeed each other like alternate states, we recognize that in this period of his life (we in this incomplete sketch are not yet aware of the seven-year periods Emerson several times intimates), Emerson focuses more on the state of Man than on the state of Nature. In fact, in these years he appears to refer rarely to nature per se. (When he does address nature directly in essays not explored in this sketch, he portrays it, according to S. Whicher, *Freedom and Fate*, not as the primarily static last issue of the spirit, as in *Nature*, 1836, but as ever flowing, ever changing, "and nothing fast but those invisible cords which we call laws, on which all is strung,") In *Self-Reliance*, 1841, he states, "Time and space [one 'word' for nature] are but physiological colors which the eye makes, but the soul is light. . . . A true man belongs to no other time or place, but is the center of things. Where he is, there is nature." Character becomes the reality that "takes place of the whole creation."

Man is actually the pendulum. Rather than swinging back and forth, he swings in and out: in toward the center of his own soul, of the anthropomorphic universe of which he is the creator in the finite; out toward the periphery where forces "not me" hold sway. The further in toward center, the more aligned is man with the universal; the further out toward the periphery, the more confined is man in the particular. The more centered one is, the more free one is from outer authority, outer forms. The clearest trumpet call of this period is for freedom. In June 1839 he writes in his journal, "I wish to write such rhymes as shall not suggest a restraint but contrariwise the wildest freedom." In September, "Freedom boundless I wish. I will not pledge myself not to drink wine, not to drink ink, not to lie, and not to commit adultery, lest I hanker tomorrow to do these very things by reason of my having tied my hands." In November, "Never was anything gained by admitting the omnipotence of limitations, but all immortal action is an overstepping of these busy rules. . . ."

In *Self-Reliance* he declares that the way to the universal sense is not through outer guides but through one's own latent conviction, "for the inmost in due time becomes the outmost." No law written on stone is to be blindly followed. For "nothing is at last sacred but the integrity of your own mind." Even if one is the Devil's child, one's freedom is to live out from the Devil within.

> Thus all concentrates [in center]: let us not rove [to periphery]; let us sit at home with the cause. . . . Bid the invaders take the shoes from off their feet, for God is here within. Let our simplicity judge them, and our docility to our own law demonstrate the poverty of nature and fortune beside our native riches.

The poverty of nature is evident in that fox and deer, much less, rock and tree, rarely appear in Emerson's expression privately or publicly in these years. And the poverty of fortune?

His journals reveal that Emerson is not free, but wishes to be free. In October 1840, deciding at the age of thirty-seven not to join Brook Farm, he writes, "I do not wish to remove from my present prison to a prison a little larger. I wish to break all prisons. I have not yet conquered my own house. It irks and repents me." The plot of ground Emerson will till is not nature's earth, to work with other men and women, but his own soul. The ground he must till is the figurative house that yet imprisons him. For the private Emerson, outer, phenomenal nature transmutes into a new incarnation of Maya, into metaphysical fortune, that which limits him.

That which limits us takes various forms, some of which Emerson is bold enough in *Self-Reliance* to call "terrors." One terror is society, which "everywhere is in conspiracy against the manhood of every one of its members." Only as non-conformist can a man be a man, without scattering his forces in dead usages. Another terror is any foolish consistency that is but "the hobgoblin of little minds," a hobgoblin anchoring one in a particular point of view rather than releasing one to sail with the winds of truth. These terrors, these aspects of fate, are not to be shunned or succumbed to, but are to be battled with, overcome. The question is not fate or no fate but will man's soul be active in relation to fate? For actually man can even make fate, can even contribute to the circumstances of the world. "The man must be so much that he must make all circumstances." For example, "Perception is not whimsical but fatal. If I see a trait, my children will see it after me, and in course of time all mankind—although it may chance that no one has seen it before me. For my perception of it is as much a fact as the sun." Man-Vishnu has a responsible role as creator on several levels of the world his children will inherit.

Man can only remain creatively independent of limiting, outward circumstances through the activity of his own soul. But as man comes closer to center, he becomes passively and vertically aligned with, in contrast to, the horizontal, outer forces of fate, the forces of a universal higher self. For what is the self-reliant man's "docility to our own law" in relation to the God within? The secret to self-reliance is Self-reliance.

> Great men have always done so, and confided themselves childlike to the genius of their age, betraying their perception that the absolutely trustworthy was seated at their heart; working through their hands, predominating in all their being. And we are now men, and must accept in the highest mind the same transcendent destiny; and not minors and invalids in a protected corner, not cowards, fleeing before a revolution, but guides, redeemers and benefactors, obeying the Almighty effort and advancing on Chaos and the Dark.

We are but organs of an immense intelligence and "when we discern truth, we do nothing of ourselves, but allow a passage to its beams." Though the self-reliant man must battle externally imposed limitations, Emerson encourages him to "accept the place the divine providence has found for you, the society of your contemporaries, the connection of events." There is a universal force in whose light each individual becomes man, in whose service is freedom. In this light, he "who has more obedience than I masters me, though he should not raise his finger." Man hovers at the threshold, between enhancing obedience to his higher "me," and diminishing slavery to "not me."

In the heart of these man-centered, self-centered years Emerson writes *The Poet* (1841). Formerly more involved with the polarity in his own soul between intellect and action, truth and goodness, Emerson now expands the middle realm of beauty through the person of the Poet. The Poet (or sayer) stands in the center between Knower and Doer. The Poet is representative, standing "among partial men for the complete man." Only now does the image of threefold man become fulfilled, an image in which the middle realm of man's being mediates between the two polar faculties, imbuing them with its warmth, affection, imagination. So that, for example, the complete man speaks not with the organ of the intellect alone, but with "the flower of the mind." The intellect is "released from all service and suffered to take its direction from its celestial life;" man speaks with "the intellect inebriated by nectar." In *Self-Reliance*, Emerson urges man into action. "Your genuine action will explain itself and will explain your other actions. Act single, and what you have already done single will justify you now. . . . Be it how it will, do right now. . . . The force of character is cumulative." The whole man needs be engaged to have the power to be free. "So use all that is called Fortune . . . in the Will work and acquire, and thou hast chained the wheel of Chance, and shall sit hereafter out of fear from her rotations."

That the soul must be active poetically as a whole implies what Emerson earlier asserts in his journal of 1839:

> Everything should be treated poetically—law, politics, housekeeping, money . . . they must exert that higher vision which causes the object to become fluid and plastic . . . to preserve them supple and alive. . . . We must not only have hydrogen in balloons, and steel springs under coaches, but we must have fire under the Andes at the core of the world.

During these years, Emerson, both privately and publicly, moved strongly through the fire of his active soul, toward transcending time and space, other limiting forms. Indeed, he appears to unhinge nature from her physical moorings, releasing the "not me," like Maya in the Hindu myth, into a metamorphosing series of incarnations in the words time and space, limitations, terror, fortune, chance, fate. In the works here explored, Emerson has essentially transformed man and nature into his experience of freedom and fate. Thirty-six to forty years old, he finds himself usually competent to do spiritual battle with the various incarnations. It is toward the center of his being that he finds the poise amidst the polarity. In April 1842, at age 39, he writes in his journal, reflecting his poise:

> The history of Christ is the best document of the power of Character which we have. . . . In short, there ought to be no such thing as Fate. As long as we use this word, it is a sign of our impotence and that we are not ourselves. . . . I have this latent omniscience coexistent with omnignorance. Moreover, whilst this Deity glows at the heart, and by his unlimited presentiments gives me all Power, I know that tomorrow will be as this day, I am dwarf, and I remain a dwarf.

That is to say, I believe in Fate. As long as I am weak, I shall talk of Fate; whenever the God fills me with his fullness, I shall see the disappearance of Fate.

I am Defeated all the time; yet to Victory I am born.

Emerson the man, between the ages of forty-one and forty-nine (1844–52), experienced few outer changes. In partial compensation for Waldo's death, a son Edward joined the two daughters, Ellen and Edith. The publishing of *Essays, Second Series* was followed by lectures of *Representative Men* in 1846 and the first publication of *Poems*. Eighteen-forty-seven led Emerson to Europe for a second time, renewing his acquaintance with Carlyle and meeting many major literary figures. Lecture tours took him further afield, to Mississippi in 1850, Buffalo and Pittsburgh in 1851, Montreal in 1852. In 1852 rage began to simmer in the as yet relatively apolitical Emerson due to the Fugitive Slave Law. As Emerson himself grew in stature in the eyes of the world during these years, his earlier concept of Vishnu-Man forging with flame at the center of the world yielded, acquiesced,  receded to a more Shakespearean, invisible man, merely beholding his Maya, his world, with the more professional detachment of a dramatist beholding his stage.

During the ages of forty-one to forty-nine, the inner Emerson became in due time the outer; the private Emerson unfolded honestly in his public addresses. His need to remain aloof, unfixed, improved his role as dramatist with an eye for the whole rather than as actor committed to a particular part. He expressed a greater weight of darkness than before, by contrast intensifying a light which, diminishing in relation to the expansive light of earlier years, now concentrates into a seed-like power. Emerson worked to increasingly penetrate the nature of fate. Freedom and fate became power and form, power needing an appreciation of the present, form necessitating illusion.

In *Experience* in 1844, one dramatic voice often bewails the separation between man and world, subject and object. "The Indian who was laid under a curse that the wind should not blow on him, nor water flow to him, nor fire burn him, is a type of us all." The only reality that will not dodge us is death. "Marriage (in what is called the spiritual world) is impossible, because of the inequality between every subject and object. . . . There will be the same gulf between every me and thee as between the original and the picture. . . ."

The universe is still the bride of the soul, but on the far side of the gulf—no realized will, no double of man. "The discovery 'that we exist' is called the Fall of Man. . . . Perhaps these subject-lenses have no power; perhaps there are no objects. . . ." Life is a bubble, a sleep within a sleep; dream follows dream with no end to illusion through which we cannot penetrate to know objects themselves. Not our life but rather our perception is threatened, for nature does not like us to observe her directly. Rather than unlocking faculties of our soul, she would have our relations to anything, anyone else be oblique, askew. "I know that the world I converse with in the city and in the farms, is not the world I *think*." Seasons, temperament, impose a limiting world we do not wish.

Yet the complementary voice knows that life, being a mixture of a power and form, will not bear an excess of either. This voice knows that, although in the view of nature temperament is final,

> into every intelligence there is a door which is never closed, through which the creator passes. . . . At one whisper of these high powers we awake from ineffectual struggles with this nightmare. We hurl it into its own hell, and cannot again contract ourselves to so base a state.

The open door invites the whispering angel when man fills the hour, with happiness; that is power. The only ballast in this "life . . . this tempest of fancies . . . is a respect to the present hour." If we would be strong with the strength of nature, "we . . . must set up the strong present tense against all the rumors of wrath, past or to come." The closer man is spatially to the inward center of his being and the more present temporally, the more here and now, the greater the individual's power will be. But the power is not simply human, for "power keeps quite another road than the turnpikes of choice and will; namely the subterranean and invisible tunnels and channels of life."

The voices of both the skeptic and the faithful now speak in harmony, both recognizing "that nothing is of us or our works, that all is of God. . . . Nature will not spare us the smallest leaf of laurel." One with resentful resignations, the other with welcome faith, both acquiesce to "accepting our actual companions and circumstances, however humble or odious, as the mystic officials to whom the universe has delegated its pleasure for us." Yet there is a guardian angel for each of us, to preserve our iota of free will. For though it may be easier to succumb to the limits, calculations of fate, "presently comes a day, or . . . only a half-hour, with its angel whispering—which discomforts the conclusions of nations and of years," which wakes us from the binding sleep of circumstances. Emerson urges us, as we swing between skepticism and faith, to have the patience that the fragmented parts will one day be members, obeying one will. For, and his journals do not contradict, in his consciously honest recognition of the terrors of experience, he still "can see nothing at last, in success or failure, than more or less of vital force supplied from the Eternal." He even, in a casual, scarcely emphasized sentence, allows that "divinity is behind our failures and follies also."

In *Experience*, in 1844, Emerson prophesied that:

> the new statement will comprise the skepticisms as well as the faiths of society, and out of unbeliefs a creed shall be formed. For skepticisms are not gratuitous or lawless, but are limitations of the affirmative statement, and the new philosophy must take them in and make affirmations outside of them, just as much as it must include the oldest beliefs.

His journals reveal him wishing away from the particulars the sparks igniting skepticism, hoping through the man-centered pole to affect the whole. "'I like man, but not men," he wrote in 1846. In 1849 he wrote:

> Culture, the height of culture, highest behavior coexists in the identification of the Ego with the universe, so that when a man says I think, I hope, I find—he might properly say, the human race thinks, hopes, finds, he states a fact which commands the understandings and affections of all the company, and yet, at the same time, he shall be able continually to keep sight of his biographical Ego.

The difficulty remains, how to act in accord with the vital force of the eternal without neglecting the beat of one's own heart, and yet: to deal consciously with the impinging particulars of fate. In January 1850, he confessed that he affirms the sacredness of the individual, yet he sees the benefit of the cities; that as he affirms the divinity of man, he yet acknowledges his debt to bread, coffee, and a warm room. His "geometry" cannot span the extremes; "I cannot reconcile these opposites."

What to do? Emerson's solution, his resolution, he expresses in 1852, in *Fate*, which for this sketch is the culmination of the years 1844–52, though not published until 1860.

> By obeying each thought frankly, by harping, or, if you will, pounding on each string, we learn at last its power. By the same obedience to other thoughts we learn theirs, and then comes some reasonable hope of harmonizing them. We are sure that, though we know not how, necessity does comport with liberty, the individual with the world, my polarity with the spirit of the times. The riddle of the age has for each a private solution.

By entering into the nature of things, of thoughts, we learn at last their power, we acquire at last their power. The *Nature* of 1836 has become, as in the middle period, circumstance. The Book of Nature is the Book of Fate. The form of the spine, the bill of the bird, season, sex, temperament—all are pages in the Book of Fate. The elemental order of sandstone, sea, and shore still exists, but more as symbol of that which resists, "thought, the spirit which composes and decomposes nature—here they are side by side, god and devil mind and matter . . . riding peacefully together in the eye and brain of every man."

Peacefully, says Emerson, in spite of the pain of opposition. For Emerson experienced a new courtship between freedom and fate beginning. By "learning the power" of a limitation we can come to accept it as measure of the growing man. "Every brave youth is training to ride and rule this dragon." As the soul purifies, the limitations refine. Yet "the ring of necessity is always perched at the top." For on ever higher planes, Fate includes the eternal laws with which even thought itself must act in accord.

> And last of all, high over thought, in the world of morals, Fate appears as vindicator, leveling the high, lifting the low, requiring justice in man, and always striking soon or late when justice is not done. . . . insight itself and the freedom of the will is one of its obedient members.

Here, as slightly hinted in *Experience*, "Fate" in its highest state literally overcomes, like an arch, the poles of man and nature, of freedom and fate. *Nature* in 1836, when Emerson was thirty-three, was infused with ethical character by the spirit. "Fate" in 1852, when Emerson is forty-nine, was the single spirit infusing both free man and the fallen, with apparently malevolent limitations to his will. Yet at this point in the essay, "Fate" illustrates that Emerson is not a thinker, proceeding on one consistent line of logical discourse. Emerson is the whole man thinking who, as Stephen Whicher notes, "apprehended ideas dramatically, not intellectually." For just after expressing the idea of Fate as vindicator, the lighting shifts, the idea is differently accentuated, revealing that, after all, "Fate has its lord; limitation its limits, is different seen from above and from below, from within and from without. . . . If fate follows and limits power, power attends and antagonizes fate." The further out from center a man stands, the more he perceives, experiences fate as limitation. Out there he needs power, power with which to move increasingly inward toward center, until limitation transcends its limits and man is aligned vertically with the presiding spirit.

To better understand this double nature of Fate we must attend again to Emerson's concept of man. In *Experience*, Emerson acclaimed that:

> The middle region of our being is the temperate zone. We climb into the thin and cold realm of pure geometry and lifeless science, or sink into that of sensation. Between these extremes is the equator of life, or thought, of spirit, of poetry—a narrow belt.

Man needs will. For in "Fate" Emerson identified that "the one serious and formidable thing in nature is will." And "there can be no driving force except through the conversion of the man into his will, making him the will, and the will him." In fact Emerson saw the end and aim of the world to be the liberation of the will from the sheaths and clogs of organization, which he has outgrown. Again, limitation is measure of the growing man. And again, apparently formidable will in nature actually has a deeper, benevolent mission. Yet will works mysteriously. For society, a form of "not me" threatens the manhood of each of its members, yet "society is servile from want of will." Limiting fate seems to work its will through particularizing into the mass, weakening the parts. Liberating power seems to express will through universalizing in the individual, strengthening the whole. In *Experience*, Emerson explored this particularizing aspect of the will in relation to sin. The conscience, with its root in the will, must feel a sin to be a particular essence, essentially evil. "This it is not," says Emerson.

"It has an objective existence, but no subjective. . . . sin, seen from the thought is a diminution, or less . . . shade, absence of light, and no essence."

To the intellect, not of cold geometry nor of simple understanding, but rather the light of reason imbued with the warmth of the temperate zone, to this intellect there is no crime, nor sin, for all is perceived in relation to a universal source. All is either less or more. Power then could not be man's free will alone, but must be guided by man's thought, to attract him away from the pole of his particular, limited self to the pole of his more universal, free self. For, he says in "Fate,"

> intellect annuls Fate. So far as a man thinks, he is free. . . . every jet of chaos which threatens to exterminate us is convertible by intellect into wholesome force (e.g., stream was till the other day the devil which we dreaded). . . . Fate then is a name for facts not yet passed under the fire of thought, for causes which are unpenetrated.

In respect to these attributes of intellect and will, it becomes clear that the weaker one's thought, the more susceptible one is to the particularizing will of fate, which pulls one out from center and down, from which perspective Fate is perceived as limiting and malevolent. Man's thinking engages his will in an active whole soul, which brings him to center and the perspective from above that all acts and events of fate can be seen in the light of one benevolent universal source. In this light one can at least realize that "tis the best use of Fate to teach a fatal courage. Go face the fire at sea . . . knowing you are guarded by the cherubim of Destiny. If you believe in Fate to your harm, believe in it at least for your good."

Although his geometry was unable to reconcile the oppositions, Emerson, with the heat of wholly animated thought, conducted with increasing intensity the courtship between man and nature, freedom and fate. ". . . fate slides into freedom and freedom into fate. . . ." The riddle of the age has for each a private solution, and "the secret of the world is the tie between person and event. Person makes event, and event makes person."

Person is the whole, event the particular. "The direction of the whole and of the parts is toward benefit. . . . The soul contains the event that shall befall it; for the event is only the actualization of its thoughts."

The soul becomes the private source, corresponding to the universal spirit, from which emanate the circumstances of life. As the Hindus felt fate to be nothing but the deeds committed in a prior state of existence, so the soul realized a responsibility for its own individual destiny, though it may know nothing provable about a prior state of existence. "A man will see his character emitted in the events that seem to meet, but which exude from and accompany him. Events expand with the character.... The event is the print of your form.... Events are the children of his body and mind."

And finally, in a phrase corresponding in intensity to T. S. Eliot's image of the fire and the rose becoming one, Emerson consummates the marriage, "We learn that the soul of Fate is the soul of us...." Not that nature in all her objects can potentially mirror us in a truth of correspondences as in 1836, but simply that the soul of the "not me" is the soul of the "me." Vishnu pursued Maya until they became man-god and woman-goddess, two in one. Over the painful chasm of the polarity arcs a uniting rainbow. A beholder of two, Emerson yet sees unity.

If Emerson's celebrations of the late 1830s were *matutina cognitio*, morning knowledge, knowledge of God, we can fairly consider them, and those of the early 1840s as well, being essentially one-sided although profoundly revealing, as knowledge of the false dawn rather than of the actual dawn. Not until the late 1840s and early 1850s, between the ages of 41 and 49, when increasingly"... on his mind, at dawn of day, Soft shadows of the evening lay," could he elaborate an actual morning knowledge, a system comprising both the skepticisms and the faiths of the modern world, preparing the way for a new moral science.

But we know that the system is not fixed, that the marriage is not static. For once one tends to rest inactively, the whispering angel descends to remind that:

> One key, one solution to the mysteries of human condition, one solution to the old knots of fate, freedom, and foreknowledge, exists ... the propounding of the double consciousness. A man must ride alternately on the horses of his private and his public nature.

Private and public is equivalent to inner and outer, related to immortal and mortal. Emerson (born under the sign of Gemini) experienced man as twins, as immortal Pollux and mortal Castor.

So when a man is victim of his fate ... he is to rally on his relation to the universe which his ruin benefits. Leaving the demon who suffers, he is to take sides with the deity who secures universal benefit by his pain.

The marriage is no end, just a sober revelation. The pendulum still swings. But with refined thought one can, rather than resist the beneficent limitations of fate, penetrate them, acquiesce, accept them and in accepting transcend one's mortal, particular self for one's universal self. "To offset the drag of temperament and race, which pulls down, learn this lesson ... that

. . . whatever lames or paralyzes you draws in with it the divinity, in some form, to repay."

The keynote resounds. "We can only obey our own polarity." Finally he was able to articulate the paradox "Freedom is necessary." The works explored in this sketch reveal Emerson to have come to the point in 1852 of neither ignoring, nor simply bowing before, but building, in active freedom, altars to the "Beautiful Necessity."

Bibliography:

Wagenknecht, Edward. *Ralph Waldo Emerson–Portrait of a Balanced Soul*. New York: Oxford University Press, 1974.
Whicher, Stephen, ed., *Selections from Ralph Waldo Emerson*. Boston: Houghton Mifflin Company, 1957.
Whicher, Stephen. *Freedom and Fate*. Philadelphia: University of Pennsylvania Press, 1953.
Zimmer, Heinrich. *Myths and Symbols in Indian Art and Civilization*. Bollingen Series, Philadelphia: Princeton University Press, 1953.

Emerson's Epistemology with Glances at Rudolf Steiner

by

Gertrude Reif Hughes

In an 1837 journal entry, Emerson pondered a version of his favorite paradox, "the infinitude of the private man." Noting that many people feel dwarfed by circumstances, he recommended that they counter their melancholy by remembering their own infinitude. "As fast as you can," he urged, "break off your association with your personality and identify yourself with the Universe." Why does such self-transcendence make one both freer and more oneself, rather than less so? Because—and this is the paradox of "the infinitude of the private man—I could not be, but that absolute life circulated in me, and I could not think this without being that absolute life."

Not only does "absolute life" confer individual existence upon man as it circulates in him, but, says Emerson, man can only have this perception because he himself *is* that absolute life. To repeat his words: "I could not be, but that absolute life circulated in me, and I could not think this without being that absolute life." These words reveal Emerson's affinity with Rudolf Steiner's philosophy of thinking. Emerson and Steiner share a radically self-referential epistemology in that both find in self-observation a starting point for reliable cognition. Each in his own way—Steiner more programmatically than Emerson—says that our own cognition is an activity which, when we ourselves observe it, reveals itself to be both objective and subjective. Our own act of thinking is unquestionably present for us to observe, and as unquestionably, it is our own activity, not something imposed upon us.

Thinking "is the unobserved element in our ordinary life of thought," says Rudolf Steiner in his *Philosophy of Freedom* (1894; revised 1918). In that work in his dissertation, *Truth and Knowledge* (1892), as well as in his 1920 lectures on Aquinas published as *The Redemption of Thinking*, Steiner describes thinking as mainly a dynamic, creative activity, in contrast to Kant, who held that the main use of thinking is to portray the given, sensory world. Steiner says, "The primary reason for the existence of thinking is not that it should make pictures of the outer world, but that it should bring to full development being. That it portrays to us the outer world is a secondary process" (*Redemption*). Like Steiner, Emerson seeks "original relation" (*Nature*, "Introduction"). He seeks a starting point for epistemology that neither assumes that the content of experience is as we perceive it, nor that it is always being falsified by thinking. The first position he calls naive (or uncritical) realism; the second, naive rationalism (*Truth and Knowledge*, and *passim*).

A proper starting point for a theory of knowledge must be neither objective, in the sense of ignoring a human knower, nor subjective, in the sense of being untrustworthy. It must be indubitable, yet pertain to the knower. In order to find a starting point for epistemology, Steiner wants to separate the directly given world picture from that which is derived by thinking. He says, of course, we never consciously experience this directly given world picture because we are always adding our consciousness and its contents. But we can take our world picture and deduct from it what we ourselves have added and thereby arrive, in principle if not in fact, at this directly given.

Before we continue, notice that Steiner, like Emerson, is not an idealist. Though sensory data cannot provide a starting point for epistemology, it is not because they are sensory but because our thinking itself is uncritically mixed in with them, whereas the starting point for epistemology must be directly given, not just hypothesized or deduced to be directly given. In fact, Steiner gives an example of an error that many would say was a sensory error but that he shows is actually an error made by cognition, not by observation. The moon on the horizon appears larger than at the zenith. This, you say, is an error; the moon doesn't change size as it rises and sets, so my senses have deceived me. The error, however, is not in the observation—the moon does indeed appear larger in one position, smaller in the other. The error comes in the interpretation that this variable appearance of the moon means that the moon actually changed size. This is the error, and cognition makes it, not observation.

Though Steiner exposes the naive rationalism of ascribing such an error to observation when it should be ascribed to interpretation, Steiner is not a naive realist. He is not a logical positivist. Like Goethe, whose scientific works he edited as a young man, Steiner cherishes empiricism, but his great contribution is to identify thinking itself as an unrecognized field for observation. Indeed, the starting point for epistemology which Steiner seeks, that about which thinking has made no prior claims or assumptions, turns out to be thinking itself. Steiner shows that ordinarily we fail to observe our own thinking; we take it for granted. In a sense, he says, it is granted; it is part of the given world picture. It differs, however, in this one respect: whereas we cannot be immediately certain whether or not we produced the rest of the given world picture, with this one part of it that is our own thinking we can be sure that we ourselves produce it. True, people have hallucinations. They sometimes believe that what they are in fact making up has independent sensory existence. But about concepts and ideas we make no such mistake, Steiner says. "We do know absolutely directly that concepts and ideas appear only in the act of cognition and ... enter the sphere of the directly given" through this activity (*Truth and Knowledge*). "A hallucination," he says, "may appear as something externally given, but one would never take one's own concepts to be something given *without one's own thinking activity*" (*Truth and Knowledge*; my emphasis). Our ideas, our concepts, then, come to us by our own activity of cognition. Our ideas we know we produce.

Notice the paradox; it is absolutely basic. Our cognition is part of the given because we can recognize it directly, that is, without having to draw any conclusions about it first. But (here is the paradox) what we directly know as given when we know our own cognition is this: that we produce it, that it is our own activity! Thus we ourselves produce this part of the given. The given contains an activity, cognition, and this activity, which we know to be our own act, produces concepts, including the concept, "There is a pre-cognitional given which is the starting point for cognition." To summarize: Cognition is both given and self-produced in that my self-production of it is what I directly know about it.

We are in the realm of paradox, but not necessarily in the solipsistic labyrinth that self-reflexivity conjures for many people (Hughes). At least Emerson, like Steiner, would deny that self-reference disqualifies one's thought from validity. On the contrary, to learn to detect your own thinking and recognize that it is yours instead of excluding it from your scrutiny because it is yours—this skill Emerson exhorts his apprentice in self-reliance to practice:

> A man should learn to detect and watch that gleam of light which flashes across his mind from within, more than the lustre of the firmament of bards and sages. *Yet he dismisses without notice his thought, because it is his* ("Self-Reliance," paragraph one; my emphasis).

In other words, Emerson agrees with Steiner that "thinking is the unobserved element in our ordinary life of thought" (*The Philosophy of Freedom*). Both Emerson and Steiner invite readers to observe their own thinking. Moreover, both relate the possibility of doing so to the possibility for freedom, the possibility for relying on no authority however illustrious, but only on oneself. This relationship between cognition and self-reliance or freedom is the goal of Steiner's epistemology and the deepest impetus for Emerson's interest in the "original relation" that he calls for in his first book and is trying to cultivate twenty-five years later in the *Conduct of Life*.

In closing, let me develop a connection between Emerson's demand for "original relation" in the introduction to *Nature* and his worship of the Beautiful Necessity in "Fate," the keynote essay of *The Conduct of Life*. As you will see, both these concepts involve the kind of radically self-critical relation between knower and known that Steiner's epistemology calls for. If you ignore this epistemological ground, Emerson's discourse sounds merely oratorical; but if you credit the demand for self-knowing cognition that underlies Emerson's concepts of "original relation" and "Beautiful Necessity," then his rhapsodies become activating insights, as he intended.

"Why should not we also enjoy an original relation to the universe?" Emerson challenges. "Let us demand our own works and laws and worship—our own connection to the world, not some inherited or derived one." In calling for "original relation," Emerson required for each single person a completely individual starting point for cognition, one undistorted—and also unaided—by others' assumptions or conclusions. Such a demand requires much from its beneficiaries as well as for them. Like Steiner's starting point for epistemology, Emerson's "original relation" can only make free an individual who knows how, or practices how, to be free.

The most austere form of original relation is the relation between individual and circumstance called fate—"the tie between person and event," as Emerson styled it in his essay on the subject (W, VI, 30). Musing on the "tie between person and event," Emerson calls it "the secret of the world" and urges his audience to penetrate that secret tie so that they can learn to see that they and their circumstances are not two but one: "A man will see his character emitted in the events that seem to meet [him], but which [actually] exude from and accompany him" (W, VI, 42). When you achieve this insight, Emerson knows, you transform something alien and limiting into something known and supporting; you recognize your circumstance as your self, your fate as your destiny.

This relationship between yourself and your world is original indeed! It is entirely yours, can belong to none other. Yes, it is dire and austere to equate that heady "original relation" Emerson is calling for in *Nature* with the "Beautiful Necessity" which he worships at the end of "Fate." But Emerson's optimism demands much, because it promises much—nothing less than each individual's identity with the "absolute life" which, he says, both constitutes each one of us and connects each to all the rest of the world. In this identity between each and all, Emerson finds epistemological ground for radical transvaluations like the equation of "original relation" with Beautiful Necessity. By showing that he shares this ground with Rudolf Steiner, I have tried to highlight how both Emerson and Steiner unsettle dualistic habits of mind and challenge some dangerously limiting perceptions and values that these habits sponsor.

Bibliography:

Emerson, Ralph Waldo. *The Complete Works of Ralph Waldo Emerson*. Centenary Edition, 12 vols., Boston and New York: Houghton, Mifflin and Co., 1903–1904. Cited as W, followed by volume number and page.
———. *Nature*. Any edition.
———. "Self-Reliance." Any edition.
———. *The Journals and Miscellaneous Notebooks of Ralph Waldo Emerson*, ed. William H. Gilman, *et alia*. 14 vols., Cambridge: Harvard University Press, 1960.
Hughes, Gertrude Reif. *Emerson's Demanding Optimism*. Baton Rouge: Louisiana State University Press, 1984.
Steiner, Rudolf, *The Philosophy of Freedom* and *Truth and Knowledge*. ed. Paul M. Allen, trans. Rita Stebbing, West Nyack, New York: Rudolf Steiner Publications, Inc., 1963.
———. *The Redemption of Thinking: A Study in the Philosophy of Thomas Aquinas*. trans. and ed. A. P. Shepherd and Mildred Robertson Nicoll. Spring Valley, New York: Anthroposophic Press, 1983 (second printing).

Toward an American Language

by

Thornton Wilder

[In 1952 Thornton Wilder, triple Pulitzer Prize winner, was invited by Harvard University to give the Charles Eliot Norton Lectures. From them ensue the next three articles, "Toward an American Language," "American Loneliness," and "Emily Dickinson."]

"No, here they are. . . ." Last night I had the lecturer's vocational nightmare: I dreamed that I had lost my notes.

Since this is a series of lectures concerning American characteristics, I must be sure to offer these young people an American lecture.

Is there a difference?

Bronson Alcott (in 1856) claimed that the lecture is an American invention. If so, it was also invented independently in Europe. Discourses have been delivered in all times and ages; but the lecture as we understand it, the secularization of the sermon and the popularization of the academic address, is probably a product of the middle-class mind. The Swiss have a passion for lectures. Conrad Ferdinand Meyer said that if the citizens of Zurich were required to make a choice between going to Heaven or going to a lecture about Heaven they would hesitate only a moment.

Yet there is a wide difference between an Old-World and a New-World lecture, and the difference arises from those American characteristics that are precisely the subject of these lectures.

Emerson, describing the requirements for lectures in the Lyceums of his day, said:

> There are no stiff conventions that prescribe a method, a style, a limited quotation of books and an exact respect to certain books, persons, or opinions.

There's the crux: no respect.

An American is insubmissive, lonely, self-educating, and polite. His politeness conceals his slowness to adopt any ideas which he does not feel that he has produced himself. It all goes back to the fundamental problem of an American's relation to authority, and related to it is the American's reluctance to concede that there is an essential truth, or a thing true in essence.

For centuries—over there—kings were held to be invested with an essential authority. The child born into a royal cradle, be it the nonentity or genius, was held to be, for mysterious and unsearchable reasons, the ruler of his people (May he live forever! May God take particular pains to save him, rather than you and me!) and held the royal authority.

Tradition commanded us to revere our fathers, not because they took the trouble to beget us and to pay our board in our earlier years, but because they wielded a paternal authority. America is now rapidly becoming a matriarchy, and fathers are bewildered to discover that they are no longer accorded any such magical sway.

For Americans there is no inherent and essential authority accruing to the elderly either. Thoreau said:

> Practically, the old have no very important advice to give to the young. Their own experience has been so partial, and their lives have been such miserable failures, for private reasons, as they must believe.... I have lived some thirty years on this planet, and I have yet to hear the first syllable of valuable or even earnest advice from my seniors.

The same indocility holds in the intellectual life. In Europe the Herr Professor and Cher Maitre and the knighted scholar and the member of the Royal Academy of . . . have enjoyed a distinction above and beyond their learning and wisdom. What better illustration of it than the fact that in Germany—in the good old days— no one less than a full professor could be invited to a dinner in society at which a full professor was present? To be sure, a mere professor extraordinarius might become a full professor next Tuesday, but on Monday he was still lacking the mystical qualification, the Mana. He was not salonfahig; *like a dog, he was not* hausrein.

American universities are still filled with vestigial Old-World elements. Our academic world is in labor trying to bring forth its first American university. There is still present among us many a tacit allusion to a state of grace enjoyed by authorities. From time to time we professors become aware that twentieth-century students are not completely sensible of this grace. The situation is far more serious:

a student's mind goes blank when authority and tradition are invoked, so seldom does he confront them outside the classroom. Many an apparently stupid student is merely a student who has been browbeaten, has been stupefied, by being overwhelmed with too much of the unarguable, unanswerable, unexaminable. The intellectual life has been presented to him as a realm in which man is not free.

In the Old World, a lecture tended to be a discourse in which an Authority dispensed a fragment of the truth. Naturally I am not talking of informative lectures—"Recent Theories on the Origin of the Nebulae," "Silversmiths in 18th-Century New England"—which are inherently reading matter, and are so delivered: but of lectures in fields where every listener can be assumed to have formed or to be forming his own opinion. When Queen Victoria, accustomed to the discretion of Melbourne and Disraeli, complained that Gladstone addressed her as though she were a public meeting; when in impatience we hear ourselves saying, "Please don't lecture to me!" what is meant is: "Kindly remember that I am a free agent. Everything you say must be passed upon by the only authority I recognize—my own judgment." An American lecture is a discourse in which a man declares what is true for him. This does not mean that Americans are skeptical. Every American has a large predisposition to believe that there is a truth for him and that he is in the process of laying hold of it. He is building his own house of thought, and he rejoices in seeing that someone else is also abuilding. Such houses can never be alike—begun in infancy and constructed with the diversity which is the diversity of every human life.

So I must remember to maintain the tone of a personal disposition. I may make as many generalizations as I wish, and as emphatically; but I must not slip into that other tone (how easy when one is tired; how tempting when one is insecure) of one in privileged relation to those august abstractions—tradition and authority.

Mr. Archibald MacLeish: Ladies and gentlemen: The Committee charged with the selection of . . . .

My good friend, our admired poet, is introducing me. During the introduction of a lecturer in America everyone suppresses a smile: the introducer, the audience, the lecturer.

This introduction is a form, a convention; it is very Old World. To Americans, conventions are amusing. They have attended many lectures; they have heard many a clarification and many an ineptitude. They have suffered often. Yet on every occasion they have heard the obligatory words: ". . . we have the pleasure of . . . it is a particular privilege to have with us this evening . . ."

Americans more and more find conventions amusing. It is amusing (and it is beginning to make us uncomfortable) that all letters must begin with the word "Dear." Hostesses are becoming impatient at writing ". . . request the pleasure of . . . ." They telephone or telegraph.

The audience is not in evening dress, but Archie MacLeish and I are. That is a convention. We explain it as being a "courtesy to the audience," but this audience which has just kindly hustled over from its dormitories sees through this. They suspect that it is an attempt to dress me in a little essential authority. What do I do next week when I must talk on Thoreau, who said, "Beware of all enterprises that require new clothes, and not rather a new wearer of clothes"?

The chief thing to remember about conventions is that they are soothing. They whisper that life has its repetitions, its recurring demonstrations that all is well—happy thought, that life with all its menace, its irruptions of antagonism and hatred, can be partially tamed, civilized by the pretense that everyone to whom one addresses a letter is dear and that every dinner guest is a pleasure. Densely populated countries—in Europe, but above all in Asia—develop a veritable network of these forms; but Americans feel little need of them. They even distrust them; they think that civilization can advance better without fictions.

Time was when one had to flatter the tyrant by telling him how kind he was; one reminded him that he was Serenissimus and Merced and Euer Gnaden, and that as a Majesty he was certainly gracious—as one says to a snarling dog: "Good, good Fido."

Americans do not ask that life present a soothing face. Even if they are in a contented situation they do not hope that life will continue to furnish them More of the Same. They are neither fretful nor giddy, but they are always ready for Something Different. In Europe everyone is attentive and pleased during ceremonial and secular ritual and these conventions of courtesy; in America people shuffle their feet, clear their throats, and size up the audience.

Archie is introducing me just right. He is telling them that I am a very hard-working fellow and that I travel about a good deal exhibiting curiosity.

The audience applauds.
Myself: Mr. MacLeish, ladies and gentlemen: In 1874, Charles Eliot Norton wrote his friend John Ruskin . . . .

Another convention.
The French do this kind of thing superlatively well. They manage in an opening paragraph to allude to the auspices which furnished the occasion, to thank the authorities which invited them, to hint at their own unworthiness, to announce their subject, and to introduce a graceful joke.

But I am an American before Americans, and immediately something goes wrong. The fact that I am happy to have received their invitation now comes into collision with my obligation to say that I am happy. And at once an air of unreality enters the auditorium. It is not a chill; it is not a skepticism; but it is a disappointment. Convention demands that I say it, but the moment I have said it, it is spoiled.

These young men and women are near enough to their childhood to remember their agony when, on leaving a party, they knew that they had to say to their hostess: "I had a very good time." A certain number of children always manage to say: "My mother told me to tell you I had a very good time."

Here we are plunged into the heart of a basic American characteristic.

If you have to do a thing, you have lost your freedom. If you have to say a thing, you have lost your sincerity. If you have to love your parent, wife, child, or cousin, you begin to be estranged from them already. If you have to go into the Army . . . if you have to study Shakespeare . . .

Life, life, life is full of things one has to do; and if you have a passion for spontaneity, how do you convert What You Have To Do into The Things You Choose To Do?

That is one of the most exciting things about being an American and about watching American life: how an American will succeed in converting Necessity into Volition. It is a very beautiful thing, and it is new, and it is closely related to our problem of authority.

I hurried over this formal salutation as best I could. There lay several months ahead during which I could show in other ways that I was happy to be among them. Most Americans solve this problem without the slightest difficulty by a resort to humor. Much American humor is precisely the resolution of the conflict between obligation and spontaneity. But we cannot all call upon that happy national gift when most we need it.

In January 1874, Charles Eliot Norton wrote to his friend John Ruskin, "I want to be made a professor in the University here," and five months later he was writing to Thomas Carlyle that one of his aims would be to quicken—so far as may be—in the youth of a land barren of visible memorials of former times the sense of connection with the past and of gratitude for the efforts and labors of former generations.

I then went on to announce that the subject for my lectures was "The American Characteristics of Classical American Literature" and that this first lecture dealt with the American Language, and that I did not mean the use of new words and idioms, nor did I mean slang or incorrectness. I meant the result of an omnipresent subtle pressure which writers and speakers in the United States were exerting on the mother tongue—within the bounds of syntactical correctness—in order to transform an old island language into a new continental one. And I proposed to show that this was not a recent effort but that the group of great writers whose major works appeared about a hundred years ago were deeply engaged in this task.

In about a quarter of an hour I am going to examine with you one of the most famous pages in American literature—the first direct view of the White Whale in *Moby Dick*. Our study of this page will not be primarily a literary one but an attempt to discover these American modes of seeing and feeling—characteristics born of a nation's history and geography before they are characteristics of style. So first let us review some of these elements of history and geography that had a part in forming the American.

When I think of those who founded this country, I soon find myself thinking of those who did not come. Of those who almost came. I think of those conversations in East Anglia, the Thames Valley, in Somersetshire—conversations which probably took place after dark and with long pauses between the exchanges:

"Farmer Wilkins, will ye go with us?" "Brother Hawkins, will ye remove with us?"

And the same questions were to be put in Dutch, in the Moravian dialect, in Gaelic. . . .

Who came? Who didn't come?

It was not, for many years, a flight from persecution or from want. At most, for the first generations from England, it was a flight from the shadow of a persecution. And it was not until many generations afterward that the travelers could be said to have come in the assurance that they would find an easier life.

Those who came were a selection of a selection in Europe. But to say that it was a selection is not to say that it was an elite. Here was the bigot, the fanatic, the dreamer, the utopian, the misfit, the adventurer, the criminal. By the middle of the eighteenth century, the phrase was already current: "He has skipped to America."

They all had one thing in common. Their sense of identity did not derive from their relation to their environment. The meaning which their lives had for them was inner and individual. They did not need to be supported, framed, consoled, by the known, the habitual, the loved—by the ancestral village, town, river, field, horizon; by family, kin, neighbors, church and state; by the air, sky, and water that they knew. The independent.

Independence is a momentum. Scarcely had the first settler made a clearing and founded a settlement than the more independent began pushing further back into the wilderness. The phrase became proverbial: "If you can see the smoke from your neighbor's chimney, you're too near."

These separatists broke away from church at home, but separatism is also a momentum. New religions were formed over and over again. Ousted clergymen went off into the woods with portions of their contentious flocks, there to cut down more trees and raise new churches. When Cotton Mather went to what is now Rhode Island, he said that there had probably never been so many sects worshiping side by side in so small an area. These were the men and women who were most irritably susceptible to any of the pressures that society and social opinion could bring.

I have recently read George Santayana's *Character and Opinion in the United States*. In it I find:

> The discovery of the new world exercised a sort of selection among the inhabitants of Europe. All the colonists, except the Negroes, were voluntary exiles. The fortunate, the deeply rooted, and the lazy remained at home; the wilder instincts or dissatisfactions of the others tempted them beyond the horizon. The American is accordingly the most adventurous, or the descendant of the most adventurous of Europeans. . . . Such a temperament is, of course, not maintained by inheritance [but by] social contagion and pressure.

A mentality so constituted will experience in a certain way and will shape its language—in this case, reshape an inherited language—to serve as instrument of its perception.

The Americans who removed to this country, then, during its first century and a half had these characteristics in common. The conditions under which they lived and the institutions which they created engraved these characteristics still more deeply into their natures.

However, those basic characteristics have suffered violent opposition. It is still a question whether many of them may survive.

The force and prestige of the original traits remain, however. One has the feeling that their expression—personal, social, and literary—has been driven underground. Perhaps they are so powerful that they will yet be able to furnish a framework—a religion, a social thought, and an art—within which an entire continent can understand itself as unity and as growth. That was the hope frequently voiced by the great writers of the middle of the last century, and it was accompanied by a great fear that this framework might not be obtained; for they saw very clearly that the European modes, however fruitful for Europeans, could no longer serve the American people.

There have been no American writers of equal magnitude since their time—nor any comparable leaders, philosophers, or artists although there have been enormous activity and many considerable talents. There are certain clarifications that only great genius can achieve. And since great genius is lacking, we would do well to return to the last occasions on which it spoke.

A number of these writers consciously discussed the problems that arose from being an American. It is rather *how* they lived and thought, however, which will engage our attention. From the point of view of the European, an American was nomad in relation to place, detached in relation to time, lonely in relation to society, and insubmissive to circumstance, destiny, or God. It was difficult to be an American because there was as yet no code, grammar, or decalogue by which to orient oneself. Americans were still engaged in inventing what it was to be an American. That was at once an exhilarating and painful occupation. All about us we see the lives that have been shattered by it—not least those lives that have tried to resolve the problem by the European patterns.

These writers have not been chosen because they were exemplary citizens, but each was incontestably American and each illustrates dramatically one or more ways of converting an American difficulty into an American triumph. Each of them was what the man in the street would call "ill"— his word for it would be "cracked"; but their illness, if such it was, should throw light on a disequilibrium of the psyche which follows on the American condition. As they were all writers, our study of them will be primarily a literary one and will bear upon the language in which they wrote.

The American space-sense, the American time-sense, the American sense of personal identity are not those of Europeans—and, in particular, not those of the English. The English language was molded to express the English experience of life. The literature written in that language is one of the greatest glories of the entire human adventure. That achievement went hand in hand with the comparable achievement of forging the language which conveyed so accurately their senses of space, time, and identity. Those senses are not ours and the American people and American writers have long been engaged in reshaping the inherited language to express our modes of apprehension.

Paul Valéry, playing, once inserted four minus signs into Pascal's most famous sentence. Pascal had said that the eternal silence of infinite space filled him with fright (*"le silence éternel des espaces infinies m'effraie"*). Valéry restated it by saying that the intermittent racket of our little neighborhood reassures us (*"le vacarme des petits coins où nous vivons nous rassure"*).

[Laughter.]

There lies a great difference between Europeans and Americans. Try as he will, the American cannot find any such soothing support in his social or natural surroundings. The racket in which he lives is greater than any European *vacarme*—not because it is noisier (any European city is noisier than an American city), but because of the disparity of things which press upon his attention.

The disparity arises because he is not deeply connected with any of them. And his inability to find any reassurance in this turbulence of unrelated phenomena which is his environment is increased by his unprecedented and peculiarly American consciousness of multitude and distance and magnitude. An American is differently *surrounded*.

It all goes back to the problem of identity. Where does the American derive his confidence that, among so many millions, he is *one*, and that his being *one* is supported and justified? A European's environment is so pervasive, so dense, so habitual, that it whispers to him that he is all right where he is; he is at home and irreplaceable. His at-homeness is related to the concrete things about him.

Gertrude Stein used to quote in this connection a phrase from the Mother Goose rhymes: "I am I," said the little old lady, "because my dog knows me."

"I am I," says the European, "because the immemorial repetitions of my country's way of life surround me. I know them and they know me."

An American can have no such stabilizing relation to any one place, nor to any one community, nor to any one moment in time. Americans are disconnected. They are exposed to all place and all time. No place nor group nor moment can say to them: We were waiting for you; it is right for you to be here. Place and time are, for them, negative until they act upon them, until they bring them into being.

Illustrations of this disconnection? Illustrations of so omnipresent a condition will scarcely persuade those who have not long observed it in themselves and in those about them; Europeans have long been struck with consternation at our inability to place emphasis on the concrete aspect of things. Taking tea with a friend in London, I am told that I must return to dine and go to the opera.

"All right," I say, "I'll hurry home and change my clothes."
"What?"

"I say: I'll go back to the hotel and change my clothes."

"Home! *Home!* How can you Americans keep calling a hotel home?"

Because a home is not an edifice, but an interior and transportable adjustment. In Chicago—in the good old days—my friends used to change their apartment on the first of May. They were not discontented with the old one; they simply liked to impress their homemaking faculty on some new rooms.

More and more farmers of the Midwest are ending their days in southern California and Florida. After fifty years of hard work in Iowa, they do not find it strange to live, to die, and to be buried among palms.

This unrelatedness to place goes so deep that, in an Old-World sense, America can have no shrines. For us it is not where genius lived that is important. If Mount Vernon and Monticello were not so beautiful in themselves and relatively accessible, would so many of us visit them? What difficulties private individuals have had, in rich America, to save the Whitman and Poe houses.

Americans are abstract. They are disconnected. They have a relation, but it is to everywhere, to everybody, and to always. That is not new, but it is very un-European. It is difficult, but it is exhilarating. It shatters many lives; it inspirits others.

There are those countries of Europe each shut in on itself by borders immemorially defended, each shut in with its own loved hills, streams, towns, and roads, each with the monuments of its past continually renewing the memory of its history, each with its language—not a self-evident thing, as natural as breathing, but a thing rendered assertive and objective because beyond the borders were all those others speaking no less assertively a deplorable gibberish. Shut in with the absorbing repetitions of customs and long-molded manners; shut in with its convulsions which themselves had the character of repetitions. Shut in, above all, with the memories of old oppressions and with the memories of the long, bloody revolts against old oppressions, against authorities and powers—once awe-inspiring, but now hollow as the bugaboos of infancy—still vestigially present, however, as disavowed menaces and seductions, invitations to escape from the burdens of freedom (*Führer! Duce! Kommissar!*).

How close together they live, in each nation, how shoulder to shoulder—not only by reason of the density of population, but because of a sort of psychic consanguinity, another aftermath of feudalism. The relation of master and serf is a "hot" relation; it is a bond of either love or hate, as is any relationship which involves command over another's freedom. It is no wonder that the English developed the stratification of the social classes, of the greatest precision and of the greatest sensitivity to encroachment; overcrowding, centuries long, has resulted in a condition where Englishmen can hear one another think. The barriers were rendered necessary to protect them from this steamy intimacy. Modern English plays and novels show us that the English live in anguish because of the indelicacy of their exposure to one another. In France life and conversation and love itself seem to us to be overruled by a network of conventions as intricate as a ballet or a game; just so the Chinese built walls of ceremony behind which they could hide from the piercing intelligence of their neighbors.

Yet such density is also warming and reassuring: "I am I because my fellow citizens know me."

Americans can find in environment no confirmation of their identity, try as they may. The American gregariousness strikes every European visitor as hollow and strained—the college fraternity ("Brothers till death"), the businessmen's clubs ("One for all and all for one"), the febrile cocktail party ("Darling, do call me up; you're my favorite person in the world and I *never* see you").

There is only one way in which an American can feel himself to be in relation to other Americans—when he is united with them in a project, caught up in an idea, and propelled with them toward the future. There is no limit to the degree with which an American is imbued with the doctrine of progress. Place and environment are but *décor* to his journey. He lives not on the treasure that lies about him but on the promises of the imagination.

"I am I," he says, "because my plans characterize me." Abstract! Abstract!

Another element entered the American experience, which has rendered still more difficult any hope of an American's deriving comfort from environment: he learned to count. He can count to higher numbers—and realize the multiplicity indicated by the numbers—than any European. It began with his thinking in distances; it was increased by his reception into this country of the representatives of many nations.

How wide and high was the America to which he came? How many thousands of miles wide and high is a country whose boundaries have not yet been reached? The peoples of Europe knew well the dimensions of their own lands; one's own land is one's norm and scale. Several of these peoples were voyagers and colonizers; their travelers had experience of great distances and vast populations; but concepts of magnitude are not communicable by hearsay. It is amazing the extent to which European literatures are without any sense of the innumerability of the human race, even those literatures which draw so largely on the Bible, which is indeed the book of the myriad. An individual genius—Dante or Cervantes or Goethe—may grasp it, but it is not in Shakespeare, for a joy in the diversity of souls is not the same thing as an awe before the multiplicity of souls. French literature is about Frenchmen, though their names be Britannicus and Le Cid; and Frenchmen are not innumerable. For a century, English writers were infatuated with the West Mediterranean people (they felt them to be splendid and damned), but their interest in them did not, to the imagination, increase the population of England or of the Earth. Nor was it increased when England came to govern colonies in all parts of the globe; those peoples beyond the sea spoke other tongues and many of them were of another color. How many is many, if the many seem to be deplorably immature and incult? The imagination plays tricks on those who count souls in condescension.

Americans could count and enjoyed counting. They lived under a sense of boundlessness. And every year a greater throng of new faces poured into their harbors, paused, and streamed westward. And each one was one. To this day, in American thinking, a crowd of ten thousand is not a homogeneous mass of that number, but is one and one and one . . . up to ten thousand.

Billions have lived and died, billions will live and die; and this every American knows—knows in that realm beyond learning, knows in his bones. American literature of the great age is filled with the grasp of this dimension; it is in Whitman's oft-derided catalogs, in Poe's "Eureka," in Melville's resort to myth, in Emily Dickinson's lyrics. It is not in Thoreau and Emerson, and its absence is all the more conspicuous when they are writing under the influence of the Sanskrit scriptures, where the realization abounds.

This knowledge is now in every American and in his glance. And there as everywhere it never ceases to call into question one's grasp on one's own identity.

Fortunately for several generations, the American has had the Bible. The Bible, like the Sanskrit scriptures, is one long contemplation of the situation of the one in the innumerable, and it sternly forbids its readers to draw any relief from what lies about them. Its characters hang suspended upon the promises of the imagination; for generations most Americans were named after them. Those (one and one and one . . .) to whom destiny has extended a promise and a plan have this consolation that they feel themselves to be irreplaceable. Each one is a bundle of projects.

It would seem as though I were about to say that the Americans are unworldly, spiritual natures like the Hindu initiates for whom the Earth is but an illusion or like the saints engrossed only in intangibles ("I count nothing my own save my harp"; "here on earth have we no abiding place albeit we seek one to come"). No, for them concrete things concretely exist, so solidly that these things do not exhale a deep emotion nor invite it. How seldom in American literature—outside of Europeanizing epigenous writers like Washington Irving—does one find such effusions as "Dear Tree, beneath which so often I played as a child," or "Newburgh, rising in glorious serenity above the lordly Hudson, would that once again I could tread thy steep streets. . . ." Americans do not readily animate things; their tireless animation is active elsewhere, in the future.

This is the disconnection from place; the disconnection from time is no less radical. Now let us search through great pages of *Moby Dick* for the literary and stylistic reflections of these characteristics.

The Melville of *Moby Dick*, a most widely admired work in American literature, is a notably interesting example for our study. Melville was not only writing within the tradition of English literature, he was writing very bookishly and stylishly indeed. No doubt he was conscious that the vogue for his books was beginning to be greater in England than in America (*Moby Dick* was first published in London). Under the mounting emotion of composition Melville's "Americanism" erupted in spite of himself. It can be seen progressively manifesting itself. The first eleven pages of the novel are the worst kind of "English English"—that is to say, the English of the contemporary New York literary cliques. There are many pages in *Moby Dick* which betray the insecurity of a writer thirty-one years old who has launched upon a mighty subject; but the page from which I am about to quote is completely successful, and its success has been achieved through the presence within it of elements inherent in the new nation's adventure.

The following pages will appear to some to be an excursion into that French pedagogical practice called the "explication de texte." It is not; there is no space here for those patient ramifications, nor is it my aim to explore this passage in and for itself. Yet I often regret the ready disparagement expressed by so many American educators of a method which seems to me to arise from the never failing French respect for métier. One of our professors in discussing it said to me that "a flower under a microscope ceases to be a flower"—a view which belongs rather to Thoreau's ecstasy-before-nature view than to Goethe's awe-before-nature. I have always felt—again with Goethe—that works of art are also works of nature and, like the works of nature, afford, under probing, new reaches of wonder. The American depreciation of the "explication de texte" may proceed from a characteristic that I shall discuss later, namely that Americans have a tendency to be far more interested in wholes than in parts.

The passage I am about to read is from Chapter 133. It affords us our first direct view of the White Whale; it is probably the most delayed entrance of a star in all literature—in my edition it is on page 538.[1] During the reading of this page, I wish you to ask yourself a number of questions: What is its movement and where have you heard it before? Does its rhythm and ordering of phrase recall you to the Bible of 1611? Or Elizabethan drama? Or Sir Thomas Browne? Or does it seem to you to sound like a prose translation or adaptation of an epic poem? Does it, indeed, seem to be trying to capture in prose the effects peculiar to poetry? But, above all, are you aware of any elements that separate it from English literature, the English spirit recounting the English experience of life?

> The whale has been sighted, "A hump like a snow-hill!" and the boats of the *Pequod* have started in pursuit.
> Like noiseless nautilus shells, their light prows sped through the sea; but only slowly they neared the foe.

Melville's emotion is gaining on him. The alliterations in *n* and *s* begin to introduce an incantatory tone which will presently be confirmed by constructions employing repetition. But the approach to a state of trance does not prevent his marking the rapidity of the boats with monosyllables, and the dragging slowness—as felt by the whalers—with open vowels.

> As they neared him, the ocean grew still more smooth; seemed drawing a carpet over its waves; seemed a noon-meadow, so serenely it spread. At length, the breathless hunter came so nigh his seemingly unsuspecting prey, that his entire dazzling hump was distinctly visible, sliding along the sea as if an isolated thing, and continually set in a revolving ring of finest, fleecy, greenish foam. He saw the vast, involved wrinkles of the slightly projecting head beyond. Before it, far out on the soft Turkish-rugged waters, went the glistening white shadow from his broad, milky forehead, a musical rippling playfully accompanying the shade; and behind, the blue waters interchangeably flowed over into the moving valley of his steady wake; and on either hand bright bubbles arose and danced by his side.

Melville's emotion is under powerful control. We are approaching a paroxysm of swooning love and shuddering horror, but so far he has mainly presented himself to us All Eyes. The emotion is present, however, in this insistence that everything is serene and in the undulation of the rhythm. Scarcely a noun is offered which is not preceded by one or two adjectives, many of which ("projecting," "soft," "white," "broad," "blue") tell us nothing new. We call this practice a mid-nineteenth-century vice, and today children are punished for it. Today such a scene—picture and emotion—would be conveyed with the economy of a telegram. But style is not only the man; it involves also the thought-world of the time, including the writer's effort to alter it. This page is an exercise in flamboyant rhetoric; it is a "purple patch," unashamed. Its triumph issues from the superimposition of novel elements upon a traditional form.

The visual details which Melville has furnished, and which he is about to furnish, are the most brilliant precision, but they do not render the scene objective, nor do they mitigate our awe and terror. The impression is that his eyes are "starting out of his head." Only the greatest authors—and Dante in chief—can thus continue to see while they are in a state of transport. Lesser authors relapse into abstract nouns and fashion from them a sort of cloudy "sublime."

> But these were broken again by the light toes of hundreds of gay fowl softly feathering the sea, alternate with their fitful flight; and like to some flagstaff rising from the painted hull of an argosy, the tall but shattered pole of a recent lance projected from the White Whale's back; and at intervals one of the cloud of soft-toed fowls hovering, and to and fro skimming like a canopy over the fish, silently perched and rocked on this pole, the long tail feathers streaming like pennons.
>
> A gentle joyousness—a mighty mildness of repose in swiftness, invested the gliding whale.

At last we have an abstract noun—four of them, and how abstractly dependent upon one another! But Melville's grasp of this visible world is so sure that we can afford a plethora of them. Abstract nouns come naturally to Americans, but they must constantly find an idiosyncratic way of employing them. New-World abstractions are very different from Old-World abstractions; they are not "essences" but generalizations. To express it most paradoxically, an American strives to render his abstraction concrete.

> Not the white bull Jupiter swimming away with ravished Europa clinging to his graceful horns; his lovely leering eyes sideways intent upon the maid; with smooth bewitching fleetness, rippling straight for the nuptial bower in Crete; not Jove, not that great

majesty Supreme! did surpass the glorified White Whale as he so divinely swam.

What! These whalefishers are hurrying to their death and the great blasphemer to his retribution, and Melville chooses this moment to linger over the behavior of some birds and to insert an elaborated Renaissance vignette?

This beautifully wrought metaphor, though not at all classical in feeling, represents a device we frequently find in Homer. The simile which arises from the presented action begins to lead an independent life of its own; it flowers into details and developments which occasionally disturb and even reverse its relation to its original correlevant. This evocation of Jupiter not only arrests our excitement; it almost cuts us off from direct vision. This would seem to be a flaw, but its justification lies in its relation to time.

There are three times transpiring on this page. There are—as in all narration—the time of the action and the time of the narrative; Ishmael at his desk recalls and re-experiences those events from the past. But the time which is passing in the mind of Ishmael the narrator is invaded by another time which can best be called the timeless. If Melville were writing an adventure story for boys, "Joe Foster, the Young Whaler," it would indeed be lamentable to deflate our excitement at this moment. But in the realm of moral issues and total experience, such human tensions are not out of place. Older readers know that life is crisis. (Goethe said that the *Iliad* teaches us "that it is our task here on earth to enact Hell daily.") The house burns down, and no Joe Foster rushes through the flames to rescue the child from the cradle; the survivors of the wreck turn black and expire upon their raft before Joe Foster appears upon the horizon; the consequences of the lives we have fashioned advance toward us with age and death on their heels. Homer and Melville remove us to a plane of time wherein catastrophe or rescue are mere incidents in a vast pattern.

But these birds and this fragment of mythology have another character. They proceed from another form of excitement. They have about them the hushed, glassy precision of hallucination. For those who come upon them in their place in the vast book, they are like the intrusions of a dream and like the irrelevances in a moment of danger. They are that moment when the matador sees the bull dashing toward him and at the same time, out of the corner of his eye, sees that a woman in the second row is wearing three red roses and that her black scarf is being fanned by the wind. The timeless is for a moment identified with the time of all those other people and things that are not caught up in our crisis—the people who pass whistling happily under our hospital window, the people who are held up at a crossing while we drive to a burial–the birds, and the nuptials of Jupiter and Europa.

Whereupon, after this far journey into the timeless, Melville brings us back abruptly to the most concrete level of his story:

> On each soft side—coincident with the parted swell, that but once leaving him,

[The autograph manuscript of *Moby Dick* has been lost. I have no doubt that Melville wrote "laving him" (washing him). After finishing this novel, something broke in Melville; he lost his concentration. *Pierre* and *The Confidence Man* are on the level of "leaving."]

> then flowed so wide away—on each bright side, the whale shed off enticings. No wonder there had been some among the hunters who, namelessly transported and allured by all this serenity, had ventured to assail it; but had fatally found that quietude but the vesture of tornadoes.

This is very extravagant writing, indeed, but, as the word "namelessly" shows, Melville is returning us for a moment to the symbolic level. We do not have to think of the Nantucket whalefishers as subject to throes of aesthetic transport. We may read:

> It is not surprising that some men have been mistaken by the apparently serene orderliness of God-in-Nature and, swept up into *hubris*, have attempted to blaspheme against it and to set themselves up as its antagonists, only to discover that . . .
> Yet calm, enticing calm, oh whale! thou glidest on, to all who for the first time eye thee, no matter how many in that same way thou may'st have bejuggled and destroyed before.

The climax employs the most rhetorical—that is to say, the most potentially absurd—of all devices: the invocation to an abstraction, to an insensible or absent being. It is characteristic of our time, and related to what I was saying about the decline of our belief in authorities and essences, that few orators can be heard saying, "Oh, Commonwealth of Massachusetts, persevere!" and few poets now address the Evening or Sweet Days of Childhood.

> And thus, through the serene tranquillities of the tropical sea, among waves whose hand-clappings were suspended by exceeding rapture, Moby Dick moved on, still withholding from sight the full terrors of his submerged trunk, entirely hiding the wrenched hideousness of his jaw. But soon the fore part of him slowly rose from the water; for an instant his whole marbleized body formed a high arch, like Virginia's Natural Bridge, and warningly waving his bannered flukes in the air, the grand god revealed himself, sounded, and went out of sight. Hoveringly halting, and dipping on the wing, the white sea-fowls longingly lingered over the agitated pool that he left.

There are some literary echoes in this passage, but they are drowned out by an influence that is not of the printed page. I find but one cadence which recalls the Bible: "suspended in exceeding rapture"; and but one reminiscence of Elizabethan, though not Shakespearean, blank verse: "Yet calm, enticing calm, oh whale! thou glidest on, to all who for the first time eye thee...."

Sir Thomas Browne is never far absent; he has had his part in the evocation of Europa, and in him Melville "fatally found that quietude but the vesture of tornadoes." To my ear, however, the movement of this passage is primarily oratorical.

Yet the observation that this passage has the air of being written for declamation does not distinguish it as a work of the New World. De Quincey, Carlyle, Ruskin, Chateaubriand, Victor Hugo, and Kierkegaard had all been writing or were about to write prose that took its tone from forensic and pulpit eloquence. There are three elements in it, however, which indicate that it is written in America:

1. It contains a number of locutions which reveal the emergence of the American language.
2. It is directed to a classless society—to Everybody.
3. It constantly betrays what I have called a certain disconnection in the American mind.

Before I enter upon a discussion of the first two of these elements (a discussion of the third as applied to this passage will be found in a later lecture), I wish to return to a consideration of the page as an example of the Grand Style Ornate. That it is a successful example of such a style does not mark it as a product of the New World, but that it is so in 1851 is, from the point of view of English literature, a matter of remark.

Americans were filled with a sense of newness, of vastness, and of challenge. As Walt Whitman put it:

> It almost seems as if a poetry with cosmic and dynamic features of magnitude and limitlessness suitable to the human soul, were never possible before.

And for this big feeling within them they needed to employ a grand style, a swelling rhetoric unabashed. And they needed it at the precise moment that England lost it.

England did not lose it because of any diminution of her exterior or interior greatness. Her exterior greatness had not yet reached its peak; and her interior greatness has never been greater than in our own time. She lost it for two reasons: one, the verbal expressions for that greatness had been under employment so long that it had begun to show exhaustion; and, two, the islanders (as I said earlier) had dwelt so long in congested proximity that a heroic view of one another was no longer possible. The mock heroic had been able to flourish side by side with the heroic in the eighteenth century, but finally it had begun to sap the heroic. British feeling in regard to all that was venerable in their institutions did not decline, but their expression of it became more and more an understatement in public and an affectionate persiflage in private. Poet laureates found it increasingly difficult to celebrate great personages and great events in the lofty language that was called for. English humor of the last half of the nineteenth century was precisely based on the mocking application to daily life of the grandiose diction of the preceding centuries.

But America was not overcrowded, and neither its geography nor its history had been for centuries the subject of literature. The heroic flourished side by side with the mock-heroic, and the mock-heroic itself seemed to be a smiling tribute to the heroic. All of the writers we are considering were highly "bookish" authors and may have been aware of the increasing hollowness of the English grand style (which accompanied an increasing precision and beauty in the description of the homely and intimate), but all advanced unhesitatingly and often into the perilous reaches of ornate eloquence. Boldest of all was Walt Whitman, who saw the necessity of desophisticating himself in order to achieve it. All of them were able to renew the validity of impassioned utterance by availing themselves of a number of novel elements.

The novel element which seems to me to be of least importance was the presence of new words and idioms. There are no examples of this in the page we are studying. "Bejuggled," which Melville had already employed in *Mardi*, is not in most dictionaries, but "juggled" has a long history on both sides of the Atlantic. But if there are no new words, there are some examples of novel usage.

"The whale shed off enticings." There is little doubt that De Quincey or even Carlyle would have written "shed enticements." "Enticings" will be followed in the next paragraph by "hand-clappings." These verbal nouns based on the present participle are relatively rare in the plural. A number, after losing their dynamic force (paintings, savings, undertakings), have entered common use, and others (understandings, risings, mumblings) are on their way to the same static condition. But we do not say laughings, shoppings, studyings, enticings, or hand-clappings. Melville in *Moby Dick* offers us intertwistings, spurnings, coincidings, imminglings, and even "what lovely leewardings!" I have counted thirty-one of them. The following year, while writing *Pierre*, he will have forgotten his infatuation with plural gerunds and will have set out to create new words in -ness, heightening the abstraction in abstract words. There we find beautifulness, domesticness (twice!), unidentifiableness, and undulatoriness—all deplorable and some of them atrocious.

(Yet genius on wings can confound any of our own theoretical objections. Emily Dickinson wrote:

> 'Tis glory's overtakelessness
> That makes our running poor.

In addition to forging our American language for us, Emily Dickinson enjoyed many a witches' sabbath with the language on her own.)

Much of this coinage in Melville is mere huffing and purring. A young man of thirty-one with barely a high-school education has remarked Shakespeare's bold inventions without having acquired the tact that controlled them. I find the plural gerunds on this page, however, completely successful.

"The whale shed off enticings." As foreigners who are learning our language frequently inform us, we Americans are forever putting prepositions and adverbial particles to new uses. Here the "off" combined with the "enticings" gives the impression of a continuous fulguration. It is not only an expression of vivacity and energy; it reveals our national tendency to restore to the past its once-present life rather than to immobilize it, to bury it under the preterite. In narration this assumes a great importance, for Americans wish to declare that all living things are free—and were free—

and the past tenses in narration tend to suggest that we, telling the story from its latter end, see them as "determined" and as the victims of necessity. When we come to discuss the American time-sense and its struggle to reshape the syntax of the English language, we shall see that one of its principal aims has been to give even to the past tenses the feeling of a "continuous present," a door open to the future, a recovery of the we-don't-know-what-will-happen.

On this page we are shown the bull and Europa "rippling straight for the nuptial bower in Crete." Water ripples; tresses ripple. Had we read in a present-day author, English or American, that "Leander rippled straight for Sestos," we would have condemned it as a vulgarity. What saves this phrase from vulgarity is the gamut of tones that are juxtaposed in this 19th century page—which brings us to our second consideration.

A novel element in our classics of a century ago is the fact that they were written for a classless society, they were written for everybody. European literature for two and a half centuries had been directed to an audience of cultivation, to an elite—Molière's farces not excepted, Dickens's (imminent) novels not excepted. The assumption on the part of our American writers that they were addressing a total society has since disappeared; we are now in the famous division between the highbrows and the lowbrows; but, given the basic considerations of our American life, such an assumption should constitute the natural function of a much larger part of American writing.

What are the signs that a writer feels himself to be addressing the total community rather than an elite? There are many; I am about to give two, both drawn from the realm of the grand style. It is well to note first, however, that this consideration has nothing to do with whether or not a writer uses long words or erudite allusions. It has nothing to do with a condescension to semi-literacy. The 1611 Bible and the works of Shakespeare are filled with incomprehensible phrases; millions pore over them daily; we read right on, sufficiently nourished by what is intelligible to us.

It is not necessary to remind you that Walt Whitman addressed himself to everyone who could read or be read to. Listen to Thoreau in *Walden* (and note the forensic tone; there is no surer sign of it than these redundant numerations):

> Simplicity, simplicity, simplicity. I say let your affairs be as two or three, and not a hundred or a thousand; instead of a million count half a dozen, and keep your accounts on your thumbnail. In the midst of this chopping sea of civilized life, such are the clouds and

> storms and quicksands and thousand-and-one items to be allowed for, if he would not founder and go to the bottom, and not make port, by dead reckoning, and he must be a great calculator who succeeds. Simplify, simplify. Instead of three meals . . .

Thoreau is addressing so vast a throng that in his effort to be heard he has lost control of subjects and verbs, scrupulous writer though he usually is.

> Cultivate poverty like a garden herb, like sage. Do not trouble yourself much to get new things whether clothes or friends. . . . Things do not change; we change.

All this is for the farmhand, the blacksmith, and the cook as well as for the Governor's lady. It is for Ralph Waldo Emerson as well as for Thoreau's mother, the boardinghouse keeper.

New Englanders have been proverbially inarticulate; but they could unlock their hearts and throats if they felt the audience to be sufficiently large. Did not Emily Dickinson say of her poetry:

> This is my letter to the world
> That never wrote to me?

Her grand style—sunbursts of Handelian rhetoric—invokes a universe:

> Mine by the right of the white election!
> Mine by the royal seal!
>
> One dignity delays for all.
> Struck was I, yet not by lightning.

Wherein do these paragraphs from *Moby Dick* reveal the fact that Melville was addressing an undifferentiated audience? They are certainly highly "bookish"—what with that elaborated classical allusion, that stylish subjunctive, and their high percentage of words from the Latin.

First, we observe that elevation and intensity are not solely and inseparably associated with noble images. The sublime does not wear a cothurnus. There are not two doors for words in America, no tradesmen's entrance: all can go in the front door. In the very same sentence in which Melville apostrophizes divinity, we are told that God has "bejuggled" many a man. It is a word from the skulduggeries of the country fair and the card game at the livery stable. We remember the horror with which Racine's contemporaries greeted the mention of a dog in tragedy, the protest of the audience against Hugo's use of the humble phrase, "*Quelle heure est-il?*" in *Hernani*. Generations of critics deplored the drunken porter in *Macbeth*. What better illustration of the limited gamut of tones available for European full-throated utterance than the observation that so many of the words that describe lofty moods are also words that stem from the designations of social rank, or that run concurrently with them and derive much of their force from connotations of status: "noble" and "*herrlich*" and "*edel*" and "*magnifico*" and "*grande*" and "*soberano*" and "majestic" and even "gentle." The United States is a middle-class nation and has widened and broadened and deepened the concepts of the wide and the broad and the deep without diminishing the concept of the high. We notice that the angelic host of birds that glorify the White Whale have soft toes. Toes, like noses, have not hitherto entered the exalted, the dithyrambic style. This page did not have the drawing room in view.

Second, most European exercises in the sublime, in avoiding the common and humble, avoid the specific. In the tirades of Burke and Carlyle on the French Revolution, in the impassioned visions of DeQuincey and Chateaubriand, the noble is associated with a high vagueness. Audiences which are composed of the selected and the cultivated and the *Gebildeten* and the *honnêtes gens* and the *cognoscenti* are not interested in life's diversity; the pressures upon them work toward the formulation of taste and convention and the Rules of the Beautiful and an ever-narrowing purity (*i.e.*, economy) in the selection of detail. But the American public was one and one and one . . . to an unlimited number. Their taste could never be codified, for it was overwhelmed by an ever-enlarging vision of the universe and its multifarious character. The bigger the world is, the less one can be content with vagueness. The catalogs of Walt Whitman, which have displeased so many immured scholars, are filled with this kind of apprehension. He hears a runaway slave

> . . . crackling the twigs of the woodpile,
> Through the swung half-door of the kitchen I saw him limpsy and weak, . . .
> The bride unrumples her white dress, the minute-hand of the clock moves slowly,
> The opium-eater reclines with rigid head and just-opened lips. . . .

Whitman can get a million people into his poem by making sure that not one of his twenty is amorphous.

What European poet, reminding us that the sunlight falls on all alike, would have selected as an illustration the reminder that it falls upon the "Squirrel in the Himmaleh"—or have drawn from the thought so chillingly abstract a conclusion as did Emily Dickinson? "But not for Compensation—/It holds as large a Glow/To Squirrel in the Himmaleh/Precisely, as to you."

Since the American can find no confirmation of identity from the environment in which he lives, since he lives exposed to the awareness of vast distances and innumerable existences, since he derives the courage that animates him from a belief in the future, is he not bent on isolating and "fixing" a value on every existing thing in its relation to a totality, to the All, to the Everywhere, to the Always? And does that not require of him a new way of viewing and feeling and describing any existing thing? And would that not require, in turn, a modification of the language?

---

1. Thornton Wilder seems to have used a copy of the edition of *Moby Dick* edited by Luther S. Mansfield and Howard P. Vincent and published in New York by Hendricks House in 1952.

The American Loneliness

by

Thornton Wilder

Walking to the auditorium where I am to lecture on Thoreau, I pass Hollis Hall in which he lived as an undergraduate.

I think we can understand why on graduation he changed his name—David Henry became Henry David, peremptorily. Like Emerson before him, he was a scholarship student. During his first year he had one coat—his mother and aunt had made it for him out of green homespun. That year the right students were wearing black. All his life he railed with particular passion against any discrimination that is based on dress. A classmate tells us that, as a student, Thoreau in conversation did not raise his eyes from the ground and that his hands were continually moist. That chapter over, he changed his name.

As I pass Hollis, I become uncomfortable; I feel those extraordinary blue eyes not on me, but directed over me, in taciturn reproach. Thoreau set down a portrait of himself, and he took pains with its details. He wished it to be known that he was direct, simple, forthright, candid, and uncomplicated. Many have taken him at his word; but no, his life and personality have more important things to tell us.

How hard it is to discuss Thoreau in the presence of the young. Many aspects of his life and thought lie in that sole territory which is inaccessible to young men and women. I never feel an incomprehension on their part when I treat of death or loss or passion; their imaginations can extend themselves—by that principle which Goethe called "anticipation"—to such matters. What is difficult is to treat of the slow attrition of the soul by the conduct of life, of our revolt against the workaday—the background of such works as Le Misanthrope *and* Don Quixote. *I must tell these young people, who are hurrying by me, that Thoreau met defeat in* his impassioned demands upon Love, Friendship, and Nature; and yet I must tell them that at the same time he was an American who fought some of our battles for us, whose experience we are to follow with a sort of anxious suspense. The rewards we obtain from the contemplation of Thoreau, however, begin their consolatory and inspiriting effect upon us as we move through our forties.

I wish I were somewhere else.

Ladies and gentlemen:

We were talking last time about how difficult it is to be an American. We spoke of the support which Europeans receive from all those elements we call environment—place, tradition, customs: "I am I because my neighbors know me." Their environment is so thickly woven, so solid, that the growing boy and girl have something to kick against. The American, on the other hand, is at sea—disconnected from place, distrustful of authority, thrown back upon himself.

Here I am again.
And suddenly, as my eyes rest on the upturned faces before me, I am encouraged. It is in many ways a sad story I have to tell. Whenever I think of Thoreau, I feel a weight about my heart, a greater weight than descends in thoughts of Poe or Emily Dickinson. Yet all of us here are Americans. My subject is the loneliness that accompanies independence and the uneasiness that accompanies freedom. These experiences are not foreign to anyone here. So forward.

Perceptive visitors to America from Europe are uniformly struck by what they call an "American loneliness," which they find no less present in that fretful and often hollow gregariousness we talked about last time.

Now there are several forms of this loneliness, and the one that occurs to us first is the sentimental form. In America the very word is sentimental, and it makes us uncomfortable even to employ it. Yet we see this kind of loneliness about us everywhere; like the loneliness which springs from pride, it is a consequence, a deformation, and a malady of that deeper form which we are about to discuss. Both proceed from the fact that the religious ideas current in America are still inadequate to explain the American to himself. The sentimental loneliness arises from the sense that he is a victim, that he was slighted when Fortune distributed her gifts (though it is notably prevalent among those who seem to "have everything"); the proud loneliness arises from the sense of boundlessness which we described as related to the American geography and is found among those who make boundless moral demands on themselves and others.

Thoreau illustrates certain American traits connected with loneliness in an extreme and exaggerated form. He finally lost his battle—the typical American battle of trying to convert a loneliness into an enriched and fruitful solitude—but before he died (at forty-four, murmuring: "It is better some things should end"), he furnished us many a bulletin of the struggle, many an insight, and many an aid.

Another of the most famous pages in American literature is that wherein Thoreau gives his reasons for going to live in solitude at Walden Pond.

> I went to the woods because I wished to live deliberately, to front only the essential facts of life, and see if I could not learn what I had to teach, and not, when I came to die, discover that I had not lived. . . . nor did I wish to practice resignation, unless it were quite necessary. . . . if [life] . . . proved to be mean, why then to get the whole and genuine meanness of it, and publish its meanness to the world; or if it were sublime, to know it by experience, and be able to give a true account of it in my next excursion.

Thoreau's books are a sort of *cento* of transcriptions and amplifications of entries in his journal. Here is what he wrote on the third day of his residence at the pond (6 July 1845):

"I wish to meet the facts of life—the vital facts, which are the phenomena or actuality which the gods meant to show us—face to face, and so I came here. Life! who knows what it is, what it does?"

There are several things to notice about these passages: among them, first, that he will put his question as though no one had ever said anything valuable before; and, second, that in order to ask what life is, it is necessary to remove oneself from the human community.

Americans constantly feel that the whole world's thinking has to be done over again. They did not only leave the Old World, they repudiated it. Americans start from scratch. This is revolt indeed. All authority is suspect. And this is boundless presumption. I quoted Whitman's words in our last session ("It almost seems as if a poetry . . . suitable to the human soul were never possible before"). Poe, clutching some mathematics and physics he had acquired during a brief stay at West Point, launched into a description of how the universe came into being, and deduced the nature of God from his theory of the galaxies. He called his work *Eureka* and did not leave us in doubt that he felt that he had succeeded where the greatest minds had failed. Professional astronomers dismiss it with a smile, but we notice that the great French poet Paul Valéry, who occupied himself with mathematics for thirty years, tells us how great a role this book played in the growth of his thought. *(L'idée fondamentale de Poe n'en est pas moins une profonde et souveraine idée.")*

Thoreau did some reading at Walden Pond, but it is astonishing how small a part it plays in this central inquiry of his life. He invokes neither the great philosophers nor the founders of religions. Every American is an autodidact; every American feels himself capable of being the founder of his own religion. At the end of the passage I have quoted from the journal there is an allusion by Thoreau to his reading of the Sanskrit scriptures. It is an ironic jest: "to give a true account of it in my next excursion." He does not believe that our souls return to inhabit other bodies, though billions have reposed in that idea all that they know of hope and courage. He makes a jest of it—for example, to him, of the uselessness of other people's thinking. There is something of this religious and metaphysical pioneer in us all. How often I have heard people say: "No, Mr. Wilder, we don't go to church. My husband and I each have our own religion—here—inside!" What student at the height of a lofty argument has not been heard to cry: "Listen, everybody! My theory is *this* . . ."?

To others this must all seem very deplorable. To Americans it is wearing and costing and often desolating; but such is the situation. The die is cast, and our interest in Thoreau is precisely that we see one of ourselves fighting, struggling, and finally fainting in this inescapable American situation. Thoreau asks, What is life? and he asks it in a world from which any considerable reliance on previous answers is denied him, and through his long inquiry he heard the closing of three doors—doors to great areas of experience on which he counted for aid and illumination, the doors to Love, Friendship, and Nature.

Here are the reverberations of these closing doors:

LOVE (27 October 1851, aged 34):
The obstacles which the heart meets with are like granite blocks which one alone cannot remove. She who was the morning light is now neither the morning star nor the evening star. We meet but to find each other further asunder. . . .

FRIENDSHIP (4 March 1856, aged 38):
I had two friends. The one offered me friendship on such terms that I could not accept it, without a sense of degradation. He would not meet me on equal terms, but only to be to some extent my patron. . . . Our relation was one long tragedy. . . .

NATURE: As early as 16 July 1861, Thoreau was saying:
Methinks my present experience is nothing; my past experience is all in all. I think that no experience which I have today comes up to, or is comparable with, the experiences of my boyhood.... Formerly, methought, nature developed as I developed, and grew up with me. My life was ecstasy....

The story of Thoreau's love is only beginning to be pieced together. The obstacles that separated him from this woman were indeed granite blocks. The expressions he gives to his love in his Journal are often strange "whirling words":

> My sister, it is glorious to me that you live! ... It is morning when I meet thee in a still cool dewy white sun light in the hushed dawn—my young mother—I thy eldest son [lightly crossed through: "thy young father"] ... whether art thou my mother or my sister—whether am I thy son or thy brother.... Others are of my kindred by blood or of my acquaintance but you are part of me. I cannot tell where you leave off and I begin.

In another passage, journal 1850, he says: "I am as much thy sister as thy brother. Thou art as much my brother as my sister."

We have reason to be surprised that the erotic emotion expresses itself in images borrowed from the family relationships. Yet such a coloring is present elsewhere in our writers of this period, in Whitman, in Melville (*Pierre*), and in Poe. In America the family is the nexus of an unusually powerful ambivalence. On the one hand, the child strains to break away and lead his own life. The young seldom settle down near their parents' home; less and less frequently do the parents end their days in the homes of their children; I have remarked that young people are increasingly eager for the moment when they are no longer financially dependent on their parents. On the other hand, the American—as we were saying—is exceptionally aware of the multitude of the human race; his loneliness is enhanced by his consciousness of those numbers. The family is at once an encroachment on his individualism and a seductive invitation to rejoin the human community at a level where he does not feel himself to be strange. Moreover, individualism has its arrogance. It has long been a tag that every American is king. Royalty marries only royalty. Other people aren't good enough. Thoreau elevates the woman he loves to this kinship. Poe's mother died when he was three; he lived the latter part of his life with his aunt and married his cousin. The blocks of granite which separated Thoreau from this "sister" were not all outside of him. The door of love closed and he never returned to it.

It was the friendship with Ralph Waldo Emerson that Thoreau described as "one long tragedy." The second friend who proved unworthy was William Ellery Channing, who seems to have enjoyed shocking Thoreau with an occasional ribaldry. Tragedy we too can call it, for few men could have needed friendship more, and few have been less ready to accommodate themselves to it. He wrote (11 June 1855):

> What if we feel a yearning to which no breast answers? I walk alone, my heart is full. Feelings impede the current of my thoughts. I knock on the earth for my friend. I expect to meet him at every turn; but no friend appears, and perhaps none is dreaming of me.

Emerson knew that he was incapable of friendship, and the knowledge caused him some pain—brief pain, for Emerson had a short way with moral discomfiture; he mounted up into pink clouds and began to give voice to abstractions. This woeful triangle skirts the comic. A letter has recently come to light which gives Channing's view of a friendship with Emerson. Channing wrote to Elizabeth Hoar from New Bedford on 23 December 1856:

> How strange it seemed to hear W[aldo] lecturing on friendship. If he knew all the hearts he has frozen, he might better read something on the fall of human hopes. . . . I have never parted from him without the bitterest regret, not for having parted, but for having come. . . .

Individualism! It is the point of honor of men and nations in this century. Every nation boasts that it is a nation of individualists and implies that the other nations are composed of sheep. ("You Americans—you all eat the same things; you repeat the same slogans; you read the same book of the month; the very streets in which you live have not even names but merely numbers and letters!") Yet no man (and no nation) is as individualistic as he thinks he is; each is so in one area of his existence, and the extent to which he is—fortunately!—conformist in others is not apparent to him. Friendship is not incompatible with individualism, as the great pages of Montaigne have shown us, but it was incompatible in the lives of our Concord philosophers. Thousands of schoolchildren were formerly required to read Emerson's chaotic essay on the subject. For generations, Emerson's style had the power to put the judgment to sleep, but one wonders what the teachers made of that farewell address to "our dearest friends": "Who are you? Unhand me: I will be dependent no more."

Thoreau's inability to come to terms with friendship was aggravated by the vastness of his expectations. To this day, many an American is breaking his life on an excessive demand for the perfect, the absolute, and the boundless in realms where it is accorded to few—in love and friendship, for example. The doctrines of moderation and the golden mean may have flourished in Rome and in China (overcrowded and overgoverned countries), but they do not flourish here, save as counsels of despair. The injunction to be content with your lot and in the situation where God has placed you is not an expression of New-World thinking. We do not feel ourselves to be subject to lot and we do not cast God in the role of a civil administrator or of a feudal baron.

Thoreau goes to the pond, then, to find an answer to the question, What is life? He will not admit other thinkers to his deliberations, and his answer will not reflect any close relation with his fellow men. With what frustrated passion, then, he turned to nature. Nature meant primarily the flora and fauna of the Concord River Valley, though he made some trips elsewhere. Now that region has no tigers, avalanches, coral vipers, Black Forests, deserts, or volcanoes. Margaret Fuller warned her Concord friends of the dangers of accustoming themselves to a view of nature which omitted both cruelty and grandeur. On his walks, Thoreau came upon some malodorous plants (26 June 1852): "For what purpose has nature made a flower to fill the lowlands with the odor of carrion?" The question seems, to us, both biologically and philosophically, a little *simpliste*.

Enough has already been written about the absence of a sense of evil in the work of the Concord essayists. It is only one of the elements that resulted in the gradually progressive grayness of the last volumes of Thoreau's journal. Far more important is the fact that Thoreau asked of nature a gift which nature cannot, without cooperation, accord. He asked a continual renewal of moments of youthful ecstasy. Unhappy indeed is the boy or girl who has not known those moments of inexplicable rapture in the open air. There is a corresponding experience accorded to those in later years—awe. In ecstasy, the self is infused with happiness; in awe the self recedes before a realization of the vastness and mystery of the non-self. Many never cross the bridge from one to the other. Thoreau despised and dreaded science; to inquire too narrowly into the laws of nature seemed to him to threaten those increasingly infrequent visitations of irrational joy. "If you would obtain insight, avoid anatomy," he wrote. With what a sad smile

Goethe would have shaken his head over these words—for it was precisely from his studies of the skeleton of the vertebrates and the structure of plants that Goethe's life was flooded, even in his eighties, with an awe which retained much of the character of a juvenile ecstasy. Indeed, Goethe at eighty would not have written the words which Thoreau wrote at thirty-three:

> In youth, before I lost any of my senses, I can remember that I was all alive, and inhabited my body with inexpressible satisfaction . . . !

As the years passed, Thoreau increasingly mourned his lost youth and the intoxication which nature had afforded him then. For a time the humming of the telegraph wires aroused transports; it was his "redeemer"; then they too lost their peculiar powers. Finally, in his last years he turned from the almost passive notation of the phenomena about him and introduced into his observations an element of progression and exploration into the unknown. He counted the rings in stumps and made notes on the succession of trees. Those who are conversant with these things tell us that he was discovering the science of ecology. He seems, however, to have derived no warming satisfaction from this innovation; his notes lie buried in his journal and the work is repeated independently by others.

I am eager to arrive at all the things that call forth our admiration for Thoreau, but I must delay a moment to point out that we have brushed against two traits in him which are not characteristic of the American: the fixed orientation toward childhood and the view of nature as engaged in close personal conversation with man. These are characteristic, however, of the region from which he came.

A portion of Massachusetts and several states of our South are enclaves or residual areas of European feeling. They were cut off, or resolutely cut themselves off, from the advancing tide of the country's modes of consciousness. Place, environment, relations, repetitions are the breath of their being. One evidence of it is a constant preoccupation with how old one is and a striking obsession with early youth (how many of the brilliant novels which have lately come to us from the South turn upon childhood). In New York and Chicago and the West, one's age is of relatively little importance; those who are active between twenty-five and sixty are contemporaries. They dine and dance and work and enjoy themselves together. This is bound up with the American sense of time, which I shall develop in later lectures. Time is something we create, we call into being, not something we submit to—an order outside us.

Similarly, there are aspects of Thoreau's relation to nature that are not those we feel to be prevalent elsewhere among us. The gods of glade and brook and pond are not the gods of plain, seacoast, forest, desert, and mountain. The former are almost in reach; one can imagine oneself in dialogue with them; they can enter into an almost personal relationship with those who have turned from the company of men. But the gods of great space are enigmatic; we are never sure that we have read aright the message of their beauty and terror; we do not hastily put words into their mouths. Yet the more we feel an "otherness" in nature, the more we recognize that we ourselves are natural. "It appears to be a law," wrote Thoreau, in April 1852, "that you cannot have a deep sympathy with both man and nature. . . . I loved nature because she is not man, but a retreat from him." There is no such law, nor have any other American voices expressed any sentiment like it, unless we take note of a moment in Emily Dickinson's life when she wrote:

> I thought that nature was enough
> Till human nature came.

Nature failed Thoreau, as it will ultimately fail anyone who wishes to divide it up, to pick and choose only limited congenial aspects of it, for ecstasy or for retreat, or who wishes to employ one aspect of it to confound another. And the question: "Life! who knows what it is, what it does?" It would seem that Thoreau had considerably compromised his inquiry by divesting himself of the testimony and the companionship of others and by repeating his question to a wooded vale.

Yet millions have testified and are testifying to the powerful clarifications that he brought back from Walden Pond. And all his triumphs came from his embattled individualism, from pushing it to the limits that border on absurdity and from facing—"face to face"—the loneliness consequent upon it. He came back with the answer that life, thought, culture, religion, government—everything—arises from subjectivity, from inwardness. Our sole self is the first and last judge of values, including the values of communal life.

> Here I traced briefly the long, gradual millenniary convergence of emphasis on the individual—religion's, government's, art's; and showed how through an historical accident the settling of America, by that "selection of a selection" of European individualists, constituted an acceleration, perhaps a "leap," in the forward movement of this centering of emphasis.

Thoreau does not urge us to live in shacks merely to save money and time; to eschew railroad trains, newspapers, and the postal service; to lay in two sets of washable clothing and a bar of soap; to refuse these jobs which deform our souls between nine and five. These are not ends in themselves. "Simplify, simplify, simplify!" All these are injunctions in order that we may refine our ear to the promptings of our subjective, inward self. The evil of community is that it renders us stupid—and cowardly. *Walden* is a manual of self-reliance so much more profound than Emerson's famous essay that the latter seems to be merely on the level of that advice to melancholics which directs them to take walks and drink a lot of milk.

Thoreau did not merely meditate about the problem of living: he costingly, searchingly exemplified it, and his work rings with the validity of that single-minded commitment. One of the rewards of independence, apparently, is that you are certain that you are the master of your choices, you are not left to doubt whether or not you are free.

Yet there is no air of triumph about the latter end of Thoreau's life. It is difficult to be an American. In some aspects of his life and thought Thoreau is one of our most conspicuous, most outrageous Americans. But the spiritual situation in which these citizens of the New World find themselves is so new, so demanding, and so uncharted, that only by keeping in contact with its total demands can one maintain one's head above the surface. A partial American will drown. Thoreau did not grasp the New-World sense of the innumerability of the human race—nor did Emerson, for all his employment of the word "universal." Thoreau had a parochial, a wood-lot view of nature and her mighty laws. Is there a Thoreau who can tell us that once one has grasped and accepted a basic solitude, all the other gifts come pouring back—love, friendship, and nature? One reads the life story of Thoreau with anxious suspense.

And Abraham Lincoln?
And Melville—and Poe?

Emily Dickinson

by

Thornton Wilder

  Gerard Manley Hopkins wrote to Robert Bridges, "To return to composition for a moment: what I want there to be more intelligible, smoother, and less singular, is an audience." And again: "There is a point with me in matters of any size when I must absolutely have encouragement as much as crops rain; afterwards I am independent." Father Hopkins' verses first reached print twenty-six years after his death.

  Emily Dickinson's closest friends included two men, each of whom, as editor, read hundreds, perhaps thousands, of poems a year with a view toward publication in periodicals; and a third, her mentor Colonel Higginson, was in a position strongly to urge their publication; yet none ventured to publish one of hers. Dr. Holland felt that her verses were "too ethereal," Colonel Higginson that they were too irregular. The Colonel could be very severe; she quotes back to him—with an air of docile gratitude and contrition—some words he had written: "Such being the majesty of the art you presume to practice, you can at least take time before you dishonor it."

  Had she been accorded an audience, would her verses have been "more intelligible, smoother, and less singular"? Not only did she write some two thousand poems, the greater part of which were seen by no other eyes than her own, but she so arranged it that most of these poems—if they were someday to be read by others—would not appear to lay claim to literary evaluation. She left them ostentatiously "unfinished," unready for print. From time to time, she seems to have started upon the task of preparing definitive copies, only to have flagged in the endeavor or to have shrunk from the presumption.

  I find a relation between an aspect of Emily Dickinson's home life as a girl and her practice as a writer. This relation has its parallel in her attitude to literary fame, to the doctrine of personal immortality, and to the greater number of her friends. This recurrent pattern in her thought and behavior can be described as the movement of "five steps forward and two steps back."

So much for the lecture which I delivered in the series and which I shall not attempt to reproduce here. I am of such a nature—being neither scholar, biographer, nor critic–that I cannot listen for long to a discussion of a great poet without being filled with impatience to hear or read one or more of the subject's poems. Great poetry, like comparable painting and music, architecture and drama, cannot be described; in a certain sense it cannot be remembered. It comes into being only when we are confronting it—and confronting it in a state of concentration. In my lecture, then, I took good care to read a number of Emily Dickinson's poems, surrounding each one with moments of silence for self-collection.

It is unsuitable, however, that I present a selection from her poetry here. So, instead of the lecture, I submit a series of reflections which came to me as I prepared for that occasion. They have the character of a progression, for they are based upon a series of questions which I put to myself, and are the answers I assembled to them. I was later to find that many of my students—and not only my students—felt little sympathy for Emily Dickinson's poetry. Some whose opinion I valued dismissed it with faint praise, some with impatience, some with contempt. It is a pleasure to remember, however, that the antipathy of the students never sprang (as it so often did in the case of their elders) from a disapproval of the irregularities in her versification. Young people are seldom moved to dictate to a writer how a poem or book should be written; they regard it—for a few years, alas—as self-evident that every person would wish to do a thing in his own way and that original thought would wear an original dress.

The tone of Emily Dickinson's letters and of many of her poems—where have I heard that before? This effusive affection combined with ostentatious humility; this presentation of the self as a little being easily overlooked, asking only a crumb, yet somehow urging strong egotistical claims; above all, the practice of alluding to great matters, to love and loss and death and God, in elliptical jokes and mannered periphrases—where have we heard that before?

Within the space of one letter to the Hollands (of "Mid-May 1854"), Emily Dickinson manages to say: ". . . if you have not all forgotten us . . . darling friends, for whom I would not count my life too great a sacrifice . . . if you won't forget me . . ."

That is to say, she shall have the honors of love; she shall love most and best; she shall enjoy stoically nourishing an unrequited passion. Mr.

Bowles is going away on a trip; she writes to Mrs. Bowles: "I'll remember you, if you like me to, while Mr. Bowles is gone, and that will stop the lonesome, some, but I cannot agree to stop when he gets home from Washington." Does that not practically dictate an answer on Mrs. Bowles's part, and an effusive one?

In a letter of condolence—and to a clergyman!—on the death of a child, she writes: "I hope Heaven is warm, there are so many barefoot ones." On such great subjects bathos is ever lying in wait for those who are not content to say a thing simply.

We have heard this tone before. It belongs to women who in childhood have received too heavy an impress from their relation to their fathers. It may be called the tone of a misplaced coquetry. Its general character is that of archness. It is perfectly in order (and arises from profound natural springs) when it is exhibited by a young woman as a response to a young man who is showing deep interest in her. It has certainly no place in mature friendship.

It is not difficult to trace the steps of this mental formation. The growing child wishes to get its way; it wishes to be succeeding and (note the word) winning. It tests out the relationships of the family toward this end. There are certain forms of appeal and persuasion that are successful with the father but have no effect whatever on the mother. The growing girl exercises her coquetry (as kittens scratch trees) on every man she meets, but particularly on those whose eyes rest attentively upon her. It is a game in which a girl concedes that she is somewhat attracted but, advancing provocatively and retreating provocatively, refuses to declare the extent. It is played with the most calculated dissimulation, and its enactment between daughter and father is mere harmless dress rehearsal for later encounters—in most cases. From time to time, however, the game has been, as it were, surprised by inappropriate intensities.

Squire Dickinson was a very grim patriarch indeed. Study his photograph. His daughter was to say of him that "his soul was pure and terrible," that "he never learned to play," and to speak of his "lonely life and lonelier death." Yet he was a complex man. Startling is the story that he set the churchbells of Amherst ringing to call the attention of the town to a particularly fine sunset. At Jenny Lind's concert,

> Father sat all evening looking *mad*, and yet so much amused that you [his son] would have *died* a-laughing. . . . it wasn't sarcasm exactly, nor it wasn't disdain, it was infinitely funnier than either of those virtues, as if old Abraham had come to see the show, and thought it was all very well, but a little excess of *monkey*.

The wife of this Abraham seems to have been a nonentity ("I never had a mother") who gradually lapsed into invalidism. Two facts should be sufficient (by the play of opposites) to reveal the extent to which the squire was a strong and frustrated man with a compelling effect upon his children: one, it appears that he had never kissed his son or daughters; and, two, his son was later to dye his blond hair red and later still to wear a red wig, the color of his father's hair.

What was it that Emily Dickinson wished to win from this man? The same thing that he wished to win from her and which he could find nowhere else—love, attentive love, and the sense of one's identity rebounding from some intelligent and admired being. Oh, he watched her, and naturally in his case the watchfulness could chiefly express itself only in rebuke. Of her reading:

> Father was very severe to me. . . . he gave me quite a trimming about "Uncle Tom" and "Charles Dickens" and those "modern literati." . . . we do not have much poetry, Father having made up his mind that it's pretty much all real life. Father's real life and mine sometimes come into collision but as yet escape unhurt.

Of her gardening:

> I got down before Father this morning, and spent a few minutes profitably with the South Sea rose. Father detecting me, advised wiser employments, and read at devotions the chapter of the gentleman with one talent. I think he thought my conscience would adjust the gender.

And she watched him.

Many a patriarchal father has misjudged his role in this game, particularly when he has long since quenched any spontaneous femininity in his wife. (Unquestionable authority is an offense against love, as it is against anything else, and it is ever seeking new territories to overwhelm.) This game can be played by the eyes alone, even in the grimmest face. New England was formerly filled with women whose imaginations had been thus overswayed. Their growth in the affective life had been arrested—some had even been frozen, as by shock or trauma—and they must continue to repeat the mechanisms of that phase forever.

Such I feel to have been Emily Dickinson's story, but Emily Dickinson was a genius—that is to say, was charged with extraordinary resources of the life force which could break through dams and repair ravage. The die, however, had been cast. The forms of speech that are characteristic of a winning child will constantly reappear, the bright remarks that set the dinner table laughing and bring a slight smile even to the most dignified father's face. Above all, the expressions of affection will be drolly indirect: "I'm lonely since you went away, kind of shipwrecked like! Perhaps I miss you!" This infantile note may recur at any moment right up to her death, and it was against this that the reparative force of her genius had to struggle. She has left us a large amount of mature poetry, and it is with something like awe that we can see the operation of genius fashioning great verse even in this tone which elsewhere can so often distress us.

One other aspect of her letters shows us how deeply her affective life had been troubled. Emily Dickinson constantly indulges in the fantasy that her loved ones are dead.

Much has been written about her preoccupation with mortality and graves, and with the promise of a beatific hereafter. Certain authorities have directed us to pay no particular attention to this strain, saying that it did not exceed the measure indulged in by many of her contemporaries. Emily Dickinson, however, was individual in her treatment of other aspects of thought and life—in love and friendship, in the description of nature, in philosophical speculation—and I am prepared to find that both in amount and in kind, her allusions to these matters were also unusual. At all events this recurring vision of her friends as "repealed" is certainly an idiosyncrasy.

Among her first letters to Samuel Bowles, she hopes the family is well: "I hope your cups are full. I hope your vintage is untouched. In such a porcelain life one likes to be sure that all is well lest one stumble upon one's hopes in a pile of broken crockery."

And later, to Mrs. Bowles: "We are all human, Mary, until we are divine, and to some of us that is far off, and to some as near as the lady ringing at the door; perhaps *that's* what alarms."

(There is the old inconsistency of the pietistic convention: it is very alarming that one's friends may at any moment become divine.) There are scores of these anticipated farewells; what is strange and disquieting about them is that Emily Dickinson almost never includes herself among the disappearing. To Mrs. Holland: "I'm so glad you are not a blossom, for those in my garden fade, and then a 'reaper whose name is Death' has come to get a few to help him make a bouquet for himself, so I'm glad you're not a rose . . . ."

And several years later: "Death! Ah! democratic Death! . . . Say, is he everywhere? Where shall I hide my things? Who is alive? The woods are dead. Is Mrs. H. alive? Annie and Katie—are they below, or received to nowhere?"

And to Mrs. Holland twenty-one years later: "God's little Blond Blessing—we have long deemed you, and hope that his so-called 'Will'—will not compel him to revoke you."

She explained this idiosyncrasy to Colonel Higginson (who had gone off to war and received the foreboding message in his camp) saying: "Perhaps death gave me awe for friends, striking sharp and early, for I held them since in brittle love, of more alarm than peace. I trust you may pass the limit of war . . ."; but the explanation is insufficient. No long experience of life is necessary to alert us to the fact that there is an element of latent cruelty in these manifestations. They confirm our sense of how deep a wound she had received.

These are the characteristic expressions of the envious and of those who feel themselves to have been "shut out" from life's major prizes. (I once heard a woman say to another: "What darling little boys you have! We all hope—don't we?—that there'll be none of these dreadful wars fifteen years from now.") One last example: What was Mrs. Holland to make of the following effusion, received at a time when she was occupied with three children and with furthering the career of her husband, who, after long struggles, was beginning to be regarded as one of the most popular writers and lecturers in the country? "How kind of some to die, adding *impatience* to the rapture of our thought of Heaven!" Here she inserts a poem beginning "As by the dead we love to sit," and continues:

> I had rather you lived nearer—I would like to touch you. Pointed attentions from the Angels, to two or three I love, make me sadly jealous.

The inappropriateness here is so great that we may well ask ourselves whether this is love at all or rather a dangerous self-indulgence in purely subjective emotion, perhaps an effort to ignite a real affection within herself—a phenomenon we occasionally find in those whose love has suffered shipwreck or been frozen with fright early in life. That she could and did love maturely we have ample evidence in the poetry, and we turn there to see how she made her escape from this perilous situation.

As a poet, Emily Dickinson started out with two great disadvantages—an enormous facility for versifying and an infatuation with bad models. Later she was to read absorbedly Shakespeare, Milton, Herbert, and the great English poets of her century, and one is aware of the influence they had upon her language, but one is also aware of how little an effect they had upon the verse forms she employed. Her point of departure was the lyric of the keepsake and the Christmas Annual and the newspaper and the genteel periodical—the avocation of clergymen and of ladies of refinement and sensibility. Even the better poets of the hymnbooks do not seem to have greatly influenced her. Although she was to make some startling innovations within this form, it is no less startling that she made no attempts to depart from the half-dozen stanzaic patterns with which she began. I choose to see in this fact an additional illustration of that arrest in her development which we have discovered elsewhere. She was extraordinarily bold in what she did within these patterns (she soon burst their seams), but the form of the poem and to some extent the kind of poem she admired as a girl continued to be the poem she wrote to the end.

She wrote to Colonel Higginson in April 1862 (she was then thirty-one years old): "I made no verse, but one or two, until last winter, sir." So far, very few poems have been, with assurance, dated prior to that time; but it seems to me that she here intended the qualification: no verse of the highest conscious intention. There are numbers of poems of about this time, and certainly early (hence, naturally, the darlings of the anthologists), such as "If I Can Stop One Heart from Breaking" and "I Taste a Liquor Never Brewed" and "To Fight Aloud Is Very Brave," which show evidence of having been preceded by a long experience in versifying. The passage from one stanza to the next is very accomplished indeed, and presupposes an extended practice, in public or in private. It appears certain to me that when, toward 1861, Emily Dickinson collected herself to write verse of the most earnest intention, she had to struggle not only against the pitfalls of a native facility, but against those of a facility already long exercised in a superficial effectiveness—in the easy pathos and in the easy epigram.

Even before she sent the first examples of her work to Colonel Higginson, she had won a critical battle over her facility. She had found the courage to write poetry which "insulted the intelligence" of her contemporaries. What shocked Colonel Higginson was not that she occasionally employed "bad" rhymes (such abounded in the poetry of Mrs. Browning); nor that she substituted assonance for rhyme; nor even that she occasionally failed to rhyme at all (that practice he had accepted in Walt Whitman, whose work he recommended to her reading); but that all these irregularities were combined and deeply embedded in the most conventional of all verse forms.

At this distance we can venture to reconstruct her struggles. A new tide had entered her being; she now wished to say with passion what she had been hitherto saying playfully, saying with coquetry. New intensities—particularly in new countries—called for new forms. A childhood fixation, however, prevented her from abandoning the stanzaic patterns for her early reading. She revolted from the regular rhyme, the eternal "my–die" and God–rod," not because she was too lazy to impose it, but because the regular rhyme seemed the outer expression of an inner conventionality. She called the regular rhyme "prose—they shut me up in prose"—and in the same poem she called it "captivity."

One of her devices shows us how conscious she was of what she was doing. She artfully offers us rhymes of increasing regularity so that our ear will be waiting for another, and then in a concluding verse refuses any rhyme whatever. The poem "Of Tribulation These Are They" gives us "white–designate," "times–palms," "soil–mile," "road–*Saved!*" (The italics are hers.) The effect is as of a ceiling being removed from above our heads. The incommensurable invades the poem. In "I'll Tell Thee All—How Blank It Grew," she flings all the windows open in closing with the words "outvisions paradise," rhymeless after three stanzas of unusually regular rhymes.

Her "teacher" rebuked her for these audacities, but she persisted in them. She did not stoop to explain or defend them. The Colonel's unwillingness to publish the work showed her that he did not consider her a poet, however much he may have been struck by individual phrases. She continued to enclose an occasional poem in her letters to friends, but they seem not to have asked to see "lots of them." The hope of encouragement and the thought of a contemporary audience grew more and more remote. Yet the possibility of a literary fame, of an ultimate glory, never ceased to trouble her. In poem after poem she derided renown; she compared it to an auction and to the croaking of frogs; but at the same time she hailed it as this consecration of the poet's "vital light." What did she do about it? She took five steps forward and two steps back. It is no inconsiderable advance toward literary pretension to write two thousand poems; yet the condition in which she left them is a no less conspicuous retreat. She called on posterity to witness that she was indifferent to its approval, but she did not destroy her work. She did not even destroy the "sweepings of the studio," the tentative sketches at the margin of the table. Had she left fair copies, the movement would have been five steps forward and one step back; had she directed that the work be burned by others, it would have been three steps back.

I am convinced that she went even further in her wish to appear indifferent to our good opinion; she deliberately marred many a poem; she did not so much insult our intelligence as flout it. As we read the more authentic work we are astonished to find that poem after poem concludes with some lapse into banality, or begins flatly and mounts to splendor. No one would claim that she was free of lapses of judgment and of taste, but the last three words of "How Many Times These Low Feet Staggered" are, poetically speaking, of an almost insolent cynicism—the first for flatness, the second for cacophony. "Indolent housewife, in Daisies lain!" or the last verse of "They Put Us Far Apart":

> Not Either—noticed Death—
> Of Paradise—aware—
> Each other's Face—was all the Disc
> Each other's setting—saw—

    That is to say, Emily Dickinson frequently wrote badly on purpose. She did not aspire to your praise and mine, if we were the kind of persons who cannot distinguish the incidental from the essential. She had withdrawn a long way from our human, human, human discriminations and judgments. As we have seen, she was singed, if not scorched, in early life by the all-too-human in her family relationships. Thereafter she was abandoned—"betrayed" she called it—by the person (or, as I prefer to see it, by the succession of persons) whom she loved most. She withdrew from us: into her house; and even in her house she withdrew—the few old friends who came to call were required to converse with her through a half-open door. She became more and more abstract in her view of people. She did not repudiate us entirely, but she increasingly cherished the thought that we would all be more estimable when we were dead. She was capable of envisaging the fact that there may be no life hereafter: "Their Height in Heaven Comforts Not" acknowledges that the whole matter is a "house of supposition . . . that skirts the acres of perhaps." But only such a company, unencumbered with earthly things, would understand what she was saying, and she took ample pains to discourage all others. The poem that begins, "Some work for Immortality, the chiefer part for *Time*" is not primarily about books sold in bookstores. In other words, those who dwell in "immensity" are not finicky literary critics.
    It is very difficult to be certain what Emily Dickinson meant by "God," though there are innumerable references to Him. Her relation to Him is marked by alternating advance and retreat. He is occasionally warned not to be presumptuous, that all the gifts He may have to show hereafter (the single work from which she quotes most often is the Book of Revelations) are not likely to exceed certain occasions of bliss she has known on earth. God, a supreme intelligence, was not a stable concept in her mind.

On the other hand, she lived constantly close to another world she called Infinity, Immensity, Eternity, and the Absolute. For her these concepts were not merely greater in degree from the dimensions of earth: they were different in kind; they were altogether other; they were nonsense. There dwelt her audience. If you set yourself to write verses for people down here on earth, in time, you were bound to miss the tone—the tone that is current in immensity. Immensity does not niggle at off-rhymes and at untidy verse-endings. Immensity is capable of smiling and probably enjoys those things which insult the intelligence of men. Walt Whitman wrote: "I round and finish little, if anything; and could not, consistently with my scheme...." It would be difficult to assemble five of the more mature poems of Emily Dickinson which one could place before an antagonistic reader and say that they were "finished poems." For those two poets, that word "finish" would smack strongly of poems servilely submitted for the approval of judges, princes, and connoisseurs. Art—the work of art—was slow in presenting itself as the project of a continent-conscious American. Hawthorne strove for it, but Hawthorne was not caught up in the realization of the New World's boundlessness; he even averted his face from it, and consciously. Poe's mind knew both the boundlessness and the work of art, and the double knowledge was among the elements that destroyed him. The work of art is the recognition of order, of limits, of shared tacit assumptions and, above all, of agreed-upon conventions. Walt Whitman and Emily Dickinson seemed to be at every moment advancing into new territories in relation to writing; the time for them had not come to consolidate what they had acquired, to establish their limits and to construct their conventions.

I have said before that Americans can find no support for their identity in place, in time, or in community—that they are really in relation only to Everywhere, Always, and Everybody. Emily Dickinson is a signal illustration of this assertion. The imagination of this spinster withdrawn into a few rooms in Amherst was constantly aware that the universe surrounded every detail of life. "I take no less than skies," she wrote, "for earths grow thick as berries, in my native town." Her tireless observation of the animals and plants about her has none of that appropriative feeling that we find in the Concord writers; she knew well that they are living their lives engaging in no tender or instructive dialog with man, and that their lives are part of a millennial chain. She "gives them back" to the universe. In this constant recognition of the immensity of dimensions of time and place, she is the least parochial of American poets and exceeds even Walt Whitman in imaginative sweeps. She could have rejoined Poe in the preoccupations that lay behind his *Eureka*.

And can we say of her that she wrote for Everybody? Yes; for when one has overcome the "low" desire to write for anybody in particular—the cultivated, the chosen souls, one's closest friends, when one has graduated from all desire to impress the judicious or to appeal to the like-minded—then and only then is one released to write for Everybody—only then released from the notion that literature is a specialized activity, an elegant occupation, or a guild secret. For those who live in "immensity" it is merely (and supremely) the human voice at its purest, and it is accessible to Everybody, not at the literary level, but at the human. It is Everybody's fault, not hers, if Everybody is not ready to recognize it. Perhaps only when Everybody is dead will Everybody be in a condition to understand authentic human speech. "Some work for Immortality, the chiefer part for *Time*." In Emily Dickinson we have reached a very high point in American abstraction. (It is characteristic of her that her thought turned often to the Alps and the Andes.) She was, as we have seen in the letters, the least confiding of women, the shut-in, the self-concealing; yet if the audience were large enough, if she were certain that Everybody would attend, her lips could unlock to floods of impassioned confession and uninhibited assertion.

The problem of the American loneliness which we discussed in relation to Thoreau is the problem of "belonging." He was a lonely man because the elements to which he tried to belong were near and few; Emily Dickinson, in all appearance the loneliest of beings, solved the problem in a way which is of importance to every American: by loving the particular while living in the universal.

The Creative Use of Language by Some of America's Great Writers

by

Christy MacKaye Barnes

There is something in the language of the best American writers of the nineteenth century not to be found in the great English authors of the same period: a tone, an undercurrent of power, motion, and of naïve, bold directness partly born out of the continent's geography—its endless, surf-washed shorelines as in Whitman and Melville, its cheerful, rocky-brook-fed valleys as in Thoreau, or in the unfelled forests where the King James version of the Bible was stamped to more than the usual depths into the lonely hearts of pioneers as in Abraham Lincoln.

Other influences came to them fresh across the Atlantic and were welcomed with open arms: the voice of Goethe from Germany and Carlyle from Scotland. It opened their impressionable minds and senses to new depths of observation and understanding of spirit, introducing them to new living communions and metamorphoses.

Ralph Waldo Emerson

With what a firm, sure-footed pace Emerson sets down the heels of his words in such aphorisms as:

Trust thyself: every heart vibrates to that iron string.

Whoso would be a man must be a nonconformist.

A foolish consistency is the hobgoblin of little minds.

Rudolf Steiner tells us that Emerson permeated his thoughts with his own activity to such a degree that in them was no trace of the negative force of "double" that also haunts the minds of our Western world. Emerson's thoughts have the clear, cold purity of glacial ice that can catch and magnify beams of sunlight to dazzling brilliance. Just so his words can create shafts of insight that strike fire in the human heart.

Henry David Thoreau

Thoreau, Emerson's friend and counterpart, viewed the universe from one small plot of countryside in Concord, Massachusetts, where he lived his entire life, yet through his *Civil Disobedience* his influence rayed out to Tolstoi and Gandhi, and down the halls of time to Martin Luther King, even to the great nonviolent protests in Eastern Europe. His townsmen, however, paid him small heed, and his words proclaiming nonviolent disobedience to the State were not even published till quite a while after his death.

His language can be like a New England brook through the bubbling waters of which we discern the forms of nature's most secret and powerful wisdom and man's awakening aspirations. His work was in the spirit laboratory of Nature. His book, *Walden*, is filled with such wisdom as the following:

> There is nothing inorganic. . . . The earth is not a mere fragment of dead history like the leaves of a book . . . but living poetry like the leaves of a tree which precede flowers and fruit—not a fossil earth, but a living earth . . . the Maker of this earth but patented a leaf. . . . The coming in of spring is like the creation of Cosmos out of Chaos and the realization of the Golden Age.

Or we find such passages as the following:

> Morning is when I awake and there is a dawn in me. Moral reform is the effort to throw off sleep. . . . The millions are awake enough for physical labor; but only one in a million is awake enough for effective intellectual exertion; only one in a hundred million to a poetic or divine life. To be awake is to be alive. We must learn to reawaken and keep ourselves awake, not by mechanical means, but by an infinite expectation of the dawn. . . . I know of no more encouraging fact than the unquestionable ability of man to elevate his life by a conscious endeavor. It is something to be able to paint a particular picture, or to carve a statue . . . but it is far more glorious

to carve and paint the very atmosphere through which we look, which morally we can do. To affect the quality of the day, that is the highest of arts.

Or he could advise: "Build your castles in the air. That is where they belong. Now build the foundations under them!"

However Thoreau is a man of many and of universal dimensions. His style can change to the scathing sharpness of a whiplash when he exposes the unlawfulness of many man-made laws as he does in his *Civil Disobedience* and in *Slavery in Massachusetts*.

> If a law requires you to be the agent of injustice to another then I say, break the law.
> The mass of men serve the state, not as men mainly but as machines, with their bodies. . . . Such command no more respect than men of straw or a lump of dirt. They have the same sort of worth as horses and dogs. . . . As they rarely make any moral distinctions, they are as likely to serve the Devil as God.

Herman Melville

In Melville's and Whitman's language one can hear the voice of the ocean. In Melville, it is the sea-storms that tossed the whaling ships on which he spent some years of his youth. Nowhere else in the English language can one hear such bold cataclysms, such dramatic torrents of language. One can hear it in the sermon spoken by a retired sea captain as he preaches to his flock of seamen from his pulpit on dry land.

> As we have seen, God came upon Jonah in the whale and swallowed him down to living gulfs of doom, and with swift slantings tore him along into the midst of the seas where the eddying depths sucked him ten thousand fathoms down and the weeds were wrapped about his head, and all the watery world of woe bowled over him.
> Yet even then, beyond the reach of any plummet—out of the belly of hell—when the whale grounded upon the ocean's utmost bones, even then, God heard the engulfed, repenting prophet when he cried.
> Then God spake unto the fish; and from the shuddering cold and blackness of the sea the whale came breaching up towards the

warm and pleasant sun and all the delights of air and earth; and "vomited out Jonah on the dry land;" when the word of the Lord came a second time; and Jonah, bruised and beaten—his ears like two sea-shells, still multitudinously murmuring of the ocean—Jonah did the Almighty's bidding. And what was that, shipmates? To preach the Truth to the face of Falsehood! That was it!

Or again you can witness Melville's superb mastery of alliteration when he captures the sea's great, calm, rippling silences of a moonlit night in the following passage, which ends with the cry of a sailor aboard a whaling ship when he sights the white uprushing gush of the spray the whale blows high into the air with, "Thar she blows!"

> It was while gliding through these latter waters that one serene and moonlight night, when all the waves rolled by like scrolls of silver; and, by their soft, suffusing seethings, made what seemed a silvery silence, not a solitude; on such a silent night a silvery jet was seen far in advance of the white bubbles at the bow, lit up by the moon, it looked celestial; seemed some plumed and glittering god uprising from the sea.
> Fedallah first described this jet . . . his turban and the moon companions in one sky. But when, after several successive nights without uttering a single sound, when after all this silence, his unearthly voice was heard announcing that silvery, moon-lit jet, every reclining mariner started to his feet and hailed the mortal crew, "Thar she blows!"

In his most dramatic passages, as in the concluding chapters of his book, he magnifies the intensity of adjectives, and with them the whole drama of his description, by turning them into adverbs. Here are a few instances of these. (Italics added)

> For an instant the whale's whole marbleized body formed a high arch, like Virginia's Natural Bridge, and *warningly* waving his bannered flukes in the air, the grand god revealed himself, sounded, and went out of sight. *Hoveringly* halting, and dipping on the wing, the white sea-fowls *longingly* lingered in the agitated pool that he left.

Ahab could discover no sign in the sea. But suddenly as he peered down and down into its depths, he *profoundly* saw a white living spot . . . uprising and magnifying as it rose.

Moby Dick, with the malicious intelligence ascribed to him, *sidelingly* transplanted himself, as it were, in an instant, shooting his pleated head lengthwise beneath the boat . . . lying on his back, in the manner of a biting shark, slowly and *feelingly* taking its bows full with his mouth.

Ripplingly withdrawing from his prey, Moby Dick now lay at a distance . . . when his vast wrinkled forehead rose some twenty or more feet out of the water.

For so *revolvingly* appalling was the White Whale's aspect, and so *planetarily* swift that the ever-contracting circles he made, that he seemed *horizontally* to be swooping upon them.

Walt Whitman

Whitman takes up the large, universal rhythms of the sea as seen from the shore, its vastness disappearing into the horizon, its great pulse of ebb and flow varying, but always giving witness of the never-ceasing life of the planet. The long lines of his poems, built often of countless namings and citations, widen our vision to cosmic distances, and lists of details weave for us a mood that bemuses and calms the soul. I imagine him chanting his poems as he creates them beside the waves of the Atlantic. Their rhythms do not have the usual regularity of poetic lines, but rather swell and diminished with the fluidity and force of the ocean itself, a happening in Nature he sees repeated in the realm of the human soul in such a way that it may suggest to us a like gesture in a still vaster world as in:

A NOISELESS, PATIENT SPIDER
A noiseless, patient spider,
I mark'd, where on a little promontory, it stood, isolated;
Mark'd how, to explore the vacant, vast surrounding,
It launch'd forth filament, filament, filament, out of itself;
Ever unreeling them—ever tirelessly speeding them.

And you, O my soul, you stand,
Surrounded, surrounded, in measureless oceans of space.
Ceaselessly musing, venturing throwing,—seeking the spheres, to connect them;

Till the bridge you will need, be form'd—till the ductile anchor hold;
Till the gossamer thread you fling, catch somewhere, O my Soul.

Whitman makes frequent use of personification and apostrophe in a way that lets the experience of "cool-enfolding Death" be permeated with serenity and joyous welcome.

DEATH CAROL

Come, lovely and soothing Death,
Undulate round the world, serenely arriving, arriving,
In the day, in the night, to all, to each,
Sooner or later, delicate Death.

Praised be the fathomless universe,
For life and joy, and for objects curious;
And for love, sweet love—But praise! praise! praise!
For the sure-enwinding arms of cool-enfolding Death.

• • •

Approach, strong Deliveress!
When it is so—when thou hast taken them, I joyously sing the dead,
Lost in the loving, floating ocean of thee,
Laved in the flood of thy bliss, O Death.

• • •

The night in silence, under many a star,
The ocean's shore, and the husky whispering wave, whose voice I know;
And the soul turning to thee, O vast and well-veiled Death.
And the body gratefully nestling close to thee.
Over the tree-tops I float thee a song!
Over the rising and sinking waves—over the myriad fields, and the prairies wide;
Over the dense-pack'd cities all, and the teeming wharves and ways,
I float this carol with joy, with joy to thee, O Death!

From SONG OF MYSELF

I celebrate myself, and see myself,
And what I assume you shall assume, for every atom belonging to me as good belongs to you.

I loaf and invite my soul,
I lean and loaf at my ease observing a spear of summer grass.
I have said that the soul is not more than the body,
And I have said that the body is not more than the soul,
And nothing, not God, is greater to one than one's self is,
And whoever walks a furlong without sympathy walks to his
        own funeral drest in his shroud,
And I or you pocketless of a dime may purchase the pick of the
        earth,
And to glance with an eye or show a bean in its pod confound
        the learning of all times,
And there is no trade or employment but the young man
        following it may become a hero,
And there is no object so soft but it makes a hub for the wheel'd
        universe,
And I say to any man or woman, Let your soul stand cool and
        composed before a million universes.

From PASSAGE TO INDIA

Passage to more than India!
O secret of the earth and sky!
Of you, O waters of the sea! O winding creeks and rivers! . . .
O sun and moon, and all you stars! Sirius and Jupiter!
Passage to you!

Passage—immediate passage! the blood burns in my veins!
Away, O soul! hoist instantly the anchor! . . .
Sail forth! Steer for the deep waters only!
Reckless, O soul, exploring, I with thee, and thou with me!
For we are bound where mariner has not yet dared to go.
And we will risk the ship, ourselves and all.

O my brave soul!
O farther, farther sail!
O daring joy, but safe! Are they not all the seas of God?
O farther, farther, farther sail!

Carl Sandburg

Despite the fact that Sandburg writes in the twentieth century, I would like to cite two of his poems because he reminds me of Whitman, although he does not have the older poet's vast sweep of words or vision. I include the first poem for its marvelous interplay of irregular rhymings, assonances and repetitions, and the second for its blunt power coupled with great simplicity and economy of words and poetic devices.

COOL TOMBS

When Abraham Lincoln was shoveled into the tombs, he forgot
    the copperheads and the assassins . . . in the dust, in the
    cool tombs.

And Ulysses Grant lost all thought of con men and Wall Street
    cash and collateral turned ashes . . . in the dust, in the
    cool tombs.

Pocahontas' body, lovely as a polar, sweet as a red haw in
    November
    or a pawpaw in May, did she wonder? does she
    remember? . . . in the dust, in the cool tombs?

Take any streetful of people buying clothes and groceries,
    cheering a hero or throwing confetti and blowing tin horns
    . . . tell me if the lovers are losers tell me if any get
    more than the lovers . . . in the dust . . . in the cool tombs.

GRASS

Pile the bodies high at Austerlitz and Waterloo,
Shovel them under and let me work–
I am the grass; I cover all.

And pile them high at Gettysburg
And pile them high at Ypres and Verdun.
Shovel them under and let me work.
Two years, ten years, and passengers ask the conductor:
What place is this?
Where are we now?

I am the grass.
Let me work.

Abraham Lincoln

The rhythms and pacings of the phrases in Lincoln's *Gettysburg Address* and in the last paragraph of *The Second Inaugural Address*, the repetitions and restraints—never overwording or dwelling on sentiment—produce in his listeners a throb of the heart, the very stuff itself of selfless dedication which the mere meaning of the word can only coolly convey—a silence that thunders.

THE GETTYSBURG ADDRESS

Four score and seven years ago our fathers brought forth on this continent, a new nation, conceived in Liberty, and dedicated to the proposition that all men are created equal.

Now we are engaged in a great civil war, testing whether that nation, or any nation so conceived and so dedicated, can long endure. We are met on a great battlefield of that war. We have come to dedicate a portion of that field, as a final resting place for those who here gave their lives that that nation might live. It is altogether fitting and proper that we should do this.

But, in a larger sense, we cannot dedicate—we can not consecrate—we can not hallow—this ground. The brave men, living and dead, who struggled here, have consecrated it, far above our poor power to add or detract. The world will little note, nor long remember what we say here, but it can never forget what they did here. It is for us the living, rather, to be dedicated here to the unfinished work which they who fought here have thus far so nobly advanced. It is rather for us to be here dedicated to the great task remaining before us—that from these honored dead we take increased devotion to that cause for which they gave the last full measure of devotion—that we here highly resolve that these dead shall not have died in vain—that this nation, under God, shall have a new birth of freedom—and that government of the people, by the people, for the people, shall not perish from the earth.

THE SECOND INAUGURAL ADDRESS, last paragraph

With malice toward none; with charity for all; with firmness in the right, as God gives us to see the right, let us strive on to finish the work we are in; to bind up the nation's wounds; to care for him who shall have borne the battle, and for his widow, and his orphan—to do all which may achieve and cherish a just and lasting peace among ourselves, and with all nations.

The Thief Who Kindly Spoke

by

Michael Miller

We are hidden in ourselves, like a truth hidden in isolated facts. When we know that this One in us is One in all, then our truth is revealed.
— Upanishad

To understand Bob Dylan's lyrics it is often necessary to listen with the ears of a child, the child you were before you were blitzed by the accumulated trash of an epoch. The mystery-charged picture-language Dylan has created in his songs is a first cousin to the wisdom language that has carried fairy tales down from the lost beginnings of time to the present. It is a language, for the most part, of pictures that correspond to inner psychic events. It is not comprehensible save through imaginative feeling and rigorously honest introspection.

Dylan released the album *John Wesley Harding* in 1968 after nearly two years of public silence following his motorcycle accident. Its quiet tone, besides marking a shift in the direction of Dylan's own music, was in sharp contrast to the wild experimentation that characterized popular music at that moment. Indeed, there seemed then to have been a dramatic competition going on among the big names in rock and roll to outdo each other with outrageous musical inventions. With *John Wesley Harding* it was as if Dylan signaled that he was not a part of all that. The comparatively softer and slower music of Dylan's album was soundly traditional. But the lyrics, subtle and mystical, were poetic creations that soared high above the fashions of the popular music scene.

One of the songs on this album, "All along the Watchtower," is a particularly good song with which to begin our exploration of Dylan's work.

Jimi Hendrix did a heavy-rock rendition of it, making it perhaps the best known and most widely-heard song from the *John Wesley Harding* album. The song itself has the advantage of being short, a mere twelve lines. Even so, it is an extremely powerful example of Dylan's mystery-language. But there is yet an even more important aspect to the song that recommends it as a good place to begin. For this song contains an essential insight into the unmanifested dimensions of man's being which is part and parcel of Dylan's spiritual perceptions. A clear understanding of this song will go a long way toward helping us unravel some of the many riddles that are set in Dylan's lyrics like so many jewels in a tiara.

Before getting into the song itself, however, I would like to make a few general observations about the song and about Dylan's method. The song is composed in four stanzas: two quatrains followed by two couplets. The first two stanzas relate a brief dialogue; then the third and fourth stanzas move on to paint a single picture viewed from a double-layered perspective. In this song, as with so many of his songs, Dylan has interwoven the obvious with the not-so-obvious in such an artful way that individual spiritual activity is demanded of the audience in order to penetrate the song's meaning.

By spiritual activity I mean not just listening or even thinking, but meditation. If it is realized that this song is the product of an honest and inner, and even prayerful, questing for personal yet universal truth, it will not seem surprising that this song requires an equally sincere and honest response from the whole man, from the inner as well as the outer self of the listener, before it will yield up its full import. As a built-in barrier, this requirement serves as something more than a mere defense: it invites spiritual communion.

Dylan could easily be accused, as he often is, of merely playing a clever game of intellectual mystification if all he intended to communicate was information wrapped in attitude. But what he is really offering is an experience of intuitive insight. "All along the Watchtower" is so constructed that a meditative listener is led gradually toward the experience of a particular intuition. When the listener thus "discovers" the meaning lighting up within himself, he has all the "proof" he needs of its truth. Argumentation is then beside the point. And in the process, the listener has become something more than he was before, both by virtue of experiencing this intuition coming out of himself and by virtue of having exercised his capacity for free spiritual activity in attaining it.

Now to the song itself. It begins thus:

"There must be some way out of here," said the joker to the thief.
"There's too much confusion, I can't get no relief."

Who has not reacted to life at some point or other with this same desperate cry, which the joker here wails to the thief? This opening immediately draws our attention to the frequently felt exasperation we have all known and experienced whenever we have felt trapped by the circumstances of our lives. But Dylan, the artist, by not stating explicitly who these two are, this "joker" and this "thief," subtly invites his audience inward to ponder over their identities. And, until we come to identify these two, the full meaning of this song and this dialogue necessarily remain hidden on the far side of a riddle.

The joker's lament, continuing in the next two lines, suggests the basic injustice inherent in the joker's situation:

"Businessmen, they drink my wine, plowmen dig my earth,
None of them along the line knows what any of it is worth."

We are all aware that we are alive here on this earth and that the burdens put on us by the business world and by the practical demands of life are using up this time of our time of living, repeatedly disrupting our equilibrium. And yet, none of the agents of those forces seems to have a clue about what any of it is worth. As this dialogue continues in the next stanza, the thief responds with an acknowledgment of the validity of the joker's observation. But he adds, by way of a challenge, the cautionary reminder that they, the joker and the thief, have now moved beyond the point of taking life as a joke. This gentle reminder is a first indication of the intimate nature of this dialogue. The thief, by making it plain that time is running out for them, intensifies the urgency of their conversation:

"No reason to get excited," the thief he kindly spoke.
"There are many here among us who feel that life is but a joke.
But you and I, we've been through that, and this is not our fate,
So let us not talk falsely now, the hour is getting late."

Either you feel that life is but a joke or you do not, the thief seems to suggest. If you are no longer satisfied with the notion that life is but a joke, and if, as well, you are keenly aware that the time of your time is running out, then you will feel the need to seek the truth now as an urgent impulse in your life. Let businessmen and plowmen do whatever they must do, and let others go on living without settling this matter for themselves, but this is not our fate. Now is not the time for speaking falsely, especially to yourself.

If you meditate on this song, you will realize that this dialogue is of a very intimate nature. Indeed, this conversation between the joker and the thief is one that takes place in some form or other within the deep recesses of every man's being, in the conscience. With the joker side of the self we are prone to think that we do not really know what's going on in life and that life is somehow unfair to us. We are apt to complain and feel sorry for ourselves. The joker in short, is the wild card; he/she can be anyone; he/she is the ordinary ego experiencing itself in isolation. The thief, on the other hand, is the darker, more mysterious side of the self. He is an "outlaw" in the Dylan sense: "to live outside the law you must be honest." And it is this thief speaking as the still, small voice of conscience, who speaks "kindly," robbing the ego of its cherished illusion.

The joker is the ego of illusion. He does not penetrate to the spiritual depths where unity is experienced. The joker, wanting to be the highest card in the deck, does not understand that he can only temporarily borrow that designation which the ace—mysteriously the highest and the lowest simultaneously—possesses as a primary quality. And even for it to be possible for the joker to act as an "ace," the real ace must first exist. Nor can the joker become a "little ace" without at the same time assuming that uncanny unity of highest and lowest. But this assumption requires the most intense humility possible on the part of the joker. For only when the joker surrenders himself, perhaps from having heard the kindly spoken words of the thief, can he function as an ace. In any case, the power of the Ace becomes present only when the joker as joker evaporates from view. But the natural tendency of the joker is to take life as a joke and to play frivolously with his own great, though temporary, potential in the game of life. Most often, he would be a knave or a deuce for the sake of simply winning a hand. Next time around he may be completely worthless.

But enough of this abstract punning. The point is that there are two sides to the self for which Dylan has found intriguingly appropriate names. The joker represents that aspect of the self that is intellectually conscious of itself in its separateness from all else. The thief on the other hand represents that aspect of the self that is spiritually conscious of itself within the unity of the Great All. These two, the joker and the thief, are at odds with each other. The joker as the ordinary worldly ego eats of the tree of knowledge and is therefore lousy with words. The thief hiding out in the cave of the soul eats of the tree of life and knows that which can hardly be spoken because it is an element of the very Word itself. The still, small voice of the conscience is the voice of the thief, speaking softly and "kindly." It gives expression to what is often beyond the capacity of facile speech.

In fact, this thief is like a little Christ within us. And like Christ who, as Dylan would put it in a later song "died a criminal's death," this thief comes from a place beyond the letter of the law, from the spirit, and he goes beyond the evidence of the senses to the substance of things unseen. It is with this thief side of our being that we know intuitively that life is not a joke and that we had better not try to kid ourselves because death is coming.

The dialogue recorded in the first two stanzas of "All along the Watchtower" is thus a picture of a primary conflict that persecutes every soul struggling with the question of its reality. This conflict is no small matter to be settled intellectually after a moment's thought. It surges continually in the subterranean reaches of the soul, calling for a commitment that can only be made with the whole of our being. Dylan accurately portrays the fine balance of this inner agony when he cites a certain validity to the ego's point of view:

> Businessmen, they drink my wine, plowmen dig my earth,
> None of them along the line knows what any of it is worth.

It is true, of course, that we are all victimized and sold short by the ways of the world. Yet we also sell ourselves short, and others as well, until we come to realize the crucial fact that life is not a joke. Once we have heard this kindly spoken message of the thief, we can then move on to develop this faculty as a living connection with our own deep reality, which extends far beyond anything the joker is able to understand. Our conscience becomes, so to speak, our connection with that vast dark region which is the unknown depths of being. Hiding away in those depths is the thief, our conscience, seeking to rob us of our illusory and egocentric possessions, our "capital."

Dylan first gives us this picture of a primary conflict raging in the soul. Then in the last two stanzas, he throws light on it from two different angles, which allows us to consider it from two contrasting perspectives. In the third, or penultimate, stanza, Dylan floods the picture of this conflict with the light from spiritual heights, while with the final stanza, he reveals the inner experience of the soul down below:

> All along the watchtower, princes kept the view
> While all the women came and went, barefoot servants, too.

Outside in the distance a wildcat did growl,
Two riders were approaching, the wind began to howl.

In Dylan's poetic language, "women" and the female gender in general symbolize the soul, while the male gender symbolizes the ego. This symbology, it may be noted, has a long history in lyric poetry, reaching back at least as far as the troubadours of medieval times, as well as the Sufi poets who were their predecessors.

The "princes" who keep the view are egos who have been crowned with spiritual vision. Looking down upon the world from their ethereal and eternal vantage point, they watch the souls coming and going, even those without shoes—which is to say, those without anything to cushion the shocks of their walk upon the path, those who must meet the rude earth with their naked "soles." Down below, however, the inner reality experienced by the soul whose ego has not yet been crowned is that outside, somewhere, a beast is growling, and that inside the wind (the spirit) is howling. All the while, there are two riders relentlessly approaching.

This is precisely our situation: Caught between the certain confusion that torments the uncrowned ego and the dark uncertainties of the soul, we see two riders advancing on us. To go with the ego, the joker, is to reduce life to a joke. But to go with the thief means opening up to the unknown, a realm which, being beyond the capacity of the ordinary ego, requires faith. The choice is always and ever ours to make, but the moment of decision is made difficult by the ever-present growling of the beast and the howling wind.

How much time do we have? Individually, three score years and ten, seventy years on the average. Some a little more, some less. It is very little compared to the millions of years humans have inhabited the earth. It is nothing within the vast stretches of time encompassing the stars. If our existence were limited to three score years and ten, we could hardly say we exist at all. Such a paltry existence would be meaningless except within the context of some larger spiritual life.

Standing here, we look to the future: death. When we consider that mysterious black hole in the future, we are naturally afraid for ourselves. Out of this fearful egotism, many become religious in the hope of immortality. But eternal life is beyond time—there before birth as well as after death (and like the blind spot in the eye, present with every passing moment). If we but turn around to examine the miracle of birth for evidence of the eternal, it becomes possible to rise above the egotistic concern for immortality, free of the fear that darkens our days. This is what Emerson did and is why he could write, "Infancy is the perpetual messiah, which comes into the arms of fallen men and pleads with them to return to paradise."

The miracle of birth and the mysterious unfolding of personality in childhood, when we view it without the restrictive limitations of contemporary science, can confirm us in a spiritual life beyond the gates of time. Although the contemplation of death might make us "religious" out of fear, the contemplation of birth can give us a sense of the eternal, which can release from that fear. And unless we can get free of that egotistical fear, we cannot experience the free spiritual atmosphere in which love becomes possible.

In early childhood we see the soul before its fall into egohood. The child acts as though the whole world were his because, living in the afterglow of spiritual unity, he experiences the world as himself. Gradually he begins to differentiate himself functionally as an individual, on the basis of his immediate body experience, until at last he begins to refer to himself as "I," usually at about the age of three. His memories of experiences in the world then begin to adhere to and form themselves around this "I" to become eventually his ordinary ego, socially identified by his given name. His pre-earthly soul life and its unselfconscious after-image in the first few years of life recede like a setting sun. At the same time his ordinary, earthly ego rises—like the moon, its cosmic symbol—into the night sky of earthbound consciousness.

And God said, "Let us make man in our image, after our likeness."

How is man the image of the Great All, in whom we live and move and have our being? Our bodies, being of the earth, are like the earth. The ego circling overhead first waxes and then wanes from youth to advanced age. And like the moon, this ego is no true light of itself, but a reflection of the true light, which shines from the other side, the spiritual side, of the body. The soul, being solar, abides with the spiritual sun, asleep in eternity, in dreaming life.

"We are such stuff as dreams are made of," Shakespeare wrote. In the night sky of earthbound consciousness we gaze upon our moon-egos and dream our lives until we experience what mystics have called "seeing the sun at midnight." But even while we are asleep in the dream of our individual lives, we are all one in the light of the spirit, even as the light from separate candles in a dark room merges to form one light.

The light shone in the darkness; and the darkness comprehended it not. The ordinary ego cannot comprehend the mystical fact that its life, its light, is from above unless it consults with its dark side and there hears the voice of the thief, the conscience. The conscience, on the dark side of the self, is our soul-life in the shadow created by the ego, and our faculty, however faintly developed, for knowing in concert with the spirit above.

To "see the sun at midnight" requires faith. And faith, as it is written, comes by hearing. The joker remains merely a joker till he begins to hear the thief. Perhaps this inner dialogue has something in common with Saint Paul's words to the Philippians, "For our conversation is in heaven; from whence also we look for the Savior, the Lord Jesus Christ."

Mary Oliver, Inspired Teacher

by

Jeanne Simon-Macdonald

  Mary Oliver's poetry is profound and startling communication. She speaks directly to her reader in a language simple to understand. It flows out of her way of life and out of her enthusiasm for life. Her writing inspires us to live more passionately.

  She is often considered a nature poet. But she is more than that. She communes with the world around her—forgetting herself in complete absorption. She enters into that vital and sometimes terrifying, amoral world of nature. She braves the night wilderness and the damp and chill of sleeping on bare ground, to experience directly, in tactile immediacy. And she braves the inner darknesses as well. She is never just an observer, but she engages with her questioning and her human responses. Her poems create a world which is neither inner nor outer, but which focuses deep human experiencing. She has the rare capacity of being awake in the moment, in all its immediacy and drama or its tenderness. She cares that we wake up to each moment too and is not averse to admonishing us to do so!

  She is a crafter of poems. Her great-grandfather was a carpenter. As he knew how to place a nail or plane a surface, so she places a comma or a dash and shortens or lengthens a line. She has studied and worked her profession. She is a craftswoman par excellence. She has written two fascinating books on prosody, without one dry concept. Rhythms and breath and sounds are her beloved tools. She figures it takes about seventy hours to create one poem! And her poems are rarely longer than two pages. That is three whole days and nights spent in communicating one short piece. Is this self-indulgent nonsense?

Or is this, in the last instance, what life really is about? Are we not here on earth to have the opportunity to perceive, to smell or touch? Is not the world recreated and known through our human experiencing—and in no other way? Is this not what we wish our poets to lead us to?

> From a low hill in the Ahti plains of East Africa I once watched the vast herds of wild animals grazing in soundless stillness, as they had done from time immemorial, as if I were the first man, the first creature, to know that all this is. The entire world around me was still in its primeval state; it did not know that it was. And then, in that one moment in which I came to know, the world sprang into being; without that moment it would never have been. All nature seeks this goal and finds it fulfilled in man, but only in the most highly developed and most fully conscious man.[1]

Mary Oliver is a poet of this vocation. Her whole being seems devoted to speaking to us so that we too might awaken to the world around and within us, becoming fully conscious human beings. Her language surprises us, her images resonate in us, and through it all her intention seems so pure. She does not entice us with beauty. Her writing is never cryptic or elitist. She writes for us with great wisdom, as a kind of dear guide and teacher, with a truly unsentimental compassion for all life.

To read the work of Mary Oliver, it may be best to begin with *New and Selected Poems*, Beacon Press, 1992. She made the choice of poems herself from her earlier books. There are two books on prosody, as well as several more recent books of prose and poems: *Blue Pastures, White Pine, West Wing,* and *Winter Hours*.

> 1. Jung, Carl. *Psychological Reflections*. Princeton: Princeton University Press, 1974.

To Each Her Honey

by

Lara Wulsin

  Mary Oliver's poetry tends to focus on a being or a scene in nature into which she breathes human sentiments. Three of her poems, "Happiness," "The Turtle," and "Milkweed," portray both women in nature and the nature of women, their suffering, and their overcoming. The three different images depicted in these poems each seem to capture some aspect of life of a feminine being in nature that seems hard or painful to the onlooker. And yet in each case there is a redeeming attitude, shared by the subjects of all three poems, that the challenging parts of life are no less important or expected than the pleasurable parts.

  "Happiness" is a blithe description of a she-bear's affair with an enclave of honey. The first five lines depict the bear's hunt for the honey, her treasure. These first lines, all trimeter, do not yet yield a clear mental picture of this bear. They do, however, give a feel for the treasure. The many long "*e*" sounds in lines 3, 4, and 5 all appear in key words, such as "sweetness," "honey," "bees," "trees." These words and sounds evoke what the she-bear is searching for. Line 6 breaks the trimeter, and for the first time appears an image of this "black block of gloom," the bear. These words linger on the tongue, enhancing her slow, dark, large figure. "Shuffled" in line 7 adds movement to the "black block of gloom," while "tree after tree" emphasizes the determination of the bear to attain her goal.

  Finally, in the following line, she finds her "honey-house deep as heartwood." The alliteration of the "*h*"s in this delicious phrase only make the honey more golden, deeper, sweeter. In lines 11 and 12, the trimeter is again broken by the she-bear fearlessly plunging in among the "swarming bees," while she "lipped and tongued and scooped out in her black nails" the honey, her precious treasure. The lilting consonants of this line help one to savor the wild ecstasy this image evokes.

As the she-bear finishes her feast in line 14, the two uses of the word "maybe" introduce the new state of the bear: "a little drunk" and "sticky," as she "hum[s] and sway[s]." Over the next few lines appear many short "u" sounds: "drunk," "rugs," "hum," "honeyed muzzle," which help to make the connection between honey and drunkenness. In lines 18 through 21 lies the beautiful, sweet image of this huge, dark, massive animal lifting her sticky muzzle and big furry arms upwards "as though she would fly." Reeling from her honey experience, she can leave the weight of her burdensome body beneath her, and can even become "an enormous bee." Here, beginning with line 21, three lines of bi-meter enter into this fantasy. Again recur the "e" sounds in "bee" and "sweetness" that appear in the first lines of the poem. This time, our she-bear is not searching for them, she *is* them.

The poem finishes amidst fields of flowers, in the lofty and intoxicated imagination of the bear. "Flower to flower" and "day after shining day" express the timeless eternity of the fantasy, therefore the unreality of the picture. I think that many women could identify with this touching image of the bear escaping from her physical body, while at the same time sucking at the very juices of life.

With "The Turtle," Oliver evokes the life of a turtle as she lays her eggs. The three strong "b"s in the first line already suggest the power and strength of this turtle as she "breaks" from the water. The abundance of "s" sounds in lines 3 and 4 help us to slide with the turtle "across the shallows and through the rushes." In lines 7, 8, and 9, the hard consonant sounds support the rough, coarse action of digging a nest, then "spewing" eggs into it. Line 10 is the first time Oliver leaves the picture of the turtle with the words "you think," which are then followed by the first line break.

Human qualities are now given to the turtle— ideal qualities: patience, fortitude, and determination. First Oliver expresses her wonder and appreciation for this female, who strives to complete her task without complaint or questioning. She then realizes that the turtle does not even think about what she is doing, for she is only playing her part in the order of nature, which proceeds unconditionally. Many "w"s and short "i"s appear in lines 16 through 20: "filled," "with," "wish," "wind." These sounds, so reminiscent of breath, emphasize that this duty of laying eggs is no more of an effort for her than breathing itself. The soft "s" sounds in line 21 are comforting, whereas "apart," "rest," and "world" introduce harshness, like the thought of the turtle being separate from the world around her.

"Every spring," (line 24) with its shortness, reconcentrates once again on the turtle, "crawling" steadily. "She does not dream" under the load of sand packed against her; she does not long for anything different or easier. The four lines and the rhyme of the last stanza echo the order that "she knows." The alliteration in lines 29 and 30 lends to the harmony of the image of her pond, her trees, her birds, all tied together. The four rhyming words: "lives in," "children," "swim," and "string" seem to symbolize this turtle's life; her surroundings, her fellow creatures, her daily activity, and the bond between all in nature, which is so important to the turtle's existence.

In "Milkweed," Oliver steps into the world of the plant as she describes a stand of old, dried-out milkweed, and compares it to "a country of dry women." In line 3 the wind toys with the "flat leaves" of the milkweed, lifting and dropping them, displaying the powerlessness of the milkweed/ women in relation to greater forces, in this case the wind. The statement in line 4 that "this is not kind" is blunt, contrasting with the longer sounds that follow: "retain," "certain," "crisp," "glamour." These longer sounds support the image that though these feminine beings have little control over their condition, they stand firmly and dignified.

The next four lines reveal the milkweed full, healthy, and in its youth, like women: "young," "delicate," "frightened," "yet capable of a certain amount of rough joy." The consonant sounds in line 8 emphasize "rough[ness]," yet the anapest of the line also gives it rhythm and a lilt, possibly reminiscent of dancing, of laughing, of men.

Line 9 breaks the reflective revelry as Oliver addresses some person, using a long stream of wishful alliterative "w"s. To whom is she speaking? Could it be her mother or father? Perhaps she longs to be able to show this person the natural way of aging and letting go and sees this group of dry and empty, dignified milkweed as a model.

Line 11 restores the picture of the milkweed/women. The hard "c" sounds in this line evoke the crispness and dryness of the old pods of the milkweed as it "crackles." The last image in the poem is of these stalks of milkweed, only skeletons of what they once were, crackling "like a blessing" over their fleeing children. This picture portrays the very human experience of letting go of those we love, which ideally includes both pain and delight.

In the three poems, "Happiness," "Turtle," and "Milkweed," one can see a progression through the life of a woman. In "Happiness," the bear is like a young girl, who, while escaping from her physical body, is at the same time able to taste the essence of life. "The Turtle" embodies a respectable woman, fulfilling gracefully her maternal destiny. She sees the world around her, while remaining focused and intent on her own activity. She merely accepts her place in the world, seeing no argument. "Milkweed" shows the nature of an old woman who, though having lost her flesh and substance, does not lose her identity and dignity and is still able to find pleasure in life. Each of these qualities, portrayed artfully in these poems, suggests ideals for women to strive for throughout the sweet and bitter moments of life.

Choosing America as a Place for Incarnation or Immigration in the 21st Century

by

Virginia Sease

Each person who finds a relation to Anthroposophy treads a unique path of study and meditation that fits his or her specific life situation. Besides this more individual aspect, however, there are general themes that are timeless in their nature and yet sometimes demand attention at a specific moment out of inner historical necessity. Now that we have entered the next millennium, such a theme, in my estimation, centers on the relation of the human being to the spiritual hierarchies. This acquires special importance for America due to the unique situation of its folk spirit.

Whereas other countries such as Italy, Norway, and France have a guiding folk spirit that is at the level of an Archangel, America does not have an archangelic being as its folk-spirit. America has a being that is higher in rank, an Archai-being, but this Archai-being has remained behind in the normal course of evolution. This is in the sense of service, not as a failure, as when certain hierarchical beings do not progress normally and thus stay at a lower degree.

The Archai-beings are designated by Rudolf Steiner as the Spirits of Personality. From an external perspective, especially if one has immigrated to America, the qualities of personality appear much stronger here than in other places in the world. One often hears the phrase: "In America *every*body is *some*body," and for those who have immigrated to America even in childhood, the great test often seems to be how to become "somebody." How can one activate one's personality, which is not even the earthly ego, in order to project a countenance? Otherwise a nagging fear creeps in that one will get "lost in the shuffle," unknown and invisible. Even when a person says "I," it serves only to differentiate himself/herself from the rest of the world. Exactly this may give the impression of extreme superficiality in America.

The eternal ego, the essential entelechy, is not encapsulated within the earthly ego. In London on the occasion of the founding of the Anthroposophical Society in Great Britain, Rudolf Steiner spoke about the relation of the "earthly I" to the "eternal I." As one delves into Anthroposophy, one can acquire the feeling that Rudolf Steiner often brought certain insights in specific places. He knew that there were people there who could take up the insights in a comprehensive manner and allow them to find a footing in their souls.

> I gaze into the darkness.
> In it there arises Light—
> Living Light.
> Who is this Light in the darkness?
> It is I myself in my reality.
> This reality of the I
> Enters not into my earthly life;
> I am but a picture of it.
> But I shall find it again
> When with good will for the Spirit
> I shall have passed through the Gate of Death.[1]

So this is the picture of the eternal I. Our own Angel-being helps to mediate between the eternal I and the earthly I of the human being. Thus we speak of our guardian angel bringing intuitions, impulses for deeds, warnings.

Another question presents itself today for many people all over the world: What is the relation of the eternal I of the human being to the Christ? At the conclusion of *An Outline of Esoteric Science* the Greater Guardian of the Threshold is revealed to the esoteric pupil as the Christ Being. And in a meditation given to an esoteric pupil at Easter in 1924 Rudolf Steiner addresses this relation:

> *In the Evening after the Review of the day:*
> From Grace
> May there stream to me Wisdom
> May Wisdom bring forth Love for me
> May Love take part in Grace
> May Love create Beauty for me
> May Beauty bring me Grace.

In the Morning: A star above one's head, Christ speaks from the star:
>Let your soul
>Be carried
>By my strong force
>I am with you
>I am in you
>I am for you
>I am your I.
>   *(Peace of Soul)*[2]

When the human being says "I" to differentiate himself/herself from other beings, the I is directed outwards. When, however, a person strives to experience the I and turns inward, then from the soul-spiritual sphere this brings one into connection—whether consciously or not—with the spiritual hierarchies. This explains why, for example, one can feel such an inward identification with one's country. Also we can see why, along the path of self-knowledge, we can come to the questions: Which spiritual beings are especially active in America, and what is their nature?

It is important to remember that, wherever an individuality incarnates on Earth, whether he/she is born in that location or moves there, two factors play an important role. One factor concerns the etheric geography of that location; the second factor is centered upon the mystery of the Double.

Concerning the first, Rudolf Steiner inaugurated an etheric geography that Guenther Wachsmuth[3] then developed further in his early writings. He differentiated four types of ether: warmth ether, light ether, sound or chemical ether, and life ether. These are parallel to the conditions of physical warmth, air, fluid, and solid earth.

Even though the ether qualities are mixed at any given place, generally one specific ether type predominates according to the geographic location. Following the indications of Guenther Wachsmuth, if we take the Atlantic Ocean as a point of departure, from the East Coast of North America to the British Isles and then over to the middle of Europe, the sound ether connected with fluidity predominates. Tradition maintains that the sound ether meets the light ether, the airy element, approximately in the area of Vienna, Austria. The light ether then extends eastward over to about the Ural Mountains in Russia, where it encounters the warmth or fire ether. The warmth ether projects from the eastern part of Russia across the Pacific Ocean, over the Hawaiian Islands to the West Coast of North America and on to the Rocky Mountains. From there eastward to the Atlantic, the major portion of North America is under the life ether, the earth element.

In view of the life-ether predominance over such a large area of North America, it seems important to consider how Rudolf Steiner described this ether in another context. In lectures in Torquay, England, in 1924, he mentioned the special task of the vital radiation, the vital ray.

> These life radiations are the rays which now must enter into our age as something beneficial; because with all of the impulses which should be given in the Michael Age, the connection with the mastery of the life radiation, the vital radiation, should gradually occur. Mainly one must learn not to work in a lifeless, dead way with that which comes from the spiritual, but directly in a living manner. To find living ideas, living concepts, living viewpoints, living feelings, not dead theories, that is the task of this Age.[4]

As this task of the Michael Age is connected with the vital radiation, we may explore its relevance for America and for a person either born in America or who has immigrated to America. A characteristic of America may be summed up as "openness." It is open for all kinds of strange phenomena, but it has also always been open to regard seriously the spirit as a reality. We may recall the story connected with the signing of the Declaration of Independence. It was a hot, humid day in Philadelphia, and the deliberations had extended over many hours. Finally, Benjamin Franklin spoke in a vociferous manner that they had all had so many thoughts about what they should do, but had they ever thought to ask the "Lord of Light" how they could proceed more fruitfully? It is especially possible in America to allow the fruits of working out of a spiritual impulse to become visible, to take on physical form.

With regard to the second factor, every person has a so-called geographic Double (not just Americans!). We are not considering now the astral Double, which sometimes has been described flippantly as the leftover baggage from previous incarnations that must be dealt with. Rudolf Steiner describes the geographic Double[5] as an Ahrimanic being who enters into the human being just before the moment of birth and remains with him until just before death. It is important that the Double does not go through death with the human being, which would affect his post-mortem situation. The Mystery of Golgotha prevented the Double from ever gaining enough strength to cross the threshold of death because as the blood of the Christ being flowed into the earth, the very substance of the earth was changed. The earth itself is, however, the attraction for the geographic Double. In accordance with the earth configuration and its etheric components, the Double chooses, as it were, the human being with whom it wishes to dwell. The human being has nothing to say about this choice!

The Double works through the human will forces, which have a natural connection to the earth, and through the forces of intellect. Whereas these beings possess a tremendously strong will and an incredibly sharp intellect, they cannot gain access to human beings in the realm of feelings. The "beat of heart and lung,"[6] as the Foundation Stone Mantram describes the middle sphere of the human being, is excluded from the influence of the Double. Thus, the Double accompanies us throughout our earthly life and takes hold of as much of our will and our thinking as we have not been able to permeate with our ego forces.

We can see an underlying connection between the geographic Double which thrives especially well when, as on this continent, the mountains run in a north-south direction in relation to both the electromagnetic pole and the life ether, which is connected to the earth element. We can think of the mighty Rocky Mountains in the West and the Appalachian chain in the East. Furthermore, in addition to the geographic Double, we must reckon with two other powerful polar opposite beings: Ahriman and Lucifer. The former tries to approach the human being from the future, stimulating a hardening into a programmed form, while the latter enters from the past and promotes complete license, often a lack of commitment, dissolution of form, and yet also encourages the artistic predisposition. How can a person in America, whether born or transplanted here, keep the essential aspect of his life configuration in place? He is constantly challenged to exercise the regulatory effect of his ego as it permeates his thinking, feeling, and will nature.

Because of the life-ether predominance on this continent, it can be especially helpful to turn to the spirits of wisdom or *Kyriotetes*, through whose sacrifice, in the distant past of Earth's evolution, the life body of the human being was formed. These beings relate especially to the rhythmic system of the human being, which is excluded from the strong influence of the geographic Double.

The Holy Rishis of the ancient Indian epoch experienced the many beings of the Kyriotetes Order of the Sun as a unity. They called that unity *Vishvakarman*. Later, in the ancient Persian epoch, Zarathustra experienced this Kyriotetes realm in the Sun as *Ahura Mazdao*, which was really like a window to see the Christ, the being of the Sun. Through the Kyriotetes the world ether streams to the earth. That is their great task.

How can we become more aware of what we might call the "countenance" of the Kyriotetes? It is not easy to come from pictures or abstract ideas into a possibility of reading their signature. To read the signature of each hierarchy represents a future task for humankind. For the Kyriotetes it is helpful to study the gesture and physiognomy of the plant world, as the group souls of the plants live in the Kyriotetes sphere.[7] Another way is to work with the metamorphic qualities of eurythmy forms. Whether one does eurythmy actively, watches a performance, or internalizes the drawings of the eurythmy forms that Rudolf Steiner created, one can enter into an inwardly mobile situation that brings the signature of the Kyriotetes closer.

We have enhanced possibilities during the Michael Age, as Michael is the intelligence or Regent of the Sun, whose regency will last approximately three hundred more years. During this time, "in a definitive form the cosmic forces of the Sun will pass over into the physical body and the etheric body of the human being."[8] This enhances the effectiveness of the task of the Kyriotetes. The etheric body has great possibilities for freedom when it is not totally involved in growth processes, reproduction processes, and so on. The free part of the etheric body can work with ideas, with ideals, and with memory. Within this free part, the forces of the Sun can become active. This provides then greater access to the cosmic etheric world where, in certain situations, the Christ being may also be perceived.

Bearing these various considerations in mind, we realize that in a place like America, which has strong geographic Double forces on the one side and the enhanced life-ether relationship to the Kyriotetes on the other, the free middle region of the human being, which comes to expression in the "beat of heart and lungs," gains ultimate significance. Rudolf Steiner gave a meditation for America, which many people have lived with for decades. Its dimensions encompass the dangers of superficial personality traits that prevent feelings from penetrating really deeply into the heart sphere, and also draw attention to the hierarchical beings that support every earnest striving.

> May our feeling penetrate
> Into the center of our heart
> And seek, in love, to unite itself
> With the human beings seeking
> The same goal,
> With the spirit beings who,
> Bearing grace,
> Strengthening us from realms of light
> And illuminating our love
> Are gazing down upon
> Our earnest heartfelt striving.

1. Given in London on the evening of September 2, 1923. The lecture leading up to this meditative verse is published under the title *Man as Picture of the Living Spirit*. The meditation is quoted in *Verses and Meditations*, Rudolf Steiner Press, 1993.

2. Permission for translation kindly given by the Rudolf Steiner Verlag, Dornach, Switzerland. See Rudolf Steiner, *Collected Works*, GA276, Dornach, 1998, translated by V.S.

3. See Guenther Wachsmuth. *Die Aetherische Welt in Wissenschaft, Kunst und Religion*. Vol 2., Dornach: 1927.

4. See Rudolf Steiner, August 18, 1924, in Torquay, in *True and False Paths in Spiritual Investigation*, Rudolf Steiner Press, London: 1985, translated by V.S.

5. See Rudolf Steiner, lecture of November 16, 1917, in St. Gallen, *Geographic Medicine*, Mercury Press, New York: 1986.

6. See Rudolf Steiner, *The Christmas Conference for the Foundation of the General Anthroposophical Society*, 1923–24, Anthroposophic Press, 1990.

7. See Rudolf Steiner, lecture of April 14, 1912, in *The Spiritual Beings in the Heavenly Bodies and in the Kingdoms of Nature*, Anthroposophic Press, 1992.

8. See Note 4, lecture of August 21, 1924.

Immigrant Contributions:
las contribuciones de los emigrantes

by

Julia E. Curry Rodriguez

To go north, *ir al norte*, continues to be a beacon of hope for many who dare to explore immigrant life and its opportunities. The United States, land of pioneering spirit and opportunity for economic and social rewards, remains the goal for many of the Earth's people.

Immigrants, both as families and as individuals, carry along with them their social values, skills, aspirations, and cultures as they travel and settle in new communities. The United States has continuously benefited from the contributions of immigrants, whether in terms of the food on our tables, the care of our children, or the intellectual discoveries and musical contributions borne of the hands of our newer residents.

Few places in the nation have not been affected by immigrants, and vice versa. The East Coast has been home to Puerto Rican garment workers, Mexican mushroom pickers, and Costa Rican intellectuals. The Pacific Northwest has benefited from the entrepreneurial expertise of Mexican women, Nicaraguan food processors, and the poetic articulations of Chicano writers. The South has been host to temporary Caribbean sugarcane workers, and also to Cuban music and cultural development. The Midwest has evolved with the organizational skills of Latino community groups working for health services and educational rights. Iowa has been the home of poets trained at the Iowa Writers' Workshop, such as Cherrie Moraga and Ana Castillo. The Southwest, perhaps the most prolific home of Mexican-origin residents, has shared in the contributions made by these immigrants. Texas with its political and social creativity became the home of the Raza Unida Party and was the place where Mexican labor activists Emma Tenayuca and Manuela Solis de Sanger united many in their quest for social justice. The people of Arizona and New Mexico, with their labor and political struggles and achievements, inspired many a child to dream of success. These are all part of the American spectrum. The nation is a matrix of its people—some newcomers, but all Americans, all contributors to this society.

The experiences of immigrant women are part and parcel of social change in America. They represent and symbolize change. Immigrant women have contributed to the feminization of the labor force and to the overall changes of conventional mores. Immigrants are important in society not merely because of the products of their labor. They also recast the way of life to which we are accustomed. They make us reflect and wonder. Immigrants are part of the future of our America, and they are important bearers of cultural norms treasured by us all.

As one revisits the accounts of immigrants, one is struck by the familiarity of their stories. Listen to their powerful voices, those of women, men, and children. Know that in their unique experience lies the root of all humanity. After all, everyone in these United States including all native tribes came from somewhere else. Realize that all humanity is linked in experience by displacement and creativity. Immigrants come into new worlds to learn from people and cultures. We continue to make contributions to our host communities, now our communities, in ways we might never know.

Who is American today? A professor at California State University, Northridge, whose mother came to the United States in the 1930s to join the ranks of the garment industry. A Salvadoran family that fled the ravages of war, the eldest daughter making a migratory path. That daughter is currently a Spanish-language newscaster in the Los Angeles area. Her younger brother pursues a doctorate at the University of California at Berkeley, hoping to make contributions to the history of Latinos in the United States. A single mother of three in the San Gabriel Valley teaching the newest Americans in a federally-funded Head Start program how to create their first pieces of art. Those are Americans, one and all. Keepers of the dreams of their parents, who brought them here or gave birth to them on U.S. soil. They nurture the dreams of people everywhere. These courageous people remind us to keep dreams alive and to carry on with abiding hope.

The Sacred in Latino Experience:
lo sagrado en la experiencia latina

by

Virgilio Elizondo

From the earliest day of my life, my people introduced me to *Papacito Dios, Jesús, María y los santos*. They were very much a part of our immediate and extended family. They were not dogmas to be believed in but personal friends to visit, converse and even argue with. In our mestizo Christianity—we do not just know about God but rather we know God personally. *No solamente sabemos cosas de Dios sino que conocemos a Dios personalmente.* We converse easily with God and appreciate the many simple, visible, and tangible representations of the spiritual world, like *estampitas, estatuas, medallitas, y veladoras*, as much as we appreciate pictures of our *Mamacita* and loved ones. They help to put us in the conscious presence of our invisible friends, guides, and protectors.

Latinos understand that life is a pilgrimage and when the pilgrimage stops, life comes to an end. This truth seems to be ingrained in our genes. From our most ancient memories, we remember being on pilgrimage. From Aztlan we marched toward the south until we arrived at the valley of Anahuac. Like the Hebrews of old, we became a great people for a brief period of time. Today, we continue our pilgrimage toward the north. Regardless of the direction, we are a pilgrim people. Even though the future is unknown, we are confident and determined. Nothing can stop us, for we are protected and guided by the spirits of earth and heaven, by the *Virgencita* who never abandon us and walk with us through the struggles of life.

The difficult moments of the pilgrimage will not stop us. We know that suffering and disappointment are part of life, but they cannot destroy us. If even God suffered the crucifixion for us, there must be something good in suffering, especially in suffering for the sake of others, that we do not fully understand. In our Latino realism, we do not go looking for suffering as if it were something desirable, but neither do we deny it or run away from it. We assume it, transcend it, and dare to celebrate life in spite of it.

We carry memories on our pilgrimages: memories of our ancestral lands and people, memories of our losses and realized hopes. Memory is the soul of a people. Without it we are just individuals living and working in a common space. The earliest creed of the Hebrew people was "My father was a wandering Aramean. . . . God brought us out of Egypt" (Deuteronomy 26:5–11). Throughout the Bible, God always calls upon the people to remember their ancestors, to remember what God has done for them. The living memory of how God has walked with us, through deserts and mountains, through triumph and defeat, through enslavement and freedom, through life and death, is the source of our strength. We have unquestioned faith in the God who is near and far away, a God who sees and hears, a God who feels in the heart, and a God who always accompanies us on the march.

And we carry our crucified Lord, the embodiment of our own crucified lives; his own unlimited power of endurance is transferred to us. They could kill him but could not destroy him. So it is with us—they can humiliate us, exploit us, kill us, but they cannot destroy us! *Aguante* is the guarantee of life! Others might see it as a weakness; we see it as the greatest strength, which transcends the many destructive forces all around us. Even when we are killed, we cannot be destroyed, for others carry on, and we continue to live in them! This is the divine energy, which keeps us moving, alive and human.

The future is *mestizo*, and to bring it about we will work, laugh, play, study, vote—to renew democracy and renew the lives of all *Americanos*. The new *mestizaje* is the joyous birth of a new humanity. No more barriers, no more racism. The past will not be forgotten but will be blended into the new bodies and cultures that will emerge out of our coming together not in battle or conquest, as in the days of old, but in love, which is the only force that can unite us without destroying us. That is the way to world peace and harmony, and Latinos struggle, dream, and work for that future.

Latinos, Too, Sing America:
los latinos, también, cantan américa . . .

by

Juan Flores

Latinos, too, sing America! The "other" America, *América* in Spanish, English, and broken tongues; songs of hope, struggle, and broken dreams. America sung in *boleros*, in *décimas, merengues* and *corridos, mariachi y mambo, plena y guaguancó Nuestra América*.

Latino songs resonate with ancestral chords and chants: drums, guitars, flutes from Indoamerica, Africa, Andalusia. *Nuestra música* takes root in the coastlands and cattle ranges of Mexico, the canefields and coffee hills of Cuba, Puerto Rico, the Dominican Republic. Its history is the story of homelands and uprooting, migrant freight cars and steamships, barbed-wire borderlands and Ellis Island holding pens, the America of beet fields and canneries, garment sweatshops and janitor pails, boxcar barrios and tenement stairways. *La migra* and Texas Rangers, United Farmworkers and Raza Unida, Brown Berets and Young Lords. Poverty and pride, racism and struggle, suffering and joy. *Nuestra historia*.

The musical life of this country is unthinkable without its glorious "Spanish tinge," the irresistible infusion of *ranchera* and *tango, cumbia* and *son* into the heartbeat of jazz, blues, country, big band, and rock. New Orleans jazz pioneer Jelly Roll Morton was the first to acknowledge it, but America's "first composer," Louis Moreau Gottschalk, before him, and Dizzy Gillespie and Bo Diddley and scores of others since, have all paid their musical homage to the rich current of rhythms and voices, dance moves and song forms forever emanating anew from the cultural wellspring of Latino culture. Rafael Hernández and Lydia Mendoza, Flaco Jiménez and Celia Cruz, Narciso Martínez and Tito Puente, Santana and Eddie Palmieri, La India and Selena, Kid Frost and Latin Empire, so the presence is old, the influences deep, and the results ongoing. In tune with the "souls of Black folk," Latino traditions and innovations help shape the very history of American musical styles and tastes, be they ragtime or bebop, rhythm and blues, or doo-wop, rock, disco, or hip-hop.

Rugged *campesino* hands fine-tune the chord of Latino laments, fingers gnarled from scratching parched soil, nails tattered on conveyor belts, sewing machines, and stubborn mop handles; Latino hands work the strings and drumskins, roll accordion and piano licks, shake maracas, and scrape gourds; hands clap and fingers snap to the blare of trumpets, trombones, saxes, and the wail of barrio voices. Tied hands and muzzled voices burst free to tune the chords and set the cadence of Latino music.

Through history, Latino music has been many musics, most forcefully the traditions from Mexico and those from the Caribbean, long flowing as parallel but independent currents from different regions of the "other" Americas. Chicanos and Boricuas each had their own sounds, one resounding in Texas and Califas, the other in the streets and clubs of los Nuyores. But in our time, with more and more diverse Latino communities coming to live side by side throughout *el Norte, nuestras músicas* are also converging, intermingling, with new hybrid sounds emerging that would have seemed strange confections but a generation ago: *salsa* with *conjunto*, Tex-Mex in *clave, merengue* rap, the sounds of "tropical" Los Angeles, Mixteco and Quisqueya New Yorkers, Miami Nicaraguans, Cubans, and Columbians, Salvadorans in Washington, D.C., Chicanos-Boricuas in Chicago, *cumbia y vallenato* from Jackson Heights, Queens. There may never be a single "Latino music," but by now it is clear that no mix is missing, all styles can harmonize, Latino beats can reverberate from different drummers.

Latinos, too, sing *América!*

Who Is Truly a Westerner Today?

by

Henry Barnes

The Western world is watching current events unfold in Eastern Europe with amazement and no little self-satisfaction. "At last," one thinks, "they have seen the light and are learning to do things our way! We Westerners have, of course, known all along that political democracy and market-driven capitalism are the way to live, and now, finally, they are catching on!" Our virtuous self-congratulation is spiced with the heady wine of a vision of enormously expanded markets for Western goods and services. But where are the voices calling on the West to awake to its own responsibilities; to recognize the need for critical self-examination of its own state of being? What about our own moral and spiritual values? As an American, one asks, what about my own society with its widening gap between rich and poor, its inner-city cancers, its failing educational system, stagnating economy and irresponsible financial legerdemain? Is this really the model for a world struggling to find itself after decades of suppression and totalitarian control in the name of an ideology that promised brotherhood and equality for all mankind? Is not the awakening in Eastern Europe also a powerful call to the West to awake to its own true nature and thus become the partner a new Europe and the wider world need?

It is in this sense that one asks: who, indeed, is truly a Westerner today? What are those distinctive attributes that are needed if the world is to be complete and whole? Are they identical with the West's own Hollywood image of itself, which the media has worked so hard to project? Or is there another "West" struggling to find itself below the surface of life today, a West rooted in the past, but seeking always to "become"?

What does it mean to be born a Westerner? In anthroposophical terms, it means that one chose—before birth and in accordance with the needs of one's karma—to build a bodily instrument, a physical, etheric, and astral organization, conditioned by specifically Western influences, an instrument with its particular limitations and one-sidednesses, as well as its particular strengths. Having made the decision before birth, one then spends one's life learning to accept and rightly use the instrument one has chosen and built up for oneself, knowing that there is no other way, in this incarnation, to enter the stream of life's experiences. It is not as disembodied spirits that we learn the meaning of freedom, but as fully-incarnated spiritual beings who say "yes" to the limitations, the capacities, the one-sidedness of one's own earthly nature. In this sense, it is not the human individuality, the ego, which is Western, European, or Asian—American, German or Japanese—but the bodily-psychic instrument through which the individuality must, in this life, express itself, and through which it can learn to know what it means to be and to become human.

With this in mind, let us try to characterize some aspects of what is truly Western in the world today, both as it is and as it can become, recognizing as we do so how easy it is to oversimplify, and bearing in mind as we look at the American, in particular, that there is a Westerner in everyone today, as there is also a latent Easterner, and a man or woman of the "middle realm."

By and large, our Westerner approaches life through his senses; he wants to "see for himself" and to know how what he sees works. It is not ideas that interest him in the first place. When he meets a new person, he "sizes him up," tries to discover "what makes him tick." He wants to know whether he is "for real" and can be trusted. Only then is he prepared to listen seriously to his ideas, and his test is: Will they work? In this sense, indeed the Westerner is a pragmatist. He observes the world and says: "Show me!" Rudolf Steiner expressed it by saying: The German has to prove everything, he must go back to first causes and explain how things evolved, whereas the American is satisfied merely to assert that it exists. Naive, instinctive pragmatism can never grasp the intangible, but, taken as one's starting point and enhanced by the inner activity of the individual, it becomes the capacity for genuine open-mindedness, for a truly childlike, but perceptive simplicity. And this simple openness—as a European friend likes to say: "This enthusiasm unhampered by experience!"—can also give the Westerner the predisposition toward an artistic approach to experience. The artist perceives concretely and works creatively with his material, and the Westerner—too often superficially—also takes things as they are and tries to "make something of them." Rudolf Steiner saw this latent attribute and spoke to it when he advised that it was through the arts that spiritual science could best be received in America. And, in this regard, it is interesting to note that the first Americans to meet anthroposophy in Europe and to bring knowledge of it back to the United States in the decade before the first World War were all musicians, young singers, almost all women, who went to Berlin to further their careers and were led by various paths to meet Rudolf Steiner in the Mottstrasse. And when one of these young singers—Gracia Ricardo—introduced her former New York vocal teacher to Rudolf Steiner's work in 1910, it was his studio in Carnegie Hall that became the first group meeting room on the North American continent. And in the pioneer years that followed, it was primarily artists who took up the work of spiritual science and planted the first seeds of a new spiritual culture in the rock-bound soil of Manhattan Island, and on the West Coast in Santa Barbara and Los Angeles. One thinks of Irene Brown, the painter, and her artist-cousin, William Scott Pyle, to whom we owe the great curtain with its motifs from Goethe's Fairy Tale, which greets us as we await the opening scene of Rudolf Steiner's first Mystery Play, *The Portal of Initiation*, in the Goetheanum; one remembers Henry Monges, the architect; Arvia MacKaye, the young sculptress, Henri and Eileen Zay, musicians, and, very specially, Lucy Van der Pals Neuscheller, the pioneer eurythmist, who succeeded for many years in the 1920s and 1930s in bringing about each Friday evening a eurythmy recital in the studio in New York City! In this regard, it is well to remember also that it was to Edith Maryon, the sculptress and English artist, that Rudolf Steiner entrusted the Section of the Visual Arts at the Christmas Foundation Meeting, even though he knew well that she was very ill and, in all likelihood, might not live. In the dreadful night of the burning of the First Goetheanum, Rudolf Steiner is reported to have said to Walter Johannes Stein that it was not so much the destruction of ten years of work that was the tragedy, but that men and women from the West would no longer meet spiritual reality in outer sense-perceptible form!

Now another aspect. The North American, in whom, perhaps, nature has concentrated her purest Westernism, inhabits a continent whose mountain spine forms the north-south axis of the earth's mountain cross. Stretching from Alaska to the tip of South America, the Rocky Mountain–Andes chain divides the eastern coast and central plains from the Pacific-facing far western regions, and between the Rockies and the Sierras one finds the American deserts—Mojave, Death Valley, the Salton Sea and the Great Salt Lake with its extraordinary concentration of mineral salts. The continental plains, rising gradually for more than a thousand miles from the vast Missouri-Mississippi River Basin to the foothills of the Rockies, grow ever drier as they rise, annual rainfall dwindling to some ten to twenty inches per year, sufficient only to sustain dryland agriculture and grazing without artificial irrigation. The continent, one might say, led the western-creeping tide of pioneers from the green and fertile Eastern coastal regions, across the Appalachians, into the rich prairie lands of the heartland, ever onward toward the mountains, into a realm of death-in-nature where the earth's mineral and magnetic forces became ever more pronounced and powerful. At the same time, the wagon trains found themselves exposed to attack not only by native Indian tribes, but also by the violent storms that raged down from the North, unbroken by east-west mountain barriers, and by tropical hurricanes and waves of humid heat sucked up from the Gulf of Mexico. Thus the pioneers, stemming originally from European stock, were drawn deeper and deeper into a continent that led them geographically into regions of intensifying mineralization, of subterranean, death-related forces from below, and climatically, into greater and greater aridity, into continental extremes of heat and cold, and into wind-swept unobstructed exposure to Arctic and tropical gales from north and south. This is the outer picture, familiar to all who know North America either from direct experience or from study, to which spiritual-scientific research adds a knowledge of the supersensible or subsensible forces that grow increasingly strong as one moves westward. These forces, as we know, are connected with the mystery of the human Double, described by Rudolf Steiner in his Saint Gallen lecture on "Geographic Medicine" and in other places. The Ahrimanic Double, as Steiner characterizes it, is connected with—empowered, one might say—by the electromagnetic forces within the earth, which intensify toward the West. It is not within the scope of this article to enter into a detailed discussion of the Double, except to point out that the struggle to know one's Double and to transform it belongs especially to a Western incarnation and constitutes part of its special challenge and its opportunity.

There is less and less "cultural cushion," as one might call it, to "break one's fall" as one moves westward. For the inwardly sensitive, spiritually searching soul on the North American continent, life becomes, in a literal sense, a "life and death affair," where there is no comfortable middle ground to fall back on as one struggles to find oneself and to awake. Knowledge of the Ahrimanic double, who seeks to stay with its human counterpart through the experience of death, certainly helps us to understand much of the tragedy of contemporary Western experience—its violence, its fascination with technology, the drug scene with its often brutal human exploitations, the crass materialism in thought, feeling, and ruthless will—but it also helps us to realize that it may be precisely in the existential struggle to overcome the double that the Western soul comes closest to the threshold and to the reality of spiritual life. Consciousness of this fact can become the strongest spur of conscience to do everything in one's power to strengthen the healing work of art and the healing knowledge of anthroposophy and its practical manifestations in medicine, education, science, and agriculture.

In the West, it is almost always the practical application of anthroposophy that one meets first, and it is often a second or third meeting that inspires the question as to the world-picture that works as a formative force in the practical activities. Although by no means uniquely Western, it is, nevertheless, the characteristic Western experience and points to the great importance of how anthroposophy lives in the practitioner: as an external "method," or as a wellspring of insight and creativity that enlivens its application. It is precisely here that the Westerner can experience the truth of Rudolf Steiner's observation that the danger for the being Anthroposophia as she moves westward is that she become "a wooden doll"! Once again, the healing power that can overcome and transform this tendency is the active practice of the arts, deepened and enhanced through meditation. It is here also that the Westerner finds help in the work of those great forerunners who ploughed the ground of the Western soul in earlier times and planted seeds that are waiting to be re-discovered today, to be transformed and made to grow.

The American, in particular, who sets out on the path of exploration to find his own contemporary roots in the past, will turn back to a peaceful Massachusetts village of sturdy farmers in the nineteenth century that harbored a company of pioneering explorers of a continent of inner experience. They blazed new trails, seldom traveled by the men and women of their day, but which just at this time are waiting to be re-discovered and to be followed.

Here, in Concord, the American will encounter that spirit-eagle, Ralph Waldo Emerson, whose thought was as transparent and clearly formed as the quartz crystal, about whom Rudolf Steiner remarked that his thinking was so penetrated by the fire of his inner experience that the double was completely overcome. It was, indeed, through the lens of his purified power of thought that Emerson observed the universe, the human soul and spirit, giving expression to his observations in daring, revolutionary terms, as, for instance, in his essay on *Self-Reliance*:

> Trust thyself; every heart vibrates to that iron string . . . . We but half express ourselves and we are ashamed of that divine idea which each of us represents. . . . God will not have his work made manifest by cowards. . . . Whoso would be a man must needs be a non-conformist . . . . To be great is to be misunderstood.

Or, again, from his essay *On Character*:

> The people know that they need in their representative much more than talent, namely, the power to make his talent trusted. They can not come at their ends by sending to Congress a learned, acute and fluent speaker, if he be not one who (before he was elected) was appointed by Almighty God to stand for a fact—invincibly persuaded of that fact in himself—so that the most confident and the most violent persons learn that here is a resistance on which both independence and terror are wasted, namely faith in a fact.

Henry David Thoreau, Emerson's friend and partner in many conversations that plumbed the depths and heights of human experience, viewed the universe from the narrow geographic confines of New England, where he spent his entire life, but his thoughts rayed out to kindred spirits like Tolstoi, Gandhi, and Martin Luther King, and today still illumine the dark clouds that have hung over Eastern Europe with a challenging and courageous light. In his famous essay *On Civil Disobedience*, which was not even published until some time after his death, Thoreau wrote:

> Oh for a man who is a man, and as my neighbor says, has a bone in his back which you cannot pass your hand through. . . . Action from principle; the perception and the performance of right, changes things and relations; it is essentially revolutionary, and does not consist wholly with anything which was. It not only divides states and churches, it divides families; aye, it divides the individual, separating the diabolical in him from the divine.

And again,

> Morning is when I am awake and there is dawn in me. Moral reform is the effort to throw off sleep. . . . To be awake is to be alive. We must learn to reawaken and keep ourselves awake, not by mechanical means, but by an infinite expectation of the dawn. . . . I know of no more encouraging fact than the unquestionable ability of man to elevate his life by conscious endeavor. It is something to be able to paint a particular picture, or to carve a statue . . . but it is far more glorious to carve and paint the very atmosphere through which we look, which morally we can do. To affect the quality of the day, that is the highest of the arts.

Our explorer and re-discoverer of the spiritual sources of Western experience will sooner or later also turn to Walt Whitman, Emerson's contemporary and poet of the Western soul, who sang the wide, all-embracing virtues of modern humanity in such passages from *Democratic Vistas*, as:

> I can say democracy can never prove itself beyond cavil until it founds and luxuriantly grows its own forms of art, poems, schools, theology.... The poet of the modern is wanted, or the great literature of the modern.
>
> The purpose of democracy ... is, through many transmigrations, and amid endless ridicules, arguments and ostensible failures to illustrate at all hazards, this doctrine or theory that man, properly trained in sanest, highest freedom, may, and must become a law, and series of laws, unto himself.

To complete our exploration we would need to speak of Nathaniel Hawthorne, at one time Emerson's and Thoreau's neighbor in Concord, whose novels probe with fearless compassion the hidden sources of evil that are so deeply and essentially human. It was of Hawthorne that Albert Steffen once remarked that his novels were accessible to the dead as well as to the living. And there would also be Herman Melville, Hawthorne's literary friend, for whom the struggle with evil, as portrayed in *Moby Dick*, was so central a theme, or Bronson Alcott, eccentric prophet of a new and creative approach to education, who also called Concord home.

But our search would be utterly incomplete if it did not include the rugged, lanky figure of Abraham Lincoln, contemporary with all these other men. In him, the Western genius shaped its greatest hero, the laconic, melancholy, deep-seeing servant and leader of his people. Dreamer, storyteller, shrewd observer, humorist, self-taught frontier lawyer and politician, whose language drew its richness and imagery from the King James version of the Bible and from Shakespeare, Lincoln reached the hearts of a nation in which brother found himself fighting against brother in the bitter years of the Civil War. It was his compassion and integrity, his deep but simple humanity that spoke to his people just weeks before his assassination on Good Friday, 1865, in his Second Inaugural Address as the re-elected President of the United States whose union he had done and suffered so much to save: "With malice toward none, with charity for all...."

These were cosmopolitan souls who participated actively in a republic of free spirits in their time and recognized each other beyond the narrow limits of political states and national languages and cultures. Thus, for example, Herman Grimm wrote to Emerson on April 5, 1856, in his very first letter in a correspondence that continued until 1871, "Of all the writers of our day you seem to me to be the one who understands the genius of the time most deeply and who most clearly feels the future. I am happy to be able to express this to you." And, on October 25, 1860, Grimm wrote, "How fortunate the country who possesses such a man! When I think about America, I think of you, and America appears to me to be first among the nations of the earth. You well know that I would not say this if it were not, in fact, my inmost conviction."

We need today such a spontaneous, free mutual recognition and admiring respect in the cultural-spiritual sphere! What might it not signify if, out of the West, there were to arise a heartfelt recognition of the greatness of the new tasks dawning for Europe, beyond the daily struggle for economic and political stability, necessary as these are. And, vice versa, how much it could mean for America, and for the whole Western world, if Europe participated with interest and heartfelt understanding in the West's struggle to find its own original identity, even if only accompanying this struggle in consciousness.

At a time when spiritual freedom is once again dawning in Middle Europe, and the rigid political and military controls begin to relax, Europe and the West should reflect upon their own true tasks and should respect and support their inherent differences. The West must find, in its own Western way, a middle, heart sphere, just as Europe, in its own way, must achieve the West within itself. Only when both fulfill their own tasks can one hope that, at some time, the brothers of the Far East and of the Southern Hemispheres may take their places as members of a threefold social organism of humanity. It is for this reason that I feel it to be so urgently necessary that the mighty call of Eastern Europe for cultural-spiritual freedom and for the transformation of the outer political and economic forms should be answered by a call from the West, a call of Western humanity to itself to awake to its own essential identity and to the tasks that await it in a cosmopolitan working together on behalf of humanity as a whole.

Waldorf Education in North America: The Curriculum and the Folk Spirit

by

Norman Davidson

On a cold morning in March 1996, I went out into my backyard at 4:30 under the clear, dark skies pinpricked with stars to see the comet Hyakutake. Binoculars revealed it glowing quietly in Libra. It is a strange experience for someone who knows the patterns of the stars to see such a ghostly patch of milky white adding itself to the familiar form of a constellation. Here was an unexpected visitor from beyond the planetary system. There was something universal about it, something beyond our personal sky. It was as if it hailed, perhaps, from the realm of the fabled Seraphim—from behind the stars themselves. These cometary phenomena announce themselves openly, even boldly, across our skies—yet physically they are of homeopathic proportion. They have but a small, hard core, and their glowing tails, while externally immense, are made up of tenuous, hardly existent matter.

Spiritual Science, or Anthroposophy, has some cometary qualities. Rather than arising out of a purely "natural" (or "matter of course") series of events, it arrives as an unexpected cultural visitor that points in the direction of the universal and the free, teaching something beyond the ordinary physical realm. Although it enters fully and dramatically onto the modern scene, it comes from afar and as a much-needed presence. Waldorf Education—an offspring of Spiritual Science—also is a kind of comet that has entered the "skies" of North American culture.

Rudolf Steiner gave to Ralph Courtney—one of the pioneers of Anthroposophy in North America—a verse that I believe was not just for the early anthroposophical community in Spring Valley, New York, but was addressed to the American spirit in general. It speaks of the inward uniting of human beings, of support from the spiritual world in that striving, and makes a distinction between feelings and "heart." It goes like this:

> May our feeling penetrate
> Into the center of our heart,
> And seek, in love, to unite itself
> With the human beings seeking the same goal;
> With the spirit beings, who, bearing grace,
> Strengthening us from realms of light
> And illuminating our love,
> Are gazing down upon
> Our earnest, heartfelt striving.

This thought of Steiner's seems an echo of what a Native American chief expressed in the last century about the emerging new America. In a speech or declaration made in Washington State to the Governor of Indian Affairs there, Chief Seattle said:

> Your dead cease to love you and the homes of their nativity as soon as they pass the portals of the tomb. They wander far off beyond the stars, are soon forgotten, and never return. Our dead never forget the beautiful world that gave them being. They still love its winding rivers, its great mountains and its sequestered vales, and they ever yearn in tenderest affection over the lonely-hearted living and often return to visit and comfort them. . . .
>
> And when the last red man shall have perished from the earth and his memory among the white man shall have become a myth, these shores shall swarm with the invisible dead of my tribe. . . .
>
> At night, when the streets of your cities and villages shall be silent, and you think them deserted, they will throng with the returning hosts that once filled and still love this beautiful land. The white man will never be alone. Let him be just and deal kindly with my people, for the dead are not altogether powerless.

Rudolf Steiner is reported to have said that the intuitive ideas of the Native American had been of great help to the white man in America, whereas the white man in Europe had been given no such help. (See bibliography: *American Indians and Our Way of Life* by Sylvester Morey.)

Steiner also spoke about the gift of the Anglo-American spirit for the development of a cosmogony, an understanding of the origins and development of evolution from a cosmic point of view. This is often misinterpreted today as being connected with some dubious aspects of star wisdom or astrology. But in his lecture of October 10, 1919, in Dornach, Steiner makes clear that he means something more in the direction of Goethean science and the principle of the metamorphosis of bodily forms from incarnation to incarnation. He is indicating the spiritual evolution of the human being, and continues:

> Science must become cosmic, otherwise it is not science. It must have a cosmic character; it must be a cosmogony. Otherwise it does not give Man the inner impulses which carry him through life.

So too must our views of education and of a folk spirit emerge out of a cosmic, universal awareness. One can speak of the genius of an inclusive American "folk spirit" (rather than a "folk soul") that cuts across and unites races in a way that an ordinary multiculturalism cannot. I recall that Steiner also spoke of the eventual emergence of a North American spirit in which all races of the world would unite and no longer be distinguished from each other by color. This could render North America a true center for the universal human being. Waldorf education can serve this ideal. The universal in the curriculum must be realized. Waldorf education is sometimes seen as a European intrusion—like the comet—into North American culture. But, in fact, at a deeper level, Waldorf education represents that which has been raised to the cosmic and given to the whole planet—a universal human element.

The theme of a common North American spirit as distinct from a collection of separate cultures has been developed by the American historian Arthur Schlesinger in his book *The Disuniting of America*. He writes:

> The historic idea of a unifying American identity is now in peril in many arenas—in our politics, our voluntary organizations, our churches, our language. And in no arena is the rejection of an overriding national identity more crucial than in our system of education. The debate about the curriculum is a debate about what it means to be an American.

The question of cosmogony or evolution in relation to American culture is an important one. Evolution is, in fact, well represented in the Waldorf curriculum but could be developed further. The genius of each culture and its part in extending the concept of what a human being is must be recognized. For example, the cultures of Africa, China, early Australia, early America, and others need to be further researched for curricular purposes. From one point of view, two different and opposite factors seem to have come together from among the many elements that contributed to the founding of North American society. One is the eighteenth-century Enlightenment in Europe with its intellectual, materialistic, and utilitarian approach to life. The other is a subtle, spiritual influence that came quietly through the Native North American. These two factors originally, it seems, touched hands and understood each other for a moment on an important social level. But on other levels they were far apart.

An example today of the persistent "enlightenment" element is provided by a 1981 resolution of the National Academy of Sciences in Washington, D.C. Founded in 1863 under the signature of Abraham Lincoln, the Academy is an official advisor to the federal government on any question of science or technology. The resolution states:

> Religion and science are separate and mutually exclusive realms of human thought whose presentation in the same context leads to misunderstanding of both scientific theory and religious belief.

The Native American influence is quite different and much more important. When I was a boy, I was familiar with the stories about Hiawatha. Later, when I came to America, I realized that they were not just "stories," but that Hiawatha was a chief of the Iroquois people and is thought to have lived in the sixteenth century. He was responsible for the republican constitution of the tribes within the Iroquois confederation, which extended over New York State and Canada. He united the five Indian "nations" within the group in a "silver chain" or "Grand Council" whose members succeeded each other in the female line of heredity. (The importance of the woman in society, it is interesting to note, has been a feature of North American society from earliest times to the present.)

Some historians claim that Iroquois orators frequently spoke at colonial meetings and that they suggested that the colonies form a confederation like that of the Iroquois. It is thought that the republican spirit of the Iroquois helped to bring about the establishment of the thirteen original states and that it influenced Benjamin Franklin and, later, Thomas Jefferson in framing the Declaration of Independence and the Constitution.

Hiawatha is also credited with a concept of universal brotherhood. I believe that this spirit of universal brotherhood in North America has as much to do with the future as with the past. One could say that the first college of teachers was formed here in North America among the Iroquois before Rudolf Steiner was even born! Actually, many aspects of a future way of working between people lie in the spirit of the invisible Native Americans in our midst. For example, since the Iroquois had no "little devils" on paper (i.e., no written language), the art of speech or oratory was specially developed at meetings and discussions. One practice was that when a person rose to speak, he or she had to start by stating the original question and summarizing the previous speeches before giving his or her own contribution to the discussion. A valuable discipline! Even practiced only inwardly, this today is essential for creating form and unity in group work.

Another aspect of Native American culture is a concern for "what" one spoke out of, for the source of one's thought. When the psychologist Carl Jung went to New Mexico, he talked with a Pueblo chief who said that white people were all mad. When Jung asked why, the chief explained that the whites said they thought with their heads. "What do you think with?" asked Jung. The chief replied, "We think here," indicating his heart.

The sense of brotherhood is strong in Native American culture. Another element is the striving for unanimity in meetings and debates. All this stands behind the natural tendency in North America to open to public discussion all matters, including the personal, a tendency that can astonish the European newcomer.

I experienced this open, discursive mood when teaching a course to the eleventh grade in the Detroit Waldorf School. After giving a presentation, I was plied with questions the next day. I soon realized that I had to change my lesson plan and allow things to grow in different directions. The mood was: "You've talked. Now we talk!"

All this has to do with how Waldorf education will develop in North America. A balance should be kept between feelings on the one hand and the "thinking heart" on the other. These two are not the same. When the heart thinks, it lives in clarity and perceptiveness, as well as in something deeply human. Clarity of thinking is our modern heritage today as much as our life of personal feeling is. We should not get lost in endless discussions. We must also let those who have had an experience of something have their say and live with that for a while, even for weeks and months.

If we do revise the curriculum for our particular needs concerning culture and character, we should be careful not to throw out the baby with the bathwater. For example, the Norse myths are there for a universal, not a racial, reason. Replacing them would require as much insight into human evolution as Steiner had when he put these particular myths into the curriculum in the first place. Yet replace them we can, and should, if it is considered necessary in relation to the environment. The curriculum of a Waldorf school in Japan, for example, must reflect the cultural environment in which it stands and not be an imported "little Stuttgart."

Concerning how elementary school lessons are taught, one notices a widespread tendency to start the day with a lengthy series of circle game activities. This obliterates one purpose of the main lesson—to carry over something inward in the students from the previous day. The carrying over of questions and feelings from the sleep life renders the first part of the main lesson time the "golden time" of the school day. The students can, after an introductory activity such as the saying of a verse, make the subject truly their own by calling up the content of the previous lesson and discussing it while they are still inwardly fresh. This carrying over, discussion, and development of the subject matter is a vital part of Steiner's method of teaching according to a two-day rhythm. The structure of the main lesson can, in fact, be a picture of the incarnating process itself.

Another important curricular question concerns the computer. When and how something is taught is as important as what is taught. The latest technology must be taught in the Waldorf school. Certainly computer technology should be familiar to the high school student. There could be a main lesson block or course on the history of technology out of which such a study could arise. This could be followed by a course on the development and technical workings of the computer since the seventeenth century, and the invention and the principle of the binary system. If these things are taught with insight and imagination, then the student will be equipped inwardly to face the encounter with the keyboard and with the spider behind the invisible threads of the electronic World Wide Web.

The North American instinctively abhors the negative side of European culture—that is, the intellectual side. But this intellectual element has sailed across the Atlantic along with the various other aspects of European culture. It is today clearly manifest in school programs that kill an alive education stone dead. This should be resisted openly and courageously by parents and teachers who have a feeling for their children's welfare and future. The child knows what is meant when you tell the story about how the Native Americans of long ago said that if you try to count the stars and don't finish counting, then you will die. Counting is intellectual, not pictorial. Culture dies when you try to count the stars. No one can count them, but to do so, metaphorically, is the basis of our modern culture.

Let us not count the stars in the Waldorf curriculum and fix them rigidly, but rather see them as pictures of the human constellation, and render these pictures rightly within each culture. We must do research as to why something appears in the curriculum when it does, and work out of that—work out of what lies behind the curriculum. Whether we change externals in the subjects taught depends on individual cultures and schools working out of insight.

One star these nights is the comet. Let the children know its exact position and its physical constitution, but let them also see it with awe as an unexpected event in the sky coming from little-known universal regions. Anthroposophy and Waldorf education also, in their way, come from little-known universal regions. May both of them shine on American culture in such a manner that the universal is understood and the American folk spirit understands itself.

Bibliography:

Barreiro, Jose, ed. *Indian Roots of American Democracy*. Ithaca, N.Y.: Akwekon Press of Cornell University, 1992.

Gifford and Cook, eds. *How Can One Sell the Air? Chief Seattle's Vision*. Summertown, Tenn.: The Book Publishing Company, 1992.

Johansen, Bruce. *Forgotten Founders: How the American Indian Helped Shape Democracy*. Cambridge: Harvard Common Press, 1982.

Lefkowitz, Mary. *Not out of Africa*. New York: Basic Books, Harper Collins, 1996.

Morey, Sylvester. "American Indians and Our Way of Life," an address given at the Waldorf School, Adelphi University, January 18, 1961. Garden City, N.Y.: Myrin Institute.

———, ed. *Can the Red Man Help the White Man? A Denver Conference with the Indian Elders*. New York: Myrin Institute Books, 1970.

Press, Frank. Preface to *Science and Creationism A View from the National Academy of Sciences*. Washington, D.C.: Committee on Science and Creationism, National Academy of Sciences Press, Washington, D.C., 1984.

Schlesinger, Arthur. *The Disuniting of America: Reflections on a Multicultural Society*. New York: Norton, 1992.

Spence, Lewis. *The Myths of the North American Indians*. New York: Dover, 1989.

Movement in America:
And So—What's Moving Us?

by

Barbara Schneider-Serio

For the last twenty or so years I have had the privilege of working in the field of movement and getting to know people through that medium. What has become clear during this time is that the way a person moves is directly connected to the way she or he speaks and vice versa. My work in eurythmy, of course, focuses on this aspect. What is the inner experience of a sound, say an "AAAh" or "EEE," or "B," "L," "SH," "M"? What does this sound call forth in me, and what gesture innately belongs to it? This makes for an interesting study when dealing with different languages, different dialects and different peoples.

Quite a few years ago, when I had just begun working in eurythmy, I spent a semester in England. Oh, how these English like to crunch their vowels! Perfectly round little "O"s, that is, God or coffee or talk, neatly perched "EE"s or "I"s and one syllable "AE"s as *man, ram, Sam*. It's a real pleasure to see these little creatures so self-contained, knowing their places, and rather enjoying the company of a few hearty consonants to get things into perfect order.

Listening to the English, and wondering how different it would be to move to an English or an American speaker, I remembered an indication for gestures for American vowels. It was to do all the vowel gestures with an indication of "AAAh." Now what belongs to "AAAH"- ness?

First, we need to open our mouths quite wide to say a proper "AAAh." (Dentists love that sound for some incomprehensible reason.) And when do I say "AAAh"? Remember the time when something just about bowled you over—seeing your newborn child for the first time . . . , meeting the person you will share your life with, watching an early sunrise through the low-lying fog surrounding the Rockies? You name it. Deep inside, you become wide open, become vulnerable, let the world come into you without obstacles, and let your most hidden soul shiver in the unexpected. And your arms just show what touches you so deeply. All they can do is open wide to let the marvel in, your whole being and body lean back to take in the world to its fullest extent and to keep the doors of your soul open. Ah, yes, what a gesture!

I was reminded of an English friend of mine describing a visit by a flustered American, "AH ma Gaad, Maally, A've last ma maney" (Oh my God, Molly, I've lost my money), and I could just hear all those "AAAh"s oozing shamelessly all over the place.

You can literally see, just looking at the jaw of a person, if it is English vowels residing there or their American cousins. How different will their owner's gestures be, following the lead of their gallant sounds? Let's have a look.

Well, yes, here we find the crisp, contained, not too emotional gestures—to the point, mind you, to the point—of the English person. And there is our American struggling to find his or her way through the landscape dotted with "AAAh" everywhere, making the gestures wide, broad. It is a big country to take to one's heart—open, somewhat unformed, full of feelings of all kinds . . . some of them belonging there, some not at all. It is a big heart, wide open; I can just see good old Walt Whitman out on the floor having a ball and just loving those " AAAh"s.

Yes, moving is delicious! With all these tidy vowels and well-ordered consonants among the English, besides a great soccer run or rugby chase, who gives a hoot about movement? Moving is a thing you have to do, not so much for pleasure or good health—whoever heard of taking care of the body in old England—but for getting to the next tea party. Well, here, the Americans live it up! Let's go, move for the fun of it, move to look tony and ripply and sleek, move to find yourself, express yourself, love yourself, play with the kids, the gals, the guys, jog, walk, parachute, climb, dance, . . . aah, become yourself, and let the movement take you!

"AAH," It feels great, but oh boy, it 's darn hard getting these consonants there to come along. Movement, well that's ok. But form, what's that? "K, B, D" . . . ends of words . . . what are those? Clear gestures? "Rrrrrrrr" rolls along prrretty well and over the prairie, down the highway over the bridge through the form past the choreography and watch out for those people over there! It's a big country, gotta keep moving.

Now watch the Germans over there, nicely sculpted consonants, well-behaved forms, everything is Just So, maybe just a bit too much will in those heels coming down.

And how about the Japanese with these beautiful, slightly bouncy steps, and gestures as neat and tidy as their writing, and as flowing?

And here come the big-step people trying to get around that curve with the minimum of just one step and across the whole room with maybe three—yeah, even New York is a big state—could qualify for a few of these European little places—like Belgium or so. Who has time for little steps? Lots to get done in little time . . . places to go . . . people to see, and let's get going with that studying here! It is the big-step people, and you bet once they got the choreography down, there is no stopping them.

Americans seem to like finding that groove together. They like that group thing, or teamwork as it is called. They are the "gotta work it out" people. As a strong contrast, visit any Continental, European train or bus station or ticketing counter—the mass of savages trying to get on that vehicle first—no matter what, no matter how, never yet having heard the call of civilization in their urge of the surge. Well, in England there's the queue; in America . . . teamwork.

In all group choreography, Americans have the wish to find the way, to curb these unruly feelings swelling in all the vowels, to get some clear organization—let's not flatten those consonants but let them teach us, too—and to find the way of the "in between". . . between each other . . . between the sounds. Where else could the essence lie? So there is a respect in the movement, and everyone is concerned with giving each other space, physical, mental, emotional. This gives the group movement its own sweet, free rhythm, where the fresh breath of the Rockies, prairies, and Great Lakes comes to life. Permeating the whole group is a spiraling movement in one accord; everyone is listening to the land and its circling and turnings. Is it following the American eagle's spiraling . . . watching, making sure everyone finds his or her space in this great land of freedom?

And let's get back to that "Aah" once again. What lies in that wide open gesture that so belongs to this place? "AAAh" opens us up to all that is around us . . . lets us be young again . . . marvel, unabashed, at the beautiful vistas everywhere. Of course it can stiffen in us and we can become professional "marvellers," inwardly unmoved but superficially friendly and seemingly open. It can keep us passively waiting for years for the next miracle, guru, or lottery to show up to lead the way. But if we truly find our way to the "AAAh," if we let that open gesture become a part of our heart's gesture, will we not be, after all, on our way?

Multiculturalism and Waldorf Education in America

by

Linda Williams

All right, here is the scene: one of the newer, more generic Detroit suburbs. I am standing at a bookstore counter, a thirtyish African-American woman with burgeoning dreadlocks. The clerk waiting on me is young, female and Asian-American. While my books are being totaled, I sneeze. The clerk looks perplexed and is not sure what to do. Hesitantly, and with an apologetic smile, she says, "I was going to say 'Gesundheit' . . ." and her voice trails off as she looks down. I realize the source of her embarrassment and smile, and offer in my best, accented German, "Danke." She laughs and the tension of the moment is relieved for both of us. The situation, however, is a typically American one: an Asian-American, an African-American, a European language. Does it all fit together? Of course it does—in America. But the clerk's embarrassment is certainly a sign of the great sensitivity that currently surrounds the issue of multiculturalism.

There are many reasons why the discussion and debate over multiculturalism have taken hold of America. We are today more conscious of each other because of shifting demographics; the increasing immigration of people of color; the civil rights and feminist movements; and the rising prominence of Asia, Africa, and Latin America in the changing global economy. But multiculturalism is almost synonymous with America herself. Even before the Europeans arrived, America was a multicultural place, containing many, varied indigenous tribes. Our task has always been to find some way to "jus' get along," as Rodney King expressed it.

The current debate is also a response to "anticulturalism" or what I call the "Wonder Breading" of America. With the advent of and the rapid increase in the use of technology, mass production, and mass transit over the past seventy years, "culture" in America is becoming homogenized. Regional differences are disappearing under the influence of the mass media. Cultural mores are being shaped by standardized images of what we should aspire to. We are all being assimilated into a culture of automation, speed, and efficiency that leaves little room for individual expression. No wonder the multicultural question has arisen. Sometimes I call it the "anycultural" question. What culture, if any, do we, can we have?

The educational world is particularly concerned with this debate. On the one hand, "inclusive" curricula seek to incorporate and recognize the contributions of frequently ignored minorities in American culture. On the other hand, many, such as E. D. Hirsch, advocate a return to the basics, the fundamentals of Eurocentric Western thought as a way to acculturate the "unacculturated."

The Waldorf school movement in America, interestingly enough, was conceived and born in an era that was similarly fraught with cultural controversy. In 1925 a group began working to bring forth the first Waldorf School in America (the Rudolf Steiner School in New York), and the school opened its doors in 1928. Those years in America were filled with irony. It was the time of Prohibition, gangsters, jazz and flappers. The heights of the Harlem Renaissance contrasted with the sobering picture of lynched African-Americans in the South. "Rugged Individualism" was a popular slogan and aspiration at a time when membership in the Ku Klux Klan approached five million. (President Harding was inducted into the Klan on the grounds of the White House.) Americans were entranced by the mobility offered by the automobile and the growing network of paved roads, while the nation, in an isolationist mood, closed its doors to the world. Native Americans finally gained citizenship, but many important socialists and communists were deported. In the arts, it was the time of Chagall, Klee, Picasso, Fitzgerald, Hughes, Cather, Woolf, Ellington and Gershwin. In the mid 1920s, motion pictures began to feature sound, and the first transmission of recognizable human features was achieved by something called television.

Within this milieu, the American Waldorf movement was born. In order to preserve its independence, Waldorf education had to join the private, independent school movement. By doing so, it joined ranks with the elitist schools that educated the Vanderbilts and the Carnegies. But it also became spiritual partners with every independent Freedman's school that helped newly emancipated slaves learn to read and with every privately sponsored settlement school for newly arrived immigrants.

During these first seven decades, American Waldorf schools have often have resembled their European counterparts. But the stamp of the American experience is helping to shape our schools into truly American institutions. Clearly, Waldorf schools have a cultural mandate, a charge to preserve, enrich, and transmit a cultural heritage. But at this point in history, our cultural imperative cannot be realized in small, private enclaves where only middle-class European-Americans are educated. Our doors will have to open to more people of color (and to people of more economic classes) because integrated education is now American education. According to a 1990 *Time* magazine article: "By 2056, most Americans will trace their descent to Africa, Asia, the Hispanic world, the Pacific Islands, Arabia—almost anywhere but white Europe." A clear majority culture will no longer exist in America within the next generation. "Meeting the other" is becoming a basic component of education today.

The Waldorf curriculum is an ideal curriculum because it has the potential of being multicultural. It can be a medium through which students meet each other and come to understand the diverse cultures to which they belong. Behind the guidelines and indications stands the picture of the human being as an integrated organism of body, soul and spirit, and of humanity as a single, interconnected reality. It is a universal view that includes rather than excludes, that embraces rather than rejects.

Also, within the Waldorf curriculum, with this all-embracing image of the human being and of humanity as a guide, the complexity of the human condition is approached in a basic way, through the arts. It is through the arts that our full humanity is affirmed. And it is through the arts that multicultural differences can be understood and appreciated.

Traditional African education was a socializing process, not an individualizing one, and one in which mind and spirit were considered inseparable. Current research on African-American children often calls for an education that de-emphasizes a Eurocentric, paternalistic, top-down format, and that encourages an experiential, hands-on, inquiry-based learning format, a cooperative education rather than one based on competition and survival-of-the-fittest.

This, of course, is exactly what Waldorf education is. Thus we in the Waldorf movement have the means to carry out effective "multicultural" education. Our holistic, synergistic, all-embracing approach is what is needed. We lack however, the content. Our stories, songs, verses and historical vignettes—the expressions we use of the archetypal experiences and pictures of human development—have been drawn mostly from European and European-American sources. Only now are we beginning to find the archetypal pictures that live in other cultures.

In the various ethnic and national cultures, there are many different expressions of the same archetypal truths, of the same universal human experiences. How can parents, teachers, and other adults decide what particular stories, pictures, music and crafts to bring to the children?

First we must find out what is essential in our own being. One effect of the homogenization of North American culture is that few of us know about our ethnic background. We need to become aware of what we have received from our heritage—be it Thai, German, Czech, Yoruban, Chinese, Sioux, or a mixture of two or many traditions. We need to become aware of the physical attributes, the qualities of soul, the world views that form the "group soul" or "folk soul" (a term used both by Rudolf Steiner and Carl Jung) of our own ethnic group.

As well we need to study and understand the unique qualities of the other ethnic groups in our culture. Exploring our own history and culture gives us the necessary framework to explore others. Also, examining the reality of "white privilege" and of the class system in America is necessary if one is to understand one's past and future paths.

When these steps are consciously taken, in faculty and/or parent-teacher organization meetings, a school or organizational culture is established that encourages real interest in "the other." This creates an atmosphere in which work to diversify the content in our schools and to answer some of the myriad questions facing our movement can begin.

And the questions are tough ones:

- How can we consciously attract and keep more children, parents and teachers of color in the Waldorf school movement?

- How will our training programs help prospective teachers meet the challenges of teaching in a multicultural environment?

- How can we become more sensitive to cultural differences and the different approaches to pedagogy these may require?

Those of us within the American Waldorf movement need more opportunities to investigate and to discuss what is going on in our classrooms, schools, and in our larger Waldorf community. Some individual schools have undertaken particular multicultural studies. We need to discuss the fruits of that research. Parents, friends, students, and teachers need to be able to share their own exciting and worthwhile experiences and knowledge and to ask questions.

To that end, all are invited to respond to this article, and to the issues that multiculturalism raises. Waldorf education is born out of experience and dialogue. Issues such as multiculturalism cannot be relegated to a few. The more voices the better.

To stimulate discussion, some colleagues and I have drawn up a list of what we call "Essential Reading for Americans." This is not intended to be a list of clear, pedagogical sources, but rather some readings that can contribute to an adult's (or high schooler's) view of what it means to be an American. Of course, this is not a conclusive list by any means—it features only the favorites of a few folks. Additions are welcome, and I hope the blatant omissions prompt readers to respond. Titles not normally available in bookstores or libraries are listed with mail-order addresses.

Suggested Reading List:

Nonfiction:
Adair, Margo and Howell, Sharon. *Breaking Old Patterns, Weaving New Ties.* Alliance Building: 1990. Available for $6.00 from Tools for Change, P.O. Box 14141, San Francisco, CA 94114.
Anzaldua, Gloria. *Borderlands: La Frontiera.* San Francisco: Spinster's Ink, 1987.
Baldwin, James. *The Fire Next Time.* New York: Vintage Books (Random House), 1962.
Delaney, Sara and Elizabeth A. Delaney with Amy Hill Hearth. *Having Our Say: The Delaney Sisters' First 199 Years.* New York: Kodansha International, 1993.
DuBois, W.E.B. *The Souls of Black Folk.* New York: Signet Books, 1969.
Ehrenreich, Barbara. *Fear of Falling: The Inner Life of the Middle Class.* New York: Harper, 1989.
Freire, Paulo. *Pedagogy of the Oppressed.* New York: Continuum, 1970.
Hale-Benson, Janice E. *Black Children: Their Roots, Culture and Learning Styles.* Baltimore: Johns Hopkins University Press, 1982.
Haley, Alex. *Roots.* New York: Doubleday, 1976.
Hooks, Bell. *Black Looks: Race and Representation.* Boston: South End Press, 1991.
King, Martin Luther, Jr. *Where Do We Go from Here:: Chaos or Community?* Boston: Beacon Press, 1967.

Lorde, Audrey. *Sister Outsider*. Trumansburg: Crossing Press, 1984.
Matthiessen, Peter. *In the Spirit of Crazy Horse*. New York: Viking, 1983.
McIntosh, Peggy White. *Privilege and Male Privilege: A Personal Account of Coming to See Correspondences through Work in Women's Studies*. 1988. Available from the Center for Research on Women, Wellesley College, Wellesley, MA 02181-8259, (617-235-0320, ext. 2500).
Niehardt, John G. *Black Elk Speaks*. Lincoln: University of Nebraska, 1961.
Peterson, Bob. "What Should Kids Learn?" In *Rethinking Schools: An Urban Education Journal*. Winter 1993, Vol. 8. Rethinking Schools Limited, 1001 East Keefe Avenue, Milwaukee, WI 53212.
Staley, Betty, ed. *Multiculturalism in Waldorf Education, Vols. 2, and 3*. Available from the Association of Waldorf Schools of North America, 3911 Bannister Road, Fair Oaks, CA 95628.
Steiner, Rudolf. *The Universal Human: The Evolution of Humanity*. Anthroposophic Press, Hudson, New York: 1990.
———. *The Mission of Folk Souls in Connection with Germanic-Scandinavian Mythology*. Garber Communications, Inc., 1989.
Takaki, Ronald. *A Different Mirror: A History of Multicultural America*. Boston: Little, Brown & Co., 1993.
West, Cornell. *Race Matters*. Boston: Beacon Press, 1993.
X, Malcolm. *The Autobiography of Malcolm X*. New York: Grove Press, 1964.

Fiction:
Cooper, J. California. *Homemade Love*. New York: St. Martin's Press, 1986.
Ellison, Ralph. *The Invisible Man*. New York: Modern Library, 1952.
Kingston, Maxine Hong. *Woman Warrior*. New York: Knopf, 1977.
Mohr, Nicholasa. *Rituals of Survival*. Houston: Arte Publico Press, 1985.
Morrison, Toni. *The Bluest Eyes*. New York: Holt, Rinehart and Winston, 1970.
Naylor, Gloria. *Mamma Day*. New York: Ticknor and Fields, 1988.
Shange, Ntozak. *Sassafras, Cypress and Indigo*. New York: St. Martin's Press, 1982.
Silko, Leslie Marmon. *Storyteller*. New York: Seaver Books, 1981.
Storm, Hyemeyohsts. *Seven Arrows*. New York: Ballantine, 1972.
Walker, Alice. *The Temple of My Familiar*. New York: Harcourt Brace Jovanovich, 1989.
Wright, Richard. *The Outsider*. New York: Harper and Row, 1953.

Columbine . . . Afterthoughts

by

Hikaru Hirata

It has been fourteen months since the Columbine tragedy. I was working as a high school faculty member at the Shining Mountain Waldorf School in Boulder, Colorado. The three seniors from the Student Council took the initiative to offer a candle vigil the following morning. All the high school students, the faculty, and the staff shared their grief and thoughts. I was glad that my students were "safe."

It is very easy to point the finger at the two students who caused this incident; however, we must cut through the initial anger and outrage and get to the core of the "suffering souls" in the youths.

Racism in the United States

Since the incident took place on April 20, 1999, which is Hitler's birthday, the first thing that came to my mind is racial prejudice—the Aryan Supremacy. Recently, as I am writing this article, racially motivated shootings took place in Indiana. I was called a "Jap" by a group of public middle school students in February 2000, here in Boulder. We all know about the slave trades, the slaughtering of the Native Americans, and anti-semitism in the United States, because those incidents are obvious and visible. Rudolf Steiner was particularly against nationalism; he was not fond of President Wilson's policies. I wonder how many of us are aware of what happened at the Paris Convention in 1919. This meeting was initiated by President Wilson to establish the League of Nations. In this meeting, Nobuasa Makino, the delegate from Japan, proposed a racial equality policy on behalf of the many Japanese emigrants in the United States, who were subjected to prejudice. For instance, Japanese workers earned fifty cents per day while white Americans earned two dollars per day for doing the same job! At times, they were "stoned" by the Americans. After the earthquake of 1906 in San Francisco, the city ordered ninety-three Japanese children to be transported to the school that was for the Asians only. When the Japanese ambassador Ueno visited the site, he was outraged because the building was standing in the middle of nowhere, making it very hard for the children to walk to the school. (This problem was solved when President Theodore Roosevelt intervened on behalf of the children.)

In 1913 the California state government created the law to take away the lands owned by Japanese people. Nobuasa Makino was very concerned about the anti-Japanese attitude of the Americans. When this idea was proposed, many delegates opposed. Makino patiently tried to persuade these opponents one by one. When the final voting took place, the result was eleven to five in favor of Makino's proposal. This proposal would have passed, but something unprecedented happened. The chairman announced, "Since we have not reached a consensus, the proposal from Japan is denied." Makino was outraged and asked, "Why, Mr. Chairman, we have been deciding, up to now, by majority!" The Chairman replied, "The issue as important as this must be decided by consensus!" This chairman was none other than President Wilson. At any rate, the League of Nations could not adopt the Racial Equality Proposal because of Chairman President Wilson's ruling.[1]

One does not need to actively persecute others to be a racist. I was told that even if one experiences a mild discomfort in the presence of the people of another race, that could be the sign of the inner tendency towards racism.

Karma of Japan and the United States

The re-discovery of the American continents by Christopher Columbus was due to the fact that he wanted to reach Japan by going "west." He was inspired by both Marco Polo and Toscanelli. Rudolf Steiner, in his lecture cycle *The Reappearance of the Christ in the Etheric*, mentions that before Columbus access to the American continent from Europe was blocked. Columbus himself "heard" the voice from heaven that he had been given the "key" to unlock the chain that guarded the continents. One can also say that the Pacific access to Japan was shielded by the American continent. It is interesting to note that the "isolation" of the American continent from the European world was, in a way, echoed by Japan isolating itself from the West during the Edo era. While there were many visitors from Holland to De-jima, "Nagasaki" in Japan during the isolation, it was the United States that forced this isolation to an end in 1854. During President Fillmore's term, Japan was visited in 1853 by Perry and in 1856 by Harris via the Pacific Ocean.

Meanwhile in the United States, the tendencies to want to go West continued long after Columbus. Although the American people did not find gold in Japan, they found gold in California. After crossing the Rockies, the longing towards Japan turned to hatred. As I have mentioned before, the Japanese emigrants suffered in California. Japan, on the other hand, attacked Pearl Harbor in Hawaii, which is the far west of the West. As we all know, this Second World War ended with the two atomic bombs blasting, one in Hiroshima, the other in Nagasaki. The uranium used in the making of these bombs was extracted from the earth in the Navaho/Hopi territory (reservation). These native people recognized this area as the "Heart of the Mother Earth," and they called the uranium the "Heart of the Mother" itself. They did warn, therefore, that by extracting the uranium, the U.S. government was cutting away the heart of the Mother Earth, which would destroy the entire world. This act is the re-activation of the Aztec/Taotl rituals of cutting victims' hearts out of their bodies but on a grander scale.

After this baptism by the Ahrimanic ashes that fell from the sky, Japan, in a way, invaded the U.S. by trying to perfect the mechanization/Ahrimanization by developing the auto and media industries. The recent invasion of Pokémon is a good example. While Japan develops the intricate train (snake) systems, the United States develops the various flying machines (winged serpent—Quetsalcoatl). What motivated this historical development between the two countries? I sense the great struggle among the various spiritual beings behind the scene. Unfortunately, the technological advancement often is accompanied by fear, control, greed, and so on. How can we remedy this? According to Steiner, the "real remedy for this is not to let the forces of the modern soul weaken and cut themselves off from modern life, but to make the forces of the soul strong so that they can stand up to modern life."[2]

Drugs, Alcohol, and Computers

What corrupts and weakens the youth? My answer is anything that is detrimental to the healthy development of the "I" in the youth. According to Steiner, alcohol acts as the "anti-I" in us. A true drug/alcohol education based on Spiritual Science is crucial.

> Alcohol is something very peculiar in the kingdom of nature, and it turns out to be not only dead weight in the human organism but, in fact, acts directly as a counterforce on it. . . . when we consume alcohol, we introduce an anti-I into our being, an I that directly opposes the actions of our spiritual I. . . . Thus, an inner war

is unleashed, and when we place the antagonist inherent in alcohol in opposition to the I, we condemn to impotence everything that proceeds from the I.... An individual who drinks alcohol behaves like someone who, wishing to demolish the wall, hammers on one side, while at the same time placing on the other side people who hammer in opposition. Consuming alcohol eliminates the I's activity on the blood in exactly the same way.[3]

Here Steiner is referring to wine drinking. What Steiner is saying about the consumption of alcohol is that it destroys the healthy ego/I building in the blood. He is also speaking about the effect on adults. One can easily imagine what may happen to the development of "I" in youths after the consumption of heavier alcohol or drugs.

I am also disturbed by the words "recreational use." It is a known fact that certain drugs and alcohol have been used in the past during initiation rituals, to have other-worldly experience; however, the rituals were considered highly sacred and not repeated. These were a one-time experience in a sacred environment, observed by the elders. The substances were never meant to be used for recreation. Furthermore, when we consider the fact that ancient people were able to "excarnate" by listening to certain tones, such as the interval of the seventh, one wonders whether the use of the drugs in the rituals may be a sign of the decline of spiritual insights. According to my understanding of Aristotle's interpretation of the tragedy as catharsis, the wine-making process is the recapitulation of the tragedy of Dionysus himself. The plucking of the grapes, stepping and crushing the grapes, the fermentation—all had to do with the idea of suffering—the suffering of the grapes, the suffering of Dionysus, the suffering of the "I"!

There has been enough said about the detrimental effects of computer use and television watching in the Waldorf movement. There are many enlightening and thoughtful articles and books available, so I shall not go into detail. Many of us know that Steiner mentioned twelve senses in us, but how many of us know exactly how many senses are activated by television watching? Can we experience the senses of smell and touch, for instance, by watching the projected image of an apple? An adult who has developed these twelve senses may not be affected so much, but for a young child who is still developing and trying to orient him/herself to the environment, the healthy and full view of the world may be in jeopardy. The senses of touch, movement, balance, warmth—all are crucial to the grasping of the world. A friend of mine indicated that television watching is encouraged by doctors for patients who just had eye surgery because even their eyes do not move around as much by watching the television screen!

One may argue that in the future, the world of science may develop such a virtual-reality television that anyone can have various rich sense experiences all at once. Could that be true? Can we experience the color and the fragrance of the flowers in the meadow with the firm feeling of the earth beneath the feet, listening to the songs of the birds, and so forth?

One thing we may never forget is that one limitation of virtual reality is in its creators'/programmers' understanding of the world. First of all, the philosophical orientation of the programmers significantly affects the virtual reality presented. There are tremendous differences between one who holds the mechanical world-view of Descartes and one with the projected worldview of David Hume. According to Descartes, even God is a mechanical extension of the world. His world is a world of machines. For Hume, the whole world exists within our mind, so to speak, regardless of what may lie physically before our eyes.

Secondly, it will be nearly impossible to input all the possible sensory data experienced by the humans and to recreate them. How can the programmer collect and program onto the chips every collective experience?

In 1984 a book titled *Technostress* was published. This book was the result of a three-year interview done by Craig Brod. I highly recommend all parents and educators to read this book. He mentions the "techno-species," which lacks human warmth, lacks flexibility, does not understand humor, is poor in expression, cold and calculated. He mentions a boy who said, "Why should I care about the enemy? The point is to kill them!"[4] He has been addicted to the space-invader game.

There is no concept of mercy in computer games. Players are bound to "destroy" the enemy by learning how to be most effective and efficient. It becomes the automatic reaction/learned instinct. Our task is not to "destroy" the computers or the industries, but to counter-balance the possible negative effects caused by the computers and televisions with rich human experiences and imaginations.

How Can We Educate Our Youth in Crisis?

I have read that some schools have started to post the Ten Commandments on campus. That alone is not enough. It is every adult's responsibility to lead the youth as the ideal human being, whether he or she is a parent, educator, or doctor. Preaching alone will not suffice. It is our deed that counts. It is our compassion to embrace the others that speaks.

Why do we teach *Parzival*? After Parzival "made the mistake" as omission by not asking the expected question, basically, everyone starts to criticize Parzival without realizing that no one can save Amfortas from his misery. Parzival was "lost" until he encountered the two sisters who were accompanying the gray knight. While the gray knight reprimanded Parzival for wearing armor on Good Friday, his two young daughters pointed out to their father that this man must be cold underneath his armor, and they invited Parzival to their place. Although he declined their offer, these daughters' words of compassion led him eventually to surrender himself to the divine. This passage is easily missed. I have personally experienced this kind of human warmth from my students.

Rudolf Steiner was not into preaching and reprimanding. There is a famous story of a junior high school girl who attended the first Waldorf school. As she rushed down the stairs and around the corner, she almost bumped into a group of teachers. Steiner was there. While one teacher reprimanded the girl, Steiner told this teacher, "Let the girl go; life will tame her." She later became a successful actress![5]

Why do we teach Goethe's *Faust*? How can this story be appropriate for the 21st century? In the Ahrimanic ritual sacrifices of the Aztecs/Taotl, the victim had his heart and stomach cut out, according to Steiner, and the "third eye," according to Guenther Wachsmuth.[6] To Steiner, Wachsmuth cites, this is the decline of the Atlantean groups into practicing black magic.[7] In our times, the cutting out of inner organs in rituals has been replaced with medical surgery. There is no doubt in my mind that many medical operations are crucial and necessary; however, are all such practices sound/valid? Furthermore, artificially flavored and colored, chemically-altered foods are affecting our organs. The excessive use of computers is numbing our minds and hearts. Through alcohol, both the metabolic system (liver) and the "I" in the human blood are under attack. Our brain and the nerve senses are under attack by the flickering images through television, motion pictures, and computers.

> It (Ahrimanic force) impresses itself upon the inclinations and desires of men, only men know nothing about it, that it lives on in their desires and in pressing upon them there.[8]

So, why do we teach *Faust*? The two points I could give are:

1. Temptation/questioning of the human values

> What is your priority in life? (Money? Power?)
> What makes you happy?

What is your ultimate goal in life?
How would you get there? (... even at the expense of the others?)

2. What lives in our "blood"?

For, as a matter of fact, the entire human being is continually drawing its sustenance from the blood, and at the same time he discharges into it that for which he has no use. A man's blood is therefore a true double ever bearing him company, from which he draws new strength, and to which he gives all that he can no longer use. "Man's liquid life" is therefore a good name to have given to the blood; for this constantly changing "special fluid" is assuredly as important to man as is cellulose to the lower organisms ... the whole cosmos lives in the form of a crystal.... The blood vessels, together with the heart, are the crystal.... The blood vessels, together with the heart, are the expression of the transformed etheric body .... In the blood lies the principle for the development of the ego .... Whatever power it is that wishes to obtain the mastery over a man, that power must work upon him in such a way that the working is expressed in his blood. If, therefore, an evil power would influence a man, it must be able to influence his blood. This is the deep and spiritual meaning of the quotation from Faust. This is why the representative of the evil principle says: "Sign with thy blood thy name to the pact. If once I have thy name written in thy blood, then I can hold thee by that which above all sways a man; then shall I have drawn thee over to myself." For whoever has mastery over the blood is master of the man himself, or of the man's ego. [9]

I have already mentioned the effects of alcohol on the "I" in the blood. What about HIV infection, cancer, leukemia, and other immunological diseases that poison our blood? Many theories have come out about the HIV virus. The uniqueness of this retrovirus is that it seems to reverse itself and eventually become part of the DNA system of the host; therefore, it hides itself within the most powerful defense system of man, within the T4 lymphocytes. While the virus grows within the infected cell, other T4 cells cannot detect the invaders. In a way, the T4 cells cannot differentiate the "I" (the healthy cells) from the "not-I" (the infected cells). Thus one slowly loses the defense, becomes susceptible to a host of infections, and eventually dies from the multiple attacks. Dr. Bernardo Kaliks in the *Mercury Journal* (#9) cites Steiner by saying that "silica is the physical foundation for the

I-organization," and according to Dr. Kaliks, our "immunological processes are connected with our lower silica-organism. In AIDS this silica process is disturbed or destroyed." One can introduce *Faust* through the understanding of the human blood and the function of the human immune system.

I have, so far, mentioned the Ahrimanic attacks through alcohol, drugs, computers, and television. To Steiner, the Ahrimanic motif is "the motif of bewitchment, of being under a spell."[10] It is our task to keep the children healthy and strong, so that their spiritual "immune" system can overcome the detrimental effects of these substances.

How Should the Educator Be

As educators, we are often tempted to become moralists. In 1923 in Den Haag, Steiner warned teachers not to introduce "moral commandments in the form of 'Thou shalt' and 'Thou shalt not'" to young children. Why not? In the previous year at Oxford, Steiner answered this question. An abstract idea as pre-digested thought is like waste material. We usually get rid of such waste material during the sleep. If this waste material is fed too much to others, it stimulates antipathy within the psyche. This becomes a big problem if this is done to young children through moral education. The more one tries to implant abstract moral ideas (waste material) and rules, the more antipathy is created in a young child. Consequently such a child becomes antipathetic to such abstract moral ideas. This child may become rebellious. However, this child is only rebelling against the waste material; therefore, we as educators must know how to deal with such a child. Also, we must be careful not to introduce such abstract ideas to a young child.

In 1955 Dr. Karl Konig gave the report of the Camphill Rudolf Steiner Schools about the education of the adolescents with learning or behavioral difficulties.

> There is nothing greater, perhaps, but of greater importance to adolescents is their teacher's faith and self-control. Many of these boys and girls are very observant of their surroundings: they know whether an adult is speaking the truth or not; whether or not he believes in what he is saying; whether he is better able to control his emotions than his pupils. This is the main issue for the adolescent with behavioral difficulties in the fight between good and evil. Is the teacher willing to devote himself totally? not ninety percent, nor ninety-eight percent. If a teacher can do this without any trace of self-pity while maintaining his full self-respect, then the adolescent will respond. His disappointment will gradually be dissolved, and he will start to believe in the honesty of other people.

> The teacher is the one person who can alter the child by altering himself, by continuous inner striving. If he speaks of God, the adolescent knows whether or not he means it; it is no use merely paying lip-service.[11]
>
> Rudolf Steiner also made interesting remarks relating to this. He spoke about "creative renunciation." He said that if a person who is into gourmet food or drinks becomes a teacher, his/her words will not "reach" the children. The words spoken by the person who has many desires will not sink into the children. Such teachers tend to accuse students for not learning, instead of reflecting on one's own self. If one understands life from the higher realm, eat only what is necessary and, especially, if he/she is trying to accept destiny, he/she will start to recognize his/her own words as having spiritual power. He/she will also gain strength in his/her gaze. Not only that, just by having the good thought near the students, he(she) can encourage them.[12]

Steiner had refreshing suggestions for future teacher training to avoid cold dogmatism in the Waldorf movement.

> Here we must say that it is essentially unimportant whether new teachers have really learned what is often taught as pedagogy, as special methods. What is important for future teachers is that, through their training, they have become capable of looking into the developing person. What is important is that they have acquired the skills that they can acquire through a thorough, real understanding of human beings. What is important is that they have become capable in the presence of each child and in each moment to newly form and re-form the educational task.
>
> For the true teacher, pedagogy must be something living, something new at each moment. Everything that teachers carry in their souls as memories robs them of their originality. New insights into the nature of developing humans that allow the pedagogy to change and be alive in those people who teach must replace pedagogical norms. We could even say that the best pedagogy (stated radically) is one that the teacher continually forgets and that is continually reignited each time the teacher is in the presence of the children and sees in them the living powers of developing human nature.[13]

I would like to mention the words given by our colleague, Christoph Lindenberg, concerning the attitude of the teachers.

1. Always, learning must become a joy. . . .
2. Always, reflecting on oneself and seeing the results of one's teaching in the students' attitudes and in their papers.
3. Have empathy towards each child's happiness and sadness.
4. Enjoy human contact so that the students can feel that they can talk to this teacher about anything and he/she can listen and tell me what he/she thinks.
5. Not only study and prepare the materials with a professional attitude, but communicate clearly and create a picture that one can see.
6. Bring out interest in the children without any pedagogical tricks; find the essence in the materials that brings out the interest and the wonder in the teacher himself or herself.
7. Always be active, not cynical and backward.[14]

Art in the School Life

I was able to paint the "Last Supper" by Leonardo da Vinci on a classroom wall of Shining Mountain Waldorf High School. I started this project during the art history class for the ninth grade in 1995. A third of the students painted the simple things in black and white. When the block was over, I did the rest. It took me over 1700 hours to create this mural. Since I consider this painting my most favorite painting of the world, it was nothing but a joy to do this. I have heard that Heinz Zimmerman had spoken about Leonardo's "Last Supper" painting in relation to the collegial relationship in the Waldorf schools. It is interesting to note that after Jesus' announcing of the betrayal, the disciples start to fight among themselves trying to decide who is the greatest. " . . . And there arose also a contention among them, which of them was accounted to be greatest." (Luke 22:24)

For this Jesus replies, " But he that is the greater among you, let him become as the younger; and he that is chief, as he that doth serve." (Luke 22:26)[15]

If we apply this to the Waldorf school, no one is greater than the other unless he or she can serve the other. Each one of us is unique and different. We must share and make the best out of it.

Back to the arts in the school. . . . There are many things that Steiner said about the importance of the arts and the artistic in the Waldorf schools. I do believe that if Hitler had been admitted to the Fine Arts Academy in Vienna, the world would have been very different. In his psychosophy lectures given in 1910 in Berlin, Steiner describes the positive psychological effect of arts on us. As an artist and a teacher, I like the following quotation by Steiner.

> If art occupies the proper place in school life, it will also stimulate the correct approach to the students' physical training, since whenever art is applied in life, it opens a person to the spiritual light necessary for inner development. By its very nature, art can become permeated with the light of the spirit, and when this has happened, it retains this light. Then, wherever art radiates, it permeates whatever it touches with the light it received from the spiritual Sun. It permeates matter with light so that, outwardly radiant and shining with the light of soul, it can express spirit. Art can collect in itself the light of the universe. It can also permeate all earthly and material substance with shining light. This is why art can carry secrets of the spiritual world into the school and give children the light of soul and spirit; the latter will allow children to enter life so that they do not need to experience work as just a negative and oppressive burden, and, in our social life, therefore, work may gradually divest its burdensome load. By bringing art into school properly, social life can become enriched and freed at the same time, although that may sound unbelievable.[16]

I have been recommending a book, *The Artist's Way*, by Julia Cameron, a poet, playwright, fiction writer, and essayist. This book portrays a twelve-week exercise to recover our creativity. Although she may not be an anthroposophist, I have found many ideas that are similar to Steiner's. These exercises benefited me very much, and my artistic style changed. I was able to express myself freely and was very excited to create for my solo exhibition, which took place in Denver in June 2000. Julia reminded me through the ten basic principles that creativity is a spiritual experience, and by being creative, as God's creations, we are continuing the Creator's creativity. We are all responsible to continue the creation through the arts.

What, then, corrupts youth? We all do, when we do not realize that we are meant to be creative, when we refuse to resolve our pain from the past, when we are motivated by fear, control, and greed.

What heals youth? When we realize that we are all creative, spiritual beings sharing the universe equally, and when we act/create accordingly with love and compassion, we are becoming true role models for our youth.

Through the direct experience of striving spirits in us and not through our preaching, youth will shine forth as the light of the world, for "the letter killeth, but the spirit giveth life."[17]

---

1. Fugioka, Nobukatsu. *Kyokasho ga Oshienai Rekishi.* (The History that the Text Book Never Teaches), Jiyusyugishikankenkyukai: 1999.

2. Steiner, Rudolf. *Technology and Art.* Dornach, Switzerland: 1914.

3. Steiner, Rudolf. *The Effects of Esoteric Development.* Spring Valley, New York:Anthroposophical Press,1982.

4. Brod, Craig. *Technostress.* (Japanese translation). Massachusetts: Addison-Wesley Publishing Co., Inc., 1984.

5. v. Baravalle, Hermann, Ph.D. *Rudolf Steiner as Educator.* New Jersey: St. George Books, 1960.

6. Wachsmuth, Guenther. *The Evolution of Mankind.* Dornach, Switzerland: Philosophic-Anthroposophic Press,1961.

7. *Ibid.*

8. Steiner, Rudolf. *Inner Evolutionary Impulse of Mankind.* Dornach, Switzerland: 1916.

9. Steiner, Rudolf. *The Occult Significance of Blood.* London: Rudolf Steiner Press, 1967.

10. Steiner, Rudolf. *The Balance in the World and Man.* Hudson, New York: Anthroposophic Press, 1996.

11.Luxford, Michael. *Adolescence and Its Significance for Those with Special Needs.* London: TWT Publications Ltd., 1995.

12. Steiner, Rudolf. *Die Evolution vom Gesichtspunkte des Wahrhftigen.* Berlin: 1911.

13. Steiner, Rudolf. *Supersensible Knowledge and Social Pedagogical Life.* Stuttgart: 1919.

14. Lindenberg, Christoph.*Waldorfschulen: Angstfrei Lernen, Selbstwusst Handeln.* (Japanese Translation). Reinbeck bei Hamburg: Rowohlt Taschenbuch Verlag, 1975.

15. *New Testament.* The Gideons International, Japan Bible Society, 1977.

16. Steiner, Rudolf. *Education and Art.* London: Rudolf Steiner Press, 1972.

17. *New Testament.* The Gideons International, Japan Bible Society, 1977.

Feminism or Humanism? Women's Studies Meets Spirit Studies

by

Gertrude Reif Hughes

Talk about feminism is sometimes perceived as trivial, unspiritual, too focused on sex, interested in what divides instead of what unites. Particularly among people who incline towards a spiritual outlook, feminism can seem limiting instead of liberating. After a talk I gave recently about feminism and anthroposophy, a woman in the audience came up and confided that she was not a feminist. The idea made her uncomfortable. She felt that calling herself a feminist would negate her more important allegiances. It would make her less humane. "I'm not a feminist," she declared. "I'm a humanist."

The woman's remark made me think. I knew that I believed in a basic unity among many beings, yet here I was, advocating a feminist consciousness. Was I unwittingly provoking contention in an already embattled society? Does a feminist perspective prevent a fully human one?

Perhaps, I speculated, it is unwise to highlight the differences between men and women when more than enough anxiety already burdens human relations, inside the house and out. Where lives are paralyzed by uncertainty over what to eat, how to conduct children's schooling, how to secure self-esteem for all individuals, and how to decide the baffling questions raised by technological opportunities and temptations, talk about feminism may seem provocative at best and divisive at worst. Maybe, I thought to myself, it is wrong to emphasize gender in a world where sex is more readily associated with violence than with love and where differences between people seem to provoke discord instead of making for an enriching variety. Certainly, harmony is needed, not more strife. As human beings, we need to find what connects us not what divides, and feminism introduces yet another "ism" in a world already rife with clashing interests. What is needed is more spirit not more flesh, more emphasis on universality, not more splitting into sects and factions.

As I pondered all this over the next several days, I began to wonder how it is that the mere announcement that one wants to emphasize women's lives, women's questions, women's contributions can cause such anxiety. For it certainly does, and not only in spiritually-minded circles. It does not matter whether you speak up at a committee meeting to ask, say, if more men or more women took part in some event that is under discussion, or whether you bring up some question about gender at a social gathering. Express an interest in women and your comment will usually be received–with or without uneasy joking—as an attempt at special pleading or factionalism. The same cannot be said of efforts to raise consciousness on related topics like racial or religious differences or class divisions. Talk about those topics can certainly make tempers flare and cause painful confrontations, but talk about gender difference is more than just controversial. It is somehow unacceptable. A feminist viewpoint is expected to justify itself each time it is offered.

While I contemplated the simple if sad fact that feminists repeatedly have to earn the right to speak out, an even simpler fact emerged: If one cannot pay explicit attention to fifty-one percent of the human race and still count oneself a humanist, then "humanism" must be conceived very narrowly. Whoever feels that feminism inhibits humanism must also feel, probably without knowing it, that women are not really human. Or, to put it another way, if feminism conflicts with humanism then what passes for humanism must be masculinism in humanist clothing.

What other phenomenon, I asked myself in exasperation, is so underrated, so overlooked, dismissed, or ignored and with so little apology, so few qualms? What other presence in daily life is routinely allowed so little recognition? My silent outburst turned out to have an answer: Spirit. Spirit is about as prevalent as femaleness and about as neglected. Like women's rights, spirituality is not discussable in polite society. A person who wants to mention divinity or morality routinely prefaces the remark with a disclaimer like, "At the risk of sounding moralistic . . . ," or "This may sound a little pompous but . . . ." Like women, spiritual beings may be worshipped or feared, but they are not accepted as a normal part of everyday life. In our culture, spirit, like femaleness, has peripheral status.

The mere act of consciously making gender or spirit a category of one's thinking about the world creates profound changes in how the world looks and what one thinks ought to be done in it. At this point in my deliberations, I realized that as a college professor who teaches women's studies and as a woman who is committed to a spiritual path and to studying Rudolf Steiner's work, I am in a very good position to compare the far-reaching results of raising consciousness about either gender or spirit and to find where, if at all, they overlap.

Take gender first. By making gender a category of analysis, a feminist consciousness recognizes the rights of women and discovers areas of life in which these rights are not taken seriously. At its most effective, a feminist consciousness notices and tries to change the "invisibility" of women and all that is designated female or feminine—whether it is found in actual men and women, or in supposedly gender-free ideals and practices. A historian asks, "Where were the women?" Suddenly domestic life, not just officialdom, becomes an arena for serious study. Parlors count as well as parliaments, feeding nations not just warring with them, raising the young not just raising taxes. Letters, recipes, memoirs, and diaries or "obscure" individuals—that is, those with no public standing—become legitimate parts of "the" record, and history takes on a very different look.

An economist asks, how is housework different from paid labor? Indeed, it qualifies as paid labor when "domestic" workers perform it outside their homes; what makes housework wage-worthy under those conditions and not when it is done by someone who lives in that home? Making gender a conscious category allows the question, what counts as work?

Insurance companies and employers who grant sick leaves need to know what counts as illness as well as what counts as work. Such questions pertain crucially to childbirth and childcare, areas of life that, under present social arrangements, usually affect women and children more closely than men. Should employers make workplaces safe for children as well as for adult workers? Is childcare a business expense like travel costs? Is childbirth illness? If not, does it qualify for health insurance and corporate leave? If so, does medical insurance cover births presided over by individuals without medical degrees? Can adoptive mothers have maternity leave or should it go to birth mothers? And how about fathers?

In a similar way, what I will call spirit-consciousness identifies the absence of a regard for spirit and recognizes the difference that taking spirit seriously can make. As soon as the sheer reality of spirit becomes a category, a viable concept in everyday life, its unacknowledged omission from ordinary cultural concerns and practices becomes noticeable, and as with gender consciousness, enormous changes in daily life can occur. All the activities based on the work of Rudolf Steiner, from biodynamic farming and gardening to Waldorf schooling and from anthroposophically extended medicine to the most basic questions governing the conduct of life, make outstanding examples of how a spirit consciousness changes all kinds of cultural practices.

Farmers and gardeners, for example, notice that it makes a difference whether you think of the earth as a living being or as just dirt. Decisions about how best to enhance the land's fertility become not just commercial questions but topics for serious scientific research and development; the use of pesticides is closely studied; organic waste materials are treated differently from inorganic ones. Spirit consciousness changes the practice of medicine, too. The relation of patients to sickness and health becomes rich with both mystery and complex possibilities for meaning when physicians, nurses, psychotherapists, and other caregivers think of their charges as beings of body, soul, and spirit. They see that the physical bodies of their patients may express inclinations and decisions that have their sources in a body-free, spirit existence where definite intentions have been conceived in urgent, if now unremembered, activity. When spirit is considered real, intimate, subtle relations between humans and their environments—natural, physical, or psychological—can be taken into account. Then correspondingly subtle diagnoses and treatments can start to result, and hitherto neglected areas receive new interest. Nutrition, childbirth, geriatrics—a spirit consciousness sheds light on those relatively neglected areas of medicine and shows their importance.

In schools, teachers change their classroom practices when they think of their students as beings whose feelings and intentions can be educated as well as their minds. When one pictures the learning processes of children and young people as a gradual incarnation by a spiritual being into a physical body, virtually every school subject and every teaching technique gets a revitalizing new impulse. Qualities are as important as quantities, and artistic work comes into its own. Instead of being reserved for enrichment or relief, music, painting, or movement turn out to be the most appropriate and effective ways to study and learn a knowledge-discipline experientially, be it history or physics, arithmetic or grammar. Spirit-aware parents and teachers see that a curriculum should not just fit children for the society into which they are born but should fit them to take up their earthly missions.

As everyone knows, whatever we imagine a human being to be, that idea generates how we live with one another. Fewer people, however, know that it takes both spirit consciousness and gender consciousness to form a viable idea of what a human being is. My women's studies students and colleagues rarely acknowledge spirit as a category. My fellow anthroposophists often overlook questions of gender or actively dismiss them. Without gender consciousness certain important discrepancies disappear from view, discrepancies between a woman's access to resources and a man's, between a woman's rights and a man's, and between a woman's sheer individuality and a man's. And of course where such discrepancies are erased, they can be disregarded. As with gender, so with spirit: without consciously taking into account the spiritual dimension of earthly life, including how our spiritual origins and destinations shape the course of our lives, and without a sense for the unique, soul-spiritual core of each single human being, we see ourselves and each other as interchangeable parts in a machine or members of a herd whose behavior, however complex and magnificent, is essentially predictable and therefore controllable. For views that neglect the reality of spirit, just as for those that neglect gender, deny human individuality.

Individuality is the crux, it is the crossing point where gender consciousness and spirit consciousness coincide and strengthen one another. Rudolf Steiner recognized a spiritually radical yet socially harmonious individualism, "ethical individualism," he sometimes called it. He saw individuality as the key to human relations of difference and of equality. His passages on ethical individualism articulate a fundamental dynamic that I call the paradox of "shared uniqueness"; in other words, uniqueness is the primary trait that we all share.

In presenting uniqueness as a social problem—a problem in doing justice to both difference and equality—Steiner highlights the issue raised by the woman who declared that she could not be a feminist because she was committed to being a humanist. In a chapter of his book, *Die Philosophie Der Freiheit*[1], entitled "Individual and Genus," he avoids making individual the opposite of society, contrasting individual with type instead. He says that when human beings view each other generically, as types, they cannot hope to understand one another. To illustrate this, he uses misunderstandings and inequities that are based on gender; so it seems as if, like the woman who preferred humanism to feminism, Steiner too would find feminism an impediment to social harmony. He writes:

"The tendency to judge according to the genus is at its most stubborn where we are concerned with differences of sex. Almost invariably man sees in woman, and woman in man, too much of the general character of the other sex and too little of what is individual." (p. 200)

Here Steiner seems to perceive exactly the situation feared by those who suspect feminism of being divisive: that emphasizing gender exacerbates the already deplorably prevalent anti-humane tendencies in social life. But as he continues, he makes gender a category in his analysis, and significant insights result. In considering the social dangers of erasing a person's individuality by highlighting the person's sex, Steiner finds that women are particularly liable to this kind of erasure:

"A man's activity in life is governed by his individual capacities and inclinations, whereas a woman's is supposed to be determined solely by the mere fact that she is a woman." (p. 200)

In short, women somehow have more gender and therefore less individuality than men!

Steiner shows how crucial individuality must be as the defining concept of humanness, but also that, ordinarily, individuality is more readily accorded to men than to women. Women are more often seen as members of the group "women" than men are seen as members of the group "men." As a result, a woman's gender more often obscures her individuality than a man's obscures his.

With the help of Steiner's analysis of individuality, in which he opposes individualism to stereotyping rather than to community, it becomes clear that feminism and humanism do not oppose one another. They are not mutually exclusive; it is impossible and unnecessary to choose between them. Rather, feminism makes it possible to understand what is at stake in calling oneself a humanist in a masculinist world—nothing less than learning to accord equal yet distinct individuality, humanness, to every woman or man whom one meets. A feminist consciousness calls for attention to women's individuality despite prevalent cultural tendencies to erase it; and a spirit consciousness recognizes that a communally responsive individuality is the soul-spiritual core of every human being, despite widespread notions that human beings have no core other than their central nervous system. Is it, then, more humane to be a humanist than a feminist? No. In fact, if Steiner's 1894 analysis of the situation applies now, at the turn of the next century—and it still seems all too accurate—one really cannot be a humanist unless one is a feminist too.

---

1. The book has various titles in English: *Philosophy of Freedom, Philosophy of Spiritual Activity, Philosophy of Freedom as Spiritual Activity,* and *Thinking as a Spiritual Path.* All are available from either Rudolf Steiner Press in Great Britain or Anthroposophic Press in the United States. Page numbers refer to the Wilson translation.

America:
The Price of Greatness

by

Edward Warren

While the Franciscan friars were Christianizing the Hopis in the American Southwest in 1629, a barrister in London who called himself "the trumpeter of a new age" was laying new foundations for natural science. Francis Bacon, the Viscount Saint Albans (1561–1626), was most concerned with man's use of the fields of knowledge through strictly scientific aims and methods to obtain dominance over the world of nature. He looked upon the mixture of science and theology as a superstitious and completely horrible state of mankind. According to Bacon, science and religion should not be confused in the study of the natural world, a study which should be directed to the glory of God and the relief of the human condition. True philosophy should not be a search for truth, but something altogether practical. Knowledge should be acquired by experience and experiment. In order to pave the way for this new philosophy of science, Bacon attacked the existing obstacles to knowledge, which he called idols. There were *Idola Tribus*—the idols of the tribe, fallacies due to man's supposition of a greater order in nature than actually exists. It also contains the fallacies inherent in human nature. There were *Idola Specus*—idols of the cave, errors due to individual prejudices, education and circumstances. There were *Idola Fori*—idols of the market place, errors arising from the power of words and the unfit choice of words. There were *Idola Theatri*—idols of the theater, errors arising from learned men who established fixed systems of thought. Amongst these, Bacon despised the "scholastics" of the Middle Ages, who never related their ideas to their experiences and thus created worthless knowledge, according to Bacon. He also denounced the philosophies of Aristotle, Plato, Thomas Aquinas, Duns Scotus, and Paracelsus as morally indifferent to the plight of mankind.

Francis Bacon wanted to create England anew. For centuries he was regarded as a symbolic figure for "universal wisdom," which was to grow forth through man's "empiric" experimentation with the natural world. Released from the bonds of religion, scholasticism, and Aristotle, man was to produce marvelous works for the benefit of mankind. Bacon's intentions were clearly expressed in *Novum Organum*, The New Instrument, 1622:

> We are not concerned with pure skill in speculation, but with real ability and the fortunes of the human race . . . . For man is not more than servant and interpreter of nature; what he does and what he knows is but that which he has observed of the order of Nature in act or in thought; beyond this he knows nothing and can know nothing. For the chain of causes can not be relaxed or broken by any force, and Nature can not be commanded except by being obeyed.[1]

Where else could England be easier created anew than in the New World? The abundance of natural resources, the flow of European immigrants, and the spirit of manifest destiny in America helped the realization of Bacon's prophecies on the progress of mankind through material growth won by observing, submitting to, and controlling the world of nature.

The colonies grew rapidly as thousands of Anglo-Protestants, Quakers, French, Swedes, Finns, Dutch, Germans, Moravians, Mennonites, Scotch-Irish, Jews, Portuguese and Spanish immigrated to the New World. Bacon's influence on two of the Founding Fathers was considerable. Benjamin Franklin (1707–1790), a member of The Royal Society of London for Promoting Natural Knowledge, and Thomas Jefferson (1743–1826) were strongly tied to the ideals of Lord Bacon's experimental philosophy. Jefferson considered Bacon, John Locke, and Isaac Newton "the three greatest men that have ever lived, without any exception and as having laid the foundations of those superstructures which have been raised in the Physical and Moral Science."[2] These two men, plus fifty-four other Americans, signed the Declaration of Independence which united the colonies in the ideal of brotherhood, though from vastly different philosophical and cultural backgrounds than the Hopi. The beginning of a new democracy, which was later constitutionalized in 1788, respected the possibility for the individual's integrity in relation to nationality, family, race, and religion.

> We hold these truths to be self-evident, that all men are created equal, that they are endowed by their Creator with certain inalienable Rights, that among them are Life, Liberty, and the Pursuit of Happiness.[3]

The new government, lands, and opportunities in America were sought by over a quarter million Europeans between 1790 and 1815. They built boats, the Erie Canal, chain suspension bridges, locomotives, rails, machines, stoves and tools as the first half of the great century of industrialism began. The United States furnished its portion of machines, which revolutionized industry. They borrowed Watt's steam engine and Stephenson's locomotive from England. While Fulton put the steam engine into a ship, Howe created the sewing machine, McCormick and Hussey invented the reaper, Morse spanned the continent with his telegram, Whitney made the cotton gin. The great railways were financed by the Vanderbilts and the Goulds. Typical of American history was the day Irish laborers who had built the Union Pacific Railway from east to west shook hands with Chinese laborers who had built the Central Pacific Railway from west to east. The 2.5 million Irish who immigrated to the United States by 1864 not only built railways but filled the New England mills and manned the Pennsylvania coal mines.

While African slaves toiled on the plantations in the southern states, the Native Americans were being systematically removed from their lands by American soldiers. Seventeen thousand Cherokees were removed from North Carolina in 1838 to lands west of the Mississippi after gold was found on their lands. They called this the "Trail of Tears." The Navajo called their trail of tears the "Long March" when they were rounded up and sent to a prison at Bosque Redondo in New Mexico by Kit Carson in 1866. The Sioux were also violently removed from their Black Hills in 1874 after vast gold resources were found.

The flow of immigrants continued after the Civil War (1861–1865) as America's industrial output increased twelve-fold. Approximately 10.7 million people immigrated from Scandinavia, Great Britain, France, Ireland, Germany, South and Central Europe, Italy, Russia, Poland, the Baltic states, Asia Minor, and Japan. Another 11.5 million immigrated between 1901 and 1920. They manned America's machines, New England textile mills, Chicago slaughter houses, New York clothing factories, and Pennsylvania coal mines and steel mills. By 1920 America was the world's leading industrial nation. Steel, oil, and banking magnates such as Andrew Carnegie, John D. Rockefeller, and J. P. Morgan, created financial empires that could reach across the entire world. Thus, workers, slaves, Native Americans, and financiers suffered or enjoyed contrasting fates in a single century which changed the fact of the North American continent.

Yet in the middle of the nineteenth century one individual—a poet, nurse, philosopher and sage—gathered his thoughts and essays on

"Democracy and the Individual," which he had been working on since 1862 when he left his post as newspaper editor in New York to visit his wounded brother on a Virginia battlefield. He had undergone a maturing process while working as a nurse in the war hospitals in Washington, D.C., comforting young soldiers, carrying sweets, and paper, writing letters, or assisting in operations. During these years, Walt Whitman (1819–1892) united himself with his country's tragedy and watched daily as President Lincoln rode into Washington on his horse on the way to the war cabinet, wearing on his face the signs and impressions of a war pitting North against the South, slave-owners against abolitionists, industrialists against agrarians, and brothers against brothers at the cost of millions of lives. After the war, in 1871, Whitman took a very hard look at America and wrote about it in his "Democratic Vistas":

> I say we had best look our times and lands searchingly, in the face, like a physician diagnosing some deep disease. Never was there, perhaps, more hollowness at heart than at the present, and here in the United States. Genuine belief seems to have left us. The underlying principles of the States are not honestly believed in, nor is humanity itself believed in. What penetrating eye can not see through the mask?[4]

Behind this mask, Whitman perceived three stages in the democratic experiment of the American people. The first stage was the establishment of political foundations upon which the rights of millions of people rested, embodied in the Declaration of Independence, the Federal Constitution, and the state governments, all constructed for universal man and not for the classes.

> The second stage related to material prosperity, wealth, produce, laborsaving machines, iron, cotton, local state and continental railways, intercommunication and trade with all lands, steamship, mining, general employment, organization of great cities, cheap appliances for comfort, numberless technical schools, books, newspapers, a currency for money circulation, etc. . . . [5]

Beyond these two stages he saw the appearance of a third stage arising from the two previous ones. It was the beginning of a

> native expression–spirit, getting into form, adult and through mentality, for these States, self-contained, different from others, more

expansive, more rich and free to be evidenced by original authors and poets to come, by America's personalities, plenty of them, male and female, traversing the states, none excepted–and by native superber tableaux and growth of language, songs, operas, orations, lectures, architecture—and by sublime and serious Religious Democracy sternly taking command.[6]

With these words, Walt Whitman described the appearance of a third stage in the American democracy that contributes to the protection of the rights of man and the material welfare of all men. It should complete the growth of the American people in their democracy and their cultural life. He calls the third stage a "native expression-spirit" with inspiration of the growth of "language, songs, operas, orations, lectures, architecture and religion." It is difficult for our modern consciousness to acknowledge the reality of a cultural source beyond our observations in the natural world. Can a spiritual being exist, amongst the millions of people living on the same piece of land, that can inspire those people to form a special contribution to all of mankind? If so, how can one learn to understand it?

Rudolf Steiner gave tremendous insight into the being of man and his evolution through Anthroposophical spiritual science. In a series of lectures given in Oslo from June 7 to June 17, 1910, he used this insight to build the concept of a Folk-Spirit that works into the individual's inner life through language, thought, and temperament. It can also inspire the cultural life of a people. Whitman approaches such realities with the following words:

> Subtly interwoven with the materiality and personality of a land, a race—there is something—I can hardly tell what it is—history but describes the results of it—it is the same as the untellable look of some human faces. Nature too, in her solid forms, is full of it–but to most it is there a secret. This something is rooted in the invisible words, the profoundest meanings of that place, race or nationality and to absorb it and again effuse it, uttering words and products as from its midst, and carrying it into highest regions, is the work of a country's true author, poet, historian, lecturer and perhaps even priest or philosopher.[7]

At the end of his second lecture in *The Mission of Folk-Spirits* in Oslo, June 8, 1910, Steiner spoke of how difficult it is to define a people's Folk-Spirit, because so many different forces are at work in a people, both normal and abnormal. He said that the character of the North American people will show that their Folk-Spirit is especially influenced by stagnation and difficulties in development. Stagnation is also voiced by Whitman in his severe judgments of the America in his day. He felt the first two stages had been brilliantly achieved, but that the third stage, which should bridge the gap between material growth and cultural progress, was less successful. Looking at his fellow man, he asked:

> Are there, indeed, men here worthy of the name? Are there crops of fine youths, and majestic old persons? Are there arts worthy of freedom and a rich people? Is there a great moral and religious civilization, the only justification of a great material one? Confess that to severe eyes, using the moral microscope upon humanity, a sort of dry and flat Sahara appears, these cities crowded with petty grotesques, malformations, phantoms, playing meaningless antics.[8]

He also looked at the social and cultural sides of the third stage:

> I say that our New World democracy, however great a success in uplifting the masses out of their sloughs, in materialistic development, products, and in certain highly deceptive superficial popular intellectuality is, so far, an almost complete failure in its social aspects, and in really grand religion, moral, literary and aesthetic results.[9]
>
> At the present all poems, literary magazines, plays, resulting from the American intellect and the formation of her best thoughts are but a useless mockery. They strengthen and nourish no one, express nothing characteristic, give decision and purpose to no one, and suffice only the lowest levels of vacant minds.[10]

Many questions arise. Can such merciless judgments be realistic? Are they fair? Are these the words of a cynical old man? Or are they words from one who really loved America and saw with high ideals the goals of the future and dared to weigh these ideals with a strict sense for reality? To what extent are they valid today?

The establishment of a democratic government, the survival of the United States through a Civil War which could have divided America into a European model of separate states, the growth of technology and industry due to natural resources and the immigration of cheap labor from all over the world, are impressive and characteristic achievements of the American experiment.

Another aspect is the role of America in world politics, especially during the twentieth century. President Woodrow Wilson (1856–1924) responded to world politics in the period from 1917 through 1919 in a way that laid the foundation for an American foreign policy and aimed at the creation of a stable world order under liberal-capitalistic internationalism. By bringing a peaceful, international order to Europe in 1917, while Europe was torn, according to Wilson, between Germany's military imperialism and Bolshevik revolutionary socialism, he envisioned that America could prove to the world its unique mission in moral and political order. Lifted high above the unenlightened past in Europe and Asia, the United States was to create a new world society. Wilson considered "Americanism" to be a country's unselfish gift to mankind. Resting on expansive commercial and financial influences, all countries united in a peaceful, international capitalism could cooperate in the growth of undeveloped countries, in guaranteeing territorial integrity and in opening trade to all on the seas. The president's advisor in Europe, Colonel House, saw the necessity of integrating Germany into this new political order and economical world system. The integration of Germany was to be established after the First World War by disarming the Germans, signing treaties to guarantee territorial integrity, promoting industrial expansion, and establishing permanent peace. Though the goals could not be reached after the First World War, towards the end of the Second World War, President Roosevelt and his secretary of state, Hull, believed in a new international order like Wilson's. They shared Wilson's antipathy for traditional European politics. After the war, Central Europe was disarmed, at Yalta territorial integrity was secured, the Marshall Plan paved the way for industrial expansion, and from establishment of NATO to the placement of cruise and Pershing II missiles in 1984, a "permanent peace" was aspired.

The American business spirit has influenced foreign policy as greatly as it has the American political process, the legal system, the press, education, and the entire country's cultural life. This has resulted in grave misuse of democracy and the balance of power in the branches of government. This mission of moral and political order, which many Americans have believed in, also resulted in an undeclared war in Southeast Asia. The executive branch of government directed the Defense Department in a war, which taught the country that half a million soldiers plus 700,000 South Vietnamese allies in total command of the air and sea, backed by the world's greatest war machine, were unable to secure even a single city from attacks of an enemy, whose strength was but a quarter of a million soldiers.

At a luncheon in Chicago on February 8, 1968, Robert Kennedy spoke out strongly against the Vietnam War. He named some of the political illusions dominating the country's involvement in Southeast Asia, illusions surrounding America's concept of the war in Vietnam which convinced us that *we* could win a war the South Vietnamese could not win themselves, that the unswerving pursuit of military victory whatever its cost was in the interests of ourselves and the people of Vietnam, that America's national interests were identical with the interests of an incompetent military regime, and that the war could be won our way and on our own terms. Illusions of such tragic consequences can be read in the words of the ideology of the Reagan doctrine:

> Safety lies in the establishment of unequivocal military dominance by the United States, including the first-strike capacity. If this means a nuclear arms race, that is Moscow's fault, not Washington's, because America's heart is pure. In any event nuclear weapons are usable and nuclear wars are winnable. We shall prevail.[11]

This ideology was answered by historian and writer Arthur Schlesinger, Jr., in his article in *Foreign Affairs* magazine:

> I no longer have much confidence in the admonitory effect of the possession of nuclear weapons. The curse of ideology is that it impoverishes our sense of reality, it impoverishes our imagination, too. It enfeebles our capacity to visualize the Doomsday horror. It inhibits us from confronting the awful possibility of the end of sentient life on this planet.[12]

During the first half of the twentieth century, Whitman's first stage, the political foundations upon which the rights of Americans rest, was not realized by all. Although American Negroes were freed by legal equality in the fourteenth and fifteenth amendments to the Constitution, restrictions on voting, plus illiteracy, kept federal rights from becoming a reality for millions of Americans. Segregation was also legalized in 1896 by the Supreme Court decision *People* v. *Ferguson*. Blacks were refused entrance to trains, schools, hospitals, restaurants, parks and water fountains. They were harassed and hung by racist members of the Ku Klux Klan. These grave inequalities resulted in a life of hate, poverty, and prejudice for millions.
Into this cultural reality Martin Luther King, Jr., was born on January 15, 1929, in Atlanta, Georgia. He dedicated his short but dramatic life to

the fight for civil rights, the fight against poverty and for world peace. By the time he was twenty-eight years old, he was world famous. His leadership in the Montgomery bus boycotts and thereafter in the Southern Christian Leadership Council paved the way for a nation-wide civil rights movement. A Baptist minister, with a doctoral degree in philosophy from Boston University, he was devoted to Mahatma Gandhi's nonviolent movement as the path for social change. From the lunch counter and restaurant sit-ins in 1960, to the Birmingham demonstrations in 1962, the march on Washington in 1963, the Nobel Peace Prize in 1964, and the voter registration march from Selma, Alabama, to Montgomery, Alabama, the Poor People's Campaign, and the anti-Vietnam War movement in 1967–1968, King worked to realize the words he spoke in his Nobel lecture on December 11, 1964, in Oslo:

> Mankind's survival is dependent upon man's ability to solve the problems of racial injustice, poverty, and war; the solution of these problems is in turn dependent upon man's squaring his moral progress with his scientific progress, and learning the practical art of living in harmony. We have inherited a big house, a great "world house," in which we have to live together—black and white, Easterners and Westerners, Gentiles and Jews, Catholics and Protestants, Moslem and Hindu, a family unduly separated in ideas, culture and interests, who, because we can never again live without each other, must learn, somehow, in this one big world to live with each other.[13]

Just as the first stage of Whitman's vision of America was not realized for all, so do the second and third stages remain goals for the future. King's "War on Poverty" was a beginning, amongst other beginnings in the 1960s, of the realization of material welfare and harmony for all Americans. His efforts to end the Vietnam War and to work for world peace, which were also left incomplete, carried seeds for a productive spiritual and cultural life in America in the future, as Whitman envisioned in his third stage. What role a fifty-five-year-old King could have played in today's world peace movement remains an open question. The possibility for this was removed on April 4, 1968, when King was shot down on the balcony of his hotel in Memphis, Tennessee.

On the night before he died, King addressed a hot and crowded audience at the Mason Street Temple. He had come to town to support garbagemen, who sought union recognition from the city authorities. His last public words gave a sense of the conviction, truth, and fearlessness so necessary today and in the future. Rain pounded down on the roof of the church. Behind him flashed a yellow neon cross, casting colors upon his shoulders and head. He spoke about the threats against life that day and said:

> It is no longer a question of violence or nonviolence in this day and age. It is nonviolence or nonexistence. Like other people I would like to live a long life. Longevity has its place. But it really doesn't matter with me now, because I've been to the mountain-top . . . and I've looked over and I've seen the promised land. I may not get there with you, but I want you to know that we as a people will get to the promised land. So I'm happy tonight. I'm not worried about anything. I'm not fearing any man.[14]

The flow of immigrants has continued, bringing millions of Germans, Austrians, Puerto Ricans, Jews, Vietnamese, Cubans, Mexicans, Afghanis, and many more to the shores of America. They have settled in an America that has replaced the Age of Industrialism with a Technical Revolution. Modern warfare, atomic energy, the space program, computers, and media such as television, video, and movies influence and direct a large part of daily life. Using a critical eye as Whitman did in 1871, the picture of a cultural life bringing forth a true gift for the rest of humanity is blurred by this caricature—a senseless, childish America bound to cultural isolation, suffering daily from Americanized, televised, popularized violence, poverty, and inhumanity to man. One can see lives wasted in racism, egotism, narcotics, and a false sense of national pride. Yet this caricature also wears a mask, behind which the lives of millions of people flourish despite social and cultural extremities and stagnation.

The prophecies of Lord Bacon, Benjamin Franklin, Thomas Jefferson, and Woodrow Wilson contributed to the protection of human rights and to the growth of material wealth by commanding the world of nature. They have dominated foreign and internal affairs in the United States. Will the prophecies of the Hopi, Abraham Lincoln, Walt Whitman, and Martin Luther King, Jr., help the American people to forge, out of the tragedies of materialism, war and inhumanity, a unity of races, nationalities, and religions in true brotherhood for all mankind?

How can we create a great moral and religious civilization to justify our great material one? How can stagnation be overcome so that we can approach the profound meaning of our land and people, so that we can utter words from its midst and again effuse that meaning in a native expression that can grow forth in our language, sciences, art, and character? How can we learn the practical art of living together? Questions such as these carry seeds for the growth of America today and in a distant future, for:

> If these, o lands of America, are indeed the prizes, the determinations of your soul, be it so. But behold the cost, and already specimens of the cost. Thought you greatness was to ripen for you like a pear? If you would have greatness, know that you must conquer it through ages, centuries—must pay for it with a proportionate price.[15]

---

1. Farrington, Benjamin. *The Philosophy of Francis Bacon*. Liverpool: 1964.
2. Peterson, Merrill. *The Portable Thomas Jefferson*. New York: 1975, p. 434.
3. The Declaration of Independence.
4. van Doren, Mark. *The Portable Walt Whitman*. New York: 1973, p. 325.
5. *Ibid.*, p. 365.
6. *Ibid.*.
7. *Ibid.*, p. 366.
8. *Ibid.*, p. 327.
10. *Ibid.*, p. 367.
11. Schlesinger, Arthur, Jr., *Foreign Affairs*. Fall 1983, Council on Foreign Relations, Inc., p. 5.
12. *Ibid.*, p. 13.
13. King, Martin Luther, Jr., Nobel Lecture, Oslo: 1964.
14. Bleiweiss, Robert. *Marching to Freedom*. New York: 1969, p. 9.
15. *Ibid.*, p. 378.

Freedom, Thinking, and Individuality: Ways to a New Style in Culture

by

John Root, Sr.

Preliminary facts:
— The work of the environmentalists foreshadows the need for a no-growth, or maintenance, world economy. Such an economy cannot be based on the present forms of competition, which would require growth as a safety valve against monopoly and its attendant economic hierarchy and political despotism.

— That the advanced few develop at the expense of the ordinary many is an archetypal principle described by Rudolf Steiner in terms of planetary and earlier earth evolution. But that the advanced few should keep the many down is no longer as self-evident as it was, for example, in ancient Egypt.

— Evolution now calls for the transformation of selfishness as part of the incarnating process, into selfless objectivity as part of the excarnating process. This change was heralded by the internalization of religion, the emergence of conscience and intellectual thinking, and ultimately the struggle for the ideal of individual freedom. The idea of the *Res Publica*, or power in the name of the people, gradually penetrated to forms of government and society in the West.

— Two books which shed light on this point of view are:
An Economic Interpretation of the Constitution of the United States by Charles A. Beard, first edition 1913; edition with new Introduction by Forrest McDonald, N.Y., 1986, and
Figures of Speech: American Writers and the Literary Marketplace, from Benjamin Franklin to Emily Dickinson, by R. Jackson Wilson, Baltimore, 1989 (first edition 1987).

For a discussion of the U.S. Constitution in terms of Rudolf Steiner's threefold social order, one very useful initial concept might be that whereas our founding fathers took the momentous step of implementing and refining the idea of the separation of powers—legislative, executive, and judicial—within the government, Steiner suggests the further momentous step of separating out the government as a whole from the culture and from the economy. For Steiner, this means that no aspect of the culture should be conducted by the state, not only religion, but also, and especially, education, nor should the state go into business or regulate any aspect of the economy that does not bear directly on the equality of rights. But as for equality of rights, the state should actually take on more duties than it already has, especially regarding labor, compensation for which should not be a function of the market but be determined by right. The economy would thus be entirely independent of government, with no expectations of privilege in the form of favorable legislation. But how has it been up to now?

The theme of what follows concerns the trouble our culture has been having in establishing itself as the direct rather than the indirect guide of social life, which cannot happen rightly if the culture does not intensify its self-awareness and make itself independent of all control from outside, as well as refraining from assuming any coercive powers of its own. The struggle to realize this has an interesting history. Symptomatic of a popular awareness of this struggle is a cartoon by Weber in the August 14, 1989, *New Yorker* depicting two crusty tycoons on vacation, one growling to his impassive companion, "I took a look at the First Amendment and some of that stuff isn't funny." Well, he has a point. If you are wealthy and are looking to gain power and influence, you do not encourage freedom of speech, press, assembly, and the like in the people you want to control.

People today still consider culture to be removed from life. It represents an ideal that must not be sullied by the real. The thought that a famous concert pianist is performing in order to make money and gain fame is not compatible with everyone's devotion to, say, Beethoven's sublime music. The thought that service personnel are being friendly and courteous to you in order to stimulate business and increase profits is uncomfortable in a similar way. You may derive some satisfaction from penetrating to someone's ulterior and hence real motives, but you are not likely to consider such motives cultural by today's standards. This attitude is changing, however, insofar as people are beginning in significant numbers to apply their ideal thinking and feeling to their real will and to come up with some hard truths they are not afraid to face; and whenever these truths become active general principles, they become part of the culture.

Thus the epochal separation of powers in our Constitution can be considered a prelude to the even greater separation into the culture as the vigorous inspiration of our civilization—deliberately and legitimately, but going no further into coercion than the inevitable force of the customs it inspires; the economy, which, set on its own, is organized and conducted by individuals and groups, but again with no coercive powers; and government, authorized and directed to enforce rules designed only to maintain equality or rights—like a referee who neither makes up the rules as he or she goes along nor joins in the game, but vigilantly blows the whistle on violations by the players. There are two categories of rules. One designs the game to highlight its particular features; the other controls the deportment of the players. Designing the "game" is a cultural matter, and the rules are then formulated by the legislature, controlling bad behavior being a function of the state. The higher and more vigorous the culture, the more the players will cultivate virtue out of a feeling of self-respect, from which a sense of cooperation will evolve that does not spoil the game but focuses and enhances the pursuit of happiness.

The framers of our Constitution (who incidentally did not compose the Bill of Rights) have traditionally been regarded as selfless idealists bent on creating a political environment wherein whole populations could experience evenhanded justice, and yet where a nation could expand in unity and become a power in the world. But in 1913 Charles Beard came out with an academic bestseller entitled *An Economic Interpretation of the Constitution of the United States*. On the basis of painstaking research, Beard claims that the framers represented a minority of wealthy, class-conscious aristocrats who wanted a strong central government in order to protect their private property rights against the lower classes, which had no unified vision of an expanding nation and its requirements, and that could be cared for by the powerful minority only if they were in a condition of dependency, not to mention downright slavery. Beard also takes for granted the materialism of the Enlightenment as extended in an unbroken line down to his own time, a materialism not yet degraded into widespread atheism or generally condoned opportunism, but that dominated economic thinking independently of cultural ideals. Beard's purpose in 1913 was, in Forrest McDonald's words, "to humanize the Founding Fathers, to show that they were not demigods but flesh and blood human beings who had lived in the real world with all its sordidness and folly." And Beard himself says, "Whoever leaves economic pressures out of history or out of the discussion of public questions is in mortal danger of substituting mythology for reality and confusing issues instead of clarifying them." Thus it was by confronting the economy that the framers really gained their fame. This took courage on their part, and in 1913 it was necessary for Beard and his intended public to penetrate the "formalities" of our heritage if they wanted to stay on top of reality.

Beard's first task is to track down the property holdings of all fifty-five delegates to the Constitutional Convention. He lists them alphabetically, distinguishing the great landowners and speculators of the South, with their vast holdings to the West, from the more directly moneyed interests of the urban Northeast. The latter wanted a hard currency so that as creditors they could be assured of value over time in the collection of their debts, and they wanted strict enforcement of contracts, including past ones, so that no one could wiggle out of his obligations by special legislation favoring debtors. They were, however, willing to benefit from special legislation in the form of protective tariffs. The southern agricultural interests needed to be assured of the continuance of slavery. Less acceptable to a large number of the delegates as a motive was the expectation that a constitution favoring creditors would enable speculators from both categories, North and South, to realize a profit by buying up (at around ten percent of par) much-depreciated government securities issued during the Revolution and redeeming them at up to forty-five percent of par.

Having focused on and identified his theme, Beard takes up his next task, to review the *Federalist Papers*, in which John Jay, James Madison, and Alexander Hamilton argue in favor of this tighter, more centralized government. This part is rich in philosophical observations, the general tenor of which is that the thriving class of successful possessors of wealth is better suited than either the old-style arbitrary aristocracies of monarchical Europe or the relatively incompetent levelers in the several states to set up a government capable of fostering the progress of a budding nation. Beard focuses particularly on Madison's famous letter No. 10, which develops the concept of the republic as the qualitative mean between monarchy and democracy. The economic element is implicit in what Madison wrote—property as a kind of yardstick of excellence; Beard merely brings it out. Property—material values—and the unrestricted acquisition thereof are the keys to a happy nation. "Indeed, every fundamental appeal in [the Constitution] is to some material and substantial interest" (p. 154). Moreover to make this feasible, the framers cultivated a general attitude of pessimism regarding the ability of the majority—the landless poor and even the multitude of small subsistence freeholders—to handle their own affairs without setting up structures that would hamper the wealthy minority in its pursuit of gain. Madison's recommendation of the republican form allows differing views about property without attempting either to inspire unanimity, which would be impossible, or to abolish freedom, which would be overkill; but through the principles of indirect voting, with property requirements for the franchise and for holding office, it would be impossible for any one faction to dominate the others in the long run. At the end, Beard can say, "The content of the Constitution as a piece of abstract legislation reflecting no group interests and recognizing no economic antagonisms is entirely false" (p. 188).

Beard's third task is to run down the roster again, now regarding the political views of the members of the Convention. Here the pickings are slim because most of them were "intensely practical men" (p. 189). But colonial society was still close enough to its class-oriented English antecedents for it to be "unnecessary for political writers to address themselves to the [nonvoting] proletariat." In the secret proceedings of the Convention, the delegates could be frank with one another about their goals, but in view of the opposition to property on the part of the debtor class, "the supporters of the Constitution had to be somewhat circumspect in the expression of their views" (both p. 190). Later developments, which swept away all property requirements for political rights, would seem to justify this concern.[1]

But in the Convention, no such scruples prevailed, as for example when Madison recorded John Dickinson's support of property rights for voting as "a necessary defense against the dangerous influence of those multitudes without property or principle, with which our Country, like all others, will in time abound" (p. 195). Beard records voices representing those multitudes, for instance "the wealthy and ambitious, who in every community think they have a right to lord it over their fellow creatures"(pp. 201, 312). But the prevailing documentation is consistently in favor of the favored. Beard gives a vivid picture of the framers at work, portraying them indeed as individuals of flesh and blood, but of course not as typical ones.

His fourth task is to follow up on the reaction to the Constitutional Convention. Suffice it to say that despite the bitter opposition to such a strong, centralized plan, the need for a competent nation in an exuberantly expanding political-economic situation prevailed in the end to establish the new Constitution. This was foreseen during the Convention when Governor Morris observed, "The time is not distant when this Country will abound with mechanics & manufacturers who will receive their bread from their employers. Will such men be the secure and faithful guardians of liberty?" (p. 208). The core of the ratification is succinctly put by Rufus King, who "explained to Madison in January 1788 that the opposition is grounded on antagonism to property rather than to outward aspects of the new system" (p. 304). One of Beard's summary statements tops off the overall theme most clearly: "The Constitution was essentially an economic document based upon the concept that the fundamental rights of property are anterior to government and morally beyond the reach of popular minorities" (p. 324).

Forrest McDonald's introduction shows how Beard's icebreaker received an intense but mixed response, was controversial for a while, then became accepted in academic circles for a while—although its theme did not filter down into secondary school history texts (even some of the ones Beard wrote)—and then became compromised in a number of particulars by subsequent, more sophisticated research. Today it is justly regarded as a turning point in American historical thinking.

The primary subject in Beard's book is, of course, the influence of the economy on political thinking. A secondary theme, however, quite strongly implied if not specifically stated, concerns the role that culture plays regarding reality. Culture designed us a Constitution based on the economy. The framers were candid with one another. There was little gap between their ideals and the life they wanted to lead. The wording of the Preamble may be obscurely elegant in places ("provide for the general welfare," for instance), but the wealthy, influential delegates got pretty much what they wanted. Even the *Federalist Papers* were not written for readers of the funnies. Those famous documents did little to comfort the landless poor. The owners of small farms could sympathize with the general concept of property because they did not, at that time, all belong to the debtor class. And today it is a tricky question: Was Governor Morris right in doubting that the masses would be the guardians of liberty? Partly. "Liberty" and "freedom" are popular expressions, and have been for more than two centuries, in an extended sense, for more than twenty centuries. But who takes them literally in their full meaning? Our culture seems unrelated to reality except in those select cases where people are restless and feeling an urge to be scientific, to face reality through observation and thinking as individuals and like-minded groups, and going on to create societies based on universal concepts. Today, independent thinkers are beginning to shake up the old world order, at least around the edges. Meanwhile, the plight of the masses, though it has not distorted the Constitution with too many outward changes, has caused government to take on a function quite antithetical to what the framers intended. They wanted a defensive government, one that left the masses on their own to live on what the wealthy, hence powerful, hence competent, had left over for them, their servile consumers and soldiers. It was enough for the revolutionaries to put divine-right monarchy behind them and transfer power to economic interests.

But now it really is "We the People," if perhaps only ironically, and government has shifted its method of dealing with the masses to one of calling the tune if it is paying the piper (mostly with the masses' money). And to keep that connection with the people alive in an industrial society like ours, it must control the main source of the culture—schooling—and raise the populace to accept the idea of hierarchy so that government can continue to impose its will on the populace economically in the "real" world. Behind the government, and exploiting it, stand the real successors of the framers, those who have the broadest vision of how private property rights are the leverage to power and influence worldwide. To that end, the major economic interests seem to be extremely busy promoting a culture beyond schooling that is not designed to lead the common person to a genuine feeling of control.

That many individuals have felt this problem intellectually on a personal scale is made clear in a remarkable book written by a Smith College history professor named R. Jackson Wilson. It has the allusive title *Figures of Speech*, where the "figures" are five (actually six, including the epilogue) famous authors, through whose careers he convincingly depicts the evolution of this struggle for control, at least in the 17th, 18th, and part of the 19th centuries. Benjamin Franklin's unheralded but highly successful effort to make writing pay in economic terms opens up the theme and exposes a dilemma that apparently could not be resolved openly. Washington Irving, William Lloyd Garrison, Ralph Waldo Emerson, Emily Dickinson, and more briefly, Walt Whitman, follow in turn.

Using mostly the *Autobiography*, Wilson traces Franklin's life as he flees Boston and his oppressive brother and carves out a brilliant career for himself in Philadelphia. Franklin the man spent his younger years emancipating himself from the underdog side of power/dependency and patronage/clientele. Franklin the printer, writer, and publisher took advantage of patronage whenever he needed it but was soon independent of that, and he was able, at a relatively early age, to retire from dependency on economic gain and to write at leisure and without constraints. Later, famous as a statesman, Franklin sought to reach with his writing a new phenomenon of his time: an anonymous "Publick." Wilson provides the background of this new readership through the eyes of 18th-century observers. "The debate turned on the consequences of a popular idea that Britain was making a fateful passage from what Adam Smith termed a crude to a civilized state" (p. 57). The division of labor resulted in a dramatic stupefaction of the mass of men. In a crude society, "all men understood implicitly how the world worked" (p. 58). Civilization, however, specialized not only labor but also knowledge, in all walks of life. Each special interest came to be pursued for some special gain. No one could claim to have an objective overview of social questions. As Franklin formulated the problem, "few in Public Affairs act from a mere view of the Good of their Country, whatever they may pretend" (p. 58). There is no immunity from this social problem. "It had once been possible to suppose that the mere ownership of land was enough to make someone independent of the particular interest that tainted all callings. But it had become abundantly clear that land in an economy of commerce and credit was a commodity like any other" (p. 59f).

Wilson concludes his study of Franklin by viewing the great sage at a historical moment when public morale had not yet come to be considered a dubious cause. "In fact, he still thought of his readers as a potential constituency for action" (p. 63). Franklin's goal "might not fit the traditional Christian notions of damnation or eternal life. But its final concern is with character and spirit—not with material gains and losses." There are "poor and powerless" who are quite moral, as well as those "who have wealth and position but have utterly lost the struggle to master the self. What mattered to Franklin was not the substitution of secular for religious goals. His concern was to devise a program of moral perfection that large numbers of people might actually work at with a measure of success, not because the spiritual end was modest but because the means were workable. And such people might then confront the world, not as isolated pilgrims, nor huddling together in withdrawn communities, but on something like equal terms" (both p. 53).

Wilson's next example, Washington Irving, has his heart set from the beginning on becoming a "writer by profession," thus winning—as he did—independence from the indulgent patronage of his family. By the time he commenced writing, the reading public had grown tremendously, and publishing had become a veritable industry, requiring marketing techniques. Irving's response to this challenge was to put up pseudonymous authors whom he endowed with quaint and charming qualities. Behind this move was a perception that could be abstracted as the growth of literary culture for diversion rather than for social thinking. "If men of letters were to become fully professional, writing openly and even aggressively for the market . . . , then what would be their social character?" Would they be shunted into "at least a symbolic relinquishment of profits and property?" (both p. 109). Such problems were neither new nor localized: "Indeed, they were common to most of the poets, artists, philosophers, novelists, essayists— intellectuals of every description—in the first half of the 19th century." And it came to this: "an insoluble problem; on one side was 'art' and 'learning';

on the other was 'worldly' or 'material' success" (both p. 113). It was possible for a best-selling author like Irving to combine art and material success, but this combination constituted a shackling of the free spirit, and like Franklin, Irving looked forward to retirement, at which time he could do what he really wanted.

About William Lloyd Garrison one might observe that, for an ambitious would-be professional, a cause—like the abolitionism for which he became famous—is as useful as wisdom and/or talent. But Garrison was moral, disciplined, and courageous, an unshackleable free spirit: "And he had made his own self his real writing subject, a subject he had immediate access to wherever he was" (p. 153). As Wilson points out, Garrison's "vocabulary of 'independence,' 'luxury,' and 'cares' echoed the autobiography of Benjamin Franklin as much as it anticipated [the transcendentalism of] Emerson" (p. 152). For culture to teach, as it should do, it has in some way to achieve what Wilson describes in his introduction as a position above the tawdry side of economics, a position that could be gained only through the quality of the works themselves. To his own great credit, Wilson points out that even elevated culture must cope with the artistic marketplace, and that it is legitimate to investigate how representative men and women have gone about it.

Whereas Garrison needed a cause, and because he ultimately became his cause and felt no inner need to retire, Emerson, who also never "retired," was compelled to work on the image of an individual unbounded by any particular cause at all, but perhaps by all good causes. So when he left the church, as Wilson points out with startling insight, Emerson took his independence seriously and confined himself to fostering in his audiences and readership the cultural ideal of the poet-hero. Presumably the virtuous, courageous, and transcendental role model for society will inspire by his sheer example, not by activism. Wilson shows how defensive this was on Emerson's part in the light of marketplace pressures. It was perhaps as though everyone in the economy wanted to retire from humdrum business into a culture that instructed, but mostly entertained, their own selves, the selves which, as Franklin so shrewdly observed, the ambitious wealthy often do not succeed in mastering.

It is the old aristocratic principle again: in England you cannot be a true amateur sportsman if you have ever labored with your hands for pay. The empress of China is said to have sported long fingernails to show that she did no work. Nevertheless, it was the work that mattered in the "real" world. Therefore, to cite an aphorism, the English dethroned their kings as tyrants, but kept them as pets. And these pets dominated the culture. Thus if Emerson needed to make a living from his writing and lecturing, he could not afford to give out that he was seeking fame and fortune if he wanted to establish his poet-hero image as authoritative. As Wilson puts it, "ministers and judges are exercising an authority that has been vested in them, while authors are trying to lay claim to authority" (p. 7).

I find it sadly ironic that publishing could itself be an industry, but anything high-minded that it publishes could not be part of the economic end of it, and that an author with something important to say would have to knuckle under to the marketability of his or her views, or that the publishers, solidly economic, would in turn have to defer to their perceptions of the cultural market if they wanted fortune, or even to stay in business. (That is the problem today: how to finance a culture that is both independent of and yet actively concerned with the economy as it affects the lives of the masses.)

So Emerson creates the image of the poet as hero, but the idealistic hero he portrays is not yet bound to any particular cause, system, or faction. The qualities the hero strives for in his progress toward self-reliance are still characterized by general virtues and values, somewhat on the order of oriental philosophy. As such, they do potentially transcend materialism and lead to something genuinely spiritual, which is always beneficial to the individual, but they do not return to social earth with any practical programs under their arms. Wilson, seeing this, says, "Most of what Emerson had to say about such things as freedom, rights, and property are not really about the civic freedoms, rights, and properties of citizens, but about the spiritual freedoms, rights, and properties of poets" (p. 202 footnote). Emerson still inspires many people with his idealism, and some of these surely act better in life because of it, but still, part of what he leaves for others to implement is apparently the perhaps subconscious notion that poet-heroes, and the culture they represent, are perennially uncommitted.

Rudolf Steiner, however, although a great admirer of Emerson's impulse and work, was not like that. What he brought back from the spirit was definitely committed to practical work, even though it was radical and went against the mainstream.

In order to understand Steiner's message about government being separated out of both culture and economics, we must, within our means, first confront the problem of culture as such. Is it to be assessed simply in terms of its manifestations in the general areas of art, the pure sciences, and religion? Or could it be approached more fundamentally, say, as the "place" where individuals are not only prepared in their early years for life in the ideal and the real worlds and how to bring them together, say, in the economy, but also as the place people turn to, continuously, for real impulses in running their lives, not just for diversion. If we take this tack, then what role should government, viewed as the arena where freedom and necessity meet to work out the need for coercion, play in a civilized society? Should government ally itself with the interests of the best, most successful elements in society and assume that in the long run they will do to the lesser elements (the masses) more good than the latter can do democratically? Obviously this was the case when our present frame of government was set up, and obviously, despite intervals of reaction like Jacksonian Democracy, progressivism, and many minor outbreaks of popular resentment by the have-nots against the haves, the few stronger elements continue to exercise closet wardship over the bulk of the population, especially through the kind of economic manipulation of the culture represented by the servile media, of which the press is the prime example. Its freedom from government censorship, as guaranteed by the First Amendment, cannot protect it from the economic pressures of advertisers or sponsors, oftentimes acting in concert with political views.

But now comes the crucial question: What must happen when the economy reaches the end of its old-style expansionist path and enters its "maintenance" phase? This has doubtless never happened before on so large a scale. When America was young, exploitation and expansion were paramount.[2] But now expansion is milling around and making trouble all over the poor planet.

Representatives of the cultural life may no longer have the same problem now with confronting the economy. Idealists are even allowed to make money. But it seems safe to say that the old system of power/dependency and patronage/clientele has escalated dramatically, through economic manipulation, despite being beaten by individuals in large numbers. Therefore society can be seen in need of a fresh new cultural impulse, a moral impulse like Franklin's, in order to accord culture the same status as the economy, but again taking the culture to mean the preparation and ongoing inspiration of the individual in its development. This means individuals as unique, free beings, not just as specimens of some sort of type. Thus the moral impulse, the quantum moral leap, needs to be characterized and identified.

The core of this particular applied impulse is the realization by individuals that in an advanced, complex civilization, the "economy" means one person providing for someone else's needs and letting his/her own needs be satisfied by what someone else can produce. This has been happening in fact for a long time, but the cultural image of the motive for work has not caught up with it. People still think they are mainly providing for themselves through the work they do for others. The spirit of cooperation is further compromised by self-interest seeking power and influence. There may still be some cultural embarrassment about the attendant egoism. Exposing self-interest to ridicule is still great sport, but egoism is losing ground, our social thinking having gone at least as far as advocating cooperation in economic matters at the expense of competition. Competition is not the spirit of maintenance. Cooperation is.

In developing his social thought, Rudolf Steiner calls for strong individuals to cooperate, not compete. To sacrifice the egoism of competition on the altar of altruism takes great moral strength and courage, especially in the pioneering stage. Steiner puts it succinctly in a lecture he gave in Zurich, Switzerland, not long after World War I (October 29, 1919): "Just as the trading system had to do with the clashing of one individual will with another, so the economic order of the Commonwealth (the Threefold Social Order) will have to do with a kind of collective will, which then in reverse fashion works back on the individual." Speaking of cooperation and association as the basis of the collective will, and noting that in an entirely different ("confused, by no means reasonable") way socialism also yearns for a collective will, Steiner continues: "How will that be possible? As we know, it must arise through the cooperation of single wills. The single wills must give a result that is no tyranny for the individual, but within which everyone must be able to feel himself free." And further in the same context, "Into that collective will must flow all that is felt by the individual man as his own spiritual, moral, and bodily nature. This is imperative." Noting that the aristocratic system was too instinctive, the trading system too haphazard, to build up a collective will properly, Steiner calls for a cultural life based on freedom (spiritual activity) implemented by the study of spiritual science: "Hence it will only be possible to establish an economic order of the community when the economic organization can be inspired by the independent spiritual life." And further, "Only a spiritual culture that has been banished from practical life can become foreign to life" (all quotations from *The Social Future*, Lecture V).

In other contexts Steiner speaks of the need to transcend the boundaries of materialism and mere rationalism. This is harder than it may sound. Materialism and rationalism have been evolutionary necessities in order to provide the individual with a basis for feeling that cognition is its own possession. This was well understood in the 18th century. As Peter Gay, in *The Enlightenment: An Interpretation—The Rise of Modern Paganism* (New York 1966, p. 419), observes, "Hume makes plain that since God is silent, man is his own master: he must live in a disenchanted world, submit everything to criticism, and make his own way." But time has passed and now evolution calls for the self-oriented ego to expand its horizons. Without losing the treasure of the cognitive self, the individual now needs to think of the economy in terms of service, not self-service. It is a very moral thought.

The call of the times is already being answered from many quarters. Two examples, partly similar, but with apparently different purposes, are worth giving. In an extremely interesting article ("The World Economy after the Cold War," *Foreign Affairs*, Vol. 69, No. 3, Summer 1990, pp. 96–112), C. Fred Bergsten, looking ahead to a global economy, claims that no one of the three big blocs—the United States, Europe (as united), or Japan—has the potential to impose itself on the others in world leadership and concludes (p. 104): "Hence effective economic cooperation will depend on the achievement of joint leadership by the Big Three economic superpowers, just as nuclear deterrence was maintained by the Big Two military powers. There is simply no alternative." And, urging his countrymen to work their way out of a net decline: "Americans will have to start viewing themselves as part of an integrated global economy, and pushing their government and firms accordingly, if they are to prosper and remain world leaders into the 21st century" (p. 106). Bergsten is still thinking of a world economy integrated and conducted by government in today's tradition, and although the concept of a maintenance economy is virtually implicit, he does not move forward to a concept of separating culture and the economy from the state.

More cultural in tone, but again looking to government initiative, is this voice speaking for world parliaments cooperating on matters of the environment and development: Robert Cahn ("The Globetrotters," *Amicus Journal*, Vol. 12, No. 3, Summer 1990, pp. 5–7) quotes French National Assembly President Laurent Fabius, who has this telling insight: "Environmental questions will not be solved spontaneously, but by voluntary, organized, directed action by men and women who think not only in terms of individuals but in terms of mankind."

Again, what is the nature of this culture? It is individuals thinking on their own about their relation to society. It is the scientific mind taking full moral responsibility for the knowledge it seeks to implement. It is free, this culture, when its members do that. Culture today shrinks from nothing. But, in contrast to the neutral objectivity aimed at when primary and secondary qualities[3] were divorced from each other by such pioneers of modern scientific thinking as Galileo, Descartes, and Locke, the free, responsible individuals do not tolerate coldness in their knowledge. They want to be engaged, like Tolstoy, who as someone said was "a writer who knows nothing of detachment from social and religious problems." Wilson, in his gentle and humane way, takes us a step further in our understanding of this cultural dilemma by exposing what one might call ulterior motives in order to help us break through the barrier between "culture" and "life." It would be interesting to see what Wilson would do with the twentieth century, where there are encouraging signs of individuals (thinking in freedom) having grasped the problem of how to make ideals real without wrapping them in propaganda, but unfortunately where the anti-individuality forces (in the masses) have pretty much been able to gloss over Lincoln's famous dictum by claiming, "Yes, Abe, but we *can* fool enough of the people enough of the time to swing the whole situation our way." For Rudolf Steiner, modern humanity, indeed "on its own," has no sure thing. Redemption is largely up to the human race.

For Wilson, "ulterior" need not connote "inferior," even though it always means "real" as against "ideal" or ostensible. If we take a cue from that, then a free culture will deal only with "ulterior" motives, where the will to deeds is at work. Thus reductionism, of which Wilson has apparently been accused, becomes a noble cause rather than casual satire. He shows his subjects within their cultural environment and makes clear what their successive problems were, problems which Emily Dickinson, for example, could resolve only by refusing to publish after a certain point, and which Whitman solves practically by marketing his own books, and also by remaining the observer standing outside the life of deeds for the economy.

Now it has advanced to the point where for many people only the real motives, for better or for worse, ulterior or not, are interesting. For idealists of this type, cover-ups are tedious and annoying. Who today admires the framers less for knowing that they had self- and class-serving interests? Beard did us and them a favor by deepening our understanding of the time.

Actions speak louder than words. Idealists who act out their ideals have integrity—not across the board, perhaps, but certainly in terms of a particular act. If they promote a maintenance economy by removing land from the commodity market and putting it into a trust, not only for conservation purposes but for any purpose, and by discouraging speculation also in other related ways; if they take labor off the market by not allowing the market to determine compensation (In threefold, there is no such thing as cheap labor. Management is cultural, not proprietary, and workers are maintained as a matter of right, at first morally felt, then on a social scale, passing over into the rights sphere.) If they put all surplus capital into a foundation trust to be fed back into the economy in the form of loans to new or developing enterprises and, on repayment, of gifts to cultural institutions, or in any other appropriate way implement their ideals in the service of what Franklin has called the Common Good, then they cannot be accused of having an ulterior, self-serving motive, and they thus belong to the New Culture. There are examples of it springing up all over the world. Perhaps the most encouraging thoughts come from publications dealing with business ethics where one might encounter the startling claim that honest, simple, straightforward, descriptive advertising is not only ethically superior to hype, but also sells more.

As the new wave gathers momentum, what will happen to our present concept of government? For one thing, it will seem increasingly inappropriate for any agency or department or branch of it to attempt to settle controversies. Controversies should first be settled culturally and only then be implemented by our repository of coercion. Impossible? Not at all! The new recycling laws were enacted only after widespread concern for the environment had settled the controversy in principle. Laws should arise out of overwhelming popular demand. That is where government belongs with respect to a vigorous culture, a culture where the human spirit, led by penetrating individual observation and conceptualizing, and inspired by common ideals that do not make the mistake of invading a person's very personal space, and, carried forward by appropriate action without fussing around too much with images, defines the lifestyle for this or that identifiable group of like-minded people. The task of government is actually not to govern. It should monitor and deal with the inevitable margin of error, where equal rights are violated by force or fraud; it should no longer presume to write the text. A German periodical recently characterized Greenpeace as a cultural institution, however activist it may be. Its primary objective is to educate, to teach, to demonstrate, not to coerce. That rings true. Culture should no more pussyfoot than it should throw bombs. It should have vision and courage in trying to pinpoint and settle controversies and so facilitate the evolutionary move toward, say, a world economy based on maintenance and without the overbearing hierarchy.

The thrust of the New Culture is by definition ethical and moral, with no need for any fundamental ulterior motive. Morality, as Wilson says elsewhere, is a function of civilization itself dealing with the complexities and confusions that beset specialization. Ethics is often a matter of little things. For instance, Forrest McDonald, in his introduction to the new edition of *An Economic Interpretation* . . . , characterizes Beard disturbingly but justifiably as an academic opportunist, who challenges his students (and readers) with bits of misinformation in order to test their alertness. That is just too academic. Writing toward our end of the twentieth century, Wilson presents his challenge without such ivory-tower gimmicks. His sharp but compassionately formulated observations can be carried forward into the present and projected into the future.

After all, education is that part of the culture that prepares the individual to realize and foster its powers of spiritual-scientific, morally motivated thinking. As Rudolf Steiner says, the cultivation of a (morally motivated) collective will, based on the cooperation of single wills, works back on the individual, and so the cultural movement unfolds at whatever pace its pioneers can set.

---

1. The wording of Jefferson's masterpiece, the Declaration of Independence, reveals a more democratic attitude toward the citizen. Jefferson was in France during the Convention, and his philosophy had, if any, only an indirect influence on the direction taken by the debates. Prior to the Declaration of Independence, the prevailing formulation of the list of rights that transcend the power of government to suppress was "life, liberty, and property." This sequence can be found, for instance, in the "Declaration of Resolves of the Continental Congress" (1774), the "Declaration of Rights of Delaware State" (1776), and the "Maryland Constitution" (1776). Jefferson, of course, has "life, liberty, and the pursuit of happiness," which can appeal to anyone, landed or landless. The same principle applies to Jefferson's famous dictum that "all men are created equal." He was not the first to treat equality so generally, but his formulation does fail to distinguish equality before the law from Locke's *tabula rasa*, whereas the "Virginia Declaration of Rights" (June 1776) strongly suggests this distinction with the phrase "by nature equally free and independent." Again, Jefferson's happy saying will naturally have had appeal to those without property qualifications for voting and office-holding. Perhaps that explains why the first section of the Declaration is so frequently invoked, even today.

2. Even Franklin felt this and recorded in his autobiography in reference to the Native American (quoted by Wilson on p. 52) the thought that ". . . indeed, if it be the Design of Providence to extirpate these Savages in order to make room for the Cultivators of the Earth, it seems not improbable that Rum may be the appointed Means."

3. Much could be said about this fateful distinction, from the reasons for its creation, and the fallacy in it, to the significantly negative consequences of its being taken up. However, here we offer merely the following for those unfamiliar with it. Galileo, in *The Assayer* (1623):

> Now I say that whenever I conceive any material or corporeal substance, I immediately feel the need to think of it as bounded, and as having this or that shape; as being large or small in relation to other things, and in some specific place at any given time, as being in motion or at rest; as touching or not touching some other body; and as being one in number, or few, or many. From these conditions I cannot separate such a substance by any stretch of my imagination. But that it must be white or red, bitter or sweet, noisy or silent, and of sweet or foul odor, my mind does not feel compelled to bring in as necessary accompaniments. Without the senses as our guides, reason or imagination unaided would probably never arrive at qualities like these. Hence I think that tastes, odors, colors, and so on are no more than mere names so far as the object in which we place them is concerned, and that they reside only in the consciousness. Hence if the living creature were removed, all these qualities would be wiped away and annihilated. But since we have imposed upon them special names, distinct from those of the other and real qualities mentioned previously, we wish to believe that they really exist as actually different from these.

Descartes, in *Meditations on the First Philosophy* (1641), Meditation II:

> And with regard to the ideas of corporeal objects, I never discovered in them anything so great or excellent which I myself did not appear capable of originating; . . . there is but little in them that is clearly and distinctly perceived. As belonging to the class of things that are clearly apprehended, I recognize the following, viz., magnitude or extension in length, breadth, and depth; figure, which results from the termination of extension; situation, which bodies of diverse figures preserve with reference to each other; and motion . . . to which may be added substance, duration, and number. But with regard to light, colors, sounds, odors, tastes, heat, cold . . . I cannot determine . . . . whether or not the ideas I have of these qualities are in truth the ideas of real objects.

Locke, in *An Essay Concerning Human Understanding* (1690), Book II, Chap. VIII:

> 9. *Primary qualities.*—Qualities thus considered in bodies are, first, such as are utterly inseparable from the body . . . . These I call original or primary qualities of body, which I think we may observe to produce simple ideas in us, viz. solidity, extension, figure, motion or rest, and number. 10. *Secondary qualities.*—Secondly, such qualities, which in truth are nothing in the objects themselves, but powers to produce various sensations in us by their primary qualities, i.e., by the bulk, figure, texture, and motion of their insensible parts, as colors, sounds, tastes, etc.; these I call secondary qualities.

Anthroposophy and the Spirit of America

by

Rick Spaulding

Magda Lissau, Kurt Nelson, and I wrote an article for the *Journal for Anthroposophy* that was published in the Spring 1998 issue. The purpose of this article on Edgar Cayce was stated in the subtitle, "A Possible Aspect of Michael's Activity in America." Part III of our article on Cayce's Study Group Readings attempted to relate the series of meditative exercises called "affirmations" given through Edgar Cayce to the path to the Christ presented by Sergei Prokofiev in his book, *The Occult Significance of Forgiveness*. That the Association for Research and Enlightenment (A.R.E., the group formed to study and disseminate Cayce's readings) may have within it study groups following a path to the Christ that is guarded by Michael himself would seem to be of interest to Anthroposophists. For some time, the question of how to adapt Anthroposophy to America has concerned the leading Anthroposophists of this country. In A.R.E., a possible ally, one completely American in its origin and development, can be discerned.

Since writing the Cayce article, we have been working on a book, *The Guiding Spirit of America*. Unlike the Cayce article, which employed Anthroposophical terminology in order to explain the meaning of Cayce's extraordinary psychic gifts and the stages of the path of initiation given through him, this book avoids such terminology. It was written for the general public, not just for Anthroposophists. We do feel, however, that the subject of this book has a specific implication for Anthroposophists and for the development of Anthroposophy in America. In fact, it is probably true that no one other than an Anthroposophist could recognize the significance of the subtitle of our book, "Dorothy in *The Wizard of Oz*." Though the idea that a character in a fairy tale could unveil the mission of the spirit of America is certainly not a common one, the view that a fairy tale contains a prophecy and a path of initiation for this country is not so far-fetched for

Anthroposophists familiar with the work of Rudolf Steiner and other Anthroposophists on Goethe's *The Fairy Tale of the Green Snake and the Beautiful Lily*.

There is one problem with the fairy tale of L. Frank Baum that even Anthroposophists can scarcely avoid. Although his tale is very much alive in the hearts of many Americans even one hundred years after its publication, more than likely it is the movie version that so lives. The plot of the movie contains barely one-half of that of the book. Even the details included (for example, the ruby slippers are actually silver shoes) have been distorted. Worst of all, the genuine imaginations of Baum have been twisted into the form of a dream from which Dorothy awakens. We tried to remedy such confusion in our book, but within the limitations of an article we hope that the above cautions, when combined with an attitude of open-mindedness, will suffice—so that the reader can relate the insights that we wish to take up to the actual fairy tale that Baum wrote in 1899.

Rudolf Steiner pointed out that Anthroposophy does live in American culture, but it often has a wooden form and puppet-like characters. Baum's fairy tale, that is, the book itself, can be characterized as possessing just such woodenness of expression and puppet-like characters. If this limitation is seen as owing to the time and place of its origin and as an accidental, not an essential, characteristic of this book, then a certain similarity to Goethe's fairy tale may be detected. *The Fairy Tale of the Green Snake and the Beautiful Lily* contains four kings, a beautiful girl with three hand-maidens, a green snake, and an old man and woman who have a dog. Baum's tale contains four witches, Dorothy and her three companions, the Wizard of Oz in the Emerald City, Uncle Henry and Aunt Em, and Toto. The whole approach of our research into the deeper meaning of *The Wizard of Oz* derives from that which Steiner took with regard to Goethe's tale.[1]

It is necessary for us to acknowledge not only our debt to Steiner, but also to other Anthroposophists who took up Steiner's indications about Goethe's fairy tale and developed them further. In particular, Dietrich Spitta researched Steiner's idea that a path of initiation is contained in Goethe's fairy tale. In an article published in the *Newsletter of the Anthroposophical Society in America* (Winter, 1994–95, pp. 6–11), Spitta showed how each of the seven stages of initiation is pictured in the events of Goethe's tale. The final chapter of our book attempts to show that all seven stages can be found in Baum's tale as well. We thought it significant that the current president of the Theosophical Society, John Algeo, had published an article (in the *American Theosophist*, 74, 1986, pp. 294–297) discussing the journey of Dorothy down the Yellow Brick Road as a path of initiation. The difference between Anthroposophy and Theosophy could hardly be made more clear. Algeo interprets the land of Oz as the earthly realm, Kansas as Nirvana, and Dorothy's journey as having as its purpose the goal of leaving the cycle of death and rebirth. The approach that we tried to take towards Dorothy's journey, as inspired by Spitta's article, led to a very different interpretation than that of Algeo.

The fundamental difference between Algeo's approach and the one that we took does not so much concern which stage of initiation is revealed by the Yellow Brick Road or which soul forces are represented by Dorothy's companions. Our disagreement with Algeo on these matters is one of interpretation. But our difference with Algeo concerning the character of Dorothy herself is basic. Our research on *The Wizard of Oz* arose from an insight that Kurt Nelson brought to one of our meetings. He suggested that Dorothy may represent the spirit of America and that the cyclone may stand for the Civil War. Kurt's insight led us to see a connection between Baum's tale and that of Goethe's, but our goal was always to develop Algeo's insight further, not to dissolve it into a theosophical allegory.

In addition to the element of self-development in Baum's fairy tale, we hoped to fathom the element of prophecy. Again the research of an Anthroposophist concerning an indication of Rudolf Steiner about Goethe's fairy tale proved to be most helpful. Steiner's discussion of the youth in Goethe's tale as representative of the Spirit of Russia led Sergei Prokofiev to find in the events of Goethe's tale a prophecy of the future trials of the Russian folk soul. In *The Spiritual Origins of Eastern Europe* Prokofiev presented his research into Russian history and connected it with the events in Goethe's tale to show how the difficulties of the present cultural age can be transformed in the sixth age. In this context, Kurt's insight was tantamount to the discovery of a version of Goethe's fairy tale that focused on the trials and tribulations of the spirit of America before she will be able to take up her world historic mission of assisting the spirit of the Russian people in preparing for the sixth cultural age. Our research in this direction led us to the idea that Dorothy is that spiritual being often called Columbia, the guiding spirit of America, and that she is opposed by another being, an anti-spirit of America, that seeks to enslave the American people.

The problem with this viewpoint is that it clashes with the view of many Americans toward their own country. The idea of an anti-spirit of America should not be dismissed out of hand, however. In his lecture cycle, *The Missions of Folk Souls*, Steiner states quite clearly that by the beginning of the twentieth century a backward archai gained ascendancy over the folk soul who had rightly guided the American people up to that time. That

Americans might be afraid of entering into this deeper view of America's destiny is understandable. Baum's tale continually points out that the Wicked Witch of the West rules through fear. It was of great importance for our group to be able to meet with Sergei Prokofiev and to discuss how best to take up this presentation of an evil force in American history without intensifying its activity or furthering the spread of fear. If the situation in America is difficult, it certainly is not worse than what the Russian people presently endure. The Wicked Witch of the West rules over a dry, barren desert region, and the poets and writers of this land have often described it as a wasteland. But knowledge is itself a power over the influence of this spiritual being, for fear comes from ignorance.

More importantly, Baum's tale is itself a source of hope. Dorothy's victory over the Wicked Witch of the West is the climax of the plot, and Baum himself wrote this modern fairy tale to inspire children. The picture of Dorothy pouring water on the Wicked Witch of the West contains what we feel is an implication of this story for Anthroposophists. The Ahrimanic being that has usurped Columbia's rightful position as guiding spirit of the American people hates water most of all and avoids it at all costs, for water is imaginative knowledge, the source of life itself. Anthroposophists are in a position to assist Columbia in achieving her victory by helping to fill the bucket that is the evil witch's downfall. The poetry of Robert Frost and the works of Thornton Wilder, especially Wilder's masterpiece, *The Eighth Day*, illustrate how Anthroposophy can foster the development of a genuine American culture even in that desert region where the rain never seems to fall.

Baum also presents a second picture that we feel contains a concrete implication of how Anthroposophy itself can develop here in America in a proper way. Since this imagination is not presented in the movie version, perhaps an explanation of its relation to the defeat of the Wicked Witch of the West is needed. After Dorothy's victory, she and her companions return to the Emerald City. There she discovers that the Wizard of Oz himself came from America, that he was driven out of the Land of the Winkies by the evil witch, and that he is willing to take her back home by the same means by which he came—in a balloon. Dorothy plans to go with him, but she ends up going to the South to meet Glinda the Good, while Oz himself successfully returns to America. This picture of the Wizard of Oz returning to America may not seem significant unless the idea that he was active once previously in this country is coupled with it. Oz is a mystery figure, but it is possible to surmise the spiritual being that stands behind the green snake, just as the archangels represented by the youth and the beautiful lily can disclose themselves.

One way to approach the spiritual being represented by the Wizard of Oz is to focus on the idea that he was once active in America. The question of his activity needs to be compared and contrasted with that of Dorothy for a concrete picture of it to emerge. When relating Kurt's insight into the being of Dorothy—that she represents Columbia—to the events in *The Wizard of Oz*, it is important to note that Oz himself has authority over Dorothy, since it is he who commands her to defeat the Wicked Witch of the West. In anthroposophical terms Oz appears as an archai, a spirit of the age, who realizes his mission through a folk soul, a messenger of the archai. If Kurt's insight into the cyclone that signals the beginning of the story—that the tornado represents the Civil War—is related to Dorothy's displacement as the guiding spirit of America by the Wicked Witch of the West, then the event referred to above as the Wizard of Oz being driven out of the Land of the Winkies by the Wicked Witch of the West can take a more concrete form. The question of the activity of the Wizard of Oz in America can be formulated: What cultural movement, active in various countries, came to an end in America around the time of the Civil War? A study of transcendentalism would reveal that the impulse of a time spirit stands behind it, for it manifested in England as romanticism and in Germany as idealism before it appeared on this continent as transcendentalism. That the transcendental movement effectively ended with the Civil War suggests that the mystery of the Wizard of Oz can be connected with the central European archai, the spirit of the fifth cultural age.

Steiner himself worked specifically with the cultural achievements that resulted from the inspirations of this spiritual being. He studied German idealism in philosophical works and produced his first great contribution to culture, *The Philosophy of Freedom*. He meditated on Goethe's fairy tale and transformed it into the first of the *Mystery Dramas*. His greatest artistic achievement, the Goetheanum, shows in its very name its connection to the height of European culture. Leaders in the anthroposophical movement have pointed to the development of the Goetheanum as a process beginning with meditation on Goethe's fairy tale and culminating in its realization as a mystery temple arising on the earthly plane. They have even suggested that America needs to recapitulate this process by building a Goetheanum in the West.

A consideration of the interrelationship of Goethe's fairy tale, Steiner's *Mystery Dramas*, and Baum's *The Wizard of Oz* can perhaps put this ideal of a Goetheanum in the West into a proper perspective. Steiner's own research into the origin of Goethe's fairy tale revealed that Goethe's inspiration derived from his reading of the *Chymical Wedding of Christian*

Rosencreutz and that Goethe's discussions with Schiller were only the efficient cause for writing the fairy tale. Steiner's own characterization of "The Portal of Initiation" suggests a similar inspiration, since he says that this Rosicrucian mystery drama came through him, not that it was written by him. John Algeo's attempt to view *The Wizard of Oz* as a theosophical allegory, as discussed above, came about because of his desire to emphasize the fact that L. Frank Baum was a member of the Theosophical Society and that his inspiration came from that quarter. If Steiner's indication about the Rosicrucian influence at the time of the founding of the Theosophical Society is connected with Baum's study of *Isis Unveiled* before composing his fairy tale, then perhaps a source of inspiration similar to those of Goethe and Steiner could be discovered for *The Wizard of Oz*. Goethe's fairy tale, as illumined by Prokofiev's research, especially relates to the Russian folk soul and the East. Steiner's *Mystery Dramas* lead to the building of the first Goetheanum in the center of Europe and point to the activity of the central European archai. Baum's *The Wizard of Oz* relates to Columbia, the American folk soul, and the West. All three may be viewed as transmutations of the *Chymical Wedding*, but in accord with a different folk or people. The ideal of building a mystery temple is achieved for Central Europe, but it looms as the ideal of the city of brotherly love hovering over the East until its fulfillment in the sixth cultural age. On the American continent, the ideal of a Goetheanum in the West would seem to await the return of the European archai and the resumption of its activity on these shores.

Before trying to emulate the last stage of a process (i.e., building a Goetheanum), it might be helpful to consider more closely the first step that needs to be taken. It is said (and most American Anthroposophists are familiar with this idea) that Rudolf Steiner suggested that if he had been born in the English-speaking world, rather than the German-speaking one, that he would have chosen Emerson's essays to build upon rather than the works of Goethe. If the source of inspiration for both German idealism and American transcendentalism is kept in mind, then this remark can be taken to refer to the preeminent representative of each cultural movement as the appropriate starting point for a genuine beginning of the process. Anthroposophists in America can do more than help talented and creative artists, writers, and musicians fill the bucket for Dorothy, as it were, with true imaginative works of art. They can take up the study of the forerunners of Anthroposophy and bring the European conceptualization of Anthroposophy into a living relationship with American culture. A study of the Concord Circle surrounding Emerson might lead to bringing Bronson Alcott's educational ideas into connection with those of Waldorf education so that a real adaptation of Steiner's pedagogical insights to the American people might occur. Margaret Fuller's social ideals, Thoreau's insights into nature and social practice, and especially Walt Whitman's role as guardian of the spirit of America might prove to be of similar importance in their respective fields.

Many American Anthroposophists worry about the question of how to defend Anthroposophy against its opponents. The only defense that can logically be expected to succeed is one that reveals the attacks to be anti-American. An Anthroposophy that brings the true ideals of Jefferson, Franklin, and the Founding Fathers into the light has nothing to fear from its opponents, at least nothing more than any other American fears when the ideal of freedom itself is under attack. If writers such as Herman Melville and Samuel Clemens and political leaders such as Abraham Lincoln and Martin Luther King are explored in any depth, then Anthroposophy will have accomplished a great deal for this land. If *The Wizard of Oz* is taken up in a similar fashion, perhaps that last stage of the process might not be so distant after all.

---

1. A comparison of Baum's characters with those in Steiner's *Mystery Dramas* could also be drawn, since Steiner himself related his characters to those in Goethe's fairy tale in the preface of "The Portal of Initiation."

America's Gold Rush: Can It Be Redeemed?

by

Dorit Winter

I live in an apartment overlooking San Francisco Bay and am most fortunate in having what the real estate agents refer to as a "killer view." In other words, it is an endlessly revivifying panorama. Angel Island, beautiful in its symmetry, green and unspoiled, sits in the Bay half-way toward the opposite shore where Berkeley is just visible over the island's shoulder. Further to the south you can see Alcatraz Island, derelict and barren, and the Bay Bridge, and Oakland on the other side of the Bay. Ferries, cargo ships and sailboats criss-cross the waters. In the distance, toward the east, the summit of Mount Diablo peeks up over the low horizon of the East Bay hills. To the north, behind a ridge, Mount Tamalpais rises up between the Bay and the Pacific. For the Ohlone Indians, who lived in this paradise of abundant game and fertile lands, Mount Tam formed the gentle pole and Mount Diablo the fierce pole of a great sacred circle. Now, as then, fog, mist, wind, water, and sunlight continually merge and remerge in an endless kaleidoscope of elemental beauty. And at the gate, the Golden Gate to this great bay, the elements swirl most intensely.

The Golden Gate Bridge, that magnificently engineered, world-renowned tourist destination, was named for the gap it spans. It is the gap itself, a narrow channel through the delicate arms of land embracing the bay, that is the Golden Gate. A sign along the Marin Headlands overlooking the gap from the north, attempts an explanation:

> Discovered in 1579 by Sir Francis Drake, it was known as the Golden Gate long before the name gained new popularity during the Gold Rush of 1849.

But this does not actually explain the name, and I have found no better explanation than my own, gained through first-hand observation from my window: twice a day at dawn and at dusk, a swath of golden light broadcasts through the narrow aperture of the gap, and the cliffs and waters of the Gate then shimmer and sparkle with golden light. The swath of light emanating westward from the rising sun and eastward from the setting sun appears to radiate almost perpendicularly through the north-south axis of the Gate around the time of the equinox.

One might think that with such daily and cosmic illumination, the gate into one of the world's great sheltered bays would have been obvious to any ship sailing up or down the coast. But, on the contrary, the Bay remained a secret undiscovered by the white man for 230 years after his first recorded coastal voyage, which took place in 1542. The name "Golden Gate" was first used by Captain Frémont of the U.S. Topographical Engineers in 1846. "Golden Gate," according to Frémont, served as a suitably impressive echo of "Golden Horn."

Why had it taken so long for the tranquil harbors, the abundant fish, fowl and deer, the peaceful Indians, the extraordinary timber, fresh waters, and fertile lands to be discovered? Was it only because the rocky coast and the very narrowness and placement of the aperture obscured its existence? Or because islands in the Bay itself blocked off the view to the distant hills in the east? Or because the evidence of fresh water from the northern delta of the Bay was masked by the saltwater tides? Or because of the widespread fog and mist? These are the prevailing conjectures, but again, I would like to offer a different explanation. Simply stated, the Bay did not want to be discovered.

Let me try to explain. Nature in the Bay Area is a very powerful presence. At its most extreme, it quakes the earth. But there is other, less dramatic testimony, even apart from the weather with its continual swirl of sea, air, and light.

In the environs of the Bay Area, particularly in Marin County just north of the Gate, great areas of land have managed to preserve themselves. The Marin Headlands, Mount Tamalpais, the Muir Woods, all these are, in spite of their astronomical real estate value, undeveloped. I do not in the least want to detract from the human achievement, the foresight, money and endless political campaigns that were, and are, waged on behalf of these preserves, but it seems to me that nature, the very elementals themselves, provided the means necessary for preservation of this land.

And here, in an area of powerful natural forces hidden for 230 years from the hungry eyes of explorers, and still (and let's keep our fingers crossed) preserved from the greedy fingers of developers, two other notable phenomena of vital interest to the Waldorf community also exist. The first is the plethora of Waldorf schools themselves, seven-and-counting in the larger Bay Area between Santa Cruz and Santa Rosa. It is a relatively small area studded by a relatively large number of relatively stable Waldorf schools. The second is Silicon Valley. Might there be a connection between these two disparate phenomena, and might this connection be related to the elemental character of the Bay Area?

The Waldorf school of the Peninsula, located as it is in the heart of Silicon Valley, is certainly at the crux of this challenging juncture, but the other schools in the larger Bay Area also exist in the cross-currents of these contrasting and adjacent cultures, as, in reality, does every Waldorf school everywhere. For Silicon Valley, though it has become a place name, also conjures up one of the most powerful phenomena of social change known to recorded history: the creation of cyberspace and the ensuing technological revolution. Silicon Valley is fueling this revolution, and since its defining characteristic is its world-wide reach, Silicon Valley represents a culture without borders, spinning its irrevocable web around the culture of everything, including that of our own world-wide movement of Waldorf schools. There is more than a grain of truth in the saying: "as goes Silicon Valley, so goes California; as goes California, so goes the United States; as goes the United States, so goes the world." We in San Francisco are on the cutting edge. Our situation anticipates yours. Thus it is that I hope I may be forgiven for focusing on what is happening in my home town.

An explanation for the location of Silicon Valley in the once beautiful Santa Clara Valley can be gleaned from Rudolf Steiner's stunning summation: "In technology, the forces of nature are active in their lifeless form" (*Man as Symphony of the Creative Word*). Silicon Valley has planted itself in an area where, as we have seen, the forces of nature are powerful. It has usurped these forces, compressed them in the silicon chip. But around the Bay, Waldorf education has, it seems to me, harnessed the forces of nature in a very different way, to benefit from them indirectly. I have no doubt that the proverbial liberalism and openness of the San Franciscans result from their continual awareness of nature's very real power. People in the Bay Area are always ever so slightly "out of themselves" in a kind of subliminal anticipation of the earth's trembling, and this edginess gives the place its edge, as it were. San Francisco did, and does, attract seekers.

The search for gold in California, undertaken first by the Spanish from Mexico, then by the mountain men from the East, and now by engineers from all over, has a fourth dimension: the "New Age" striving for spirit revelation. People are still coming to the Bay Area looking for gold.

Some find it in technology and get rich. But many, and I am speaking from ten years of experience with the public who find their way into the San Francisco Waldorf Teacher Training, are looking for a spiritual path. Most of those entering the teacher training have already tried other paths, including the rampant materialism of Silicon Valley.

Before continuing, I want to make sure you understand that this is not going to be a diatribe against technology. To that end, let me tell you a little about my own tech-conversion. In 1996, because of the large number of refugees from Silicon Valley seeking spiritual enlightenment in the San Francisco Waldorf Teacher Training, I felt I needed to do some research on the subject of technology. The resulting article was published the following year in the *Golden Blade*, England's journal for anthroposophy, under the title "Karma and the Internet."

I wrote, or should I say, processed "Karma and the Internet" using Word Perfect 5.1 on my primitive lap-top, a 386SX with one megabyte RAM. Within a year of writing the article, I was technologically up to snuff with a seventeen-inch monitor and a powerful desktop, and a few months after that, in other words, last November, the San Francisco Waldorf Teacher Training published its splendid Website. At least one of this fall's incoming students found us first through *sfwteachertraining.org*, and inquiries are pouring in.

Furthermore, as I prepared my history of art main lesson last fall for the ninth graders of the San Francisco Waldorf High School, there was many a late night when I found the Internet to be a nifty place for research. You can find anything on the information highway. You can get exquisite prints of the Sistine Chapel or the Sistine Madonna, download and print any self-portrait of Van Gogh or Rembrandt, and research just about any facet of the life of any artist. Then too, in preparing the summer session literature class, I wallowed in Shakespeare on the Web. Did I want four particular sonnets on a page? Nothing could be easier than to choose them, reformat them, and print them. Voila! You can find anything on the Internet, including all of Shakespeare's sonnets. And what's more, there is a kind of thrill, a certain rush, about having all that material at one's finger tips. I use the Internet, I have email, and the teacher training has a Website. No, let it not be said that I am a Luddite.

Nor, for that matter, was Rudolf Steiner. From early childhood he was fascinated by technology. The nib of the fountain pen interested him more than the words his father asked him to write. And as the son of a railway employee, he learned early about the telegraph and the steam engine. No, he did not eschew the technology of his day, and, as I learned in the course of writing the Internet article, he anticipated our technology and its radical impact with startling precision.

"Man," said Rudolf Steiner in 1914, ". . . will chain a second being to his heels. Accompanied by this second being, he will feel the urge to think materialistic thoughts, to think not through his own being, but through the second being who is his companion" (*The Balance in the World and Man*). It is, you must agree, a devastatingly accurate picture, right down to the PC, "the personal companion" being described. But I also discovered that

> It would be the worst possible mistake to say that we should resist what technology has brought into modern life. . . . The real remedy is . . . to make the forces of the soul strong so that they can stand up to modern life. A courageous approach to modern life is necessitated by world karma, and that is why true spiritual science possesses the characteristic of requiring an effort of the soul, a really hard effort. (*Art as Seen in the Light of Mystery Wisdom*)

What could be clearer than this antidote for SV (that is Silicon Valley, not Spring Valley) syndrome? A really hard effort of soul is necessary. But there is a catch. SV syndrome is insidious. It leeches the soul. The more technology we use, the less we want to use it less.

Just recently I came across an even more telling description of where we are now, and I could not help but be stunned.

> Yes, look at all we've achieved! Wireless applications carry our thoughts, applications encircling the entire earth, about which previous epochs could not even have dreamed. But what have we gained thereby? We send the most trivial, most empty thoughts from one place to another; we have harnessed the highest powers of human intelligence, so that we can use all kinds of perfected appliances to transport food from one part of the globe to another, and we have harnessed the power of our intelligence so that we can quickly, very quickly, circle the globe, but we have nothing in our heads that is worth sending from one place to another. For thoughts that we carry about are cheerless, and in truth, they have become even more cheerless ever since we began to carry them in our present conveyances instead of carrying them in the old snail paced conveyances. ("Faith, Love, Hope," in *Love and Its Meaning in the World*)

Doesn't this sound as if it could be part of a recent editorial lamenting the "trivial and empty thoughts" we send from one place in cyberspace to another? In fact, it is Rudolf Steiner in 1911, speaking about a very far distant future, a future our present technology is merely forecasting. And once again, the very choice of words, as in "snail" mail, makes you wonder. I am at pains to point out Rudolf Steiner's perspicacity on the subject of technology, because the complaint is sometimes heard that we anthroposophists are behind the times and should "get with it." Well, it does seem that Rudolf Steiner, at least, was not just with it, but ahead of it.

While Waldorf education is scrambling to earn its high-tech qualifications, there are others out there with the very best of technological credentials, already warning, in all earnestness, of the computer's potentially dehumanizing powers, especially in education, and who are looking to us to stand firm as bastions of human intelligence in a world increasingly dominated by RAM.

One of these is Clifford Stoll. He has published another book specifically on the use of the computer in education. It is called *HighTech Heretic Why Computers Don't Belong in the Classroom and Other Reflections by a Computer Contrarian*, Doubleday 1999.

This is certainly a man after our own Waldorf heart. And by now, he has, indeed, enrolled his children in the East Bay Waldorf School. But the reason I mention all this is that he, in personal conversations, made it plain to me, that if Waldorf education begins to go mainstream, becomes, in other words, too wired, he may have to look elsewhere for his children's education.

Let me mention another Bay Area personage on the cutting edge of the cutting edge of technology. She is Moira Gunn, columnist for the *San Jose Mercury News*, a Silicon Valley newspaper, and host of her own radio show called, "Technation; Americans and Technology." Here is what she writes in a June editorial:

> Millions of American office workers now use a personal computer, and they are reporting an unprecedented incidence of health-related problems. While the federal government has worked hard to bring all our schools online, we have begun to fear for how the World Wide Web may be adversely affecting our teenagers. High-trading Internet stocks presume a high-flying wired economy, and yet, is it also possible that we have an unseen underclass of "technology have-nots" who are destined to a future of menial jobs? If they have any jobs at all?

Here is a computer engineer with impeccable credentials, someone who makes a living from being as technologically "with it" as you can be, pierced by the horrifying recognition that nothing less than the center is in danger of annihilation. The center, that is, of the human being. The center between the "high-flying wired economy" and the "underclass of . . . menial jobs." The middle is being obliterated, the middle class, the middle man, the middle of man, the soul. Going . . . going . . . gone are the tradesmen, artisans and craftsmen; increasingly, the vocational and service industries consist of push-buttons; the bakers, mechanics, and toll collectors, even the pilots are being replaced by machines. Artists have always been peripheral, that has been their strength, but now they too are being marginalized out of existence. In every sphere, the "menu mentality" that equates creativity with choice is insidiously persuasive. Gene technology, which atomizes, splices and synthesizes to create gene-tech food, gene-tech medicine, gene-tech animals, and gene-tech humans, also encourages an atmosphere in which synthetic thoughts prevail. This is part of the binary revolution. Creativity of every kind is being replaced by technologically spawned synthesis. Digital used to mean "by hand," and earning one's living by the toil of one's hands used to be honorable. But factories now consist of machines run by machines, and we have digital wars, digital research, digital art, all of which use point and click methods and mock the soul. While the humanities atrophy in conventional school systems, and the arts are already more dead than alive, we lose the center between the nerdy geeks and the brazen jocks, a center without which the tragedy of Littleton, Colorado, will spread.

The center, the human heart, the human soul, that is what Waldorf education is about. It is a dynamic, not a static, center, one continually seeking balance. And that center is what people are looking for. Certainly people entering the teacher training are looking for it. They arrive with spiritual thirst, spiritual hunger. They seek the "living nourishment" of anthroposophy.

There is no such thing as "anthroposophical education." There is only our striving as anthroposophists to become educators in the truest sense, out of the living center, which nourishes all of us. As we find in ourselves the requisite authority, we shall, I have no doubt, be ready to provide insight into the true content of education, as process, as art, as activity in the teacher igniting activity in the student through truth, beauty, and goodness.

For 233 years, sailors missed the Golden Gate. We now have another narrow aperture, a chink in time, during which we can still find the Gate, travel along the swath of gold which, being spiritual, is always there for us, if we would but become inwardly active as anthroposophical students and teachers.

Biographies of Contributors

David Adams holds a Ph.D. in Art History Education. He has taught art history at several state universities and art schools and currently teaches at Sierra College. A former Waldorf school teacher and administrator, he is also a writer, editor, graphic designer, and the director of the nonprofit Center for Architectural & Design Research in Penn Valley, California.

Christy MacKaye Barnes received her B.A. at Rollins College with a diploma in Speech Formation at the Goetheanum, Dornach, Switzerland, in 1940. She was a class teacher at the Rudolf Steiner School, New York, from 1952–1958, and taught English/Literature in the high school from 1958–1977. Retired. Resident: Harlemville, N.Y. Publications: *Wind in the Grass*, Harper, 1931, with introduction letter by Edwin Arlington Robinson; *A Wound Awoke Me*, Adonis Press, 1994; Former editor *Journal for Anthroposophy*; *For the Love of Literature*, Anthroposophic Press (contributor).

Henry Barnes received his B.S. at Harvard University in 1933, and his M.A. at the Teachers College, Columbia University, 1947. He attended the Waldorf Teachers Seminar, Stuttgart, 1933–1934. He was a class teacher, taught high school history, Faculty Chair, at the Rudolf Steiner School, New York from 1940–1977. Publications: various articles; *A Life for the Spirit, Rudolf Steiner: In the Crosscurrents of Our Time*, Anthroposophic Press 1997; *Percy MacKaye, Poet of Old Worlds and New*, Adonis Press, 2000.

J. Leonard Benson (Ph.D., Basle University, Switzerland) is Professor Emeritus of Classical Archaeology and Art History at the University of Massachusetts, Amherst. Author of numerous books and articles and a study of the interactions of Greek art and Greek philosophy to be published on the Internet by the Libraries of the University of Massachusetts, Amherst, in the spring of 2000.

Norman Davidson was born in Scotland, where, as a boy, he supported the cause of Hiawatha with a collie dog, bow and arrows, and numerous campfires in the woods fringing the Pentland Hills on the south side of Edinburgh. Later he fashioned his crow feather into a pen and became a journalist for ten years, then laid aside the pen for the spoken word when he taught in Waldorf schools for sixteen years. In 1986, the call of the land of Hiawatha came again, and he became director of teacher training at Sunbridge College, Spring Valley, New York. He is the author of *Sky Phenomenon: A Guide to Naked Eye Observation of the Stars*.

Tom Dews, a graduate of Davidson College (B.A.), and Emory University (M.L.S.), is an English teacher and librarian at Kimberton Waldorf School in Pennslyvania. Over the past seven years, he has developed a folk music elective for high school students, emphasizing ensemble playing and improvisation.

Virgilio Elizondo, a native of San Antonio, Texas, has an STD./Ph.D.. degree from the Institut Catholique (Paris, 1978); an M.A. degree in religious studies from the Ateneo University (Manila, 1969); and a B.S. degree in chemistry from St. Mary's University (1975). He was founder and first president of the Mexican American Cultural Center and founder of Nuestra Santa Misa de las Americas, an international weekly televised mass for the Americas. Dr. Elizondo has been a professor or a visiting professor at various major universities throughout the United States and at the major pastoral institutes throughout the world. He is currently senior research scholar for a project on the study of San Fernando Cathedral as the cradle of the Mastizo Christianity of the United States.

Juan Flores is a professor in the Department of Black and Puerto Rican Studies at Hunter College and in the Sociology Program at the CUNY Graduate School. From 1994 to 1997 Dr. Flores served as director of the Center for Puerto Rican Studies at Hunter College. He received his Ph.D. from Yale University in 1970. His doctoral training and early teaching career at Stanford University were in the field of German literature and intellectual history. He is the author of *Poetry in East Germany* (*Choice* magazine award), and *Divided Borders: Essays on Puerto Rican Identity*. He is also translator of *Memoirs of Bernardo Vega* and coeditor of *On Edge: The Crisis of Contemporary Latin American Culture*. In the spring 1998 semester, he was visiting professor of Ethnic and Latino Studies at Harvard University.

Joseph Glosemeyer had a life-changing experience in California forty years ago, beginning a search throughout much of the United States, pursuing spiritual dimensions in life. He settled with his wife on a small acreage in Choctaw, central Oklahoma, thirty-two years ago, where he practices biodyanamic gardening. Living in close proximity to the Native American sense of place, both within and without, as well as the wisdom of Rudolf Steiner, raised the question of the relationship between the individual and the land upon which he or she lives. The Oklahoma City bombing of April 19, 1995, occasioned an earnest attempt to answer that question, which has resulted in the essay in this collection.

Hikaru Hirata earned an A.A. degree from Marymount College, and he received his Waldorf Teacher Training at Rudolf Steiner College in Fair Oaks, California. From 1995–1999 he taught studio art, art, and music history at Shining Mountain Waldorf School in Boulder, Colorado. He also teaches art history at the Boulder Anthroposophical Institute. He has exhibited widely in Japan, Germany, New York, California, and most recently in London, England, and Denver, Colorado.

Gertrude Reif Hughes is professor of English and Women's Studies at Wesleyan University in Connecticut. She received a B.A. from Mount Holyoke College, M.A.T. from Wesleyan University, and Ph.D. from Yale University. She is the author of a book on Ralph Waldo Emerson, and she has also written essays on poetry by numerous American women, including Emily Dickinson, Hilda Doolittle, Gwendolyn Brooks, Adrienne Rich, Mary Oliver, Rita Dove, and Joy Harjo. An alumna of Rudolf Steiner School in New York City, she has served as president of Anthroposophic Press and of the Rudolf Steiner Summer Institute in Maine.

Michael Miller was born in Dayton, Ohio, and moved to Denver, Colorado, in 1983 where he first began to publish. He has published poetry, short fiction and essays in a number of small magazines and journals. "The Thief Who Kindly Spoke" is chapter three of his unpublished book, *Hard Rain/ Slow Train: Passages about Dylan*. Excerpts from other chapters were combined into an article published in the Belgian journal, *Initiations* (Number 8, Spring 1992) under the title "La Voix Du Barde Royale" ("The Voice of the Kingly Bard").

David Mitchell was born in Salem, Massachusetts, the cradle of American history. He has been a Waldorf class teacher and a teacher of life sciences in Waldorf high schools in England, Norway, and the United States for over thirty years. He is chairman of Publications for the Association of Waldorf Schools of North America and is part of their leadership committee. He received his Waldorf training at Emerson College, England, and earned a B.A., Cum Laude in English at the University of Massachusetts. He has done graduate studies at the University of Oslo, Norway, and Heidelburg University, Germany. He has edited over forty titles, and his most recent writings include: *Will-Developed Intelligence, Resource Guide for Waldorf Teachers,* and *The Wonders of Waldorf Chemistry.*

Hilmar Moore is a native Texan. He has worked as a lecturer, teacher, and administrator for the Anthroposophical Society and the Waldorf Institute, operated a market garden, and today is a body worker. He lives in Austin, Texas.

Julia E. Curry Rodriguez received a Ph.D. in sociology in 1988 from the Department of Sociology at the University of Texas at Austin. Her research addresses immigrant women, immigration, racial and sexual stratification, and a variety of issues pertaining to Chicanos and Latinos in the United States. She is currently a research associate at the Chicano/Latino Policy Project of the Institute for the Study of Social Justice at the University of California, Berkeley. She has held positions as assistant professor in the department of Ethnic Studies at the University of California, Berkeley, and in the Sociology Department at Arizona State University.

John Root, Sr. taught for twenty-five years at the Rudolf Steiner School in New York City and is a former adjunct faculty member at the Antioch Waldorf Teacher Training program in Wilton, New Hampshire. He is currently president of Berkshire Village, a community for mentally handicapped adults located near Great Barrington, Massachusetts.

Barbara Schneider-Serio was born and raised in Germany. From a young age, she was involved in ballet, gymnastics, modern and jazz dance. She visited the United States for a year of social work before beginning university studies in Germany and has stayed ever since. She attended the School of Eurythmy in Spring Valley, New York, and received her diploma after completing the four-year course in 1983. She then taught in the Waldorf School in Ithaca, New York, and founded her own performing ensemble while there. In 1988, she was asked to join the faculty of the School of Eurythmy in Spring Valley. She became a member of the Eurythmy Spring Valley Ensemble with whom she has been performing throughout North America and Europe.

Virginia Sease was a Waldorf teacher in Los Angeles and a member of the Pedagogical Section Council in North America. She now serves as a member of the Executive Council (Vorstand) of the world-wide Anthroposophical Society in Dornach, Switzerland, and is leader of the Section for Eurythmy, Speech, and Music.

Jeanne Simon-Macdonald is a teacher of eurythmy at Sunbridge College, Spring Valley, New York. She has worked as a therapist, teacher, and performer internationally for over 20 years, giving many performances in recent years based on Mary Oliver's poetry.

Rick Spaulding holds an A.B. in English (Harvard University) and a M.Ed. (Loyola). He taught at the elementary school level for seven years, and as an English teacher in a Chicago public high school for 21 years. His work in Anthroposophy includes serving as a discussion group leader of a public study group focusing on Steiner's basic books (12 years) and, since 1981, lecturing on various literary figures and their works.

Philip Thatcher was born in Reno, Nevada, in 1939, and he emigrated to Canada in 1964. He has taught history, English, and drama at the Vancouver Waldorf High School since 1984. He has also served on the Council of the Anthroposophical Society in Canada, and as an editor of *Aurore*, the journal of the Society, since 1994. In the spring of 2000, he published the novel, *Raven's Eye*, the first volume in a trilogy of quest stories.

Edward Warren was born October 27, 1953, in Scranton, Pennsylvania. He majored in English and modern history at Harvard University and the University of Oslo. He studied Waldorf education at the Goetheanum in Dornach, Switzerland. He spent twenty years in the Waldorf school movement in Switzerland and Norway as a student, class teacher, and high school teacher in English, history and religion. He has conducted research for twenty-three years in teenage personality development. For the last two years he has worked as manager of professional development for McKinsy and Company. Author of *Thinking as a Spiritual Activity*, Ted is currently working on a second book.

Thornton Wilder (1897–1975) was born in Madison, Wisconsin. He grew up mostly in California, with substantial time in China. He started writing plays in high school and continued during his time at Oberlin College and at Yale College. After teaching at the Lawrenceville School in his twenties, he earned an M.A. in French at Princeton University. He received Pulitzer Prizes for his second novel, *The Bridge of San Luis Rey*, as well as for his plays, *Our Town* and *The Skin of Our Teeth*. Wilder was awarded the German Peace Prize in 1957 and the Presidential Medal of Freedom in 1963. A peripatetic traveler, he became one of the most global of citizens. Hence, the perspectives which he offers in the Charles Eliot Norton Lectures at Harvard in 1951–1952, on the making of an American language, arise from an unusual grasp of both center and periphery, of his country and the world. His later novels, *The Eighth Day* and *Theophilus North*, only amplified his contributions as a major force in the cultural life of the twentieth-century Western world.

Linda Williams taught at the Urban Waldorf School in Milwaukee and is currently a class teacher at Detroit Waldorf School. She graduated from the Waldorf Institute of Mercy College in 1986, and completed her M.A. in education at Mercy. An Assistant Professor at the University of Detroit Mercy, Linda heads the elementary program for the Waldorf Teacher Development Association and is working on her doctorate in literacy education at Michigan State University.

Michael Winship has worked as a musician in Europe for many years and as a Waldorf high school history teacher. Currently associate professor of history at the University of Georgia, Michael wrote *Seers of God: Puritan Providentialism in the Restoration and Early Enlightenment* (Johns Hopkins University Press,1996) and is soon to publish *Making Heretics: Militant Protestantism and Free Grace in Massachusetts, 1636–1641* (Princeton University Press).

Dorit Winter is founder and director of the San Francisco Waldorf Teacher Training of Rudolf Steiner College. Her most recent books are *Because of Yolanda*, Golden Gate Publications and *Sheets of White Light,* a collection of short stories, Rudolf Steiner College Press, 1999.

John Wulsin grew up in Cincinnati, and has lived in Japan, Switzerland, Austria, France, and England. He received his Waldorf training at Emerson College, England, and earned an A.B. at Harvard University and an M.A. at Columbia University, both in English and American language and literature. He has taught for twenty-five years, twenty-one teaching English and drama at the Green Meadow Waldorf School, Spring Valley, New York, while teaching poetics at the Eurythmy School of Spring Valley for twelve years. Recent publications include *Laws of the Living Language* and *Proverbs of Purgatory*, both available through AWSNA Publications.

Lara Wulsin wrote her essay as a senior at the Green Meadow Waldorf School. She is now a senior at Wesleyan University in Connecticut where she majors in English.